TERROR AND REPRESSION IN
REVOLUTIONARY MARSEILLES

Terror and Repression in Revolutionary Marseilles

WILLIAM SCOTT

Lecturer in History
University of Aberdeen

BARNES & NOBLE
BOOKS
10 East 53d St., New York 10022
(a division of Harper & Row Publishers, Inc.)

Published in the United Kingdom 1973 by
THE MACMILLAN PRESS LTD

Published in the U.S.A. 1973 by
HARPER & ROW PUBLISHERS, INC.
BARNES & NOBLE IMPORT DIVISION

ISBN 06-496134-6

Printed in Great Britain

Contents

List of Maps

This is based on the *Plan routier de la Ville et Faubourg de Marseille en 1790, levé par Campen*, reproduced in M. C. O. Teissier, *Les Anciennes Familles marseillaises* (Marseilles, 1888). The boundaries of the Sections, which were several times redrawn in the course of the Revolution, have not been fully retraced by historians: those published in the *Atlas historique: Provence* [...] ed. E. Baratier *et al.* (Paris, 1969), being inaccurate in some respects. Since the staff of the Archives communales are at present producing a definitive version of the Section boundaries, it was thought advisable to indicate only the general location here.

Preface

This study is centred round an analysis of the work of the Revolutionary Tribunal at Marseilles, which operated from the end of August 1793 to April 1794. A fairly extensive account of events leading up to the Terror at Marseilles is provided, dealing principally with the 'federalist' revolt of the summer of 1793, the repression of which forms the main subject of the book. Thus I do not attempt to give a full history of Marseilles during the revolutionary period; a total history of a city of the size and importance of Marseilles – even if one might reject its claim to be the 'Second City of France' – is certainly greatly needed, if only to remedy the neglect of Marseilles in almost every general work on the Revolution; but this is clearly beyond the scope of the present study.

Nor, despite its title, does it claim to be a full treatment of the Terror at Marseilles, concentrating as it does on the judicial aspect of a phenomenon which had extremely complex political, economic, social and psychological aspects. Even within the judicial sphere (itself of crucial importance, of course) it is not easy to evaluate the impact of the Revolutionary Tribunal. We know little of how people who did not come into direct contact with it reacted to its activities, yet one of its main functions was to deter others from counter-revolution. Perhaps the lack of evidence of overt resistance suggests that it was fairly successful in this respect, though other factors were undoubtedly at work here. It is also difficult to see how one might measure the effect of eliminating some hundreds of citizens from the life of Marseilles and its region. While books and articles on the causes of the Revolution proliferate, few are dedicated to a thorough analysis of its results and consequences, making it all the more difficult to place the impact of the judicial Terror at Marseilles in the context of the Revolution as a whole.

In my treatment of the papers of the Revolutionary Tribunal, I have been a *modéré* – trying to avoid, on the one hand, slicing up my material into statistically imposed categories which might

provide shapes conveniently squared-off to fit into the construction of a model of the Terror as a whole, but at the expense of
the sometimes recalcitrant and idiosyncratic nature of the
material employed; on the other hand, I have tried to resist
the accumulation of case histories for their own sake – it is
hoped that the individual and the particular has not always
been highlighted to the detriment of the general.

In the context of the present stage in the historical treatment
of the Revolution, the position of Marseilles is of exceptional
interest. For here was a city where the revolutionary struggles
took place in an advanced urban milieu, where the eighteenth-
century expansion of trade and industry had led to the development of a numerically important and economically self-
sufficient bourgeoisie. This had interests and attitudes in common which tended to contrast and sometimes to conflict with
those of the first two Orders of the State; and yet it was itself
divided according to various interest groups and – with the
Revolution – according to differences of opinion regarding the
tactics whereby objectives were to be attained and, if attained,
defended. Almost at once, the attacks on the nobility and clergy,
though initially forceful and subsequently always underlying
successive stages of the Revolution, were pushed into the background by divisions within the bourgeoisie. At Marseilles the
Revolution was the work of the bourgeoisie and, though the
bourgeoisie's unity was imperfect (and even then short-lived)
and though revolutionary militants were increasingly drawn
from rather restricted groupings, the main political struggle
was contained within the ranks of the bourgeoisie. But precisely because of splits within the bourgeoisie, problems of the
relationship between the revolutionary leaders and 'the people'
were posed with great acuity, in different forms at different
stages of the Revolution.

Thus, though the revolutionary breakthrough at Marseilles
was made possible by popular riots, both rural and urban, in
the early months of 1789, and though Marseilles' contribution
to the revolutionary effort of France was of a 'popular' nature
(in the form of expeditions by its National Guard, by its Battalions which marched to Paris, and by the large number of
volunteers who joined the revolutionary armies), the impact of
the masses was generally directed by leaders drawn from the

ranks of the revolutionary bourgeoisie. There were no popular insurrections of great consequence after 1789. The federalists, by their selfish policies, failed to gain – or at least to keep – a popular following, while the frankly reactionary and quasi-royalist outcome of their revolt (though sparking off the most significant popular rising of this period) completely discredited the meetings of the Sections, which alone might have provided the basis for sustained popular participation in politics. Consequently, there is little indication that a *sans-culotte* movement existed in the period 1793–4. There is still less evidence for the emergence of *enragé* activity or influence. The revolutionary government seems to have almost monopolised political life from the autumn of 1793 to the summer of 1794.

From this, it appears that any treatment of the Revolution at Marseilles must be concerned, directly or indirectly, with a central theme of the continuing debate on the nature of the French Revolution, namely the problem of the role and definition of the revolutionary bourgeoisie. This problem certainly calls for rigorous study of 'social structure' – and some work is now being done on this for Marseilles – but this, of course, is not the only approach. The papers of the Revolutionary Tribunal cast much light, if sometimes from a rather oblique angle, on the social and political relationships of revolutionary Marseilles and on how these were viewed not only by committed revolutionaries and counter-revolutionaries but also by men and women whose preoccupations were not always of a highly political order. Thus, although many matters are only lightly sketched in in this study, many of the most important issues of the revolutionary period were evoked before the Tribunal at Marseilles: in its papers therefore, and in my treatment of them, are reflected many of the preoccupations and concerns which interest modern students of the Revolution.

My first acknowledgement must be to Marseilles itself, surely the most varied and best situated city of France. I would like to give a collective expression of gratitude to all who have helped me in the various archives and libraries of Marseilles – the Archives communales and départementales, the Bibliothèque Municipale and the Musée du Vieux-Marseille (all of which, incidentally, have been much enlarged and modernised since I first visited them). No less helpful have been the staffs of the Bibliothèque Municipale of Clermont-Ferrand, the Archives Nationales and Bibliothèque Nationale – and, of course, the British Museum. At the John Rylands Library, Manchester, and at King's Library of the University of Aberdeen, I have enjoyed the utmost courtesy and assistance.

I wish also to acknowledge the generosity of the Carnegie Trust for the Universities of Scotland in giving me a grant which financed one of my trips to the Midi.

I am greatly indebted to Professor Richard Cobb, my supervisor at Oxford. Professor A. Goodwin and Professor N. Hampson have likewise been generous in their encouragement and suggestions. Miss Linda Robertson, of Aberdeen, kindly read my typescript and offered useful criticism and advice. The work of Mrs Margaret Gissop of Manchester; of Mrs Ann Gordon, Mrs Mabel Watt, Mrs Christine McLeod and Miss Maureen Malcolm, all of Aberdeen, and that of my wife, Helena, has been absolutely indispensable in preparing this book for publication.

Finally, I would like to thank Mr Richard Harris, whose fine hospitality at 90c Highgate High Street has provided me with the best possible base for expeditions to the British Museum and further afield.

Aberdeen
January 1973   W. SCOTT

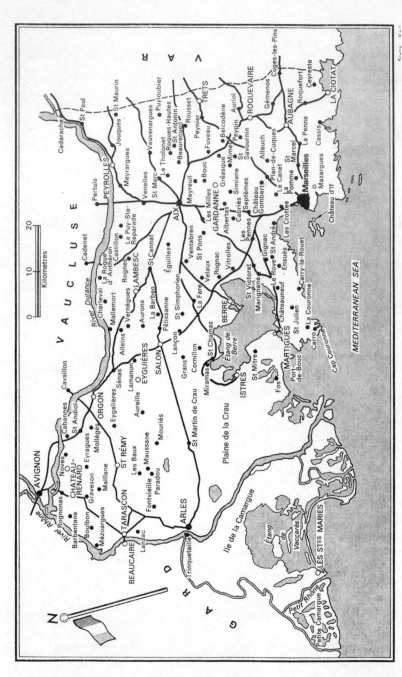

1   The Department of the Bouches-du-Rhône

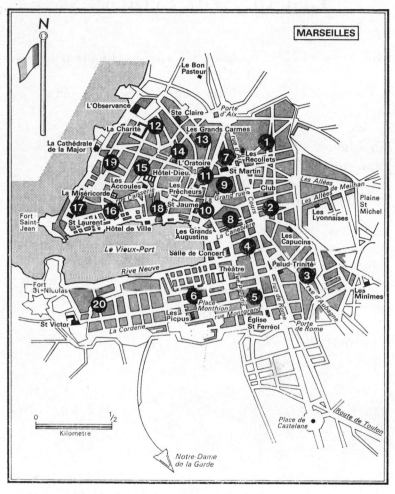

2   Plan of Marseilles. The figures show the location
of the central Sections

List of Abbreviations

ABR   Archives départementales des Bouches-
                        du-Rhône.
A. Comm.   Archives communales de la ville de
                        Marseille.
A. Nat.   Archives Nationales.
Bib. Mun.   Bibliothèque Municipale (of Marseilles).
Dept. Admin.   Departmental Administration of the
                        Bouches-du-Rhône (also Department).
Jnal. Dépts. Mérid.   *Journal des départements méridionaux.*

CHAPTER ONE

Marseilles' Revolutionary Expansionism[1]

'Les patriotes de tous les pays sont Marseillais.'
Barbaroux

The fame of Marseilles, towards the end of the eighteenth century, was European in scope; yet travellers approaching the city for the first time became increasingly perplexed as to why so large and celebrated a town had developed in so unfavourable an environment. Since leaving Lyons, their endurance had been tested by a long and often arduous journey down the Rhône valley, much of the way on bad roads passing between infertile hills. In Provence, the peasantry looked particularly miserable and ill-fed; in various localities, diseases and fevers were rife; towns and villages, not all recovered from the plague of 1720, were broken down and decrepit – one traveller remarking of Saint-Chamas that 'everything and everyone looked so wild, and the place was in such a ruinous condition that I could scarce believe I was not among the Arabs in Egypt or the ruins of Persepolis'.[2] The great flat expanse of the Crau was a scene of desolation; while Marseilles itself was surrounded by an amphitheatre of steep and barren hills, which gave space to only a small extent of fertile coastal plain. Only the elegance of Aix-en-Provence contradicted the general impression of

[1] Works generally useful for this section include: *Marseille à la fin de l'Ancien régime*, ed. F. Dollieule (Marseilles, 1896); C. F. Achard, *Description historique, géographique et topographique des villes . . . de la Provence*, (Aix, 1787), and *Dictionnaire de la Provence et du Comté Venaissin*, 4 vols. (Marseilles 1786–7) and, especially, *Tableau historique de Marseille et de ses dépendances* (Lausanne, 1789); J. B. B. Grosson, *Almanach historique de Marseille* (yearly from 1770 to 1790).

[2] Philip Thicknesse, *A Year's Journey through France and part of Spain*, 2 vols. (London, 1789) II, 42–3.

wildness and strangeness which was, to outsiders, the most
striking feature of Provence.

Seeking guidance, travellers turned naturally to history for
an account of the fame of France's most ancient city. They
learnt that 'when the rest of Gaul was in a state of barbarity,
Marseilles long subsisted as an independent republic governed
by excellent laws'. The trading city founded by the Greeks
colonised much of the western Mediterranean: its people
succumbed to Roman might only after a long struggle; and
even then 'they long enjoyed the important benefits of a free and
independent republican state; during that happy period, they
not only flourished by commerce and opulence, but were also
distinguished for learning, arts, and sciences.' Even during the
troubles of the Middle Ages, the proud city retained many of
its privileges: and twice it repulsed the armies of the Emperor
Charles V, armies which marched down from the north to
enslave it. During the Wars of Religion and later, at the time
of the Frondes, its citizens had taken up arms to recover their
ancient liberties.[1]

Such were the most striking episodes of the city's history.
From them emerged the picture of a proud and tenacious
people who had – at the southern extremity of France –
struggled with great persistence to maintain its independence
against prolonged and dangerous attacks, a people abundantly
conscious of its history and constantly determined to resist
encroachments on its liberty. This was the aspect of the town's
history most consistently highlighted by its historians and
which, by the end of the eighteenth century, had almost
assumed the proportions of a myth which might even yet help
to provoke the townspeople to action or sustain them in
adversity.[2]

But was this fierce love of freedom still an active force among
the Marseillais? After all, for more than a century, Marseilles
had developed peacefully and prosperously. And though the
gradual development of monarchical absolutism had largely
deprived the city of political privileges and any large measure

[1] Lord Gardenstone, *Travelling Memorandums made in a tour upon the Continent of Europe, in the years 1786, 87 and 88,* 3 vols. (London, 1791) I, 103 ff.

[2] See below, the use of this history by Moïse Bayle, deputy of Marseilles
to the Convention, p. 140.

of self-government, there had been no active resistance to this trend.

This may partly be explained by the very prosperity of the great port, which made rebellion increasingly unnecessary or even dangerous, and partly by the fact that the city was allowed to retain some of its former privileges, thus escaping too brutal a humiliation. These two factors are closely connected, since the most important privileges were commercial in nature. Indeed it was Louis XIV who, pursuing the twofold purpose of keeping the traditional turbulence of the Marseillais in check and increasing their prosperity, bestowed upon the port the most important privilege of all – the virtual monopoly of the Levant trade. Commercial prosperity served to dull the citizens' awareness of lost political independence as a mercantile aristocracy evolved, with ambitions rather different from those of the nobles who had formerly fought for the communal, even republican, rights of their city. Since the government backed Marseilles' privileged position – against the envious clamour of other ports – the town's patricians largely abandoned all troublesome pretensions to autonomy. Nobles and the upper ranks of the bourgeoisie were increasingly bound together by commercial interest, forming a compact, self-contained society caring more for wealth and pleasure than for public affairs, which they abandoned, with only token protests, to royal agents.

And, undoubtedly, wealth from trade did give the patricians of eighteenth-century Marseilles ample compensation for vanished political agitation – real power within the city, an incomparable standard of living, and a flourishing intellectual and social life.[1] Such a context was much too comfortable for the survival of *frondeur* activities. A *frondeur* spirit did survive; but this was directed mainly against rival seaports, rather than against the government itself. For prosperity did not kill off Marseilles' particularism, – it transformed and in a way intensified it, by stimulating pride in peaceful commercial and

---

[1] A. Chabaud, *Essai sur les classes bourgeoises dirigeantes à Marseille en 1789. Extrait de la Commission d'histoire économique, Assemblée générale de 1939, tome* I, pp. 47–144 (Paris, 1942). Also the *Série* Q, in the Archives départementales, containing the inventories of the belongings of merchants who had emigrated or been executed.

artistic emulation rather than in troublesome outbursts of revolt.[1]

And, in other respects also, the economic situation of the great port kept alive its inhabitants' conviction that they had interests which were not identical with those of Provence or of France as a whole. As a free port, Marseilles benefited from its isolation from the rest of France to pursue a lucrative entrepôt trade. Also, the city had established a quite exceptional hold over the Levant *échelles* – in fact, Marseilles rather than Versailles had real control of France's interests in the eastern Mediterranean.[2] Also, as a major importer of corn, Marseilles acted as a granary for much of the Midi, a situation which bolstered the city's feeling of power, giving it an 'overlordship' over the southern provinces.[3] Thus the very structure of its trade, together with a *conjoncture* often at variance with that of France as a whole,[4] gave reasons for independence of outlook, reasons which found forceful expression in the *cahiers*, where particularism took the form of harking back to half-eroded franchises and condemning the desires of other ports to share the rich prizes of the Levant trade. The Marseillais were annoyed at having lost some of their city's privileges but their fear that it might lose them all – and particularly its commercial privileges – kept its leading citizens from rash acts against the government.

And just as the government in its turn respected, in essentials, the unique economic situation of the port, so it refrained from abolishing the last vestiges of the city's 'political' autonomy. Thus, even now, citizens could only be invited, not ordered, to pay taxation, no citizens were to be forced to submit to a 'foreign' jurisdiction and no troops were to be admitted without

[1] For Marseilles' trade, see G. Rambert (ed.), *Histoire du commerce de Marseille publiée par la Chambre de commerce* ... (Paris, 1949 etc.) especially vols. 4, 5, 6, 7.

[2] M. Zarb, *Histoire d'une autonomie communale: Les Privilèges de la ville de Marseille du Xe siècle à la Révolution* (Paris, 1961) pp. 149ff. Till the mid-seventeenth century, Marseilles had also engaged in the practice of commandeering corn-ships in the Mediterranean, Zarb, p. 268.

[3] R. Romano, *Commerce et prix du blé à Marseille au XVIIIe siècle* (Paris, 1956).

[4] A communication by Charles Carrière, summarised in *Provence historique*, tome 18, Jan.–Mar. 1968, p. 193.

the consent of the Municipality. The preservation of these rights, to a greater or lesser degree, reconciled citizens to the loss of even wider freedom.[1]

One visitor, Lord Gardenstone, celebrated this happy union between mercantile wealth and public liberty, observing that the citizens of Marseilles 'have been allowed to enjoy valuable public rights and privileges; and they have made a wonderful progress in industry, population and opulence'; the city 'possessed all the advantages, comforts, and blessings of a republican state, without its disorders and under the steady effectual protection of a powerful monarch.' Lord Gardenstone evidently thought that Marseilles and Versailles had reached a reasonable *modus vivendi* in which the overriding claims of commercial wealth were endangered neither by a brutal enforcement of absolutist ambitions nor by the excessive advancement of particularist claims.[2]

Yet, in matters of public liberty as in economic affairs, there still remained a regret that the wings of their town's autonomy had been clipped to a very considerable extent – that, for instance, the *Intendant* of Aix had acquired a position of great power even within the council-chamber of the town. And, just as economic demands in the *cahiers* were expressed in particularist terms, so too were claims relating to political autonomy. Thus the *cahier* of the Third Estate affirmed the dual nature of the townspeople, citizens of two *patries*, Marseilles and France, each with conflicting claims upon its subjects. It modestly stressed that Marseilles would demand, of its ancient rights, only those compatible with the interests of the Nation, but warned the government that their city was a free city, an 'état à part' which had never been conquered or assimilated into France.[3]

And so, at a time when provinces and towns – especially large ones – were demanding a big voice in the regeneration of France – and in the benefits proceeding from that regeneration – the history and situation of Marseilles ensured that the great seaport should speak with a particularly strong voice and a

---

[1] The erosion of the privileges of Marseilles is best described in Zarb, op. cit.

[2] Gardenstone, I, 109.

[3] J. Fournier, p. 369, *cahier* of Third Estate.

distinctive accent. Moreover, other factors, noted with keen-
ness by outsiders, with self-satisfied complacency by *Phocéens*,
contributed to the originality of Marseilles at the outbreak of
the Revolution.

Some of these factors were attributed to the fact of its continued remoteness from the capital. Laurent Lautard, for
instance, has an amusing paragraph describing how a Marseillais, on his return from Paris, was treated as if he came from
a strange and foreign land – and the 'old Marseillais' himself
did nothing to disguise his contempt for Paris fashions and
modes of thought.[1] A more important expression of the distance between Paris and Provence, however, was the difficulty
some travellers had in making themselves understood by the
southerners, who spoke a patois 'more intelligible to a Nea-
politan than a Parisian.'[2] According to Chardon, writing in
1806, it was only in the last thirty years that the French language was 'welcomed' by the people of Marseilles: and, even
when he wrote, persons of a certain age, however elevated
their social and professional rank, persisted in speaking this
patois.[3]

While the Prefect Thibaudeau later remarked on the
propensity of the Marseillais, when abroad, to disclaim connection with France,[4] and while stories of the Provençaux' good
opinion of themselves were numerous in Paris, mutual incom-
prehension was the rule – 'Vous aurez d'étranges esprits à
gouverner en Provence', said Louis XIV to one of his agents
unfortunate enough to be sent south.[5] It remained true that,
to the cultivated Parisian, the Marseillais were strange and, on
the whole, unlikeable creatures, contaminated by their contacts
with the east. To explain their uncouthness, there was an old
saying, 'Aix-en-Provence, Marseille en Turquie, Toulon en

---

[1] L. M. Lautard, *Esquisses historiques: Marseille depuis 1789 jusqu'en 1815*,
2 vols. (Marseilles, 1844), I, 23.

[2] Nathaniel Wraxall, Junior, *Memoirs of the Kings of France . . . to which is
added A Tour through the Western, Southern and Interior Provinces of France*, 2 vols.
(London, 1777), II, 332.

[3] J. Chardon, *Tableau historique et politique de Marseille ancienne et moderne*
(Marseilles, 1806) pp. 156–7.

[4] A. C. Thibaudeau, *Mémoires, 1799–1815* (Paris, 1913) p. 104.

[5] A. J. E. Fabre, *Les Rues de Marseille*, 5 vols. (Marseilles, 1867–69) III,
351.

Barbarie'.[1] The harsh, ugly accents of the people, their swarthy complexions, the cosmopolitan crowds which strolled along the quays, all served to intensify the northerner's prejudices against the Marseillais.

Many visitors however did try to come to terms with the city and to accept its values (whereas others quickly departed in disgust). To try to define their feelings, they compared it with other towns of their acquaintance, particularly with its neighbour, Aix-en-Provence. Not all preferred the calm elegance of the smaller city (whose population was about a quarter of Marseilles' 106,000) – its fine houses, wide avenues, and gracious fountains. Nor were they all impressed by the position Aix held as capital of Provence, seat of *Parlement* and University, archbishop and *Intendant*. Indeed, Lord Gardenstone, arriving at Marseilles from Aix, saw the bustle and cosmopolitanism of the port as much more in keeping with the forward-looking, expansionist spirit of the age,[2] while Nathaniel Wraxall commented of Aix that 'The city has that air of silence and gloom so commonly characteristic of places devoid either of commerce or industry, and forms a most striking contrast to Marseilles, where opulence and population are universally visible.'[3] A Polish nobleman, Count Moszyński, noted that many bourgeois families were leaving Aix in search of a fortune in the trading city. For him, the fine buildings ill-suited a town which had an air of decrepitude about it.[4]

Thus, to the fine buildings, and imposing institutions of her august and aristocratic neighbour, Marseilles opposed her commercial wealth – to Aix's *Parlement* and archbishop, she opposed her Chamber of Commerce. Her great merchants appreciated the comments of the many visitors who admired the intricacies of soap-making or who toured the port. And much of this pride in the trade of the city permeated down to those

---

[1] M. Margarot, *Histoire ou relation d'un voyage*, 2 vols. (London, 1786) II, 147.

[2] Gardenstone, I, 99. 'Here we see no great palaces, magnificent churches, theatres, nor extraordinary fine paintings – no prince, no court; but we see objects more endearing and respectable to uncorrupted minds and the honest lovers of mankind.'

[3] N. Wraxall, II, 329–30.

[4] Count Moszyński (ed. F. Benoît), *Voyage en Provence d'un gentilhomme polonais, le comte Moszyński, 1784–1785* (Marseilles, 1930).

whose share of it was not very considerable: this is seen by reading the eloquent *éloges* which can be found in the *cahiers* of even the most humble artisans. After all, trade and the varied industries to which it gave rise, kept all types of workers, artisans and tradesmen in jobs, however much they might complain of actual conditions of employment, however much they might lament the declining state of particular industries.

But other evidence suggests that this unity of views – pride in and defence of the city's particular trading position and, by extension, of its political liberties – was more apparent than real for the bulk of the townspeople and that their celebration of their city's unique virtues rang rather hollow in the face of more immediate problems. When the mob burst into the electoral assembly, on 1 April 1789, to demand the repudiation of the *Intendant*, was this really an assertion of Marseilles' right to municipal independence? For the populace, the *Intendant* was, above all, the protector of those men who, in positions of authority, used their power to fill their own pockets, to profit from the high price of foodstuffs and to perpetuate abuses in the administration of the town. But while many of the electors recognised this motive (some welcomed it, others feared it), to most of them the *Intendant* was primarily an agent of the central government, who could control municipal debates and whose position as inspector of commerce gave him wide powers in the economic life of the city; and it was for this reason that they acquiesced in the rejection of his authority.

In fact, citizens united in the fairly general demand for the restoration of former privileges, were sharply divided on more pressing problems – problems relating to the internal administration of the town. Thus the *ouvriers cordonniers*, who had bitter reasons for brusqueness, would not pay even lip-service to the need to recover former municipal independence; they wanted more tangible reforms and did not care who provided them – indeed, they expressly begged the king to assume full control of Marseilles, to unite his city with Provence, so that it might be better administered than in the past.[1] So blunt a repudiation of ideas prevalent, in a dilettante fashion, in upper-class circles, was unique; but, taken with other bitter denunciations of the municipal régime, it does suggest that large sections of the

---

[1] J. Fournier, p. 104.

townspeople were concerned not with the status of their town in a regenerated France, but with more immediate problems concerning day-by-day living conditions within the town.

Besides the numerous grievances expressed by members of various guilds who complained of adverse conditions affecting their own branches of industry, attention was above all drawn to abuses in the financial administration of the city. The tax-barriers which surrounded the town were subjected to a savage pounding from practically every section of the community, but, for really devastating denunciations, the *cahiers* of the poorer artisans exceed all others, quoting figures to show how the farms increased the price of basic foodstuffs (bread, meat and wine) and raw materials, thus contributing to the stagnation of several artisanal trades and to the general misery of the labouring classes.[1] Far from benefiting the lower classes, this symbol of the particular status of Marseilles brought prosperity only to a corrupt oligarchy and to its associates in politics and the judiciary.

This attack on the town-farms was accompanied by demands for a more democratic system of town-government. It was for instance suggested that the guilds should elect representatives to the town-council. This was seen partly as a return to earlier and more liberal régimes[2] but mainly as a means to clean up the financial affairs of the town and to shift the burden of taxation from foodstuffs on to land and urban properties, thus tapping the city's commercial wealth for the benefit of the community as a whole.

Thus there existed a very strong current of popular indignation having as its target abuses specific to Marseilles. While particularist feeling did influence the ways in which this indignation was expressed, a mere return to an alleged golden age of municipal autonomy could not provide the basic answer to the problems of the bulk of the townsmen: only for a short time would such a reactionary slogan prove, for some people, adequate promise of improved conditions.

[1] J. Fournier, pp. 4 ff., the *arquebusiers*; p. 14, the *arts de la soie*; pp. 33–4, the *maîtres caissiers*; p. 376, the Third Estate.

[2] The municipal settlement of 1652 was often mentioned, by which guilds sent representatives to the municipality. For these *doléances*, see J. Fournier, p. 7, pp. 44 ff. etc. etc. Also A. Crémieux, 'Le particularisme municipal à Marseille en 1789', *Révolution française*, LII, 1907, pp. 191–215.

So, to explain the unusual intensity of the revolutionary struggle within Marseilles – beginning with the violence of the early months of 1789, and leading to the extreme Jacobinism of 1792–3 and to the federalist reaction to that extremism in the summer of 1793 – other forces besides particularism must be invoked; but these forces can be seen in relation to the particularist framework within which they tended to find expression.

And, in fact, one highly important aspect of local patriotism did have strong, tenacious roots in the social and economic conditions of the town – the turbulent 'republicanism' which outsiders, whether French or foreign, had attributed to the Marseillais throughout their history. It was almost as if Marseilles was seen as a political volcano, at France's southern border, which, though it had not erupted since the Frondes, was regarded with apprehension in periods of peace and prosperity, and with a sort of panic in times of political disturbance. To combat the unruly character of the townspeople, Louis XIV had constructed or rebuilt the two forts which flanked the entrance to the Vieux-Port; but this spirit of turbulence remained. Wraxall found that 'The common people have a brutality and rudeness of manners more characteristic of a republican than a monarchical state'[1] while Count Moszyński declared that the townsmen were 'wholly republican' and 'ready to revolt at the least threat of their privileges'.[2] A Swiss gentleman, visiting Marseilles in 1787, wrote that the common people of the town regarded themselves as the citizens of a republic and looked down on the French, who were treated almost as slaves.[3]

For some observers, this unruliness and brutality were enlivened by more genial qualities: to Dulaure, for instance, the townspeople, thanks to the heat of the sun, were gay, lively, easily carried away both by pleasure and anger – 'inflammable' is the epithet he applies to them.[4] And indeed many outsiders called in the sun as an explanation of the volatile nature of the Marseillais.

In speaking of the common people in this fashion, these writers were thinking especially of the inhabitants of the old

---

[1] N. Wraxall, II, 332.   [2] Moszyński, op. cit., p. 82.

[3] H. Barré, *Marseille en 1787 et en 1891* (Marseilles, 1895); also S. Vialla, *Les Volontaires des Bouches-du-Rhône* (Paris, 1913) p. 20.

[4] A. J. E. Fabre, *Les Rues de Marseille*, 5 vols. (Marseilles, 1867–69) III, 353.

town which, overlooking the Vieux-Port from the north, formed
a redoubt in which old values survived more strongly than in
the more spacious and opulent new quarters on the other side
of the harbour. And though differences between the two halves
of the city – differences in which physical geography was closely
related to deeply ingrained attitudes – should not be exaggerated,
especially as factors of political motivation, they were none the
less considerable.

The *vieille ville* (the site of the earliest settlement on the
French coast), remained unrivalled until, from the reign of
Louis XIII onwards and especially in the second half of the
eighteenth century, new quarters were constructed at the head
of the Vieux-Port and on the land under the shadow of Notre-
Dame de la Garde. The tortuous streets of the old town, its
steep alleyways and narrow passages between tall houses which
shut out the sunlight, formed the greatest possible contrast to
the well-planned elegance of the more recent areas. Visitors
differed only as regards the precise degree of unpleasantness of
the ancient, more crowded area of the town. Wraxall had no
doubts that 'The old city is one of the most nasty and ill-built in
Europe. I have never had courage enough to penetrate its
recesses, which are insupportably filthy'[1] and all agreed that
unwary visitors risked a deluge from some 'abominable cascade'
or being 'over the shoe with filth'; all lamented the absence of
lanternes and latrines. Though there seems to be little evidence to
suggest that then, as in more recent times, the old town was
regarded by the citizens of more salubrious areas with a disgust
amounting almost to fear, observations on its unwholesome
aspects were not confined to strangers – Achard remarking on
the foul smoke-laden air which, he thought, engendered unruly
passions and dangerous acts.[2]

Moreover, a glance through the rough notes of the police[3]

---

[1] N. Wraxall, ii, 333. See also P. Thicknesse, *A Year's Journey through France
and part of Spain*, 2 vols. (London, 1789) pp. 56–7: 'surely, exclusive of its fine
harbour and favourable situation for trade, [Marseilles] has very little to
recommend it, but riot, mob and confusion. Provisions are very dear and
not very good.'

[2] C. F. Achard, *Dictionnaire de la Provence*, ii, 29 ff., article on Marseilles.

[3] A. Comm., 2143, *Police: brouillard de notes, 1792, No. 4*; Moszyński,
p. 100, mentions a 'Tribunal des pauvres' which met on Sundays to sort
out popular quarrels.

gives some measure of the life led in this area of the town – fights were common; domestic brawls infuriated neighbours, who called in the police; 'chiens méchants' terrorised passers-by; children were lost or abandoned; the police spent much time tracing lost relatives, absent wives or husbands; complaints about noise were frequent. Conditions of hygiene are indicated by a petition from a butcher who complained that residents above his shop 'habitually' threw out filth which spoilt his meat. Visitors complained of the lack of police, the large numbers of beggars and diseased and mutilated people in the streets.

The presence of the Mont-de-Piété,[1] together with numerous charitable institutions, notably the enormously enlarged Hôtel-Dieu and the vast Hôpital de la Charité, suggests the largely popular nature of the older part of the town. Since the plague of 1720, the loss of population (almost half the citizens, or 40–50,000 people, not more than a thousand of whom were above the rank of worker or artisan),[2] had more than been made good, both by natural growth and immigration, so overcrowding must have been almost intolerable.

Thus[3] the northern quays of the Vieux-Port presented a much more animated sight than those to the south; and the streets leading up from the harbour were busy with merchandise being distributed throughout the old town. The Maison Commune faced directly on to the waterfront, and in its rooms the great merchants met in the *Loge* to conclude every type of mercantile business. The area round about was extremely busy,

---

[1] A. François Simon, *Le Mont-de-Piété de Marseille* (Marseilles, 1939).

[2] *Histoire de la Provence*, ed. E. Baratier (Toulouse, 1969) p. 359.

[3] Besides the well-known geographical dictionary of the *abbé* Expilly and the previously cited work of Achard and almanacs of Grosson, we have consulted Augustin Fabre, op. cit., and A. Bouyala d'Arnaud's *Évocation du Vieux Marseille* (Paris, 1964), as well as various articles cited in the bibliography. See also P. Masson, *La Provence au XVIIIe siècle*, 3 vols. (Paris, 1936); G. Rambert, *Marseille, la formation d'une grande cité moderne* (Marseilles, 1934); J. Chardon, *Almanach historique, politique et commercial de Marseille* (Marseilles, 1803–1804); J. Chardon, *Tableau historique et politique de Marseille ancienne et moderne* (Marseilles, 1806 and subsequent years); C. F. Achard, *Tableau historique de Marseille et de ses dépendances* (Lausanne, 1789); J. J. Mazet, *Le Guide marseillais, contenant la liste alphabétique des noms, maisons de commerce et demeures de MM. les négociants, marchands, manufacturiers . . . de la ville de Marseille* (Marseilles, 1789) etc.

with men of all professions represented in its crowded streets –
from fairly substantial merchants, lawyers and exchange
brokers, to their clerks, sailors, warehouse-porters and the like.
Essentially, however, this district between the Grand'rue, the
rue Caisserie and the harbour,[1] was one of small-scale businesses
satisfying a varied clientele – cobblers, tailors and hatters were
predominant, as far as numbers were concerned, but all types
of *marchands* were easily available, with grocers, chemists and
drapers also numerous. The presence of jewellers, watchmakers
and glovers, as well as dealers in foreign wines and in engravings,
suggests, moreover, that the commerce of this area was not
confined to satisfying the most banal needs of the townspeople –
indeed, if we are to judge from Grosson's street-guide, specifically designed to help strangers find the best places to buy all
types of goods,[2] this area of town was undoubtedly the most
'commerçant', provided with the widest possible range of
commercial establishments.[3]

Further to the west, however, one came to quarters from
which luxury and comfort were banished, where, around the
church of Saint-Laurent, and beneath the walls of Fort Saint-
Jean, fishermen and sailors, many from Genoa and other
foreign ports, had long established their principal settling-
ground. Compared with the seafarers, men of other professions
were few. Warehouse-porters, caulkers, customs officials lived
there in limited forces, but very few professional men, merchants,
bourgeois or *propriétaires*. Nor, at the other end of the scale, was

[1] This area was centred on the Maison Commune where Section 18,
La Loge, was to meet. To the east was Section 10 (Saint-Jaume), while
Section 8 met in the Grands Augustins, at the town end of the Vieux-Port.
To the west, Section 16, of the Grande Miséricorde, extended to the eastern
boundary of Section 17 – the fishermen's Section of Saint-Laurent.

[2] Grosson, almanac for 1781, pp. 251 ff., *Liste indicative des principales rues,
où se trouvent les magasins des divers objets de marchandise de détail, pour la commodité
des étrangers*.

[3] Besides the secondary sources and contemporary almanacs and guides,
indications as to the distribution of the population of Marseilles were found
in ABR, L1063–L1071, containing lists of citizens who, according to their
Sections, demanded *cartes de sûreté* in the Year II; and L1982, providing
fragmentary census-returns for various districts of Marseilles at various times
from 1793 onwards. Obviously, no attempt has been made here to use these
sources exhaustively or scientifically but they do provide some measure of
statistical control over our 'literary' sources.

there any concentration of industrial workers.[1]

In fact, many of Marseilles' industries were situated rather further from the harbour, in the area north of the rue Caisserie, a bustling road which formed the southern boundary of the *vieille ville* proper.[2] Within the town, industry, mostly on a small-scale basis, was fairly well dispersed and largely diversified; but some areas did have an unusually high concentration of industrial workshops. The unpicturesque and undescribed district immediately within the northern walls, and especially around the nunnery of Sainte-Claire, is a case in point, containing numerous soap factories, tanneries, sugar refineries and bleaching houses. In its closely-packed streets lived the families of tanners, soap workers, starch makers as well as hatters and undifferentiated 'ouvriers'. Also – underlining the industrial as opposed to commercial nature of this area – a substantial number of manufacturers (of starch, woollen goods, tobacco, stockings, glue and soap) lived there, in marked contrast to the very small numbers of merchants, *bourgeois*, clerks and property-owners. Masons, tanners and warehouse-porters, as well as the cobblers who lived in large numbers throughout the old town, formed the rest of the labouring classes of this area,[3] many of whom, no doubt, went outside the town walls to work in the soap, sulphur, pottery, glass, tanning and bleaching establishments of the *banlieue* Saint-Lazare, on either side of the road to Aix.[4]

Between this area, the north-western districts of the city, and the largely commercial streets leading down to the harbour, was situated, on fairly high ground, the very heart of the old town, stretching between the churches of Les Accoules, Les Prêcheurs and Saint-Martin. This was perhaps the most densely populated quarter of Marseilles; but only the presence of the Palais de Justice attracted professional men – notably *avocats* and *procureurs* – though even they sometimes had offices here, but preferred to live in the more attractive areas nearer the harbour

[1] This area was to be Section 17, of Saint-Laurent.

[2] Invaluable for the study of the location of industry at Marseilles is the *Plan topographique de la ville de Marseille*, of M. Desmarest, begun in 1802 and finished in 1808.

[3] Sections 12 (L'Observance); 13 (des Grands Carmes); 14 (L'Oratoire); 15 (L'Hôtel-Dieu) and 19 (La Major) were situated in this area.

[4] To be Section 24.

or in the new town. Otherwise, as Achard and Grosson pointed out, men of distinction were inclined to abandon districts where the streets were narrow and dirty, the houses dilapidated, without courtyards and gardens. And so this area was inhabited not only by the ubiquitous cobblers, perhaps even more numerous here than elsewhere in the old town, not only by small-scale tradesmen such as tailors and hatters, and heavy manual workers – masons and warehouse-porters – but also by a class of rather seedy dealers in old clothes, old furniture and old ironware, whose nefarious activities were described with obvious distaste by their more respectable fellow-citizens. The churches of Saint-Martin and Les Prêcheurs were central points in this somewhat depressed area, the latter being regarded as the very centre of the old town, and thus serving, in March 1789, as a meeting-place for the election of deputies to the States-General, and as a forum where the citizens demanded action to bring down the high price of bread. This last fact, in particular, underlines the popular nature of this district – where also were to be found several of the most important markets of Marseilles.[1]

The whole *vieille ville*, with the partial exception of the streets closest to the harbour, was characterised by the low proportion of men of wealth and distinction who chose to reside there. It was not until one crossed the rue d'Aix into the north-eastern quarter of the city that, in more spacious surroundings, one encountered a significant increase in the number of property-owners, merchants and *bourgeois*. The change is fairly striking – for in the section of the town immediately to the west of the rue d'Aix, centred on the church of Saint-Martin (later Section 7), a list of citizens suggests that there were some six times fewer *propriétaires* than in the adjacent Section (No. 1) to the east of the rue d'Aix, and that the number of *bourgeois* was proportionately almost as low.[2] Also, the better-frequented Section boasted a sizeable class of merchants who were hardly re-

---

[1] Les Prêcheurs formed the meeting-place of Section 11, soon to distinguish itself for its revolutionary zeal. Section 7 was to meet in the church of Saint-Martin, while Section 9 met in the chapel of the Pénitents de Saint-Antoine.

[2] For Section 7 – Saint-Martin – ABR, L1066; Section 1, Recollets, L1064.

presented in its neighbour. Also, perhaps a fair indication of commercial activity, the number of clerks was substantially higher in the eastern section.

And, going southwards, even more well-to-do quarters are reached, especially the area on both sides of the rue de Noailles, a continuation of which, the famous Canebière, led down to the head of the Vieux-Port. The most majestic thoroughfare of Marseilles, the Cours, bisected this area, impressing visitors by the width of its tree-lined carriageway, by the splendid regularity of its buildings and by the fashionable nature of the crowds which strolled along it. In this area lived some of the wealthiest merchants of Marseilles – Seimandy and Hugues *l'aîné*, both extremely rich, lived in the place de Noailles; Simon Laflèche, alderman (*échevin*), resided just off the rue de Noailles; Étienne Martin, a future mayor, had a house in the nearby rue du Tapis-Vert, while the director of the *Compagnie royale d'Afrique* lived in the parallel rue Thubaneau. And these men, active in the commercial life of their city, were within easy reach of their colleagues – merchants, *bourgeois*, exchange brokers, *propriétaires* and manufacturers – and of men and women who served them in all sorts of capacities, clerks, tailors, hairdressers, cooks, innkeepers, café owners, jewellers, watchmakers, sculptors and tradesmen of all description: not to mention high class prostitutes. All these were categories which seem to have expanded in size during the century. Apparently many tradesmen had migrated from the old town to satisfy a more wealthy and demanding clientele: and the Cours and the Canebière especially were fashionable streets, catering for discriminating tastes, for men who bought books, engravings, imported wines, leather goods; for women seeking articles of fashion or expensive furnishings for the sumptuous houses of the new town[1] – for the type of people, in short, who read the 'small advertisements' in Beaugeard's *Journal de Provence*.

But perhaps the most elegant streets, of all those in Marseilles, led southwards from the Canebière, particularly the rues de Rome, de Paradis and Saint-Ferréol which, with the equally splendid lateral streets, formed the most distinguished area of the city – devoted to art and pleasure in the Salle de Concert and

[1] This area comprised Section 2 – Saint-François – and, further from the port, Section 23 – des Capucins.

the Nouvelle Salle de Spectacle, to luxury, to commerce and to stylish, even noble, living.[1] Many eminent citizens resided here: the great Roux de Corse, most famous of all merchants of Marseilles, had owned a vast *hôtel* in the rue Montgrand and nearby was the residence of a scarcely less distinguished merchant, Basile Samatan. In the district of Saint-Ferréol, the most opulent of the three Sections forming this area, the names of merchants and property-owners predominate, while exchange brokers were more numerous here than in other areas and clerks formed an extremely important category. There was also a large number of craftsmen and artists here and in the adjacent district of the Salle de Concert, where, however, closer proximity to the south side of the harbour was revealed by a larger number of warehouse-porters, caulkers, corders and the like. This proportion increases as one goes towards the Fort Saint-Nicolas at the entrance to the Vieux-Port, an area in which many soap factories were established, where along the Corderie ropes were twisted, where in great warehouses wines and spirits were stored. Here also were situated the shipbuilding yards, with their work-force of caulkers, carpenters, workers in iron and in wood. Unlike the old town, however, the streets were wide and regular and the townspeople were not huddled together in excessively cramped conditions.[2]

So, in this hurried tour of the city, we have seen that it may be divided up into various zones, some richer or poorer than others, some with a predominantly commercial, others with a primarily industrial character. Obviously the boundaries between these areas were not clear-cut – nor did they always bear a very rational relationship to the constituency districts (or Sections) into which the town was to be divided. Not all the streets of the old town were dirty recesses deserted by rich merchants, as is shown both by Grosson's almanacs and by Mazet's series of commercial directories which gave the addresses of the most important people in Marseilles' economic life.[3] The fact that the transference to the new town of the Maison Commune, the Bourse and the Palais de Justice, had

[1] The richest area was to become Section 5 – Saint-Ferréol; Section 6 – Picpus – and Section 4 – Salle de Concert – were adjacent.

[2] Section 20 – Saint-Victor, after the famous and ancient abbey of that name.   [3] J. J. Mazet, op. cit.

been proposed and rejected, shows the reality of, and the limitations to, the drift of wealthy and influential people to the new town.[1]

Moreover, Mazet's guides also underline the fact that industries were to be found not only around the Porte d'Aix but also near the Portes de Rome and de Paradis. In fact, Grosson, so painstaking in listing, street by street, the whereabouts of shops, left the visitor to his own devices when it came to visiting manufactories, explaining that, as they were so numerous and so widely dispersed, they could not easily be missed.

Nevertheless there did exist a marked difference between a wealthy district such as that of Saint-Ferréol, with its gracious modern church built in a tree-shaded square, and the Section of Les Prêcheurs, its old church surrounded by the mean and overcrowded streets of a poor parish; between districts whose largest building was the Hôtel-Dieu or Hospice de la Charité and those whose residents lived only a short step from the Theatre and Concert Hall.

Chardon wrote that the merchants and office-holders who lived in the new town, source of all pleasures and amusements, gave hardly a thought to the poor districts, yet the old town was the most heavily populated, housing seamen and workers of all description, without whom the city's trade could not survive – and it was the old town which was the city of the *Phocéens* and their descendants.[2] Achard and Grosson likewise lamented the ill-repute and contempt into which the *vieille ville* had fallen from so noble beginnings.

It is however difficult to decide the extent to which the differences between various districts gave rise to differences in attitude as between their inhabitants. There was undoubtedly a link between the poor living conditions of the bulk of the townspeople,[3] and the social and economic grievances expressed in the *cahiers*. Some of the most vehement attacks on the tax-farms and the old municipal system came from corporations

[1] A. J. E. Fabre, *Notice historique sur les anciennes rues de Marseille* (Marseilles, 1862) p. 17. See also his lists showing that many men eminent in the commercial life of the city still lived in the old town, pp. 15 ff.

[2] J. Chardon, *Tableau historique* . . . (1806) p. 139.

[3] The census of 1790 gave the population of Marseilles, including the *campagne* immediately adjacent, as 106,585; 49,973 of these lived in the small area of the old town (Sections 7 to 19).

whose members – cobblers, warehouse-porters, hatters, tailors and the like – were extremely well represented in the older quarters. Certainly the men and women of the old town formed, at the outset of the Revolution, a potentially explosive section of the population, with their own pressing grievances and their own turbulent methods of gaining satisfaction.

Important in their own right, these men were perhaps equally important in providing the revolutionary leaders with men and slogans to levy against the old régime. Men drawn not from the highest nor yet the lowest rank of society, residing in the new town as often as the old, found in popular discontents an effective weapon with which to dispossess the men in office. The streets of the *vieille ville* were thronged with men whose demands threatened the comfortable positions of the well-to-do merchants and lawyers of the rue Paradis and Allées de Meilhan, and who, enrolled in the National Guard, the Battalion of 10 August, or the armies of the Republic, extended their activities far beyond the shores of the Vieux-Port.

It is the interaction of these social and economic factors and the fierce local patriotism of the revolutionaries of Marseilles, the clash between these dynamic factors and the increasing immobilism of large sections of the affluent community of the town, which underlie the revolutionary history of Marseilles and help explain the particular physiognomy of the revolutionary struggle, providing a situation of conflict both between social groups within the city and between the city and the wider world of revolutionary France.

*　　*　　*

In briefly sketching the early course of the Revolution at Marseilles, we concentrate on those factors which seem to be found to a more significant degree here than in most other cities of France. The revolutionary struggle was here fought out with particular intensity, conflicting parties drawing their strength from deep-rooted social divisions. A particularly rapid progress towards extremism on the part of the revolutionary leaders was paralleled by a stubborn current of social conservatism among their richer fellow-citizens. At first expressed in open opposition to the 'patriots', terrorised for a time into silence, this current emerged openly in the federalist revolt of 1793. Also, going hand in hand with the movement towards revolutionary extremism culminating in revolutionary excesses, was the growing impetus of revolutionary expansionism. This expansionism, the dynamic expression of the traditional particularism and turbulence of the Marseillais, finding a new outlet in a time of troubles, likewise drew much of its strength from the grievances of the popular classes of the city (the National Guard providing an all-important link) and was likewise used by the revolutionary leaders to beat down obstacles to the complete triumph of their principles. The Marseillais were thereby encouraged to believe that they had a duty, as well as a necessity, to march always in the vanguard of the Revolution, not only to keep pace with Paris, but to outstrip the capital, and above all to convert all Provence, by force if need be, to the most advanced policies of the Revolution. Fired with their vision of Marseilles as a power-house of revolutionary energy, the leaders mounted a double assault, aiming not only at gaining power for themselves within the city, but also at winning for their city complete control of the Revolution throughout Provence. With this end in view, Aix was dethroned from its position of privilege and power, the hard-pressed patriots of Arles and Avignon were 'liberated' by armed columns, those of Paris were aided, on two occasions, in overthrowing the king; and by the autumn of 1792 towns as far apart – and as important – as Lyons and Nice were urged, by envoys sent within their walls, to raise themselves to the exalted revolutionary standards of the Provençal port.

These acts formed a kind of Jacobin federalism which, drawing strength from past traditions, preceded and prepared the way for the reactionary federalism of 1793. For many citizens, one type of federalism led imperceptibly into the other; for federalist aspirations were deeply ingrained in the character of the Marseillais, whatever their revolutionary opinions. But though this aspect of the revolutionary activity of the Marseillais is obviously of vital importance in considering their readiness to reject the leadership of Paris, there is a sense in which it is incidental to the history of the revolt of 1793, since it is the reactionary content of this revolt – as much as its federalist form – which proved so attractive or abhorrent to the conflicting parties who used both Paris and Marseilles as battlegrounds. The large element of social and political conservatism to be found in the events of 1793 stemmed from the earliest stages of the Revolution, arising inevitably from the scenes of violence and mass-enthusiasm which heralded more widespread disturbances: as waves of agitation spread throughout Provence, reaching a peak of intensity in the spring of 1793 – when the Jacobins of Paris and Provence seemed about to plunge France into complete 'anarchy' and when the trade and industry of the great port had received a most serious blow from the onset of the maritime war – the forces of conservatism were impelled once more to assert themselves in order to bring to an end the period of agitation and disturbance.

Thus Marseilles was both divided deeply within itself and alienated at one time or another from the course of the Revolution in other parts of France. Never a backwater in the torrent of revolutionary politics, the southern city soon became an object of interest, concern or alarm to the whole of France, so that by the autumn of 1792 its citizens were regarded either as bloodthirsty brigands or as saviours of the Republic.

*   *   *

Certainly the Revolution started at Marseilles as it was to continue, the city at once becoming an object of concern to the central government and an object of emulation to all patriots.[1] Political polarisation was rapid.[2] In Provence, a restricted

[1] The following section summarises, in an extremely condensed form, research undertaken in the Archives Nationales and, especially, in the Archives communales of Marseilles, research which it is hoped to publish more extensively elsewhere. Among crucial secondary works are R. Baehrel, *Une Croissance: la Basse-Provence rurale*, 2 vols. (Paris, 1961) and J. Égret, 'La Pré-Révolution en Provence, 1787–89', *Annales historiques de la Révolution française*, 1954, pp. 97–126. In the Municipal Library of Marseilles, the *Recueil de François Michel de Léon* (No. 4717) provides a splendid corpus of printed documents.

[2] Interesting narrative accounts of the course of the Revolution at Marseilles are provided by Laurent-Marie Lautard, *Esquisses historiques: Marseille depuis 1789 jusqu'en 1815*, 2 vols. (Marseilles, 1844); C. Lourde, *Histoire de la Révolution à Marseille et en Provence depuis 1789 jusqu'au Consulat*, 3 vols. (Marseilles, 1838–39); S. Vialla, *Marseille révolutionnaire* (Paris, 1910). Indispensable is *Les Bouches-du-Rhône, Encyclopédie départementale publiée ... sous la direction de Paul Masson*, 16 vols. (Marseilles, 1914–37). See also

section of the nobility – the fief-owners – backed by the upper clergy, conducted a last-ditch defence of their privileged position in political life. This position – especially their virtual control of the provincial Estates – was bitterly challenged in the winter of 1788–9 at meetings throughout the province, attended not only by men of bourgeois status – lawyers,merchants,members of the liberal professions, tradesmen – but also by artisans and peasants (including both property-owners and *travailleurs*, or rural wage-labourers, who owned little or no property). With the effects of the bad harvest of 1788, aggravated by a severe mortality of olives, popular rioting occurred, directed against the *seigneurs*, with attacks on châteaux, but also against the rich of all three Orders and against royal tax-collectors. According to the *Intendant* and the military commander,[1] these attacks were directed against 'la bonne bourgeoisie' as well as against the *seigneurs*, against the bourgeois *consuls* of the townships, often as oppressive as the nobles, as well as against bishops and tax-collectors. And many bourgeois, who had, as agents, lawyers and advisers of the *seigneurs*, integrated themselves within the feudal régime, felt the onslaught of agitation by artisans and men drawn from the poorer sections of the peasantry. Though many nobles and administrators blamed bourgeois propaganda for arousing the lower classes, these widespread riots, culminating towards the end of March 1789, forced some sort of *rapprochement* between nobles (the fief-holders, for example, abandoning the defence of their fiscal privileges) and *roturier* landowners. In the face of pressure from below, there is evidence to suggest that even the better-off peasants (*ménagers*) rallied to the forces of order and co-operated with nobles and bourgeois in forming 'bourgeois' guards to contain lawlessness in the countryside. The long-term effect of the riots seems to have been to weaken the position of the nobles – already

---

Histoire de la Provence, ed. E. Baratier (Toulouse, 1969) and the *Atlas historique : Provence, Comtat Venaissin, Orange, Nice, Monaco*, ed. E. Baratier, G. Duby, E. Hildesheimer (Paris, 1969). Ferréol Beaugeard's *Journal de Provence* gives a vivid account of events. For the earlier period, G. Guibal, *Mirabeau et la Provence*, 2 vols. (Paris, 1887–91), is also extremely valuable.

[1] The *Intendant* was Charles-Jean-Baptiste des Galois, seigneur de la Tour; the military commander, Victor-Maurice de Riquet, comte de Caraman. Many of their reports are to be found in A. Nat., H1238, H1240 and H1274.

weakened somewhat by social and economic developments in the eighteenth century – and to strengthen the position of the bourgeoisie in the countryside.

The riots had repercussions within Marseilles. Though the city was cushioned from the worst effects of the fluctuation of corn prices because of its rôle as an importer of corn on a massive scale, bread cost 5 *sous* in March[1] and the tax-farms were strongly denounced for needlessly increasing the price of foodstuffs and raw materials, thus causing stagnation or recession in several basic trades and industries. As the guilds met for elections to the States-General and to draw up *cahiers*, those most affected by the bad economic situation found ready champions among the patriots, whose main immediate objective was to replace the old oligarchical government of the city. Men who were to play varying rôles in the Revolution now mounted the political stage for the first time and with powerful effect. In January, Mathieu Blanc-Gilli, a merchant, had published an *exposé* of the immense profits of the tax-farmers, together with a plan for a more equitable system of taxation. On 20 March, in the church of Les Prêcheurs, Étienne Chompré, *chancelier* of the consulate of Rome, made a violent denunciation of the tax-farms and the *Intendant*. Charles Barbaroux and Étienne-Jean Lejourdan, both young *avocats*, helped draft the *cahiers* of several guilds.[2]

Agitation culminated on 23 March, when, after various irregular meetings where *doléances* were drawn up, a crowd attacked the house of a tax-farmer and the *hôtel de l'Intendance*. The Municipality proclaimed big reductions in the price of bread and meat and admitted electors of the Third Estate – soon to be joined by deputies of the nobility and clergy – to form a 'reinforced council'. In response to the rioting, a

---

[1] R. Romano, *Commerce et prix du blé à Marseille au XVIIIᵉ siècle* (Paris, 1956) pp. 49 ff.

[2] Mathieu Blanc-Gilli became a member of the Legislative Assembly but was expelled after 10 Aug. 1792, for opposing that insurrection. Étienne Chompré, born Paris in 1742, was in prison when elected to the first revolutionary Municipality (Feb. 1790): later, he was elected *greffier* of the Criminal Tribunal of the Bouches-du-Rhône and kept this post when this body became the Revolutionary Tribunal in Aug. 1793: see below, pp. 145–6.

Étienne-Jean Lejourdan did not play so prominent a rôle as his colleague Charles Barbaroux, the celebrated deputy to the Convention.

patriotic guard was formed – the first in France – which both protected the property of the rich merchants and became the centre-point of patriotic agitation. The mayor – a noble – and some of his colleagues fled, as did the *Intendant*. Some of the richest merchants of the city – Samatan, Hugues, etc. – joined with some leading nobles, clerics and royal office-holders to appeal for royal intervention, picturing the city as given over to violence and rapine. As a result the military commander established himself at Marseilles (20 May) and quashed the Reinforced Council, though patriots were still added, from time to time, to the old Municipality at moments of intense popular pressure. The patriotic guard – 'la jeunesse citoyenne' – was replaced by an avowedly bourgeois guard, half of whose officers were nobles, half bourgeois – including some of the town's richest merchants.[1] Royal troops entered the city and provided *force majeure* for a tribunal of enquiry under the *grand prévôt* Bournissac.[2] This tribunal imprisoned many of the leading patriots, including Chompré, François-Trophime Rebecquy and Omer Granet,[3] and forced others to leave Marseilles. Its justice was denounced as arbitrary and repressive and helped to unite virtually the whole town behind the patriots – with the exception of those nobles, clerics, office-holders, army officers and prominent merchants who gave evidence against the patriots. These however became increasingly isolated in a hostile city and trembled at news of disturbances in the countryside of Provence as well as at events at Paris. The guilds held meetings, drafted petitions and proclamations against Bournissac. The patriot leaders, largely ignoring nobles and clerics who were numerically, economically and ideologically weak at Marseilles,[4]

[1] Much useful information on merchants and their rôle is to be found in A. Chabaud, *Essai sur les classes bourgeoises*, op. cit. For the fate of two eminent merchants, Joseph Hugues and Basile Samatan, see below, pp. 137, 158, 302–3.

[2] Noel-Étienne-François-Antoine Senchon de Bournissac, *prévôt-général de Provence*: executed by judgement of the Revolutionary Tribunal at Marseilles; see below, p. 208.

[3] François-Trophime Rebecquy, future member of the Convention, who denounced Robespierre's alleged aspirations to dictatorship, left Paris for Marseilles during the federalist revolt, but after its defeat drowned himself in the Vieux-Port (1 May 1794): François-Omer Granet, a prosperous *tonnelier*, future Montagnard in the Convention.

[4] See A. Chabaud, op. cit.

directed their attacks against the richest merchants, accused of
wanting a revolution for themselves alone, in order to mono-
polise public office. They were denounced for benefiting from
the unjust tax system, which spared their lands and trading
profits, and thus defending the corrupt Municipality of the
Ancien régime. The patriots, many of whom were themselves
merchants, though of 'the second class' – others being *fabricants*,
master artisans, members of the liberal professions – attacked
the 'commercial aristocracy' for monopolising wealth, apeing
the nobility by purchasing titles and investing in land and
honours (to the detriment of investment in trade and industry).
And certainly some of the most eminent merchants had become
noble, many had large landed estates, and some used their
landed fortune as a foundation for their pretensions to wield a
virtual monopoly of political power.

Unfortunately for their cause, however, the municipal
elections of January–February 1790 brought the patriots to
power. The new Municipality, backed by the frequent meetings
of the guilds and by the district assemblies (or Sections) to
which the national electoral qualification was only slackly
applied, declared unambiguous hostility to Bournissac and
made his task impossible. Several members of the new Municipality were, in fact, in prison under Bournissac's orders: but
patriotic and popular pressure forced their release and the
grand prévôt and the military commander were forced to flee the
town. Thus the new Municipality was now completely in
control. The aristocratic Bourgeois Guard was replaced by a
truly National Guard, for which artisans seem to have provided
the bulk of manpower. Now Marseilles fully recognised the
National Assembly: a new era of politics began. The Municipality was headed by a merchant and the major part of its
membership was made up of merchants, with manufacturers
and *bourgeois* also well represented. Sixteen out of forty-two
notables (assistant town-councillors) were merchants: and men
of this profession were active and numerous in electoral
assemblies, in the National Guard and in the Club (which first
met on 11 April 1790, with the mayor presiding). Certainly
members of the restricted group of top-ranking merchants
were largely absent but at Marseilles, at least, the success of the
Revolution depended on the active participation of members of

the industrial and commercial classes. In fact, the new town-council occupied a position between the mercantile élite on the one hand, and the populace on the other. It criticised the rich merchants for trying to sabotage the Revolution by failing to pay taxes, attacked the Chamber of Commerce as the centre of resistance by selfish egoists to the progress of the Revolution, and even led attacks on the foremost merchants for their defence of the slave trade and their opposition to the extension of political rights to the free coloured population of the colonies. And yet, while keeping a distance from the richest citizens, the Municipality – which depended on financial support from the merchants and which foresaw the greatest danger of popular disturbance if their essential trading interests were harmed – also pursued policies which were far from democratic or socially levelling. It seemed to be just as ruthless as its *Ancien régime* predecessor in arresting and expelling 'vagabonds' and in preventing agitation on wages by repressing all forms of workers' combinations. Thus the patriots did much to reassure the merchants that their essential interests – peace, law and order – would be protected. And indeed, despite much political agitation and undoubted political plotting by the merchant aristocracy, commerce prospered under the new régime[1] and merchants took advantage of new conditions by making lavish purchases of *biens nationaux*. After the vehement propaganda of 1789 directed against the opulent, reconciliation between patriots and the richest citizens was far from complete; but, on the other hand, divorce or separation had been averted.

*   *   *

However, a further strand in Marseilles' revolutionary history – the expansionist activity in which patriotic leaders co-operated with wide sections of the city's population – also served to alarm the richer townsmen.

Already, in resisting attempts to destroy the Revolution, the townspeople had embarked on the first of the expeditions outside the town which were to give them a reputation for unbridled revolutionary zeal: for, on 27–28 July 1789, a band, some

[1] See, for example, C. Carrière, 'Les entrées de navires dans le port de Marseille pendant la Révolution', *Provence historique*, tome 7, 1957, pp. 202–5.

hundreds strong, after seizing arms from the Hôtel de Ville, marched to Aix and released from prison about seventy men who had rioted in March. This expedition contributed both to the unease of the rich citizens of Marseilles and to the city's notoriety with the government, as a source of danger which might lead to the conflagration of the whole of Provence.

Perhaps it was for this reason that the capital of the Bouches-du-Rhône was placed at Aix, despite strenuous representations by the deputies of Marseilles. When Aix had been capital of Provence and seat of an *Intendant* and archbishop, the difference in the political status of the two cities had been tolerable to, and indeed welcomed by the Marseillais; for it symbolised the unique freedom of their city from governmental control. But now that Marseilles had, formally at least, renounced those privileges incompatible with the true union of Frenchmen, (5 November 1789), now that the town had to find a new position within a unified and uniform France, its representatives demanded the position of power and prestige to which its size and wealth entitled it.[1] Thus, when the division of France into departments was debated, the Marseillais wanted their city to form the capital of an undivided Provence. When this scheme was seen to be impracticable, Marseilles wished to place itself at the head of a department distinct from that governed from Aix. Unfortunately (from both the local and national points of view) Marseilles was subordinated to Aix in the department of the Bouches-du-Rhône. This seemed a triumph of old values over new, a decision which fatally implicated the National Assembly in the governmental attempt to crush the Revolution in Provence by use of *Parlements*, *prévôts* and other paraphernalia of the old régime. Certainly the debate in the National Assembly aroused high feelings and the final decision came as a bitter blow to the Marseillais, confirming their conviction that the government was fundamentally hostile to their claims and reinforcing their view that they would have to look after their own interests in the most forceful way possible. And this effect was also unfortunate since it encouraged the most dynamic organs within the city – the Municipality, Club and National Guard – to flout the government's authority. This

[1] The 'demotion' of Marseilles was a serious reverse to the constant campaign of the patriots for the provision of more judicial posts in the city.

involved Marseilles in a vicious circle, from which it hardly escaped during the Revolution: the constantly-alleged neglect of its interests by the government forced the city to adopt, on its own initiative, extreme policies which often served to aggravate the distrust felt by the government for the turbulent southerners. Demoted to the rank of townships such as Salon and Apt – soon to be deprived even of its venerable bishopric – Marseilles, as might have been expected, reacted violently.

Every effort was now made to force the government to recognise the claims of the second city of France. The town went so far as to elect new deputies to replace those first sent to the States-General, now thought of as too moderate; but these elections were quashed by the National Assembly.[1] A few days later, on 17 May 1790, a meeting at Brignoles in the Var, assembling delegates from adjacent departments convoked on the initiative of the Municipality of Marseilles, pledged itself to a common programme in the defence of the Revolution; the National Guard was to be free to go wherever it was needed (paying no attention to administrative boundaries); arms could be taken from State arsenals; royal troop movements were to be kept under observation.[2] It is not surprising, in view of these intentions, that the Municipality of Marseilles was accused of wishing to take control of Provence, and establish a southern Republic detached from France.[3] This speculation on Marseilles' intentions was compounded by plans to send its National Guard against the royalists at Nîmes and Jalès; it seems that men were indeed assembled for this purpose, but to what effect is uncertain.[4] The offer of national guardsmen for the colonies – June 1791 – marks the geographical limit of Marseilles' intended intervention.

Pamphlets were issued stressing the importance of Marseilles to the nation as a whole. One of these used a form of black-mailing technique by prophetically threatening that if the port

[1] *Encyclopédie départementale*, v, 11; among those elected were Chompré, Bausset and Blanc-Gilli (May 1790).

[2] For this assembly, see A. Comm., 1D1, 15 May 1790 – instructions given by the Municipality of Marseilles to its deputation; and A. Dept., L3327, *Précis des opérations de l'assemblée à Brignolles*.

[3] A. Comm., BB292, letter of Municipality, 30 May 1790.

[4] A. Comm., 4D1, Municipality reports to its deputation at Nat. Assembly that it has chosen 1200 men to defend Nîmes against the royalists of Jalès.

fell to the counter-revolution, it would be impossible to limit the damage inflicted on the Revolution – for Marseilles could, by interfering with the corn trade, starve half the population of France within a month and, by cutting off the supply of raw materials for the country's industries, force millions of workless people into counter-revolutionary insurrection. Marseilles, finally, could offer its harbour to France's enemies, thus giving them a base from which to wage war against the Revolution.[1] Certainly the pamphlet stressed that it would be difficult for counter-revolution to gain initial control. But this situation would alter if the energy of the patriots were relaxed for one moment: only if the city kept Provence as a whole under its strong control, could catastrophe be averted.

More alarming to the politicians of Paris, even more exhilarating to the patriots of France, were the attempts of the Marseillais to destroy the enemies of the patriots at Aix, Arles and Avignon. The two latter towns especially were rent by internal divisions. The origins of these divisions hardly concern us here; but the Marseillais followed with great anxiety the varying fortunes of the factions in Avignon and the Comtat Venaissin.[2] The Municipality expressed its detestation of the fanaticism of the Catholics of Nîmes:[3] they were also extremely alarmed by the royalist conspiracies centred on Jalès. They did not fall into the government's error of underestimating the importance of the struggles. Civil war between Carpentras, capital of the Comtat, and the patriots of Avignon led to clashes between armies of up to 7000 strong and to a fifty-day siege of Carpentras itself. It was to reinforce the patriots of Avignon that, on 14 July 1791, five hundred armed men left Marseilles for the papal possessions, thus aiding the patriots to seize control of Avignon and preparing the way for the union of the papal city with France and its incorporation in the department of the Bouches-du-Rhône. This was a triumph for Marseilles.

Similarly, Arles, divided by fierce struggles between the

[1] British Museum, F64**(24), *Adresse à l'Assemblée nationale par les amis de la Constitution de la ville de Marseille*, n.d. Drawn up by Blanc-Gilli.

[2] Lourde gives quite a reasonable view of events in Arles and Avignon as seen from Marseilles – 1, 174 ff., 11, 69 ff., 98 ff. etc. Also S. Vialla, *Marseille révolutionnaire*, and *Les Volontaires des Bouches-du-Rhône*.

[3] A. Comm., BB292, in a letter of 11 May 1790, to the leaders of the Catholic Assembly at Nîmes.

'monnaidiers' and the clerical-royalist 'chiffonnistes', presented a challenge to the revolutionary fervour of the Marseillais. From mid-1791, the *chiffonnistes* led a successful attack on the patriots. Affected by events in Nîmes, Arles gave refuge to refractory priests and *émigré* nobles and their sympathisers barricaded themselves in the city. The Arlésiens seized rifles and cannon destined for the defence of Toulon. They were accused of giving shelter to foreign troops and of hoarding corn harvested from the fertile regions round about. To the Marseillais, always fearful of food shortages and constantly clamouring for more arms for their National Guard, apprehensive of Spanish or Savoyard attacks upon the Rhône, and convinced that Toulon was in-adequately armed if it was to fulfil its rôle of protecting Mar-seilles' trading fleet, such actions seemed treasonable. And yet the government seemed unmoved by the urgency of Marseilles' demands for punitive action – indeed, the way in which it dis-posed its troops seemed to afford protection to the counter-revolutionaries.[1] Finally, on 25–26 February 1792, despairing of protection from Paris, the Marseillais marched to Aix, where they disarmed the Royal Ernest Regiment which, having provided Bournissac with armed backing during the provostal enquiry, had been so unpopular in Marseilles as to be moved to Aix, where however it posed a direct threat to any armed column marching against Arles. With this regiment disarmed, the road to Arles lay open, and an armed contingent, several thousand strong, was sent there in March 1792 and, driving out the *chiffonnistes*, re-established the domination of the patriots.

These expeditions galvanised the revolutionary energy of the department. Many communes provided detachments of their national guard to join the column sent to Aix, while the fame of the National Guard of Marseilles stimulated recruiting throughout the department. But such enthusiasm did nothing to calm the rage of Narbonne or the alarm of successive Ministers of the Interior. Frequently the town's governors had

[1] British Museum, F64**(5), *Rapport fait à l'Assemblée nationale par les députés extraordinaires de la Commune de Marseille;* F656(3), *Observations de la Commune de Marseille sur l'état actuel du Département des Bouches-du-Rhône.* On 20 Feb. 1792, deputies from Marseilles spoke at the Legislative Assembly on behalf of their city's policy.

to refute accusations from Cahier and Roland that the city was determined to plunge France into civil war. As good Jacobins, they protested that they were the victims of calumny, that, as their patriotism excelled that of other communes, they were the prime target for counter-revolutionary slanders.[1] Certainly Paris must have been full of tales of the exploits of the Marseillais, for at the height of the agitation, the Minister of War was forced to refute rumours that an army six thousand strong was on the way to Paris to destroy the Constitution and proclaim a Republic.[2] But of course such rumours were premature by only a few months and, as early as May 1792, Pierre Baille had stated that most people in France looked on Marseilles as the main hope for the preservation of freedom.[3]

But it was not only the deeds of the Battalion of 10 August which marked the climax of the revolutionary expansionism of the southern patriots, though no one would wish to deny the electrifying effect which the march of the *fédérés* had upon both *modérés* and Jacobins.[4] To some, the Marseillais were equated with bloodthirsty cannibals. (One writer reports that any man caught kicking a dog would be pursued with awe-struck whispers of 'Voilà un Marseillais'.) All the scum from a very scum-ridden city had flowed into Paris and cast a blight upon the Revolution. To others however the Marseillais were to be emulated. Within the city itself, both points of view were to be found. The despatch of the Battalion had finally confirmed the now absolute domination of the Jacobins over their supine enemies. The Municipality, under the seventy-two-year-old firebrand Mourraille,[5] had led the anti-royalist campaign and had given enthusiastic backing to the Battalion; the Club, by

[1] The Legislative Assembly vindicated the Marseillais, by, on 19 Mar. 1792, declaring Arles in a state of rebellion. But conditions worsened, and it was not till after 10 Aug. that Marseilles was 'acquitted' of oppressive and vexatious conduct in Arles and Avignon.

[2] Lourde, II, 337 ff.

[3] Pierre Baille, in the Club of Marseilles, 21 May 1792. Pierre-Marie Baille, born c. 1753, was a member of the Department; elected to the Convention, he was sent to the Army of Italy in April 1793, but was thrown in prison by the Sections of Toulon and committed suicide.

[4] For this episode see J. Pollio and A. Marcel, *Le Bataillon du 10 août* (Paris, 1881).

[5] Jean-Raymond-Pierre Mourraille, 1720–1808, elected mayor 14 Nov. 1791.

its addresses and its envoys sent out across Provence, by means also of its fiery newspaper,[1] had rallied the city to the policies of the Jacobins. Now the Club's premises were too small, especially as passive citizens had long been eligible for membership.[2] Those who dominated the political scene included Barbaroux, as yet only the holder of a humble municipal post, François-Trophime Rebecquy, Moïse Bayle[3] and François-Omer Granet, as well as a score or so of clubists drawn mainly from the professional classes, men too young or of too humble a status to have achieved even municipal distinction under the *Ancien régime*.[4] These were the men who had won Avignon for France and Paris for the Revolution. They showed their ruthlessness – and their disinclination to make the safety of the Revolution depend on the lethargy of Paris – by deporting the refractory priests of Marseilles a month before such a measure was even passed at Paris.[5] They also prohibited the despatch of money from the public coffers to the Treasury. Their control of the city was virtually unchallenged: the rich merchants were forced to plant ceremonially a tree of liberty in front of the Bourse (30 July). The city, as one royalist scathingly observed, came to resemble a forest, as in July and August the façades of rich *hôtels* were decorated with revolutionary foliage – but the

---

[1] *Journal des départements méridionaux* . . . founded in Mar. 1792 by Pierre Micoulin and Alexandre Ricord *fils*, addressed to 'artisans laborieux et honnêtes, cultivateurs estimables, ouvriers intéressants'.

[2] A. Comm., 2I42, Club's petition of 19 Apr. 1792.

[3] Moïse-Antoine-Pierre-Jean Bayle, born near Geneva, of French Protestant stock: gained living as *teneur d'écriture*; then elected to the Municipality and *procureur général syndic* of the Department (Sept. 1791). Published on 2 Aug. 1792 *De l'inutilité d'un roi dans un gouvernement libre et représentatif*. Elected to the Convention, led the 'left-wing' of the deputation of the Bouches-du-Rhône against Barbaroux and Rebecquy; 9 Mar. 1793, sent with Joseph-Antoine Boisset to recruit men in the Bouches-du-Rhône. See below, pp. 65 ff., etc.

[4] Men like the school-teachers, the Maillet brothers; *hommes de loi* like Pierre Laugier and Leclerc *fils*; Étienne Seytres, *notaire*; priests such as Joseph-Marie Turcan and Jean-Baptiste-Antoine Boutin . . . Some of these will play a prominent part in the Revolution at Marseilles.

[5] Voted by the Municipality, 23 July 1792 – with the participation of the bishop and clubists etc.; an apparent eye-witness said that about 400 left, Bib.Mun., MS. 048728, *Correspondance entre MM. Baleste et Roustan de Marseille et M. Mourgues de Martigues*.

marquis de Fonvielle also noted the sudden increase in emigration on the part of merchants and nobles.[1] Moreover, the murder, on 21–23 July, of some ten people in the city streets for allegedly plotting against the patriots discouraged a trial of strength between aristocrats and their opponents.[2] The mayor, Mourraille, was said to protect merchants from the murderers in the interest of the corn supplies of his city.[3] Henceforth, the richer citizens kept their opinions to themselves and no doubt groaned inwardly at the disastrous news from Paris of the triumph of their fellow-townsmen.

The patience of the leaders of the merchant-community had been sorely tried. At the start of 1792, the Municipality, by a rather imprecise and demagogic attack on speculators and hoarders – threatening them with 'des vengeances qui n'auraient pas été celles de la loi'[4] – had aroused fears that all merchants were under suspicion. The Department however sprang to the defence of the merchants, condemning the Municipality, attacking Marseilles for not paying taxes, calling on the Ministry of War for more troops to control disturbances in Marseilles and throughout the Bouches-du-Rhône, agitated by religious troubles and by popular resistance to a tax load considered worse than that of the *Ancien régime*.[5] (In return, Marseilles denounced the Department to the National Assembly for favouring hoarders and speculators and sabotaging the city's National Guard.)[6] The attacks on hoarders alarmed many poorer citizens whose livelihood depended on commerce:[7] there were several incidents in which warehouse-porters –

[1] B. F. A. Fonvielle, *Mémoires historiques de M. le chevalier de Fonvielle de Toulouse*, II, 370. See also Bib. Mun., MS. 048728, op. cit.

[2] The clubists thought they were to be the victims of a 'massacre général'; *Jnal. Dépts. Mérid.*, LXII, 26 July 1792. For this episode, see P. Espert, 'Un faux complot à Marseille', *Provincia*, XIX, 1939, pp. 59–92. Those murdered included two clerics.

[3] Lautard, I, 138.

[4] A. Comm., 5F6; the phrase occurs in a municipal proclamation of 28 Dec. 1791.

[5] A. Comm., 5F6, correspondence between Dept. and Municipality; Collection Michel de Léon, letter from Dept., to Minister of War, 4 Jan. 1792.

[6] A. Comm., 4D2, Mun. to Nat. Assembly, 3 Feb. 1792.

[7] *Journal de Provence*, XV, 4 Feb. 1792 – municipal proclamation attempting to restore calm after its denunciation of hoarders.

incited, it was said, by merchants – attacked the Club.[1] There were continued complaints that rich citizens were not paying their taxes, though each expedition of the patriots stirred them into some activity in this field. Such enthusiasm however was short-lived and one patriot demanded that a horde of rich citizens who tried trickery to obtain *cartes de section* should be excluded from the Sections if they had not paid their taxes, while more cards were demanded for the workers of the manufactories in his area.[2] When rumours circulated of approaching Russian and Spanish naval squadrons, the rich were bitterly condemned for their selfish refusal to serve in person in the National Guard.[3] Worse, complaints were made against employers who tried to prevent patriots going on expeditions by threatening to take away their jobs; such men were to be inscribed on public lists of suspects. For future levies of men, merchants were asked to guarantee jobs for returning volunteers.[4] By the start of August however the Municipality was able to report that

> Les négociants et en général la classe des citoyens favorisés par la fortune paraissent avoir été pénétrés de cette grande vérité, qu'ils ne sont rien et qu'ils ont tout à craindre, s'ils ne se réunissent à la cause du peuple.[5]

Little wonder then that the commercial and industrial classes complained about the difficulties of carrying on their activities in such an atmosphere of uncertainty: public force was inadequate to protect the corn trade from popular troubles; corn exporters were threatened with popular vengeance; roads had become very bad; manufacturers were having difficulty in getting raw materials; inflation was forcing up wages.[6] This was at a time when the Municipality suppressed the Chamber of

[1] Collection Michel de Léon, *Tribunal de police correctionnelle* condemned two *portefaix* who took part in attack on Club, 1 Feb. 1792. Also A. Nat., F⁷4603, letter from Chabaud to Blanc-Gilli, 14 Feb. 1792, on *négociants* and *portefaix*.

[2] A. Comm., 2I42, letter of Bausset, president of Section 6, 21 Jan. 1792.

[3] Collection Michel de Léon, proclamation of Municipality, 10 May 1792.

[4] A. Comm., 1D3, deliberation of Municipality, 30 July 1792; 13D8, municipal proclamation of 13 Aug. 1792.

[5] A. Comm., 4D2, Municipality to Granet, 31 July 1792.

[6] A. Comm., 2I42, petition of corn traders, 1 May 1792; 13D6, meeting of manufacturers to discuss their problems, 13 Apr. 1792.

Commerce[1] and when demands on the purses of the merchants increased with the levying of thousands of volunteers. At the end of July, a patriotic subscription demanded the 'superflu' of the fortunes of rich citizens, to equip the soldiers. 'Si vous voulez conservez le tout, sachez faire le sacrifice d'une partie' was the reassuring message of a municipal proclamation.[2] But the leading merchant Rabaud co-operated as treasurer of this subscription. Merchants continued to defend the cause of commerce, which did not harm the 'social order', and especially the import of corn, which was essential to the survival of the Marseillais, whatever their political complexion.[3] And, according to a modern authority, commerce continued at a high level, despite the political polarisation within the city.[4]

This uneasy polarisation of forces was not the only important effect of the march to Paris: a precedent had been set. On two subsequent occasions, battalions were levied in attempts to impose the will of Marseilles upon the capital. There was some continuity of personnel between these levies but what was more important was the continuity of federalist aspiration which impelled their creation.

Of equal importance in consolidating the position of the Jacobins in the Bouches-du-Rhône was the forcible transference of the Departmental Administration and the Criminal Tribunal from Aix to Marseilles. The Department had long been a thorn in the flesh of the patriots, despite the fact that Moïse Bayle, Pierre Baille and Trophime Rebecquy were members. Exposed to the verbal lashes of the Minister of the Interior, it had given only lukewarm support to the aggressive policies of Marseilles. [5] It had sent guns to defend Carpentras against the patriots of Avignon: in January 1792, it had appealed to the government

---

[1] L. Bergasse, *Notice historique de la Chambre de Commerce de Marseille* (*1599–1912*) (Marseilles, 1913).

[2] A. Comm., 13D7, proclamation of 31 July 1792.

[3] Archives de la Chambre de Commerce, B21, *Délibérations du bureau provisoire de commerce*, motion passed on 17 Aug. 1792, by Section 24, approved by Bureau, 24 Aug.

[4] C. Carrière, 'Les entrées de navires', op. cit., pp. 202 ff.

[5] See, in Bib. Mun., MS. 49068 – letters from Roland, Minister of the Interior, condemning the aggressive policies of Marseilles. A. Nat. F⁷4603, letter from Moïse Bayle to Blanc-Gilli, deploring the inaction of the Department, of which he was a member.

to send more troops into the department and had declaimed against the *gens sans aveu* who infested Marseilles and pushed the city into acts of brigandage.[1] Little wonder, therefore, if it was accused of being indifferent to the growing power of the counter-revolutionaries of Arles, if the shortage of arms in Marseilles and the poor state of the coastal batteries and the arsenal of Toulon were blamed on its neglect. Consistently the Department had failed in what the patriots regarded as its main task – to get the government to accord all possible protection to the interests of Marseilles.[2] On the 22–23 August, therefore, the Department was moved twenty miles southward, escorted by the National Guard of Marseilles.

This open defiance of the Legislative Assembly had far-reaching consequences. Revealing the impotence of the government, it led the patriots – and perhaps the Marseillais in general – to overestimate their own strength, to think that as one of them remarked, a few months later, all things would be granted to Marseilles if it shouted loud enough, or took them for itself. From now on, the sanctions which a flouted government could wield against a disobedient city were consistently made light of – first by the Jacobins, subsequently by the federalists. In this situation, criticism of governmental inertia and misconduct could be more ruthless, and liberty of action throughout Provence even more lightly circumscribed than hitherto. Moreover, at Aix the Department seemed much more directly under the authority of Paris than at Marseilles, where the power of Municipality and Club kept that of the Minister of the Interior at bay. And, once in the tempestuous atmosphere of Marseilles, it was inevitable that, in November 1792, men of the most advanced opinions should gain complete control.[3]

---

[1] Lourde, ii, 196 ff. A. Nat., F7 3659[2] (Bouches-du-Rhône: Troubles) letter of Dept., of 4 Jan. 1792; reports by government agents on situation in Provence, etc.

[2] The accusation regarding the theft of arms is cited in S. Vialla, *Marseille révolutionnaire*, pp. 165 ff.; also in British Museum, F656(3).

[3] ABR, L278, Augustin Maillet *cadet*, a 35-year-old schoolmaster, was elected president of the Criminal Tribunal and Joseph Giraud, originally from Arles, public prosecutor; Alexandre Ricord *fils*, 22-year-old journalist of the Club; Honoré Paris, a 42-year-old *officier de santé* from Arles, who was to become one of the leading terrorists of the department; and Louis Barthélemy, a soap-manufacturer who in June 1792 accused his fellow

Thus the Jacobins of the Bouches-du-Rhône, unlike those of many other departments, could, after August 1792, count on the enthusiastic support of the highest organ of local government and this in itself gave their actions a renewed impetus and a more devastating and lasting effect. The 'Three Administrations' – Department, Municipality and District – plus the Criminal Tribunal, which gave jobs to three of the most prominent clubists of Marseilles, worked in harness to destroy all opposition to Jacobinism both within the city and throughout Provence.

Thus most of the activities of the Marseillais, in this period of *la patrie en danger*, were destined to bolster their city's position as a bastion of the Revolution. For instance, Barbaroux' idea of a 'République du Midi' undoubtedly had some reality at this period. He later wrote that envoys sent throughout the Midi in July to stimulate recruiting and to gain support for addresses against the monarchy were part of a concerted plan to preserve France's freedom if the North should fall.[1] Certainly those present at the meeting of the Administrations of Marseilles which sent out these men shared Barbaroux' conviction that the government, because of internal divisions and corruption, could not act with that ruthlessness which alone could destroy France's enemies – some of which enemies, moreover, in the case of the Piedmontese, the *émigrés* of Turin and the Spaniards, were more immediately dangerous to Provence than to Paris.[2]

Obsessed with the belief that Marseilles was particularly vulnerable to attack both by land and sea, from east and west, convinced also that this fact was not fully appreciated at Paris, the Municipality and Club had made a tremendous effort at self-help, as far as recruiting was concerned.[3] And since recruits served in the *Armée du Nord* – protecting Paris – Marseilles felt

---

industrialists of hoarding, were elected members of the Department by the Electoral Assembly of the Bouches-du-Rhône, 12–28 Nov. 1792.

[1] *Mémoires de Barbaroux* (ed. Alfred Chabaud) (Paris, 1936) pp. 121 ff.; see also C. Perroud and A. Chabaud (editors), *Correspondance et mémoires de Barbaroux* (Paris, 1923).

[2] A. Comm., 1D3, *Conseil général de la commune*: for instance Maillet *cadet* was sent to the departments of the Ain and the Rhône-et-Loire and 'inspected' the Army of the Midi at Bourgoin in the Isère. Others were sent out on equally wide-ranging missions.

[3] For figures see S. Vialla, *Les Volontaires des Bouches-du-Rhône* (Paris, 1913).

all the more entitled to speak forcefully on matters of national concern. Moreover, pride in their *volontaires* made the Marseillais all the more ready to cry treason and neglect if adequate measures were not taken for the safety of their troops. The way in which these soldiers were levied likewise contributed to the pride of their city, for often the initiative had come from Marseilles; the government was referred to only in abusive terms, for failing to provide both volunteers and national guardsmen with arms and for making inadequate provision for the defence of the coasts – this last being a most grievous neglect, since by sending men to the north-eastern frontiers, Marseilles was exposing itself all the more to naval assault. Also, the levying of these troops involved – or served as an excuse for – sending out envoys throughout the Midi, envoys who carried with them the doctrines of the patriots of Marseilles and who urged towns of the importance of Lyons to raise themselves to Marseilles' standard of fervour. These envoys – clubists and members of the administrative bodies – became accustomed to regard themselves as arbiters of the nation's destiny and every victory was portrayed as the work of the Marseillais, every defeat as the triumph of their enemies.[1]

Thus, in the autumn of 1792, the Jacobins were everywhere victorious. At Avignon – itself a symbol of the triumph of revolutionary expansionism – the Electoral Assembly which chose deputies to the Convention had been completely dominated by extremists, and had elected advanced revolutionaries such as Barbaroux, Granet, and Moïse Bayle, who had pledged themselves to work for the destruction of the monarchy and the execution of the king.[2]

And finally, at Marseilles, in a far-reaching affirmation of that city's determination to manage its own affairs without outside interference and to do everything possible to impose its will on the future of the Revolution as a whole, two important decisions were reached. A Popular Tribunal was formed to deal

---

[1] Thus Maillet *cadet*, at the fall of Nice at the end of September.

[2] ABR, L278, Electoral Assembly held at Avignon from 2 Sept. 1792, absolutely dominated by the patriots of Marseilles, applauded the September Massacres, sent out expeditions to crush counter-revolutionaries of the countryside. See below p. 53. The newly-elected deputies vied with each other to pronounce the most vehement discourse against the monarchy.

with outbreaks of lawlessness in the city and surrounding areas.[1] Meeting for the first time on 1 October, composed of men elected by the Sections, now in permanent session, the Tribunal never received – never sought – the approval of the Convention. Throughout its existence, it therefore symbolised Marseilles' independence *vis-à-vis* Paris. The other decision, of 3 September, likewise taken by the Municipality, though on the initiative of the Club, as the immediate reaction to news of the fall of Longwy, was to send a Second Battalion to Paris to bring pressure to bear on the legislature to ensure that the results of 10 August were not – as seemed to the Marseillais only too likely – squandered away by the Parisians and the new legislature. Leaving on 16 September, this Second Battalion reached Paris on 20 October and played a vital rôle both in the controversies surrounding the trial of the king and in the equally controversial questions regarding relations between Paris and Marseilles.[2] Both the Popular Tribunal and the Second Battalion therefore were federalist in conception and in consequences. Both played a rôle in preparing the federalist revolt.

[1] See P. A. Robert, *La Justice des sections marseillaises. Le Tribunal populaire, 1792–1793* (Paris, 1913).

[2] See F. Portal, *Le Bataillon marseillais du 21 janvier* (Marseilles, 1900).

CHAPTER TWO

The Jacobin Offensive

(a) WITHIN THE CITY

How then did the Jacobins use the power which they had won in Provence? In answering this question, fuller knowledge of the people who dominated the Club of Marseilles would have been helpful, since, by the autumn of 1792, the Club was the most dynamic body in the region.[1] Certainly we know that the score or so men whose names are most prominent were drawn from the group of professional men, not from the rich merchants of the city nor from the mass of the population. Some like Turcan,[2] Boutin,[3] and the *abbé* Bausset had been clerics; the Maillet *frères* were teachers who had held office as justices of the peace; Étienne Chompré and François Isoard[4] were also school-teachers while Alexandre Ricord *fils* and Pierre Micoulin

[1] Only a few minutes of the Club survive, with few indications of membership: see especially ABR, L2071.

[2] Joseph-Marie Turcan, aged 28, 'ci-devant vicaire à la Trinité', in Departmental Administration, autumn of 1793.

[3] Jean-Baptiste-Antoine Boutin, ex-*capucin*, elected in 1791 to parish of Saint-Louis; sent to the Gard and the Hérault on 23 July 1792, to rally the Montagnards of the Midi; said to have married in 1793 and was sent to the *Commission populaire* of Orange as a Girondin.

[4] Louis-François-Dominique Isoard, aged 29, son of a poor mason; Oratorian; as a *clerc* served at mass in the church of the Accoules; had continuous career of revolutionary zeal – Apr. 1792, setting up clubs in the Basses-Alpes; Sept. 1792, arresting men implicated in the Monnier conspiracy, centred on Grenoble; Oct. 1792, conciliating patriots at Apt; Jan. 1793, to Berre to destroy a counter-revolutionary plot; Feb. 1793, to Salon, as envoy of Department, when that town was in rebellion against the Montagnards; involved in the Club's 'Campaign of Terror' Feb.–Mar. 1793; escaped arrest by the federalists; went to Paris; returned in Sept. 1793 as agent of Committee of Public Safety (to take down church bells); involved in a General Assembly of the Clubs of the Midi at Valence and then at Marseilles; *procureur général de la commune* till 14 *frimaire* II, fell foul of Barras and Fréron; later was arrested, tried by the Criminal Tribunal of the Bouches-du-Rhône and condemned to death, 2 *vendémiaire* IV.

were the journalists of the Club. Pierre Laugier[1] and Antoine Maurin[2] were *hommes de loi*. It was their education which gave these men leadership of the Club and entry to administrative office – Maillet *cadet*, Joseph Giraud, ex-Oratorian, and Étienne Chompré staffing the Criminal Tribunal. It was men such as these, articulate with voice and pen, keen in debate, and extremely ambitious, who devoted their time to political activity and gave leadership to the shoemakers, carpenters and shopkeepers who made up the majority of the Club's membership.[3] Often escaping from the routine of heavy administrative duties, these men were able to operate with great freedom, audacity and irresponsibility: they could criticise freely and ruthlessly, their denunciations could be imbued with great virulence and sting; their envoys could be sent far afield and could act with great initiative for, in a way, they were accountable to no one but themselves and discipline would come from their own hearts and heads, rather than from outside – if it came at all. Only by arousing a general outcry against themselves in city and department could they be held in check – and this they succeeded in doing by April and May 1793.

Their chief concern was with the defence of the Revolution against enemies at home and abroad, with the elimination of suspects and the recruitment of volunteers. To attain these ends, they were prepared to use ruthless measures – they were prepared to throw the net widely and cared little if, with a hundred dangerous plotters, they caught one or two worthy and respectable citizens. Thus a Jacobin offensive against suspects was launched; and this grew in strength and scope, till in March and April 1793, many citizens of the department came to feel threatened, both in their lives and properties, by a 'reign of terror' which, if not indiscriminate, was at least excessively wide in its scope. The Club saw the elimination – or at least neutralisation – of lukewarm citizens as its *raison d'être* and it pursued this task with relentless energy, convinced that once suspects were tracked down and punished, peace and prosperity would

[1] See below, pp. 261–5.   [2] See below, pp. 165–71.

[3] In an analysis of some 200 out of 250 patriots later indemnified for their sufferings under the federalists, Dominique Radiguet shows that most were small-scale employers, artisans, professional men etc. D. Radiguet, *Foules et journées révolutionnaires à Marseille, août 1789–25 août 1793* (unpublished *Diplôme d'études supérieures*, Faculty of Letters of Aix, 1968) pp. 128 ff.

be won for the Republic and ruthless and often cruel measures would become unnecessary. Until then, however, the Club gave a very wide definition to the class of suspects and it was this which alarmed and eventually antagonised many citizens. To the clubists, the 'riches égoïstes' and their lackeys who waited upon events were the most dangerous, because insidious, enemies of the Revolution.[1]

The clubists of course were not alone in fearing counter-revolutionary plots. In the aftermath of the Monnier conspiracy – a royalist rising which, betrayed, broke out abortively at Jalès in July 1792 – some 1500 arrests were made throughout the Midi. At Marseilles, the murders of the end of July had been followed in September by the lynching of four more citizens, accused of conspiracy. They included two leading patriots of 1789. Rumours circulated of intended prison massacres. The murders, thought regrettable but necessary by many patriots, caused an increase in the emigration of rich citizens which heralded ill for Marseilles' prosperity during the winter. So the Jacobins tried to reassure the rich by defending commercial activities and by repudiating the intention of punishing rich townsmen who had signed counter-revolutionary proclamations. In fact, for some time, wise counsels prevailed; for the sectionaries thought it wise to restrain popular fury against suspects by the creation of the Popular Tribunal.[2] This was set up by the Municipality at the request of Section 1 – fairly affluent, and always forward in efforts to preserve the rule of law – and met for the first time on 1 October.[3] It had a twofold and delicate task; on the one hand to prevent outbursts of popular passion,

[1] *Jnal. Dépts. Mérid.*, passim; ABR, L2071, Club's deliberations, 28 Feb.–18 Apr. 1793; L2072–6 scattered papers of the Club. These, and a few other isolated *liasses* form the meagre bulk of the surviving documents of the Club. Most were no doubt burnt when the Club was destroyed by the federalists on 3 June 1793.

[2] For the Popular Tribunal and the events leading to its establishment see P. Robert, *La Justice des sections marseillaises. Le Tribunal populaire, 1792–1793* (Paris, 1913). Barbaroux was said to have had a big rôle here. One might question the depth of Barbaroux' professions of humanity, however, since he had exulted in the murders committed in July and seemed to look forward to nearly two hundred more. A. Aulard, *La Société des Jacobins*, IV 163–4.

[3] A. Comm., Marseilles, *Série Affiches*; 11 Sept. 1792; ABR, L3100–L3108, papers of Popular Tribunal.

on the other, to deal severely with the law-breakers. Throughout the autumn, it judged men accused of having conspired against the Republic, most of whom it released, to scenes of popular rejoicing. It was aided in its task by various *comités de surveillance* which, established in the Sections, or electoral districts, disarmed suspects and kept a watch over *gens sans aveu*.[1] In the face of such measures, 'everything vicious hid or was exterminated'. Yet, within the city (not yet to speak of the department) armed robberies and threats of hanging, nocturnal disturbances, highway robberies and brawls continued: on 13 January 1793, for instance, the *curé* Mathieu Olive, a refractory priest returning from Italy, was murdered in the city streets. By January and February 1793, the Popular and Criminal Tribunals had become so ineffective as weapons against disorder and crime that the authorities were reduced to making helpless pleas to citizens to take active measures of self-help against attack. In desperation, on 25 February, the Municipality, after ordering some minor measures of police, declared that, if these measures were not successful, they would resign from the government of the city.[2]

It was in response to this situation of confusion and impotence – or, perhaps, to take advantage of it for their own ends – that the Club responded in February by setting up their *Comité central* and in March by demanding increasingly wide-ranging measures against suspects. The *Comité central*, established on 12 February, and including Hugues (not to be confused with the rich merchant of that name) and Isoard among the most forceful of the clubists, dealt with *les affaires secrètes*, chief of which was the denunciation of suspects.[3] This measure, and a demand on 4 March that the Sections should give *certificats de civisme* only to those whose zeal was approved by the Club,[4] showed that the clubists wished to make themselves arbiters as to which people, or groups of people, should be designated as suspects, troublemakers and law-breakers – categories which to them were identical.

This was because events in March played into the hands of

[1] ABR, L1941, (Section 8), 19 Sept. 1792; L1945, (Section 17), 11 Oct. 1792, etc.
[2] A. Comm., *Affiches*, 25 Feb. 1793.
[3] *Jnal. Dépts. Mérid.*, CXLIX, 12 Feb. 1793.   [4] ABR, L1977.

the extremists. In Marseilles, as at Paris, people were worried
about food prices; the onset of the naval war hit the trade and
industry of the port, increasing prices, making raw materials
scarce, throwing men out of work. As the price of bread rose,
the authorities prohibited the 'export' of corn to Provence –
thus contributing to distress in many localities and to con-
sequent bad feeling – yet without allaying fears of shortages
within the city.[1] There were constant complaints about the
bad quality of bread. The Marseillais were especially enraged
at delays in receiving subsidies voted by the Convention.[2] The
issue of *assignats* – 'des assignats, toujours des assignats!' – was
blamed for the rise in prices and for swelling the fortunes of
speculators and hoarders: even a popular movement at Paris
had not caused the *Comité des finances* to tackle the financial
problems in a serious manner.[3] As for unemployment, a plan
to make the workers repair roads without pay – said to be
suggested by the government – met with a derisive reply from
Marseilles; it seemed to introduce the *corvée* (which, in fact,
was unknown in Marseilles under the *Ancien régime*).[4] Hectic
activity however was being demanded for the expedition against
Sardinia – which returned to Toulon on 8 March after a complete disaster; the desperate privateering war was more successful, though the great merchants played little part in fitting out
ships.[5] Traditional fears for the security of Marseilles and
Toulon reached new heights of anxiety, the Minister of the
Marine being constantly accused of planning to deliver France's
fleets to the enemy; merchants protested at the lack of escorts
for their ships – those about to go to the Isles and those import-
ing corn from North Africa.[6] Chaos in the *échelles* contributed to

[1] A. Comm., 46F12 (*Bureau des subsistances*). This decision, taken early in
February, troubled the government and dismayed many towns and
villages of Provence accustomed to look to the port for provision of corn.

[2] A. Comm., 46F13.

[3] A. Comm., 2I14, protest of Section 4, of 14 Mar. 1793, approved by
all Sections of Marseilles.

[4] ABR, L1973, Section 13, protest to Dept., 5 Jan. 1793.

[5] C. Carrière, 'Les Marseillais étaient-ils des corsaires?', *Conférences de
l'Institut historique de Provence*, 1966, No. 4, pp. 204–6; and C. Taillefer,
'La guerre de course à Marseille de 1793 à 1802', *Provincia*, 1963, *tome* 5,
No. 258, pp. 113–15.

[6] Archives de la Chambre de Commerce, B21; petition of the merchants,
11 Mar. 1793.

feelings of insecurity. Nearer home, *émigrés* were believed to be returning in large numbers, while deserters from the armies were thought to be planning a descent on the city and plotting to starve Marseilles of food supplies. Patriots were alarmed that the departure of so many men to the frontiers was undermining their hold on the city and causing those remaining to serve so frequently in the National Guard that they were becoming tired and unwilling.[1] Moreover, Lyons was said to be on the point of delivering itself to the enemies of the Republic, thus extending the catastrophe of the Vendean revolt.[2]

Such disasters, or threats of disaster, preoccupied the clubists, especially the members of the Central Committee. Fears reached a climax when, on 16 March, a letter from Moïse Bayle, describing the dangers which were nearly overwhelming the Republic, announced the establishment of a Revolutionary Tribunal at Paris.[3] Immediately the Club demanded the prompt levying of an unlimited number of troops and, equally important, the appointment of a treasurer to receive contributions from the rich for the war-effort. Envoys were to be sent out to hasten the levying of troops, the Municipality was to be asked to suspend the granting of passports – to prevent suspects leaving the town – while laws against *émigrés* were to be rigorously enforced. The Club then received with joy the news that the Three Administrations[4] and its own delegates had voted the establishment of a Revolutionary Tribunal to replace the Popular Tribunal, considered too lenient towards suspects. The fact that all the members of the new Tribunal – who included Hugues and Isoard – were predominantly clubists served further to reassure them. Finally, the Municipality proposed the suppression of the *cercles bourgeois* – organs which collected money for charitable purposes – and expropriated the money to finance the recruiting drive. Next day, the Three Administrations and the clubists voted to set up a *Comité de secours* to

[1] A. Comm, 4D12, Municipality to Dept., 18 Feb. 1793.
[2] Most of the above preoccupations can be followed in ABR, L2071, *procès-verbal* of the Club, 28 Feb.–18 Apr. 1793, and in the correspondence of the Municipality, A. Comm., 4D2.
[3] ABR, L2071, 16 Mar. 1793.
[4] The Municipality, the District, and the Department, meeting together. For their decisions, see ABR, L48, *Registre des Procès-Verbaux des Trois-Corps Administratifs de la Ville de Marseille*, 16–17 Mar. 1793.

levy forced loans and revolutionary taxes upon those *gens aisés* whom avarice and egoism had inhibited from contributing to the war-effort, the money thus obtained being destined for the equipment of recruits, for the National Guard, and for the batteries which protected the coasts. And, as a final measure of public security, a disarmament was effected on 19 March. Authorised by the Municipality, since arms were in the hands of people who cared little for the future of the Revolution, this disarmament was conducted with firmness but, seemingly, with little brutality.[1] But it fell especially hard upon the *gens aisés*, many of whom had arms but rarely turned out for the National Guard.

Thus by mid-March a militant form of Jacobinism was triumphant in Marseilles. The campaign against enemies of the Revolution had left the city at the mercy of the Jacobins, whose enemies had been disarmed and were threatened by forced loans and by the quick justice of a revolutionary tribunal composed of those who most violently denounced the rich and indifferent.

These developments undoubtedly alarmed large sections of the city's population, for whom the Popular Tribunal had stood as a bulwark against the repetition of the murders of July and September in Marseilles and the Massacres of September in Paris. That such a body should be replaced by one composed of men who openly justified the September Massacres[2] appeared as the prelude to a blood-bath which would overwhelm all respectable citizens. As yet however protest was ineffective. But a few months later, in May, June and July, men who had been terrorised into silence by the measures of March were able to speak out before a revived Popular Tribunal staffed by opponents of the clubists. In the almost complete absence of speeches by the clubists, it is from the evidence given by these witnesses, in the summer of 1793, that we can best judge the effect the disarmament of suspects and the plan for a revolutionary tribunal had upon the uncommitted people of Marseilles. Even if those who testified before the Popular Tribunal exaggerated the bloodthirstiness of the clubists, this in itself

---

[1] *Jnal. Dépts. Mérid.*, CLXIV.
[2] *Jnal. Dépts. Mérid.*, CLXIV, Club, 30 Jan. 1793; and CXLVI, Club, 4 Feb. 1793.

tells us something about the fears which gripped a large part of the city's population. The large number of witnesses, drawn from all social classes, shows the extent of these fears, while the vehemence of their denunciations – and the concordance of one with another – reveals the depth of the rift between the clubists and their opponents.

The main allegation was that the measures taken in March formed the prelude to a 'general massacre' of all law-abiding citizens and the signal for a new insurrection, directed not against nobles and priests, but against all opponents of 'anarchy' and 'brigandage'. Étienne Seytres, *procureur de la commune* at the time of the disarmament, alleged that the clubists had wished to assemble seventy or eighty companies of the National Guard, to surround the Cours, to seal off the city by closing the town gates thus enclosing many countrymen in town for the market, and to confine people to their houses. Disarmed citizens were to be put in a church and held under arrest. Seytres and other members of the Municipality said that, this done, a new September Massacre was to begin – 'two thousands heads' being the alleged target. Mourraille, the mayor, gave corroborative evidence.[1] Other witnesses told of the lists of proscription drawn up by the Central Committee of the Club.[2] A locksmith was alleged to have said that he had received orders to build 'une guillotine ambulante' but attempts to make him incriminate the Club failed completely.[3] A phrase of Maillet *cadet* – doubly unfortunate in coming from the president of the Criminal Tribunal – was quoted as summing up the attitudes of the Jacobins – 'Il veut, dit-il, que l'on coupe des têtes et pourquoi non? Il vaut mieux pendre qu'être pendu.'[4] The Popular Tribunal even cross-examined all the undertakers to see if they had been requisitioned for nocturnal burials in preparation

[1] See ABR, L1044, *Lettre de Mourraille à ses concitoyens*, 27 May 1793, disclaiming responsibility for the disarmament.

[2] ABR, L3104; Popular Tribunal, evidence of Cler Bonnet, 16 May 1793. Later it was stated that the law of 29 Mar., ordering the posting of residents' names on doors, was intended to facilitate massacres.

[3] ABR, L3104, Popular Tribunal, evidence of Antoine Pillon, etc., 21 May 1793.

[4] ABR, L3100, *Le Comité général des trente-deux Sections de Marseille remet au Tribunal populaire à l'appui du grand acte d'accusation les pièces suivantes . . . Contre Maillet cadet*, 1 July 1793.

for the 'general massacre': their answers were unanimously and emphatically negative.[1]

Obviously it is difficult to disentangle the truth from such openly partisan denunciations. Not all clubists, of course, used temperate language and, since Marat was their idol, perhaps the threats of hangings said to emanate from the Central Committee are to be treated with the seriousness accorded to similar threats of the Friend of the People. What is beyond question is that the clubists demanded measures which were far too ruthless and wide-ranging to win the whole-hearted approval of those who had controlled the destinies of the city, that they provoked these people to a reaction against Jacobinism, with its very real threat of terror, and forced people who had hitherto been indifferent to the political struggle to enter political activity, and to enter on the side of the enemies of the Jacobins. The 'riches égoïstes' and others, whom the Club had, in mid-March, tried to terrorise into supporting the Revolution or be hanged, exerted themselves not only in defence of their properties but also in defence of their lives. And they carried with them into the struggle a host of men who, though they had little property to fight for, would, and did, fight for their lives and peace of mind.

(b) IN THE DEPARTMENT

These men, numerous in Marseilles, were joined by people from the department; for outbreaks of violence in the countryside paralleled those occurring in the city – and news of these outrages, often exaggerated, redoubled terror within the city itself.[2] In each case, the clubists of Marseilles were increasingly implicated.

The records of the Criminal Tribunal during the autumn of 1792 show that violence was quick to come to the surface, that

[1] ABR, L3100, Popular Tribunal, evidence of Pierre Beaulieu, 11 July 1793.

[2] The best illustration of this is to be found in Bib. Mun., Marseilles, MS. 048728 (op. cit.) – correspondents in Marseilles report on 17 July that the mayor and two municipal officers of Pertuis have been killed; 19 July, 400 men from Marseilles put down rebellion at La Ciotat; 1 Aug., 13 people murdered at Toulon, including four departmental officers; 8 Aug., 4 refractory priests murdered at Manosque; 10 August, a *courtier* was hanged for speculation; 21 Aug., 500 Marseillais go to Manosque. . .

violent crimes – *voies de fait* of every description – were numerous, conflicting parties being quick to use fire-arms. Quarrels often took political overtones,[1] rumours and threats sped through the countryside, raising widespread alarm; deserters roamed the hills terrorising farms and villages and, most serious of all, administrative bodies were treated with open contempt by men who usurped their rights, arresting people, forcing citizens to pay them money.[2]

The mere mention of a few of the graver incidents indicates the area involved and the frequency of the disturbances in a region left in a state of turmoil by the expeditions against Arles and Avignon. At Pertuis, on 15 July 1792, five men were murdered, including a municipal officer; four days later, four hundred men were called out to put down a disturbance at La Ciotat, a town divided by struggles between rich citizens and workless artisans.[3] Towards the end of July, thirteen men, including the public prosecutor of the Var and members of the departmental authority, were murdered at Toulon. At Carpentras on 4–5 August four prisoners were seized and shot: soon after, the *seigneur* of La Penne was killed while, at the end of the month, five hundred Marseillais rushed towards Manosque after two envoys of the Club of Marseilles had been arrested following the murder of four priests and, returning by Aix, witnessed other bloody clashes. At Eyguières about eight men were killed in an armed conflict on 23 August. Throughout October, complaints flowed in to local administrations of attacks on 'persons and properties', of troubles stirred up by priests, and by bourgeois who put up a stubborn resistance to the recruiting drive. In many areas, long-smouldering fires of agrarian discontent led peasants to attack bourgeois who encroached on common land; elsewhere, exchanges of land, planned a long time previously, were now effected by force and patriots were seizing their share of land (and wood, furniture,

---

[1] Or religious ones. In Mar. 1792, the Protestant church of Apt (in the Vaucluse), was sacked by national guardsmen of Gordes etc., who attacked Protestant pastors who refused to say mass. A. Nat., F7 3659².

[2] ABR, L3023, L3059, Criminal Tribunal of the Bouches-du-Rhône.

[3] A. Comm., 1I73, undated document attacking rich citizens of La Ciotat; 1I75, Municipality of Aubagne, 27 July 1792, stated that La Ciotat was in rebellion and feared interruption of communications between Marseilles and Toulon.

wine . . .) which the Nation had confiscated from the aristocrats. Armed sorties went out against châteaux, where nobles
were thought to be making last-ditch stands, and warriors
seldom returned from such expeditions empty-handed. It was
stated that the 10 August had 'authorised' these attacks.[1] Old
scores were being settled, old debts extracted by force and judges
were being compelled to pay back fines imposed under the
Ancien régime. Complaints that the new taxation favoured the
rich at the expense of the poor led to conflict. The fact that the
authorities spent so much of their time sending off letters in all
directions repeatedly urging 'respect to persons and properties'
tends to confirm the desperate report of a royal agent that the
course of justice was completely disrupted and that the body
politic was falling apart.[2]

Against such a background of disorder – at a time when the
deficits of the 1791 and 1792 harvests were making themselves
felt – the Club of Marseilles sent out its agents, frequently in
attempts at pacification, but often to found affiliated clubs and
to speed up the levying of men and money for the armies.[3]

In the face of indifference on the part of peasants and bourgeois, such expeditions often became punitive sorties directed
against those who did not take the Jacobin view of the Revolution, and propaganda forays designed to win the support of
local municipalities and clubs to the addresses sent to the
Convention demanding the death of the king. The clubists
thought of these sorties as military campaigns – *chevauchées* from
one besieged bastion of Jacobinism to another; and, exulting
in their power, they aroused hostility not only from the opponents of the Revolution but from those whose former loyalty

[1] ABR, L1975, the club of Peypin d'Aigues, in the Vaucluse, to Club of
Marseilles, 24 Jan. 1793: explaining the devastation of their château in
Sept. 1792.

[2] A. Nat., F7365 9[2], 26 July 1792. See this dossier and also F7365 9[3] for
most of the incidents referred to in this section. Also ABR, L500, L588,
L590, L599 (*fonds* of Districts of the Bouches-du-Rhône, dossiers of troubles).

[3] A fresh levy of 6000 men was voted on 20 Sept. for the Army of Italy.
The frequency of the sending-out of envoys from the Club of Marseilles
can best be seen in *Jnal. Dépts. Mérid.*; in ABR, L45, deliberations of the
Department, which invested many clubists with powers to supervise
recruiting; L2076, *La Vie politique de François Isoard*, n.d. (*nivôse* II), etc.
S. Vialla, *Les Volontaires des Bouches-du-Rhône*, pp. 173 ff.

could not stand the strain of reiterated demands. Throughout Provence, club called to club[1] and Jacobin to Jacobin. Marseilles responded, sending agents far and wide, levying taxes for the war-effort, recruiting men, founding rural clubs, intimidating priests and bourgeois and arresting suspects. In August, Isoard and Tourneau caused uproar at Manosque and were rescued from an enraged populace only by the threat of a full-scale invasion from Marseilles; in September, Isoard and colleagues were engaged in rounding up suspects as far away as Grenoble,[2] while another batch of envoys were sent to recruit for the *Armée du Midi*.[3]

Even if these agents were welcomed in the outlying regions they were generally fêted by only a section of the population; and, since they came with peremptory demands and used fairly ruthless methods (disarmament, arrests, shows of force by the National Guard) to back up local Jacobins, their activities provoked a widespread outcry – an outcry which was soon heard in Marseilles. Complaints reached the town Sections which, concerned above all with the preservation of law and order, a task which they had entrusted to the Popular Tribunal – whose judges they elected – demanded the punishment of those going through the countryside 'sous le nom des Marseillais', forcing people to contribute money and destroying their property.[4] The Municipality feared that the activities of the clubists – or unruly men acting in emulation of the clubists – would alarm rich landowners, causing them to stop contributing money to the war-effort and to abandon the cultivation of their land, thus causing widespread rural unemployment.[5]

[1] The *Atlas historique*, pp. 166–9, has interesting information on the geographical incidence of Provençal clubs. Their density seemingly had little to do with language, literacy or divisions between Protestant and Catholic areas; but there was a correlation between a high density of clubs and a high percentage of population living in towns and *bourgs* rather than in isolated hamlets. In the Bouches-du-Rhône, 90 communes out of 110 had clubs; *Histoire de la Provence*, p. 413.

[2] P. Robert, op. cit., pp. 26 ff.

[3] S. Vialla, *Les Volontaires des Bouches-du-Rhône*, pp. 173 ff. These included Jean Savon who was later to become notorious, see below, pp. 69 ff.

[4] Complaints in Section 8, 7 Nov. 1792, ABR, L1941; Section 17 heard that Section 1 had demanded that the offending *commissaires* be sent before the Popular Tribunal, L1945, (Section 17), 20 Nov. 1792.

[5] *Journal de Provence*, 27 Sept. 1792 – municipal proclamation of 22 Sept.

The Club took notice of these complaints, instituted an enquiry, proclaimed its conviction that those who had legitimate grievances (for instance, in disputes about land) would find satisfaction in the law courts, and, finally, made a strong repudiation of excessive revolutionary zeal, now that France's enemies were being held at bay.[1] Unfortunately for the cause of the Club however, its enquiry seems to have been extremely perfunctory and a man who complained of exactions by its agents was brusquely informed that such complaints were designed solely to 'put the Revolution on trial'.[2] Such statements, and the ease with which the clubists justified themselves (before their own colleagues), seemed to cast doubt on the Club's professed intention to punish abuses committed in its name – an impression confirmed by an important declaration of eight agents, including the much-travelled Isoard, who, in November 1792, declared that those who complained of the clubists putting the Revolution on trial and would soon question the 'legality' of 10 August and the imprisonment of the king. 'Déjà l'aristocratie bourgeoise levait sa tête dans toutes les communes du département; déjà les commissaires de la société étaient partout de vils exacteurs; déjà Marseille, qui les avait envoyés, devenait l'objet de toutes les criailleries de l'incivisme'.[3]

This declaration provided a warning that, faced with a grave crisis to the Revolution, the Jacobins would not shrink from brutal action. Such a crisis did occur, as we have seen, in February and March 1793: and so, just as this period marked the climax of the Jacobin offensive within the city, it also saw the most determined effort of the clubists to enforce their views on the department. Of all the expeditions of this period, that to Salon had the greatest impact in galvanising widespread resistance to the Jacobins. Trouble had reached a peak in September

[1] ABR, L2076, *Adresse de la Société populaire de Marseille aux citoyens du département*, 26 Oct. 1792. But one commissioner said that he *had* demanded an end to attacks on property, but that this displeased the peasants who wished to get revenge for former oppressions.

[2] *Jnal. Dépts. Mérid.*, CXII, 14–15 Nov. 1792; and subsequent sessions; for the complaint of Bertrand d'Apt (for whom see below, pp. 183 ff.), see *Jnal. Dépts. Mérid.*, CXVI, 24 Nov. 1792.

[3] *Jnal. Dépts. Mérid.*, CXVI, 24 Nov. 1792, signed by Isoard, Turcan, Antoine Riquier, etc.

1792, when the Jacobin Electoral Assembly meeting at Avignon to choose deputies for the Convention, sent detachments of the National Guard to investigate the ill-treatment of patriots at Eyguières, a village to the south-east of Avignon.[1] This expedition met with violent resistance, in which at least eight men were killed, a small army having been formed by men from Salon, Eyguières and the surrounding villages. Despite later explanations that this resistance had been the natural reaction of peasants protecting their crops from 'brigands', a 'political' interpretation was at once put on these events and Salon was denounced as the home of 'l'aristocratie des richesses' and the refuge of an infinity of former nobles and *parlementaires*.[2] Thus the Department, in close touch with the Club, sent Abeille, Grimaud and Bazin to restore order there.[3]

The weight of repression was to fall on the richer citizens – they were to pay the cost of a small army of occupation – but such were the abuses in the collection of this very hefty tax, and so vexatious was the conduct of the soldiery, that resistance to the Jacobins extended well beyond the wealthy citizens – in fact a crowd of citizens of all social classes, the majority peasants, came to Marseilles in February to protest at the reign of terror imposed on their town.[4] For a time, the clubists were expelled from Salon by the townspeople. New disorders broke out, in which at least five people were killed, without the agents of the Department making any effort to discover the murderers.

In their journeys throughout Provence – and nowhere more so than at Salon – the clubists had become convinced that resistance to revolutionary measures came from men whom they described as 'bourgeois' or as members of 'l'aristocratie bourgeoise' who had replaced the now-decimated ranks of nobles and priests as foremost opponents of the Revolution. Like the

---

[1] ABR, L278, Electoral Assembly of the Bouches-du-Rhône, meeting at Avignon, 1792. Eyguières, *arrond.*, Arles, *chef-lieu de canton*.

[2] ABR, L2076, *Les Électeurs du District de Marseille à leurs concitoyens.* N.d. See also L3044–L3047; and depositions before the Popular Tribunal, expecially L3104.

[3] ABR, L45, Departmental Administration, 29 Nov. 1792; 16 Dec. 1792; and L126, register of correspondence of Dept., 16 Dec. 1792 etc. Little is known of Jean Bazin, of Lambesc, member of Dept., Sébastien Abeille or François-Paul Grimaud.

[4] ABR, L45, Dept. Admin., 12/13/14 Feb. 1793.

nobles and priests, the bourgeois of the small towns of Provence were dangerous because of their hold over the minds of the peasants and small tradesmen of the countryside – they enjoyed the prestige of education and financial ease, they were good customers of local tradesmen and necessary employers of rural labour, and they were in close touch with events outside the experience of most peasants in Provence (often having worked in Marseilles or Aix before retiring to the countryside). Their social rank was hardly ever defined by the Jacobins but, if we are to judge from those who later denounced the clubists before the Popular Tribunal, it would seem that professional men – doctors, surgeons, lawyers of all descriptions – landowners, *fermiers*, and tradesmen and artisans formed the bulk of this category.[1] In contact with events in Marseilles, often inheriting the mantle, as well as the land, of the *seigneurs*, the bourgeoisie held the peasantry under their sway and, hearing of attempts to coerce the rich inhabitants of Marseilles, could easily stir up the countrymen to resist the clubists by spreading alarming rumours that the rapacious city-dwellers were coming to seize their property or take their lives. The *cultivateurs* were regarded – and perhaps despised – by the Jacobins as an inert mass,[2] whose natural goodness might all too easily be corrupted by the money and speeches of the wily bourgeoisie. Moreover, rich

[1] For descriptions of the 'rural bourgeoisie' of Provence see P. Lafran and G. Plantier, *Saint-Chamas des origines à 1851* (Les Amis du Vieux Saint-Chamas, 1955); M. G. Gagneux, 'Un village provençal urbanisé: Marignane à la veille de la Révolution', *Actes du 83ᵉ Congrès national des Sociétés savantes, Aix-Marseille, 1958* (Paris, 1959), pp. 471–482; M. Agulhon, *Pénitents et francs-maçons*, gives many indications regarding the social composition of Provençal – mainly Varois – localities.

[2] But the density of clubs in Provence suggests that the Jacobins exaggerated a little, (see above, p. 51 n.). We have few indications regarding the social composition of the clubs. M. Agulhon, *Pénitents et francs-maçons*, pp. 284 ff., reports that many clubs in the Var contained a large majority of the adult male population, i.e. a large number of agricultural workers: but *ménagers*, artisans and bourgeois seem to have been politically dominant. Their sessions were more frequent in winter than summer. Often however they were village assemblies debating harvest conditions, etc. The prospect of the division of common lands caused increased attendance. See ABR, L2065, Club of Éguilles (*arrond.*, Aix; *canton*, Aix-Sud); in the Year III there were 312 members, most of whom had been 'received' before 1793: the vast majority were 'cultivateurs', with a small representation of rural artisans.

and poor had an obvious community of interest in resisting men who came to take money and men for the wars.

Evidence of antagonism between the clubists and the rural and small-town 'bourgeois aristocracy' is revealed by speeches of the clubists themselves, though the real significance and depth of this antagonism emerges most clearly in the denunciations which, in the summer of 1793, men threatened by the Jacobin offensive made before the Popular Tribunal. For instance, in October 1792, the *Journal des départements méridionaux* described the happy state of the villagers of Peypin who had the good fortune, not shared by most other villages, of being without bourgeois.[1] Later, Mauger Manneville and Augustin Delaporte, both prominent clubists, were sent to Salernes, not to levy taxes or men, but to smooth out differences between the two opposing classes of the village – the *bourgeois* and the *cultivateurs*. Their report describes, in graphic and no doubt exaggerated terms, the persecution which they had suffered at the hands of the bourgeois – 'Nous disons la classe bourgeoise, car il y a encore des classes dans ce canton, où l'égalité n'est pas connue . . .' To them, a bourgeois was an enemy of the people who treated the poor badly, speculated in grain, forced the peasants to sell him their crops on unfavourable terms and adopted contemptuous attitudes towards his social inferiors.

Condemning the unbridled greed of their enemies, the clubists concluded, 'Si c'est un crime d'avoir pensé qu'après la ci-devant noblesse, la bourgeoisie est la classe qui pèse le plus sur le peuple, nous persistons dans ce crime et dans nos principes.'[2] The countrymen were seen as completely dominated by the bourgeoisie. The clubists reported that one cause of the alleged reluctance of the peasants to attend the clubs was that if they went, they would infuriate the bourgeoisie. They dared not do so, since they were mostly in debt to the bourgeois. At least one scheme was floated to liberate the peasants from these debts – according to a plan of the club of Aubagne, patriotic citizens of Marseilles were to pay them off in *assignats*, thus

[1] *Jnal. Dépts. Mérid.*, xciii, 3 Oct. 1792 (Peypin, *arrond.*, *canton*, Roquevaire).

[2] ABR, L2072, papers of the Club of Marseilles, *Rapport des commissaires de Marseille à Salernes*, n.d. Salernes is in the Var (*arrond.*, Draguigan; *chef-lieu de canton*).

winning the peasants for the Revolution.[1] In general however the clubists did not really show much understanding of the discontents of the poorer peasants, though often they demanded the speeding up of the sale of *biens nationaux*.

Impelled by a fierce patriotism, the clubists did do much to rouse a determination to continue the war-effort at the highest pitch, collecting money for privateers and *volontaires*, collecting metal from church bells, complaining of the run-down state of the arsenal at Toulon, attacking the Minister of the Marine for failing to provide naval escorts for French merchantmen.[2] At the height of their effort, the Club even proposed to take over the task of recruiting from the *Représentants* sent from the Convention on 9 March – though Fréron successfully squashed this usurpation of powers.[3] Yet one does not have to believe every accusation levied against the clubists to see that Salon in particular had suffered grievously at their hands. The tax on the Salonnais was heavy for a small town, most of whose inhabitants were not implicated in resistance to the Jacobins. The soldiery were a blight on the country people, whatever their social rank and political opinions – breaking into the lands of those who had been forced, by threats of hanging, to flee; ransacking houses, driving away flocks, destroying crops and helping themselves to provisions. Those citizens who, fearing for their lives after the murder of five of their townsmen, fled to Martigues or further afield in Provence were declared *émigrés* and, if they returned to prove their residence in the country, had to pay exorbitantly before they were struck off the lists of *émigrés*.[4]

At La Ciotat, where the *curé* had condemned the bourgeois

[1] ABR, L1974, plan of Club of Aubagne, 15 May 1792.

[2] ABR, L2071, register of Club, 28 Feb.–18 Apr. 1793, passim.

[3] ABR, L2071, Club, 26 Mar. 1793; 27 Mar. 1793. Stanislas-Louis-Marie Fréron, son of the famous polemicist, himself editor of *L'Orateur du peuple*, was renowned for his extremist pronouncements and extravagant oratory; a deputy of Paris, he was sent with Paul-François Barras to the Basses- and Hautes-Alpes, on 9 March 1793; these two deputies passed a couple of days at Marseilles at the end of March, exhorting Marseilles to rise a third time, in order to back the Parisian attacks on the Girondins. They returned to Marseilles in the autumn of 1793. See below, pp. 130 ff.

[4] Besides the dossiers of the Popular Tribunal, those of the Criminal Tribunal (investigating these matters in the Year III), contain a lot of material – e.g. ABR, L3044–47; L3064; L3066; L3040, etc.

for speculating in *assignats* to the detriment of 'les ouvriers', the 'citoyens aisés', once the Jacobins had been ousted from power, stated that under their domination they had been less free than under the *Ancien régime* and that they had had to make great sacrifices for the indigent classes. At Caderouse in the Vaucluse, the sectionaries blamed the Jacobins for pillaging the goods of their *seigneur*, using his furniture in the town hall and club, monopolising the leasing of the lands of the clergy, keeping non-Jacobins away from the auctions by displays of force, sub-letting the land at immense profit, throwing out the poor peasants who were cultivating the land.[1]

Such excesses were attributed by the witnesses before the Popular Tribunal, not just to blind greed or soldierly drunken-ness, but to a Jacobin offensive against the bourgeois aristo-cracy. This was a theme which united the various incidents and atrocities which were evoked before the Tribunal not only by the bourgeois themselves but by a much larger number of peasants and small traders. Thus Grimaud is alleged to have urged 'qu'il fallait pendre tous les bourgeois et tout première-ment le curé, que les cultivateurs deviendraient les maîtres et que lorsque les bourgeois ne voudraient pas leur donner du travail, il fallait les rosser à coups de bâtons'.[2] All the envoys of Marseilles were accused, often by the peasants, of urging the *cultivateurs* to seize and redistribute the land of the bourgeois, to confine them to a certain amount of property. And since the Popular Tribunal did not confine its enquiries to Salon, the Jacobins of Saint-Chamas, of Orgon, of Mornas and of many other villages were accused of similarly stirring up the peasants against their priests and their bourgeois. According to the wit-nesses before the Tribunal, the hanging of the bourgeois and the priests was the Jacobin remedy for all the ills of the whole department.

Events at Salon and elsewhere exemplified, therefore, the activities which were to bring about the downfall of the Jacobin cause in Provence. The Jacobins were isolating themselves in an

---

[1] ABR, L1974, club of La Ciotat to Club of Marseilles, 24 Apr. 1792; and Section 1, 23 May 1793; Caderouse – undated report to Sections of Marseilles.

[2] ABR, L3105, Popular Tribunal, evidence of Sauveur Ollivier, 2 July 1793.

increasingly hostile department: they were continually increasing the ranks of those who were to take part in the federalist revolt. The agents of the Club, coming hard up against what they considered rural indifference to the Revolution as they saw it, were incapable of seeing this as anything other than a political plot against the Revolution. To them, the Revolution was a career of denunciation, of militant speeches, of long journeys through Provence, of hazardous missions to the Armies of Italy or of the Pyrenees, of all-night sessions in the Club or the Department. From these men, the Revolution demanded, and obtained, absolute devotion. When therefore they encountered people to whom the success or failure of the Revolution was a matter of little concern, of no real importance one way or the other, they felt entitled to equate apathy and laziness with ill-will and conspiracy. Inhabitants of a city where political emotions were at fever-pitch, the clubists were dismayed to find that the bulk of the country people did not go to the local Jacobin clubs, but preferred to go to church on Sundays, that their preoccupations centred round the weather, the harvest prospects, and matters of village politics which often had little connection with revolutionary politics. And their insistence that recalcitrant peasants were 'paid by the bourgeois', together with the large number of peasant witnesses before the Popular Tribunal, suggests that the Jacobins themselves realised that their appeals to the cupidity and land-hunger of the countrymen had failed to reconcile them to the sacrifices demanded by the revolutionary war and had therefore failed to dissolve the bond of common interest which, in the short term at least, united them to the bourgeoisie.

*   *   *

Thus, in the countryside as in the city, all those who feared for their lives and property were alienated from the Revolution by the policies of the clubists who seemed bent on plunging France into anarchy. In the face of the activities of the clubists, evidence of lassitude and exasperation increased – complaints of too frequent service in the National Guard, both in city patrols and on expeditions to places such as Salon. Exasperation with the government increased:

Citoyens, le peuple commence à acquérir des lumières; il commence à comprendre que les ministres, que plusieurs mêmes des représentants de la Nation qui sont bien nourris et bien vêtus, se soucient fort peu de la misère du pauvre, qui est nu et meurt de faim.

Thus the citizens of Section 13, one of the most popular of Marseilles, expressed their discontent at the sacrifices imposed on them. What use, they asked, was there in replacing one despot with a thousand?[1] Resistance, once passive, became an active force which, organising itself, did open battle with the Jacobins and for a time defeated them.

And this defeat was all the more serious in that it was inflicted not only on the social ideas and tactics outlined above, but on a whole political crusade. For the ruthless activity of the clubists, in their attempts to get men and money for the Revolution, would have been useless had it not been combined with a 'political' assault on the champions of immobilism, on the allies of the lukewarm and the indifferent, on, in Jacobin terminology, the perfidious Representatives of the People who, at the very heart of the Republic, were attempting to neutralise the national effort against the league of tyrants.

(c) IN THE REPUBLIC

This 'political crusade' was directed against the king and against those deputies of the Convention who protected his cause. Revolutionary Marseilles had been united behind the *fédérés* of 10 August and had elected deputies who had pledged themselves to finish the task of their fellow-townsmen – for instance Barbaroux, who greeted his election by offering a dagger which, if he did not deliver France from the odious race of kings, was to be plunged into his heart as a traitor to his townsmen's cause.[2] As the autumn dragged on, revolutionary tempers at Marseilles – as we have seen – became excited. Parallel with attacks on lukewarm citizens in town and department, came bitter denunciations against the delays of the

[1] ABR, L1973, remonstrance of Section 13, 5 Jan. 1793.
[2] ABR, L278, Electoral Assembly of the Bouches-du-Rhône, Avignon; 2–10 Sept. 1792.

Convention and virulent addresses which show that, here as elsewhere, Marseilles was not content with a subsidiary rôle and that its citizens were no more averse to criticising the short-comings of their elected assembly than they had been slow to denounce the double-dealing and treachery of their appointed monarch.[1] An address, drawn up by Ricord *fils* and sent by the departmental electoral assembly in November, made the restoration of peace and prosperity depend on the king's death, which was being delayed by scandalous faction-fighting within the Convention. Remember, it continued, that the Marseillais retained the right to recall and punish those deputies who betrayed the Nation's cause.[2] Nor were recriminations confined to the slowness of debates within the Convention, as is shown by an address of the Municipality which at the end of December fulminated against the privileges which the presence of the legislative assembly conferred on Paris: 'A peine avons-nous pu prévenir le manque de subsistances pour alimenter nos voisins et, tandis que toutes les faveurs sont prodiguées à une ville superbe et arrogamment ingrate, Marseille est lâchement abandonnée, plus lâchement encore calomniée.'[3] The delays in the Convention were attributed to its situation at Paris, a city which aspired to dominate the whole Republic and which afforded refuge to the more dangerous counter-revolutionaries; only the extermination of the traitors within the Convention, or its transference to a more trustworthy town, would end the divisions in the country.[4]

Who were these traitors in the Convention? Opinion in Marseilles was as yet uncertain. Barbaroux was undoubtedly the most popular of the city's deputies. In the Convention, he won the town's gratitude by demanding, for instance, that the nation should assume responsibility for its municipal debt, should provide more generous subsidies with which to buy arms and corn, and should preserve its *Bureau de commerce* and the *franchise du port*, by interesting himself in such diverse matters as

[1] ABR, L1945, Section 17, 7 Dec. 1792; A. Comm., 4D2, *Conseil général de la commune*, 26 Dec. 1792, etc.

[2] ABR, L278, Electoral Assembly of the department, Marseilles, 28 Nov. 1792.

[3] A. Comm., 4D2, *Conseil général de la commune*, 26 Dec. 1792.

[4] A. Comm., 4D2, *Conseil général de la commune*, 29 Dec. 1792.

the upheavals in the Levant trading posts, the expansion of the Black Sea corn trade, the digging of a canal from the Mediterranean to the North Sea, the improvement of the defences of Toulon and increased compensation for the victims of the 10 August. All these causes were vitally important to the Marseillais and explain why Barbaroux' relationship with the Municipality – of which he had been a member – should be exceptionally close.[1]

Of his political attitudes, his attacks on the Commune of Paris, his demands for a departmental guard, his complaints that Paris got millions of *livres* for the purchase of corn by threatening insurrection, his insistence that the Convention should remove itself from the capital – a city which wanted everything for itself and ignored the wishes of the rest of France – these attitudes were readily appreciated in his home town which was likewise convinced that Paris was grievously neglecting its interests.

But, though the Marseillais distrusted Paris, their distrust, at this stage of the Revolution, was expressed in the belief that Paris – refuge of many counter-revolutionaries – and the Convention, refuge of as yet undesignated traitors, were sabotaging their efforts to get the king executed with all speed. In other words, their lack of faith in Paris proceeded largely from their own extreme republicanism. With Barbaroux, on the other hand, distaste for Paris was increasingly bound up with a revulsion against extremist policies, a revulsion which, as is well known, led him, under the influence of the Rolandins, to embrace the cause of the 'appeal to the people'.

The evolution of Barbaroux' views – like those of Rebecquy – was as yet masked for the Marseillais, for whom he was still the man who, at the Electoral Assembly at Avignon, had declaimed most forcibly against the monarchy and had rejected 'la république fédérative' as a viable constitution for France. But the Second Battalion of *fédérés* became, in December 1792, the centre of a propaganda battle between Barbaroux and Rebecquy – who hoped to win its soldiers to the cause of the appeal to the people – and Granet, Moïse Bayle and Pierre Baille, who demanded the execution of the king, 'purely and simply'. Letters from Dominique Girard, commander of the Battalion,

[1] Barbaroux, *Mémoires*, pp. 107 ff., etc.; *Correspondance*, pp. 246 ff.

kept the Municipality of Marseilles informed – or half-informed – on these struggles.[1] On the whole, Girard defended Roland, Louvet and Barbaroux against the intrigues of the Jacobins of Paris and Marseilles, blaming the Montagnards and their ally, the mob, for the fact that the Marseillais were subject to a constant campaign of vilification by the Parisians – for instance, when Marseilles asked for a grant with which to buy corn, the factions in Paris accused the city of wishing to provide only the Midi with corn, starve the North and set up a new form of government in the South. Girard consequently denounced the Parisians and their idols.

Contemporary observers noted this friction between the Marseillais of the Second Battalion and the militant revolutionaries of Paris. John Moore remarked that the *fédérés* were feared by the extremists in the Convention, who tried to stir up the *sans-culottes* against them; he reported that the Marseillais had been invited by the Rolandins to protect the Assembly from the mob, that, so far, they had resisted Montagnard attempts to send them to the frontiers. Moore saw the *Conventionnels* becoming polarised into two parties, a process in which he assigns the Marseillais a crucial rôle; for, he reports, the Rolandists would have been overthrown had not the very name of the Marseillais kept the 'suburb patriots' in check.[2]

But, reviewing this period in his memoirs, Barbaroux ascribes the failure of the campaign for the appeal to the people to the success of the Montagnards in winning part of the Battalion to their point of view: thus, when he ordered the Marseillais to defend the Convention to protect the deputies' freedom of speech, they refused, thereby enabling Robespierre, Danton, and the crowds at their disposal, to intimidate the honest deputies.[3] Obviously the speeches of Bayle and Granet, demanding the unconditional death of the king, had borne fruit among the *fédérés*.[4]

[1] See A. Comm., 4D44, *Registre des lettres reçues de Paris*, letters of various dates, (e.g. 5 Dec. 1792; 4 Jan. 1793). For Dominique Girard, see below, pp. 282–3.

[2] John Moore, M.D., *A Journal during a residence in France, from the beginning of August to the middle of December 1792*, 2 vols. (Dublin, 1793) II, 111–13.

[3] Barbaroux, *Mémoires*, p. 198.

[4] ABR, L2076, *Discours que prononça Granet . . . au Club du Bataillon Marseillais à Paris*, n.d.

These debates are all the more important since the letters of the *fédérés*, and accounts of their *esprit public*, were one of the principal sources of information regarding events in Paris to be available to the citizens in the south. And, perhaps even more important, the clubists of Marseilles regarded the Second Battalion, when it returned home at the end of March, as the principal bearer of the germ of federalism to the revolutionary stronghold in the south.[1]

Because of conflicting news from Paris, then, a period of some perplexity preceded the arrival of hard-and-fast news that Barbaroux, Rebecquy, Duprat[2] and Durand-Maillane[3] had voted for the appeal to the people and that De Perret[4] and Durand-Maillane had voted for the eventual banishment of Louis. Before this news arrived, addresses had been sent, with extreme urgency, denouncing those who by adopting the appeal wished to divide Paris from the departments and so provoke a civil war; and who, by favouring 'la démocratie pure', would destroy the representative system of government and, by repeated *appels*, plunge France into continual anarchy.[5] This was described by the clubists as the rankest federalism, setting one *assemblée primaire* against another, one region against another, thus giving the royalists, thought to dominate regions not far from Marseilles, new opportunities to cause divisions within the Republic and to provoke bitter debates which had been decided once and for all – by the Marseillais – on the 10 August. Finally, a new note of social conflict was heard when one clubist

[1] See below, p. 65; and pp. 282–3, for the trial of Girard as liaison-officer between Barbaroux and the federalists.

[2] Jean Duprat, born Avignon, in 1760, active in union of Avignon with France; mayor of Avignon, June 1792; a friend of Barbaroux, in the Convention, came increasingly under the influence of the Girondins. Attacked arrests of 2 June, was arrested and executed on 31 Oct. 1793.

[3] Pierre-Toussaint Durand-Maillane, born Saint-Rémy 1729: advocate, sat in National Assembly; played large rôle in drawing up Civil Constitution of the Clergy; in *Comité de législation* of the Convention; was secretary of Convention on 30 May 1793. Lay low during Terror, prominent in the thermidorian reaction in the Midi; member of *Conseil des Anciens*, d. 1814.

[4] Claude-Romain-Lauze De Perret, born at Apt (now in the Vaucluse) 1747, of a noble family, *conseiller du roi*; worked actively for 10 Aug., but, like Duprat, came under influence of Barbaroux and was likewise executed on 31 Oct. 1793.

[5] ABR, L2041, Club of Marseilles to Club of Aix, 18 Jan. 1793.

observed that only 'les honnêtes gens' favoured the appeal to the people. These also were the views of Moïse Bayle, Pierre Baille, Bernard Laurens, Granet, Gasparin, Rovère and Pellissier who voted for death, purely and simply.[1]

News of the split within the deputation caused consternation at Marseilles; but all the administrative bodies, all the Sections, rallied to the *devise* of the Club: 'Mort du tyran: point de fédéralisme'.[2] Only the royalists, who had abandoned the political forum – and often the town – to their enemies, did not share the general rejoicing at the failure of their cause. Only the royalists – if they could do so without calling attention to themselves – refused to sign a barrage of petitions demanding the recall of the perjurors who had so abjectly betrayed the interests of the Nation. The flamboyance of Barbaroux' gesture at the Electoral Assembly was not forgotten – he, especially, was taunted with having betrayed the people's trust;[3] and even Mourraille, who had every reason to appreciate his friend's services to his city, disavowed his colleague, and, willingly or not, broke off all correspondence with him.[4]

As the Club's frontal attack on the *appelants* gained momentum, all policies thought of as Girondin or Rolandin were disavowed. Alarmed at Rolandin penetration into the ministries and armed forces, the clubists demanded the expulsion from

[1] Bernard Laurens, from the Basses-Alpes, ex-surgeon; in Committee of General Security for a short spell in Jan. 1793; no very prominent rôle during Terror: Thomas-Augustin Gasparin from Orange, of an old Protestant family; member of Legislative Assembly; active on missions to the armies; influential opponent of Vergniaud, Guadet, etc.; in June and July, member of Committee of Public Safety; sent on 9 Aug. 1793, to the Armies of the Alps and of Italy, and played a rôle in the repression of the federalist revolt. Joseph-Stanislas Rovère, a *marquis* from the Vaucluse, of dubious revolutionary integrity and financial acumen; member of Committee of General Security; 24 June 1793, sent on mission to Bouches-du-Rhône, implicated in shady dealings in *biens nationaux*; recalled in disgrace 25 Nov. 1793; opponent of Maignet; implicated in royalist plots, banished after 18 *fructidor*. Marie-Denis Pellissier, born at Saint-Rémy, 1765, more constant in his revolutionary principles than most of his colleagues, opposed most of the excesses of the thermidorians, member of the 500, executed 1816.

[2] ABR, L365, Club, 23 Jan. 1793; L1940, Section 7, 29 Jan. 1793, etc.

[3] *Jnal. Dépts. Mérid.*, CXLVIII, 8 Feb. 1793.

[4] *Jnal. Dépts. Mérid.*, CLIV, 23 Feb. 1793 and CLV, letter of the Municipality of 24 Feb. 1793.

the Convention of Brissot, Roland and their clique.¹ Letters from the Montagnard deputies explained that the Rolandins supported all measures favouring 'l'aristocratie de richesse' and were therefore sabotaging the Montagnards' efforts to raise money for the armies; they were blamed for the wranglings in the Convention, for the food riots at Paris and for every reverse to republican arms.²

With the receipt of news from Paris on 16 March, the campaign against the *appelants*, like that against their allies in Provence, reached a climax. Marseilles, it was recalled, had risen twice to impose its will on the Revolution, once deposing and once executing their king; now was the time for a third insurrection, this time to destroy the criminals of the Convention. Chompré demanded that the Club should inform the Assembly that it recognised only the Montagne, but a citizen pointed out that this, by depriving some regions of their representation, would be an abhorrent act of federalism. Nevertheless, the whole city – Club, Administrations and Sections – supported a fulminating address demanding the withdrawal of all deputies who had voted for the appeal.³

Added impetus was given to this campaign by the arrival, on 27 March, of the Second Battalion, whose men, often at loggerheads with their commander, gave vivid and conflicting accounts of the intrigues to which they had been subjected at Paris.⁴ Further fuel was added to the fire of Jacobin indignation against the Rolandins when four of the most advanced Montagnard deputies, Moïse Bayle, Boisset, Barras and Fréron arrived.⁵ These deputies, sent on 9 March, had wide powers to

---

¹ *Jnal. Dépts. Mérid.*, CLIX, 6 Mar. 1793.

² ABR, L2071, Club, 5 Mar. 1793.

³ ABR, L2071, Club, 16–17 Mar. 1793; *Jnal. Dépts. Mérid.*, CLXIV, 18 Mar. 1793, etc.

⁴ *Jnal. Dépts. Mérid.*, CLXVIII, CLXX, 28, 30 Mar. 1793. And see below, pp. 282–3.

⁵ Paul-François-Jean-Nicolas Barras, from Fox-Amphoux, in the Var; of noble family – 'ils sont vieux comme les rochers de Provence' – served against British in India; member of Dept. of Var; helped capture Nice and organise Alpes-Maritimes; represented Var in the Convention; 9 Mar. 1793, with Fréron to the Basses- and Hautes-Alpes; then to Army of Italy. Returned to Marseilles in Sept. 1793. See below, pp. 130 ff. For Fréron, see p. 56.

Joseph-Antoine Boisset, from the Drôme (b. 1748), represented that

arrest suspects and to dismiss the 'gangrened' members of the Administrations, and, for this reason, were subjected to an intense brain-washing campaign by the local Jacobins, who succeeded in the not too difficult task of harnessing their energies for the final assault against the *modérés*. In fact, the speeches of these deputies repeated themes which the Marseillais had long made their own – it was hardly necessary to awaken the Marseillais to the need to reduce the power of the Rolandins over the ministries, the finances of the State and the press. They did, however, contribute to the increasingly violent 'debate' about federalism.

To Moïse Bayle, for instance, Barbaroux' ambition was the dictatorship of a 'Southern Republic'.[1] To Barère, however, in the Convention, it was the Jacobins of Marseilles who had shown themselves federalists, in their petition demanding the recall of the *appelants*, and refusing to acknowledge laws made by all members of the Convention.[2] But to Danton this petition showed that Marseilles had declared itself the 'Montagne de la République',[3] while Barras affirmed that 'Paris a besoin de l'impulsion de Marseille pour se lever une troisième fois'. To crush the *appelants*, unity between Paris and Marseilles was essential.[4]

And, with money taken from the bourgeois *cercles*, more envoys were sent out by the Club – Maillet *cadet* going as far as Lyons to urge that perfidious city to take measures already implemented at Marseilles.[5] Again the Marseillais were fulfilling their chosen rôle of urging others to attain their level of revolutionary commitment. It was also hinted that these envoys might be used to prepare a popular uprising in the Midi, if the *appelants* were not expelled from the Convention.[6]

Thus by the end of March the city was becoming the centre of a vast campaign to win the Midi for the Montagne. The

department in the Convention, many missions recruiting in the southern departments; became friend of notorious thermidorian Cadroy.

[1] ABR, L2071, Club, 30 Mar. 1793.

[2] *Moniteur*, XV, p. 765; No. 82 of 23 Mar. 1793; Convention, 21 Mar. 1793.

[3] *Moniteur*, XV, p. 808; No. 87 of 28 Mar. 1793; Convention, 27 Mar. 1793.

[4] ABR, L2071, Club, 28 Mar. 1793.

[5] ABR, L2071, Club, 28 Feb. 1793; and L3100, *Le Comité général au Tribunal populaire*, 1 July 1793 and *Jnal. Dépts. Mérid.*, CLVII, 1 Mar. 1793 and CLXVI, 23 Mar. 1793.   [6] ABR, L2071, Club, 25 Mar. 1793.

arrival of Bayle and Boisset, together with the brief visit of Barras and Fréron, had given the Club renewed dynamism; and the close relations between it and the *Représentants* increased its status in the town – increased the arrogance of the clubists and made them more threatening to their enemies. To these factors may also be ascribed the new-found breadth and range of the Jacobins' attacks on their opponents – on the ill-conceived declaration of war on Holland, Britain and Spain, the abandonment of Belgium, the lack of protection for France's hard-hit commerce, the propaganda campaign to mislead the departments as to the intentions of the Parisians – a campaign which, taken with their opposition to 10 August, their idea of a 'République du Midi', their plan to move the Convention to Tours and their projected departmental guard, provided a good Jacobin definition of Girondin federalism, especially when it was added that the absurd Girondin Constitution consecrated the domination of 'l'aristocratie des riches', and killed the right of petition.

Obviously such a denunciation, drawn up by Maillet *cadet* at the end of March,[1] reflected an acute fear that the *appelants* would prevail unless new measures capped those of the middle of the month. So, on 11 April, the Club produced a plan for a *Comité de défense générale* to co-ordinate the efforts of the clubs of the Midi against the *appelants* and their allies – in other words, to call on the considerable forces of Jacobin federalism to defeat those of the Girondin federalists. With this end in view, each southern department was to appoint two deputies to join with the Club of Marseilles to take measures to preserve the unity and indivisibility of the Republic. Together with two members of the Jacobins of Paris, they were to bring pressure to bear on the local administrations to take all necessary measures of public safety – if the administrations resisted, the clubists would appeal over their heads to the *Représentants en mission*, who were to make full use of their wide powers of coercion. The main duty of the clubs was to supervise the levying of troops and to detect plots against the Republic.[2]

[1] ABR, L2076, *A toutes les Sociétés populaires et à toutes les Municipalités* ... *Marseille, le 1 avril 1793.*

[2] ABR, L2071, Club, 11 Apr. 1793. Note the similarity between this plan and the project of the *Assemblée générale des clubs du Midi*, meeting at Marseilles, in the autumn of 1793 – see below, pp. 132–4.

This plan was never carried out – it was too ambitious and aroused too much opposition in the town. Had it been effective, it would have placed Marseilles and perhaps the whole Midi at the mercy of the Club, which would gather all revolutionary powers for itself and, using the arm of terror, impose the Montagnard creed on all Provence. As it was, Bayle and Boisset, hearing that several patriots had been murdered at Beaucaire (in the Gard, across the Rhône from Tarascon), were levying 6000 men to prevent the disturbances – heralding, they feared, a new Vendée – from spreading into the Bouches-du-Rhône.[1] The clubists welcomed this army as a new weapon to be used to terrorise their opponents, especially since Jacobin *commissaires* accompanied it, bearing powers to dismiss all public officials who were 'corrupt' and to send them before the clubist-dominated Criminal Tribunal.[2]

It was not in the department, but in Marseilles itself however that such powers provided an example for the clubists, who, on 10 April, exploded a bomb in the political life of the town by unleashing a battery of denunciation against Mourraille, the mayor, and Étienne Seytres, *procureur de la commune*.[3]

Despite his pre-eminence in his city's anti-royalist campaign, Mourraille had fallen foul of the Jacobins on several occasions. In January, he had led municipal opposition against the Department's project of sending a third battalion to Paris in order to bring pressure on the Convention to stop internal disputes and hasten the execution of the king.[4] In the Club, he had to rebut allegations that he had taken up the cause of a party 'hostile to liberty'; and, though he was forced to break off communications with Barbaroux, their past correspondence, fruit of a continued respect for Barbaroux' constant services to the city, confirmed the Club in its belief that Mourraille, after expending his political energy in the assault on the

---

[1] ABR, L45, Dept. Admin., 3 Apr. 1793; ABR, L120, departmental *arrêté* of 3 Apr. 1793. Some 1000 Nîmois were said to have invaded Beaucaire, (whose municipality was alleged to protect nobles and refractory priests).

[2] A. Comm., *Affiches, arrêté* of Bayle and Boisset of 21 Apr. 1793.

[3] ABR, L2071, Club, 10 Apr. 1793.

[4] British Museum, F655(10), *Observations de la Commune de Marseille au Département des Bouches-du-Rhône*, 8 Jan. 1793. He argued that one battalion of Marseillais was already in Paris and that the departure of another would weaken the city's defences.

monarchy, had himself become a bastion of immobilism and reaction, in other words, a supporter of the *appelants*. And suspicions were strengthened, when, on 8 April, a deputation from the Club, trying to get the quick departure of the new battalion of 6000 men, was received 'with brutality' by the mayor.[1] Thereupon, all attacks were justified: Mourraille was accused of having held Marseilles under the sway of his 'empire despotique', of having terrorised citizens to re-elect him in January 1793, and of having failed to keep public order. The enthusiastic response of the Sections to these denunciations suggests that the last one, in particular, was not without some justification.

That this is so, is further suggested by the accusations launched against two *portefaix*, Jean and Laurent Savon, who with their accomplices were arrested for having extorted money by threats of force. Evidence against them – as exiguous as that cited against Mourraille – seemed to point to a connection between the municipal officers and the *portefaix*, for Jean Savon admitted that Seytres had given him money to pay off his debts and to enable him to uphold his immodest style of living. Moreover since the Municipality controlled the National Guard and the Savons had used their uniforms to intimidate people into giving them money, such accusations fitted in well with denunciations against Seytres for embezzling public money, and against the mayor and procurator for taking part in fraudulent sales of confiscated land and for obtaining municipal posts for law-breakers and ne'er-do-wells.[2]

All Marseilles was thrown into confusion by these events. The Sections enthusiastically endorsed the Club's attacks on Mourraille and Seytres and began collecting evidence both against the town councillors and the Savons, thought to be linked in a single conspiracy to control the city by dictatorship and injustice.

[1] *Jnal. Dépts. Mérid.*, CLXXIII.
[2] For this affair, see the *Compte rendu* of Bayle and Boisset, A. Nat., AF II 90⁶⁶⁴. Also ABR, L1932, Section 1, 14 Apr.; L2071, 13 Apr.; L1949, Section 13, 15 Apr. 1793. The brothers Savon were accused of going round with ropes, threatening to hang people. They had been employed by Club and Department as envoys throughout the Bouches-du-Rhône, in the autumn of 1792. Their reputation was similar to that of Jourdan Coupe-Tête.

For the Club, the arrest of Mourraille and Seytres marked the culmination of the campaign against their opponents within Marseilles, while the suspected connection of the two men with the Rolandins and the attacks on 'Rolandin' mayors of other large towns,[1] showed that their arrest also marked a new stage in the campaign against the *appelants*. On the other hand, the arrest of the Savons – murky as the circumstances are – may be taken as a first blow against the threatening omnipotence of the clubists, who were connected by links of friendship with them.[2]

[1] ABR, L2071, Club, 10 Apr. 1793 – demands for the suppression of the municipalities of all large towns.

[2] In Jan. 1793, at the time of municipal elections, Mourraille denounced a faction which lived off crime and brigandage and which brought illegal pressure to bear on electors. This faction was centred on Section 13 – a Section where Savon was extremely powerful. Mourraille was likely to have been less a friend of the Savons than an administrator who was forced to tolerate their goings-on. A. Comm., 1D3, Mourraille's speech to Municipality, 20 Jan. 1793.

CHAPTER THREE

Sections against Club

So far, the interests of the Club have been stressed because that body provided the shock troops of the Montagnard offensive which dominated political life in the early months of 1793. However, the very extent of this movement led to its downfall, which occurred, with surprising suddenness, towards the end of April. For, parallel to the campaign of the Club, had occurred a slow but steady increase in the power and influence of the Sections of Marseilles. For a long time, the Sections had merely provided a sounding-board for the Club; little by little, however, their reactions became more and more significant in the city's politics and they themselves were to take initiatives which had hitherto seemed the monopoly of the Club.

It is this process which we are now to follow. As with the Jacobin offensive, the Sections' growth in power began in the autumn of 1792 and so events studied hitherto from the point of view of the Club must be reviewed from that of the Sections. Not that these two points of view are necessarily different or distinct – far from it, since many clubists were active in the Sections and vice versa. But it will be our task to see where they approach each other as well as where they diverge. Firstly, we look at the powers and organisation of the Sections, then at how they used these powers in the important events which we have already partially described.

Established in the autumn of 1789, the Sections functioned as *assemblées primaires* for elections. They were very active as general debating assemblies throughout the winter of 1789–90;[1] but thereafter their activity seems to have slackened rather, despite the early admission of passive citizens.[2] They were declared permanent by the city authorities on 23 July 1792;

[1] See above, p. 25.
[2] A. Comm., BB294, Municipality admits to Dept. that tax qualifications for entrance to Sections have been abandoned, 26 Oct. 1790.

and, boosted by the results of 10 August – especially the elections to the Convention – began to act as serious political organs.[1] Their adhesion, on 10 August, to the deliberation of the Section of Mauconseil in Paris (that the Nation had lost confidence in the king),[2] and the prolonged and keenly-debated elections to the Convention gave them opportunities to organise themselves and take stock of their resources, thus beginning a move towards increased self-consciousness heralding increased self-confidence. The keeping of regular registers giving accounts of their activities, the process of electing presidents and secretaries, the sending of deputations to sister-Sections, to the Club and Administrations, the levying of subscriptions from their members to meet their modest expenses and above all the formation of various committees within the Sections themselves – all these activities soon forged a tradition of sustained endeavour by the twenty-four Sections of the city and the seven Sections which, till another was added, represented the *campagne*, the suburbs and countryside immediately dependent on Marseilles.

Matters of *police générale* occupied much of their time, while the setting up of committees to disarm suspects, to make censuses of *gens sans aveu*, gave them experience in organisation and debate. The idea of giving members *cartes de section* showed a growing degree of self-awareness and cohesion and revealed a wish to make membership of their assemblies the test of a

[1] It does not seem that the Sections were flooded with new men after the results of 10 August had had time to make themselves felt. The lists available for comparison of the membership of the Sections are too fragmentary to admit of elaborate statistical analysis. Also, it is obvious for instance that more people would appear in the Sections to take part in the crucial elections to the Convention than would appear to undertake more routine tasks. Nor is it anywhere evident – contrary to what the Montagnards were later to assert – that those who did appear for the first time in the period after 10 August, (i.e. Sept., Oct., Nov. and later), altered the course of the Sections' debates in a 'counter-revolutionary' direction. Indeed, throughout these months the Sections gave full support to the Club in its campaign against the king, and later in its campaign against the *appelants*. See lists in ABR, L1934–35, Section 2 (the most complete); L1946, Section 21; L1943, Section 12; L1936–7, Section 4; L1945, Section 17; L1932, Section 1. Unfortunately, the lists for 1792–3 do not give any indication as to the social composition of the sectionaries. Nor do the records of the Revolutionary Tribunal give the Sections of those who appeared before it.

[2] ABR, L1943, Section 12, 10 Aug. 1792; L1941, Section 8, 10 Aug. 1792, etc.

person's patriotism and social responsibility.[1] The *comités de surveillance* provided in each Section a nucleus of men well experienced in police matters; and such men were the driving force behind attempts to bring pressure on the Municipality to increase measures of police and to punish troublemakers more severely.

The part the Sections played in the establishment of the Popular Tribunal increased their standing, for it was in Section 1 – always on the look-out against law-breakers[2] – that a member, on 30 August 1792, outlined plans for the Tribunal;[3] and in fact the Municipality organised the court in exactly the manner prescribed[4] by this member, each Section electing one person to the *Tribunal d'accusation* and one to the *Tribunal de jugement*.[5] The Sections had thereby imposed their will on the Administrations and even on the Convention (since the establishment of such a tribunal was the prerogative of the legislature). Moreover, the Popular Tribunal, which soon eclipsed the departmental Criminal Tribunal, provided the Sections with an organ which they considered with justification as their own creation and which moreover served as an essential element of continuity, since interest in its activities (as well as the efforts of their *comités de surveillance* in co-operating with the Tribunal) served to unite the Sections among themselves in the all-important drive to keep public order. The moderating rôle of their court, in the autumn of 1792, was a source of considerable pride – on 10 October, Section 13 wanted to petition the Convention to set up similar courts throughout France.[6]

Consultation with the Sections increasingly provided the Administrations with a unique means for sounding public opinion – in no other body, or group of bodies, were so many

[1] ABR, L1941, Section 8, 19 Sept. 1792.

[2] ABR, L1932, Section 1, 30 Aug. 1792; Section 1 was a fairly bourgeois district.

[3] ABR, L1932, Section 1, 30 Aug. 1792.

[4] See above, pp. 38–9.

[5] Its historian, P. A. Robert (*La Justice des sections marseillaises*, p. 222), affirms that its judges came not from the most humble sectors of the population, but were 'de petits bourgeois, modestes et aisés' – *notaires, hommes de loi, oratoriens, bourgeois, commis, artisans chefs de métiers*, etc. See above, pp. 42–3.

[6] ABR, L1940, Section 7, 16 Oct. 1792.

citizens gathered to discuss political, social and economic problems.[1] Two commissioners from each Section sat in the meetings of the Three Administrations with *voix délibératives*[2] and this practice gradually built up a group of men who knew what was going on within the Administrations and who, together with those sectionaries who held public office and attended the Club, were able to give a lead in most political controversies.

A host of miscellaneous measures kept the assemblies occupied, *subsistances* providing a field for great activity.[3] Their firmness in demanding the destruction of royalist emblems and in celebrating the 10 August did much to exacerbate hatred of the monarchy[4] while their approval of the addresses demanding the quick trial of the king and deploring the dissensions in the Convention not only showed their awareness of the most important matters affecting the Republic but confirmed their identity of views with the Administrations and the Club on these matters.[5]

In criticising the acts of the envoys of the Club, the Sections spoke on behalf of Marseilles, whose name was being discredited by these clubists. They further reaffirmed their characteristic concern for the rule of law, for individual liberty and their hatred for 'les principes agrariens', by demanding that the Club punish its unruly members.[6] As regards events at Salon, the preservation of calm and social harmony was once more their main preoccupation. The Popular Tribunal was

[1] Though the numbers who attended the individual Sections in the autumn of 1792 were not always very high. In Section 2, (ABR, L1934, L1935) after some 200 to 300 had attended the elections to the Convention at the end of August, figures slumped badly (57, 65, 39, 71, 25, 32, 34, 69, 130, 46 – forming a typical sequence in September). Until mid-March 1793, figures of membership were, with few exceptions, below 100. From other lists, this seems fairly typical.

[2] ABR, L1940, Section 7, 28 Sept. 1792.

[3] ABR, L1945, Section 17, 5 Sept. 1792; 18 Sept. 1792, etc.

[4] ABR, L1940, Section 7, 14 Oct. and 7 Dec. 1792.

[5] See, for instance, ABR, L1941, Section 8, 26 Aug. and 17 Sept. 1792; L1945, Section 17, 16 Oct. 1792; L1941, Section 9, 9 Nov. and 7 Dec. 1792; L1936, Section 4, 15 Jan. 1793; L1945, Section 17, 18 Jan. 1793 (against the *appel*, etc.)

[6] ABR, L1932, Section 1, 16 Nov. 1792; L1945, Section 17, 20 Nov. 1792. And see above, p. 51.

itself a manifestation of the Sections' determination to protect individual liberty, a determination which led them increasingly into conflict with the policies of the Club.

The ambitions of the Club to get more and more power over the surveillance of suspects worked for a time in harmony with the Sections' concern for justice. When, in early March, the Sections accepted the Club's request to be consulted if their assemblies had doubts about the *civisme* of men applying for *certificats*, they acknowledged the Club's experience in this field,[1] though they themselves had organised numerous committees to watch over potential troublemakers. They also supported the decision to establish a Revolutionary Tribunal and a Committee of Forced Loans[2] and endorsed the Club's address of 17 March against the *appelants*. Thus the Sections were dominated by men of a Jacobinism as ardent as that of the clubists. By now, however, they had acquired their own identity and ambitions – thus when Section 4 endorsed the decision to set up a Revolutionary Tribunal, it added the proviso that its members were to be elected by the Sections,[3] thus contradicting the deliberation of the Three Administrations which had already appointed the members of the Tribunal.[4]

In demanding that the staff of the proposed Revolutionary Tribunal should be elected by the Sections, large claims were advanced for their 'sovereignty':

> Que d'après ces principes inhérents à la souveraineté du peuple et sans lesquels aucun état démocratique ne peut exister, tout pouvoir émanant directement du Souverain, à lui seul appartient le droit de le conférer de la manière dont il l'entend et même à le révoquer, quand il le juge convenable.[5]

Their campaign to appoint the members of the Revolutionary Tribunal helped to cause the abandonment of this project and thus the ambitions of the Sections thwarted the will of the Club.

Nevertheless the Sections enthusiastically welcomed the Club's attacks on Mourraille and Seytres[6] and obtained their

[1] See above, p. 43.
[2] ABR, L1940, Section 7, 26 Mar. 1793; L1946, Section 21, 26 Mar. 1793; L1943, Section 12, 26 Mar. 1793.
[3] ABR, L1941*bis*, Section 8, 17 Mar. 1793.
[4] See above, p. 45.
[5] ABR, L1987, Section 3, 17 Apr. 1793.   [6] See above, p. 69.

arrest. They likewise aided the Club in obtaining the arrest of the Savons and co-operated with Bayle and Boisset and the Club and Administrations in levying the army of 6000 men.

Within a couple of weeks however this harmony was irrevocably shattered. It seems that after the arrest of Mourraille and Seytres, a large number of people became alarmed as to the future course of the Revolution. The plan for the Revolutionary Tribunal and the Committee of Forced Loans was still ineffective but had not been abandoned. The Montagnards of the Club were calling for a new revolution and the actions of their envoys in the department – above all at Salon – seemed to announce that this revolution was imminent and that it was to be directed against those who had hitherto stood aloof from the Revolution – the rich, the indifferent and the lazy. The levy of 6000 men in early April seemed a threat that civil war might break out in the Midi and seemed a private army in the irresponsible hands of the Montagnard deputies and their associates in Club and Department. The attacks on the *appelants* had reached a climax; and many of the most wealthy and influential citizens of Marseilles had been friends of Barbaroux and Rebecquy. At Paris, Marat and Robespierre seemed on the point of triumphing; and their triumph was regarded in some quarters as heralding a reign of anarchy and the complete collapse of all social order. The discontent of the upper ranks of Marseilles' society was aggravated by the collapse of Mediterranean trade with its harmful effects on Marseilles' industry. The fall of Mourraille and Seytres, who had many friends in patrician circles, served as a warning of what was to come, while the mission of Bayle and Boisset had proved even worse than had been feared, the *Conventionnels* surrounding themselves with clubists and with Paris, the president of the Departmental Administration, accused of preaching the 'loi agraire'.[1]

By mid-April therefore, a large number of Marseillais, finding themselves the designated victims of a new revolution, stirred

---

[1] Honoré-Genès Paris, born 1740; doctor with publications to his credit; came from Arles; called 'le père Duchesne du Midi'; sent by Maignet to *Commission populaire* of Orange; condemned as terrorist in Year III; released by Fréron; fled to avoid vengeance, but murdered at Milan, 1796. (Information from G. Martinet, 'La vie politique à Marseille en 1795 et 1796', *Provence historique, tome* 16, Apr.–June 1966, pp. 126–76.)

themselves to action and sought some way of parrying the dangers which threatened them. In the Sections, they found organs pre-eminently suited to their needs; for it was easy for them to infiltrate meetings which were open to all citizens of the *quartier*. Moreover, an influx of members would not disturb their machinery which, having acquired increasing impetus during recent months, virtually ran itself. New men would be welcomed into the Sections, whose ambitions could be fulfilled if membership rose substantially – and moreover any increase in membership was an encouraging demonstration to the sectionaries of the more eminent place which they now held in the town's political life.

As early as 25 March, the Club demanded that the Sections bar the entry of men who had been disarmed.[1] On 19 April, a member of Section 3, referring to 'la grande affluence des citoyens qui se rendent aux Sections', said that this annoyed the enemies of the sectionaries – that is, the clubists, who were trying to end their daily meetings by alleging that agitators had slipped into them in order to 'put the Revolution on trial'.[2]

The question of the increased frequency of the Sections' meetings was inextricably bound up with the question of their increased membership for many criticisms were levied at one and the other of these processes. The clubist François Isoard complained that, whereas before 10 August some thirty or forty people had attended each Section, now four or five hundred people attended.[3] According to Bayle and Boisset, 'aristocrats' who had not frequented the Sections before 10 August had been forced to appear by the execution of the king, and many more had entered since the disarmament. Many patriots had meanwhile gone to the armies and those remaining did not suffice to defend the people against the wiles of the aristocrats. Bayle and Boisset further alleged that the aristocrats dominated the Sections by bribing 'les ouvriers' and so they demanded that the Sections should not meet each day because this was inconvenient for the workers. They also counselled 'plus de sagesse dans les délibérations'.[4]

---

[1] ABR, L2071, Club, 25 Mar. 1793.
[2] ABR, L2011 *bis*, Section 3, 19 Apr. 1793.   [3] ABR, L2076. N.d.
[4] A. Nat., AF II 90⁶⁶⁴, *Compte rendu* of Bayle and Boisset (June 1793); ABR, L1940, Section 7, 21 Apr. 1793; L1936, Section 4, 21 Apr. 1793.

Thus there is a strong indication that it was thought in April that new men were entering the Sections in increasing numbers. The registers of these assemblies cannot be said to give over-whelming evidence as to the extent of this movement.

For some Sections, no registers survive and, while some registers (incomplete) do not cover this crucial period, others provide no lists of those who attended. Those registers which do make an attempt to list those present often provide inadequate and confusing evidence. The registers of Section 1[1] – a fairly modern Section, between old and new quarters, containing a high proportion of *propriétaires* and *bourgeois*, and a fairly big contingent of merchants – show new men entering after 10 August but thereafter attendance seems to stabilise itself in the winter of 1792–3. Unfortunately there are no lists for the crucial period of March and April or for subsequent months, though, from the names which appear in the register, it is evident that many of the leading sectionaries, (Joseph Arnaud, *notaire*, Joseph Suffren, *bourgeois*, Joseph Issaurel, *bourgeois*, etc.) had been members at least since the elections to the Convention.

The adjacent Section 2, comprising some of the most fashion-able streets and residences in the city, home of some of the wealthiest merchants, provides more numerous lists, virtually complete from 28 July 1792 to 16 April 1793 when, unfor-tunately, they dry up.[2] But from early March 1793 to 16 April, attendance rises from well under a hundred to 402: when figures resume in July, attendance sometimes attains 300 and frequently reaches the upper 200's – numbers previously attained only during the elections to the Convention. The lists show that there was next to no influx of new men after 10 August (the increase in numbers being due mainly to the attendance on three days of men who had already appeared from time to time in the Section). And even in the lists in April, the number of new men appears extremely low – perhaps the majority had attended the Section before the elections to the Convention; certainly the vast majority had attended when Section 2 endorsed the campaign for the death of the king, the

---

[1] ABR, L1932–L1933, Section 1. There are numerous difficulties involved in identifying men from session to session, since, for example, only surnames are given.

[2] ABR, L1934–L1935, Section 2.

attacks on Barbaroux, the arrest of Mourraille and the Savons. And even after April 1793, the names of those who played the most prominent part in Section 2 are of men who had attended before the effects of 10 August made themselves felt. Thus Section 2 hardly provides adequate evidence to confirm the observations of Bayle and Boisset. And if one recognises that some changes in personnel were inevitable (men moving from or to Marseilles, from one Section to another, men dropping out through illness or death), the changes reflected in the lists seem very moderate. This impression is confirmed by the register of Section 21 – a semi-rural area, situated to the south of the town outside the Porte de Rome – which does not indicate an important influx of new sectionaries, though lists are too fragmentary to provide a reliable indication of numbers.[1]

In Section 17's register, we see no invasion by 'new men' after 10 August and no massive expansion of numbers – 60 on 13 April, 69 on 18 April, 54 on 21 April; these are the only indications given before lists stop altogether. And even after April most of the leading sectionaries, those appointed to the *bureau* and to committees and deputations, had attended before 10 August. This Section, situated at the very extremity of the Vieux Port, on the side of the *vieille ville*, was inhabited largely by seamen and fishermen, with very few *bourgeois*, merchants or *propriétaires*, though enough to provide the vital *état-major* of educated men.[2] Section 12, at the extreme north-west of the town, included many of the most characteristic industries of Marseilles – tanning, dyeing, soap and starch manufactories – and their workers naturally lived nearby, as well as a few *fabricants* and a host of cobblers and humble tradesmen. Unfortunately the few lists available do not reveal the social composition of those who attended the Section, though there was a fair sprinkling of new men among those who attended early in April.[3] In Section 4, meeting in the Salle de Concert, and bordering the Canebière on the side of the new quarters, devoted mainly to small-scale businesses and trades catering for a well-off clientele, and with quite a number of artists and craftsmen, there was a sprinkling of new men in September 1792 and more in January but very few thereafter – thus the vast

[1] ABR, L1946, Section 21.   [2] ABR, L1945, Section 17.
[3] ABR, L1943, Section 12.

majority of those who attended in May had done so in January and February, when Montagnard policies were approved.[1] For Section 23, a very modern and fashionable area typified by the spacious Allées de Meilhan, we have figures for May 1793 and subsequent months which, like those of adjacent Section 2, show that 300 people sometimes attended, while over 200 were often present; but how this differs from the situation in April we do not know.[2]

These figures are confirmed by random indications from other Sections. Part of a register of Section 6, an opulent district in the new quarters, discloses that 430 voted on 13 April, rising to 500 on 19 and 23 April, falling to 300 on 25 April and reaching 800 on 27 April; but otherwise no long-term trends are revealed.[3]

Thus, to say the least, evidence is confused and fragmentary, and in no case is it possible to make a direct comparison between membership before and after the critical weeks of the second half of April. The only conclusion to be drawn is one which stresses the continuity of personnel before and after April 1793, even when numbers may have increased after this date. What is certain is that most of those who led the Sections after April had attended them when they fully supported Montagnard measures. Men like Pierre Laugier, Louis Meyfrédy and Antoine Maurin had been leading clubists and Jacobin sectionaries and yet were to play leading parts in the anti-Jacobin movement.[4]

On the other hand, the career of the marquis de Fonvielle shows how one man reacted to the situation at Marseilles. An opponent of the Revolution from its earliest days, at Sète and Montpellier, Fonvielle came to Marseilles in the early months of 1792 and described the murders and emigrations of the summer and autumn of that year and the wave of terror which broke out during the trial of Louis XVI when the clubists created such consternation in order to force the lukewarm to petition for the death of the king.[5] After this, however, the clubists split into two factions: one party left the Club for the

[1] ABR, L1945, Section 17.   [2] ABR, L1947, Section 23.
[3] ABR, L1972, Section 6.   [4] See below, pp. 165 ff., etc.
[5] *Mémoires historiques de M. le chevalier de Fonvielle de Toulouse*, 4 vols., (Paris, 1824) II, 366 ff.

Sections – this was the faction which had attacked Mourraille. In the Sections, they adopted a more moderate tone, in keeping with the attitudes of the majority of sectionaries. They thus attracted wider support than was enjoyed by the fire-breathing Jacobins. Soon the moderate – and more talented – clubists were absorbed into the Sections. Up to this time, Fonvielle had been neither to the Club nor to the Sections. 'On me rapportait tous les jours que les honnêtes gens s'y portaient en foule, on me disait qu'il fallait aller les seconder.'[1] Persuaded by the prominent merchants Samatan, Grenier and Seimandy, he went to Section 2, which was always one of the most vigorous champions of the sectionary cause and perhaps staffed by men of exceptional energy and command – as Fonvielle himself proved to be.[2] There, he rejoiced, with several *négociants* among his friends, to hear words of peace which the Revolution had seemingly banished from France for ever. Finding the new atmosphere surprisingly congenial, therefore, at least one 'modéré', not to say royalist, had entered the Sections for the first time at this period. He ascribed the rush to the Sections to the fact that the Club wished to make lists of those who had refused to sign addresses calling for the execution of the king. According to him, those who frequented the Sections made good use of the tactics of denunciation and agitation which they had learned in the Club, and by declaiming against disorder, managed to gain the whole population to their side. Since these men were superior to the Jacobins in talent and education, Fonvielle hoped that France would find in their new influence the end of its political turmoil.

The reaction of the Sections to the accusations of the Jacobins suggests that Fonvielle was not alone in the espousal of their cause; for though the Sections repudiated the aspersions cast on the patriotism of their members, they did not deny that their meetings were both more frequent and more crowded. On the other hand, Fonvielle's account suggests strongly that the whole movement began as a split within the Club, rather than with the

[1] Loc. cit., pp. 399 ff., pp. 406–11.
[2] And his activities are reflected in a register of Section 2, ABR, L1935. After fulfilling a mission to the Drôme, the Lozère, the Ardèche, and the Haute-Loire to form a departmental coalition to support Marseilles' plans, he emigrated when the cause of the Sections was lost.

arrival in the Sections of men who had played no previous part in politics.

Attacks on the patriotism of their members, upon the frequency of their meetings, and upon the wisdom of their deliberations enraged the Sections, who consequently rejected the demands of Bayle and Boisset to exclude new men from their meetings.[1] Section 10 rejected their demand that only citizens who had been granted *certificats de civisme* should be allowed to attend, stating the possibly genuine conviction that every citizen had the right to go to the Sections in return for the obligations which he fulfilled towards the Republic and affirming that the exclusion of some citizens would lead to arbitrary distinctions being drawn between 'good' and 'bad' citizens.[2] The demand of Bayle and Boisset was denounced as impracticable, 'parce qu'il n'y a aucun caractère certain pour reconnaître le bon républicain et l'ennemi de la République.' Their premises were not accepted by the Sections, for whom an increased membership, meeting more frequently, suggested the desirable conclusion that more people were concerned with the safety of the Republic. Thus, while Section 6 seemed to comply with the requests of the *Représentants*, by meeting less frequently and demanding *certificats de civisme* from its members, within a few days the clubist Maillet *cadet* was ousted from the office of president and earlier measures were reversed.[3] Nearby Section 4 likewise decided to limit its meetings to two a week, except for 'le cas urgent' – but 'les cas urgents' being more and more frequent, permanence of assembly continued to be the rule.[4]

[1] ABR, L1945, Section 17, 24 Apr. 1793.

[2] ABR, L1934, Section 2, 23 Apr. 1793.

[3] ABR, L1972, Section 6, 23 Apr. 1793. This seems to be the only case of a sectionary coup; though, in Section 23, on 30 April, a significant change occurred when Joseph Giraud, public prosecutor of the Criminal Tribunal and an energetic clubist, was replaced as president of the Section by Pierre Laugier, one of the presidents of the Popular Tribunal, who was to be a prominent sectionary: ABR, L1947, Section 23, 30 Apr. 1793. Both these Sections were of more than average distinction (i.e. wealth) in the city, both situated in the newer areas, Section 23 being a fashionable area outside the town walls, a Section which was to be the source of several vehement anti-Jacobin petitions (see below, p. 124). Thus they provide interesting evidence of how two aristocratic Sections could be dominated – up to a point – by a couple of clubists.

[4] ABR, L1936, Section 4 – also fairly prosperous – 19 Apr. 1793.

And it is certainly not clear why the *Représentants* accused men who had entered the Sections in the autumn and winter of 1792–3 of counter-revolutionary leanings, for it was during this period that the Sections had supported all the Club's policies. Even Section 18 (meeting at the Loge in the Hôtel de Ville where merchants met to transact business) later to gain a disastrous reputation for slavish adherence to federalist principles, and to be punished heavily for this, had distinguished itself in January and February by the particular virulence of its addresses against the king and the *appelants*,[1] while the same can be said of Section 1 or Section 23. Only in mid-April did the Sections' policy diverge from that of the Club. It therefore seems impossible to ascribe this divergence wholly to the presence in the Sections of 'new men'. In fact, the events of March and April turned 'old men', as well as new, against the Montagnards. The criticism of their assemblies by Bayle and Boisset – coming at a time when they were most conscious of their power – would in itself have provoked a reaction from Montagnard policies. Other actions of the *Représentants* served to intensify and prolong this reaction.

The closure of the Sections of Aix caused alarm at Marseilles. On the orders of Bayle and Boisset men accused of terrorism were released from Aix's prisons just when they were about to be judged. The Sections of Marseilles thought the action of the *Représentants* at Aix heralded similar action at Marseilles. They therefore protested.[2]

Moreover the attack on the Sections of Aix came at a time when, owing to their increased membership and more frequent meetings, those of Marseilles were more confident than ever. They claimed a 'sovereignty' which gave their will precedence over the wills of the *autorités constituées*, which, it was thought, drew all their authority from the *assemblées primaires* which had elected them. The Sections delegated power to the *autorités*, but

[1] See, for instance, ABR, L1943, Section 12, 29 Jan. 1793; A. Comm., iD3, *Conseil général de la commune*, 14 Dec. 1792; ABR, L1933, Section 1, 5 June 1793.

[2] ABR, L1934, Section 2, 21 Apr. 1793 and A. Nat. AF II 90⁶⁶⁴, *Compte rendu* of Bayle and Boisset. Also ABR, L1932, Section 1, 26 Apr., 1793; L1940, Section 7, 24 Apr. 1793, etc. Early in 1793, several prisoners were murdered at Aix by the Jacobins: the Sections of Aix had arrested the Jacobins.

these could expect obedience only as long as they expressed the general will of the people, as proclaimed in the *assemblées primaires*: as soon as the organs of government contradicted the will of the people, they forfeited their powers which reverted to the Sections.[1] Thus the closing of the Sections of Aix seemed doubly tyrannical: 'La souveraineté du peuple a été méconnue à Aix en faisant fermer les Sections'.

The affairs of Mourraille and Seytres and of the Savons provided the Sections with other opportunities to advance their cause; for, to find evidence against these men, they had formed a *Comité central* of two members of each Section and had intensified the work done by the secret committees of the individual Sections.[2] But divergences between Club and Sections soon emerged. For whereas the Club had engineered the downfall of the mayor to give the clubists an opportunity to advance the Jacobin reign of terror, the Sections wished to use it to reassert their traditional concern for the maintenance of good order. For them a new epoch was heralded by the downfall of the mayor – 'enfin le temps de parler librement et sans crainte était arrivé'.[3]

While the Sections pressed on with this line of attack, the Club faltered: it wished to downgrade the whole affair, even to delay consideration of the matter, whereas the Sections, while denying that they wished to put the Revolution on trial, wished to get to the bottom of the affair by arresting the Savon brothers' accomplices, no doubt thought to be members of the Central Committee of the Club.[4] On 27 April, however, Bayle and Boisset authorised the Popular Tribunal – not the clubist-dominated Criminal Tribunal – to judge Mourraille, Seytres and the Savons. This, together with the creation of the Central Committee to co-ordinate the Sections' policy, marked a victory for the Sections – for those who proclaimed that 'il est temps que l'anarchie de quelques hommes de sang cesse'.[5]

[1] ABR, L1946, Section 21, 17 Apr. 1793; L2011 *bis*, Section 3, 19 Apr.; L1932, Section 1, 19 Apr. 1793 – where Section 24 said of the administrators – 'ils ne sont que les délégués des Sections, qu'ils aient à être plus circonspects s'ils sont jaloux de conserver la confiance de la cité'.
[2] ABR, L2006, minutes of the meeting of the *Comité central* of 17 Apr. 1793.   [3] ABR, L1934, Section 2, 12 Apr. 1793.
[4] See ABR, L1932, Section 1, 18 Apr. 1793; L1936, Section 4, 19 Apr. 1793.   [5] ABR, L1934, Section 2, 27 Apr. 1793.

Moreover the levy of 6000 men increasingly seemed destined to aid those who wished to dominate the town. Thus the Sections, at first favourable to this levy, now led by the very opulent Section 5,[1] combated it on the grounds that abuses were committed in levying men and money for it: that it was unnecessary since 'il n'en existait réellement aucun trouble que pour ceux qui avaient intérêt qu'il y en eut'.[2] It was also criticised for taking men from commerce and industry. A proclamation of Bayle and Boisset and an *arrêté* of the Department of 27 April denounced arbitrary exactions;[3] but the Department was forced by the Sections to recall the troops, despite orders of Bayle and Boisset to the contrary. The levy was disbanded, though some men joined the Departmental Army which set out for Paris some six weeks later.[4]

The Bourbons – including Philippe-Égalité – were sent to prison in Marseilles by a decree of the Convention of 8 April.[5] Already the Club had debated their fate and several schemes had been advocated – banishment, execution and so on.[6] Fréron alleged that the Rolandins were trying to use Philippe-Égalité as successor to Louis XVI[7] and, because of this, the Club decided to press for the execution of the Bourbons imprisoned in the Temple.[8] Granet, in sending news of the Convention's decision, said that it was passed against the opposition of Barbaroux and the Girondins, who wanted the Bourbons sent to Bordeaux: Granet, and the Club of Marseilles, rejoiced that they had been sent to a city where the Montagnards dominated, where they could therefore do no harm to the Republic, whereas, had they been sent to Bordeaux, the Girondins would have

[1] ABR, L2071, Club, 18 Apr. 1793.
[2] ABR, L1934, Section 2, 29 Apr. 1793.
[3] A. Nat., AF II 90⁶⁶⁴, in the *Compte rendu* of Bayle and Boisset – *arrêté* of 23 Apr. 1793; ABR, L46, Dept. Admin., 27 Apr. 1793.
[4] A. Comm., *Affiches*, Dept. Admin., 6 July 1793.
[5] See A. Nat., BB 30 163, for documents relating to the transference of the Bourbons to Marseilles: also ABR, L498, for the interrogations of the royal prisoners by the Criminal Tribunal. Those sent were Louis-Philippe-Joseph Égalité (to leave Marseilles for the guillotine at Paris); his sister, Louise-Marie-Thérèse Bathilde d'Orléans; his cousin, Louis-François-Joseph Bourbon (Conti); his sons, the duc de Montpensier and the comte de Beaujolais.   [6] ABR, L2071, Club, 11 Mar. 1793, etc.
[7] ABR, L2071, Club, 27 Mar. 1793.
[8] ABR, L2071, Club, 9 Apr. 1793.

proclaimed Égalité king.[1] In Section 2, Bayle said that he regarded the sending of the Bourbons to Marseilles as proof of the Convention's confidence in the patriotism of that city; but in Section 7, he described the Bourbons as 'un mauvais présent que les deux tiers de la Convention, qui étaient dans les mauvais principes, nous faisaient, en ajoutant qu'on envoyait dans notre sein une pomme de discorde'.[2]

The Sections were confused as to the meaning of the transference of the Bourbons to Marseilles, regarding it as a Montagnard ruse to 'preserve' them in order to make Égalité king. In that case, the hatred of royalty, very strong in the majority of townspeople,[3] served only to intensify the feeling of unease occasioned by the arrival of the Bourbons in the city, and to intensify fears regarding the Montagnards who, once the Bourbons were at Marseilles, were regarded as engaged in frequent secret intrigues with Égalité.[4]

For these reasons therefore, the deputies of the Convention had made themselves unpopular with the Sections. They had surrounded themselves with clubists and espoused their policies: their army of 6000 men seemed an instrument of terror; their closure of the Sections of Aix seemed an ill omen for those of Marseilles. Their criticism of the Sections of Marseilles infuriated their members and made them more determined than ever to assert their powers. The Bourbons were indeed 'une pomme de discorde', while the cases of Mourraille, Seytres and the Savons likewise revealed tensions between Sections and Club. To the men who controlled the Sections, all these measures pointed to the existence of a Montagnard plot aimed at causing dissension in the city and department, subverting social order and seizing power in the ensuing confusion. In the face of mounting hostility from the Sections, Bayle and Boisset left Marseilles secretly and took refuge at Montélimar.[5]

[1] ABR, L2076, 9 Apr. 1793.

[2] ABR, L1934, Section 2, 21 Apr.; L1940, Section 7, 21 Apr. 1793.

[3] A. Nat., AF II 3[18] – report of the *commissaires* who took the royal prisoners to Marseilles. The Bourbons grew more and more frightened as they approached Marseilles.

[4] ABR, L1248, 26 May 1793; L3104, Popular Tribunal, deposition of Jacques Luc, 18 June 1793, to the effect that Chompré was conferring in secret with Égalité.

[5] A. Nat., AF II 90[664], *Compte rendu* of Bayle and Boisset.

This was hailed by the Sections as a great victory over the forces of anarchy and intrigue. Henceforward the battle was to be more open as they sought to defend the power which they had won. The expulsion of the *Représentants du peuple* was a triumph of the Sections against the Club and against the Montagnards of Marseilles; it was also a triumph against the Convention.

CHAPTER FOUR

The Fall of the Club

Throughout May, Marseilles was split by a battle between two factions. To the sectionaries, their opponents were 'anarchistes', 'brigands', 'intrigants', 'factieux', 'maratistes', and clubists. To the clubists, the Sections were full of 'modérés', 'aristocrates', 'riches égoïstes' and 'honnêtes gens'; but while these men saw themselves as upholders of law and order against anarchy, the Club retorted that they denounced as anarchical any revolutionary measure demanding sacrifices of money or influence. Between the two factions, the Administrations were reduced to impotence.

Already the Club had offended the Sections by its display of resentment at the increased frequency of their meetings and by its distrust of the new members who attended them. The Club's rôle seemed reduced by the greater frequency of their meetings, especially as many clubists now attended the rival assemblies,[1] whose pretensions were not reduced by this development. Thus relations between the Club and Sections had not been improved when Bayle, in the Club,

> donne une courte définition de la souveraineté du peuple, qui ne réside pas dans une Section, dans les Sections de toute une ville, de tout un département, mais dans la généralité des Sections de la République entière . . .[2]

But with the departure of the two *Représentants* things went from bad to worse. Thus the Sections received from Montélimar an *arrêté* of Bayle and Boisset,[3] dated 2 May, declaring them in counter-revolution, suppressing the Central Committee and the Popular Tribunal, and attacking the increasing powers of the Sections –

Se disant SOUVERAINES, elles agissent comme si la Souveraineté

---

[1] ABR, L2071, Club, 18 Apr. 1793.
[2] *Jnal. Dépts. Mérid.*, CLXXX, 24 Apr. 1793.
[3] Printed in *Journal de Marseille*, tome 37.

nationale leur appartenait en propre . . . les mots LES SECTIONS SOUVERAINES DE MARSEILLE manifestent ouvertement une tendance vers le fédéralisme.

This enraged the Sections. Section 24, one of the most vehement in resistance to the Convention and its deputies, claimed that the Sections had

> une Souveraineté relative dont un citoyen ou une portion de citoyens peut revendiquer l'exercice, toutes les fois que les droits, qui lui ont été transmis et cédés par le pacte social, sont violés à son égard; faculté qui lui est accordée par la loi, sous le nom de 'droit de résistance à l'oppression'.[1]

It affirmed therefore that the Sections of Marseilles, according to the first Right of Man and the Citizen, had declared themselves in a state of Resistance to Oppression. The city as a whole repudiated the *arrêté* and, in an address to the Convention, justified itself, claiming that, now Marseilles was freed from the domination of a handful of agitators, the real voice of its citizens spoke up loudly against anarchy and against attacks on property. Consequently the Sections all attacked the disarmament of 19 March as arbitrary and the levy of 6000 men as likely to have caused bloodshed. A further address[2] defended the Popular Tribunal as having rendered exceptional services to the country and to humanity and re-pledged their confidence in a mayor who was now deemed to be thoroughly worthy of their esteem.

The Sections claimed to have risen in the cause of 'humanity' and so tried to preserve order in the city and, in doing so, strengthened their own powers, since it was they who now designated suspects and who came to control the judicial organs. The various secret committees of the Sections replaced the Central Committee of the Club, doing the same work in the same way. A General Committee was formed of ninety-six members, three from each Section. This body soon controlled Marseilles;[3] for it formed a focal point for all sectionary

[1] Printed in *Journal de Marseille*, tome 37.

[2] ABR, L3101, *Les Républicains assemblés en permanence dans les 32 Sections de Marseille . . . à tous les Républicains qui composent les diverses sections de la République française*, 11 May 1793.

[3] ABR, L1955.

activities and co-ordinated the policies of the individual assemblies. The Sections circulated petitions among themselves and, when these petitions had won widespread support, sent them to the General Committee for execution, though often the General Committee took initiatives of its own. Meeting for the first time on 9 May, led by Pierre Peloux and Antoine Castelanet, it managed to preserve for some time a high degree of homogeneity among the deliberations of the various and varied Sections.[1]

The Popular Tribunal – another institution which fostered sectionary solidarity – momentarily stopped work after the *arrêté* of 2 May but it was re-established to get to the bottom of the intrigues which surrounded the affairs of Mourraille, Seytres and the Savons.[2] When on 15 May the Convention declared the Tribunal – suspended by decree three days before – illegal, the Sections decided to press on regardless,[3] but the judges of the Tribunal obeyed the law and laid down their functions until the Convention should decide to confirm the legality of their court.[4] Nevertheless, between 8 May and 27 May (when the judges resigned their office),[5] the Popular Tribunal did valuable work to consolidate the sectionary régime, proclaiming in pamphlets which, for their moderation, must have won over many of the uncommitted, that the defence of individual liberty and the reign of law was not a prelude to the return of the *Ancien régime* and warning that, on the contrary, a longer period of anarchy would have led inevitably to despotism.

The Popular Tribunal acquitted Mourraille and Seytres and

---

[1] ABR, L1955, *Comité général. Articles de règlement.* Pierre Peloux, a *négociant en soies, suppléant* to National Assembly, took his seat in Sept. 1789; emigrated after failure of federalist revolt. Antoine Castelanet, a *notaire royal*, was elected *suppléant* to National Assembly, took seat 16 June, took oath of *Jeu de Paume*, in 1790 defended royal troops against Mirabeau's attacks on their conduct at Marseilles; emigrated after fall of federalism, probably to Spain.

[2] ABR, L1947, Section 23, 15 May 1793; L1946, Section 21, 7 May 1793.

[3] ABR, L1946, Section 21, 18 May; L1943, Section 12, 18 May 1793, etc.

[4] ABR, L3100, Popular Tribunal, meeting of 27 May 1793.

[5] ABR, L3100, *Adresse des tribunaux populaires d'accusation et de jugement,* 10 May 1793.

condemned to death the Savons and one of their accomplices.[1] This was what the Sections wanted; for it was seen as the just punishment of the most notorious anarchists and as a warning to their associates.[2] Moreover, the Popular Tribunal put the Jacobin view of the Revolution on trial as witness upon witness unanimously condemned acts of Jacobin zeal. The disarmament of 19 March, the vote of the Revolutionary Tribunal and the Committee of Forced Loans were seen as an attempt to plunge Marseilles into a blood-bath; the levy of 6000 men was an instrument of civil war. Esmieu affirmed that Mourraille had been dismissed because he showed that there were no troubles at Beaucaire. He attacked Paris, president of the Department, for demanding

> L'expulsion des Sections de tous les citoyens qu'il appelait aristocrates mais dont on redoutait les lumières, le courage et la probité.[3]

Thus the arrest of a score of prominent clubists on the night of 18–19 May was probably a direct consequence of evidence heard before the Popular Tribunal – certainly those who were arrested by order of the General Committee included those most directly implicated in the events denounced before the Tribunal: Maillet *cadet*, president of the Criminal Tribunal, Giraud, the public prosecutor, Albert Gérin, a member of the Municipality, Galibert and Louis Barthélemy, members of the Department, the *abbé* Bausset, and Ricord *fils* and Micoulin, the journalists of the Club. Other clubists, including Chompré, were arrested later.[4] Some fled to Paris: they reported that there were about six hundred determined patriots in Marseilles who, with aid, could restore the city to the Revolution. Though no one spoke of the monarchy, a restoration – they alleged – might well be in the minds of the merchants.[5]

Combined with out-and-out repression, the Sections also embarked on a highly effective propaganda offensive. They

---

[1] ABR, L3100, Popular Tribunal, judgement of Savon, etc., 15 May 1793.

[2] See *Journal de Marseille, feuille* of 18 May 1793.

[3] ABR, L3104, Popular Tribunal.

[4] ABR, L3037, *Comité central des sections*, 23 May 1793.

[5] A. Nat., AF II 24[198], report of patriots of Marseilles, 23 June 1793.

forced the Municipality and the Department to issue proclamations praising their good intentions and their devotion to
the Revolution and they sent envoys throughout the department to propagate their principles.[1] Some of these envoys were
to follow the tracks of the clubists, in order to investigate their
predecessors' actions and find evidence to use in their trials
before the Popular Tribunal.[2] Sometimes small towns and
villages asked the Sections to send deputies to overthrow the
local domination of the Jacobins. These envoys found the towns
and villages under the power of a handful of terrorists. Generally
they were treated as liberators – 'anges tutélaires' – by the
majority of the inhabitants. At Aubagne,

> On livra aux flammes en présence de la Municipalité les
> réverbères qui n'avaient été placés que pour victimer les
> innocents, jeter l'épouvante dans le cœur des amis de l'ordre
> et de la paix et extorquer des contributions.

Everywhere the terrorists were denounced for preaching 'la loi
agraire', an execrable principle for a time when

> chacun sait qu'un vrai républicain est un homme sobre,
> vigilant, et juste, un homme qui, content du bien qu'il
> possède, ne cherche pas à envahir celui d'autrui.[3]

From far and wide tributes and requests for aid flowed into the
Sections. The miners of Saint-Savournin, who supplied Marseilles' industries with coal, together with the poor peasants
asked the Sections for support against their ex-*seigneur* in a
dispute over feudal dues, just as the previous September (1792)
they had asked the Club to intervene.[4] At Saint-Chamas, the
trading and industrial bourgeoisie rallied to the Sections and
now came forward with their money and stocks to keep their
fellow-townsmen well supplied with corn.[5] From many local-

[1] ABR, L1940, Section 7, 11 May 1793; L1947, Section 23, 7 May
1793, etc.

[2] ABR, L1944, Section 16, 9 May 1793; L1934, Section 2, 11 May 1793, etc.

[3] ABR, L1959, Aubagne, a *chef-lieu de canton* in the *arrond.* of Marseilles.

[4] ABR, L1975, Saint-Savournin, *canton* of Roquevaire, *arrond.* of
Marseilles: Section to Sections of Marseilles, 30 June 1793; to Club of
Marseilles, 9 Sept. 1792.

[5] P. Lafran and G. Plantier, *Saint-Chamas des origines à 1851* (Les Amis du
Vieux Saint-Chamas, 1955) pp. 145 ff.

ities, letters praised the Sections for restoring order at Marseilles.

Moreover, to back up their offensive, the Sections made use of the talents of Ferréol Beaugeard, whom they adopted, at his own somewhat obsequious request, as official journalist. Beaugeard offered to print in his *Journal de Marseille* the debates and decisions of the Sections, to attend the meetings of the General Committee, and to print whatever he was asked to – and nothing else. This offer was accepted and, on 21 May, we read in Beaugeard's journal that it will contain in future details of the work of the sovereign Sections.[1] This journal, together with an official *résumé* of their debates,[2] was of the greatest importance in providing them with a coherent justification of their actions, a defence which became the common history of each Section, thus binding together the individual Sections in a common bond. This gave them greater confidence and enabled them the more readily to control the minds of the Marseillais.

However, besides the constant denunciation of acts and threats of terrorism, other aspects of sectionary policy helped them attain a position of dominance within Marseilles. One aspect of their campaign – and one which, as the clubists later admitted, had deluded many patriotic citizens into supporting the federalists – was to denounce the Jacobins as partisans of Orléans and of Marat and to praise the *appelants* for being far-sighted enough to have seen the dangers into which the policies of their opponents were leading the Republic. The Sections urged that the Popular Tribunal should put Orléans on trial:[3] Section 24 demanded the trial of those who plotted to put Orléans on the throne, and therefore the arrest of Marat, Robespierre and Danton;[4] while Rebecquy, *appelant*, informed Section 16 of a plot by Danton and Robespierre to declare Orléans king.[5]

---

[1] ABR, L1972, rough draft of the meetings of the General Committee, 18 May 1793; L1984, Beaugeard to the Sections of Marseilles, n.d.; *Journal de Marseille, feuille* of 21 May 1793.

[2] Bib. Mun., Marseilles, *Fonds de Provence*, 1881, first appeared 27 May 1793.

[3] ABR, L1947, Section 23, 11 May and 19 May 1793.

[4] ABR, L1944, Section 16, 21 May 1793; L1933, Section 1, 21 May 1793.

[5] ABR, L1944, Section 16, 22 May 1793. Rebecquy had resigned from the Convention on 10 Mar. 1793, because Robespierre's demands for a dictator had gone unpunished.

The Sections thus reversed the attitude of Marseilles to the great conflict which split the Convention, blaming the Montagnards, of whom Bayle, Boisset, Barras and Fréron were thought to be typically bad specimens, for the ills of the Republic and of Marseilles. Orléans, who presided over the Montagne; Marat, who wished to turn France into a place of desolation; Danton, who had stolen large sums of money from the Nation and had shared the treason of Dumouriez; and Robespierre, who had the effrontery at the tribune of the Convention to demand a dictatorship – Marseilles had rejected these men in favour of the wisdom and virtue of Condorcet, Sieyès, Paine and Pétion.[1]

From now on, news from Paris was to come from Girondin sources, as the Sections were to do all they could to block Montagnard channels of communication. Thus the great mass of Marseillais received news from Paris as before, but from a different 'Paris'. Most of them, not knowing how to read, having little time or taste for political meetings or discussions, did not grasp this change. Having, according to the new leaders in Marseilles, been 'misled' by Jacobin propaganda, they were now to be 'enlightened' by that of the Girondins. By censoring all incoming information (as best they could) the Sections were able to win the support, or at least the acquiescence, of the bulk of Marseillais – who rarely, if ever, went to the Sections.

This part of the sectionary offensive was inestimably aided by the splendid record of Barbaroux in the Convention in the early months of 1793 – a time when he showed that devotion to his native city could survive not only the attacks of the Montagnards in the Convention but could also triumph over brutal repudiation by the leading citizens of Marseilles.[2] Barbaroux was especially concerned with obtaining measures to aid Marseilles' commerce and to safeguard its food supply. He had supported – or initiated – every proposal for the provision of funds for the Marseillais to import corn. His friend Rebecquy

[1] ABR, L1947, Section 23, 18 May 1793.
[2] For this see *Mémoires de Barbaroux* (ed. A. Chabaud) (Paris, 1936) – especially Chabaud's fine introduction; and C. Perroud and A. Chabaud (editors), *Correspondance et Mémoires de Barbaroux* (Paris, 1923) especially pp. 250 ff.

had likewise demanded such measures and had pointed out, on 23 November 1792, that whereas bread was sold in the Midi at 5, 6 or even 8 *sous*, it was *provided* at 3 *sous* at Paris.[1] On 25 February, at Barbaroux' insistence, 2,200,000 *livres* were granted to Marseilles to buy corn while, on 31 March, he persuaded the Convention to preserve Marseilles' *Bureau de commerce* (successor to the Chamber) and its *Bureau de santé*, both organisations vital to the maintenance of the great port's Levant trade. His concern for its trade was wide-ranging, for, among other projects, he championed measures to stimulate the corn trade with Russia, and a vast nation-wide plan to spread prosperity evenly to the very extremities of France by means of an integrated programme of public works, roads and canals – 'Ouvrez donc les canaux que je vous propose et vous n'aurez plus en France de Nord et de Midi'.[2] On 27 April, speaking against the proposed tax on grain, he used the occasion not only to give a detailed *exposé* of his views on the way to supply France with corn but also, with less justification, to launch attacks on Paris. For, he maintained, the attempts of the Midi to buy corn in Burgundy were thwarted by those who said that the Marseillais came to starve Paris –

> C'est ainsi que les inquiétudes sur les subsistances, propagées en tous lieux par les malveillants, nous préparent peut-être des déchirements intérieurs.

He drew attention to the fact that bread cost 5 *sous* a *livre* at Marseilles:

> Ce n'est qu'à Paris, au sein de l'abondance maintenue au dépens de la République, que sont nés les systèmes désastreux de la taxe des grains. Au contraire, dans les départements pauvres, tourmentés de la disette et oubliés par la Convention nationale, on a tout souffert plutôt que de briser le lien social par la violation des propriétés.

---

[1] *Moniteur*, XIV, p. 557, No. 330 of 25 Nov. 1792; Convention, 23 Nov. 1792.

[2] British Museum, F1179(3), *De l'influence de la guerre maritime sur le commerce et l'organisation des travaux publics* (May ?, 1793): also F479(8), *Opinion de Charles Barbaroux sur les causes de la cherté des grains et les moyens d'y remédier*, n.d.

In fact he denounced the *maximum* on corn as divorced from all economic realities; and, in particular, underlined the fact that if it reduced the price of corn, foreign suppliers, seeing profits decline, would discontinue supplying the French market. This point had obvious relevance to Marseilles – erstwhile granary of the Midi.[1]

He seems never to have deserted his belief that only complete free trade in corn – with decent profits assured to the merchants –would eliminate dearth by the creation of a unified national market closely linked to international patterns of trade. He wanted national unity in this respect, so that there would be no question of one area using the problem of food supplies to coerce another, and so that prices would be much the same everywhere. Free trade would boost agriculture, lead to improvements, bring about the gradual abolition of poverty and begging. This situation would arrive, not as a result of government intervention, but by the natural effects of free trade. This policy was combined with a commercially aggressive foreign policy – to capture the American grain trade from the English; to establish French trade in eastern Europe; to send a naval squadron to capture Trieste or Fiume.[2] It was also combined with measures designed to encourage the development of industry, for he saw France's manufactures as the most abundant source of prosperity and the prime mover in France's trade: here again, his policies were aggressive – the Rhine–Rhône canal would either ruin Holland or force her to join with France and would enable France to win the European carrying trade. As for bread subsidies, 'Bientôt les hommes corrompus voulurent être nourris sans travailler', he remarked, talking of the fall of the Roman Empire.[3]

Barbaroux seemed fired with the vision of a France whose economic supremacy over the other powers of Europe was unchallengeable. To this end he utterly repudiated federalism: in a letter to Marseilles – dated 18 June – he rejected any such policy which would, in his opinion, destroy France's power:

[1] *Moniteur*, XVI, p. 243; No. 119 of 29 Apr. 1793, Convention 27 Apr. 1793.

[2] British Museum, F476(12), *Opinion de Charles Barbaroux sur les subsistances*, n.d. (Speech of 8 Dec. 1792, at Convention).

[3] British Museum, *De l'influence de la guerre maritime.*

Ainsi la France morcelée cesserait de peser dans la balance de l'Europe, et nos richesses passeraient, avec notre commerce, dans les mains des Anglais.[1]

It is not at all clear what reception these wide-ranging aspirations found within the business community of Marseilles but it is certain that on specific issues his ideas met with a ready response, for they coincided with those expressed in the Sections.

Of two other speeches of Barbaroux which would surely have won the approval of the mercantile aristocracy of Marseilles, one expressed his opposition to a forced loan on the rich which, he said, would not leave the merchants enough capital to continue their commerce, thus endangering the prosperity of 'toutes les classes';[2] the other blamed the deterioration of France's financial position on the excessive emission of *assignats*. Speeches such as these, taken with his attacks on the prolongation of the powers of the Committee of Public Safety[3] and on the excessive powers granted to the *Représentants en mission* (especially since he described Bayle and Boisset as 'torrents dévastateurs' and 'rochers détachés de la Montagne' in their mission of destruction)[4] soon regained for Barbaroux the esteem of his fellow-citizens and the re-pledged confidence of the Municipality; and undoubtedly lost the Montagnards and clubists an enormous amount of sympathy. He urged the Marseillais to press home their attacks on the Montagnards – to find evidence that the envoys of Montagnard Marseilles made speeches tending to provoke the poor against the rich. The law suspending the Popular Tribunal should be obeyed but such tribunals should be set up throughout France –

C'est le cri général des départements, qui ne veulent pas que leurs meilleurs citoyens soient livrés à un tribunal établi à Paris entouré d'assassins de la faction et maîtrisé par eux.[5]

---

[1] *Mémoires de Charles Barbaroux*, ed. Berville and Barrière (Paris, 1822), p. 102, letter of Barbaroux, from Caen, 18 June 1793.

[2] ABR, L1968, Barbaroux to Rebecquy (a copy), 20 May 1793, (report of a speech).

[3] *Moniteur*, XVI, p. 367; No. 133 of 13 May; Convention, 11 May 1793.

[4] *Moniteur*, XVI, p. 332; No. 129 of 9 May; Convention, 7 May 1793.

[5] P. Vaillandet, 'Lettres inédites de Barbaroux', *Annales historiques de la Révolution française*, 1933, pp. 338–53; letter of end May – start June (?), to a friend at Marseilles, pp. 349–50.

The reconciliation between Barbaroux and the Municipality was facilitated by the fact that the Commune felt that Marseilles' interests had been neglected by the Convention. It continually had to demand that Toulon should be better defended, so as to provide security for Marseilles and its ships, whereas Bayle and Boisset boasted of taking escorts from a convoy of merchantmen bound for the Levant, using them to convoy munition ships to the Army of the Pyrenees.[1] It asked for arms to defend the city and surrounding towns; it repeatedly asked the Convention to provide money for the importation of corn, and in doing so lectured the government on the special position of Marseilles, a city which usually supplied corn to the southern departments but which, now that the harvest was bad in the surrounding areas, might cause widespread disturbances if not adequately supplied.[2] It also lamented that its debts were increasing and should be shouldered by the Nation: a multitude of creditors – often from the poorest classes – was approaching destitution.[3] As we have seen, its addresses to the Convention, ostensibly concerned with obtaining the judgement of Louis XVI, were equally important in expressing Marseilles' perennial conviction that its interests had been neglected, while those of Paris, 'ville superbe et arrogamment ingrate', had been consistently satisfied[4] – satisfaction obtained, wrote Barbaroux, by the threat of popular insurrection.[5]

Moreover the fact that, when the Montagnard deputies were entrusted with the task of speaking on Marseilles' behalf – Barbaroux' services having been rejected – the Convention had failed to satisfy the city's demands, also redounded to the credit of Barbaroux – Marseilles echoing for instance his complaint that none of the surplus corn in the north of France was 'circulated' through Burgundy and Languedoc to the south.[6] Shipping delays, a bad harvest and the effects of war had

[1] A. Nat., AF II 90⁶⁶⁴, *Compte rendu* of Bayle and Boisset.

[2] A. Comm., 4D2, Municipality to Minister of War, 18 Sept. 1792.

[3] A. Comm., 1D3, municipal deliberation of 18 May 1793.

[4] See above, p. 60. A. Comm., 4D2, *Conseil général de la commune*, addresses of 26 Dec. and 29 Dec. 1792, etc.

[5] A. Comm., 4D44, Barbaroux to Municipality of Marseilles, 6 Feb. 1793; also 25 Feb. 1793.

[6] A. Comm., 4D2, Municipality of Marseilles to Granet, Laurens, Moïse Bayle and Pierre Baille, 1 Mar. 1793.

aggravated this situation. The failure of the expedition to Sardinia, on which many Marseillais served, and the dilapidation of the arsenal and fleets of Toulon were attributed to the negligence of the government. The alleged return of *émigrés*, the mass emission of *assignats*, the rising price of grain, slowness and negligence in sending decrees of the Convention, even the crippling burden of the municipal debt – these were likewise blamed on Paris.[1]

Thus Barbaroux and Rebecquy had earned the good opinion of the Sections and the Municipality – being asked, in particular, to persuade the Convention to legalise the Popular Tribunal. But the reputations of Robespierre, Danton, and especially Marat sank under the weight of the usual Girondin denunciations. Like Robespierre, Marat was denounced for having demanded a dictator to guide the Republic to victory. Section 23 – many of whose citizens were the opposite of Marat in terms of social standing – urged his *mise en accusation*, urging that anyone who spoke in favour of a king or *maître* should be punished by death.[2] Such a profession of republicanism was designed to parry allegations that the Sections, because of their 'aristocratic' leanings and their support for the *appelants*, would favour a monarchical restoration. They were also aimed at Montagnards who, they thought, wished to put Orléans on the throne.

Finally, frequent pronouncements on matters of social concern served to aggravate the breach between Sections and Club – pronouncements which go far to confirm the Jacobin picture of the Sections as dominated by men of the upper ranks of Marseilles' society. A plan to erect a monument to commemorate the victory of the Sections of Marseilles shows this clearly. Proposed on 13 May in Section 5,[3] it put into the mouths of the 'people of Marseilles' an indignant repudiation of those who incited them against the rich – the rich are our brothers; without them, we would all be poor. Another instance is furnished by a speech in Section 6, on 2 June, when the orator defended the rich as the indispensable support of the poor and as the

---

[1] A. Comm., 4D2, Municipality of Marseilles to the Convention, 25 Mar. 1793; and an undated letter shortly afterwards.
[2] ABR, L1944, Section 16, 22 May 1793.
[3] ABR, L1984, Section 5, 13 May 1793.

benefactors of humanity. Anyway, he continued,

> la carrière de la fortune est ouverte à tout le monde. Chacun peut y parvenir sans devenir criminel, le talent n'a plus d'entraves et le soleil ne refuse sa lumière à personne.[1]

This, the language of the *gens aisés*, suggests that the clubists' propaganda may not only have been justified but may have been making converts amongst those who treated the rich 'unjustly'. The Sections, in making one of their main policies the apology of riches, (though none, seemingly, went so far as Section 1 of Aix, which complained of 'l'aristocratie de la pauvreté'),[2] seemed to invite attacks from the clubists on this aspect of their philosophy.

Moreover it is noticeable that these apologies for wealth stem mainly – though not exclusively – from Sections whose population was of above-average affluence – Section 5, perhaps the most opulent of all, the very centre of elegance of the new town; its neighbour Section 6, slightly less distinguished because nearer the port, but nevertheless sharing the residences of some of the town's most wealthy merchants; Section 23, newest quarter of all, outside the town walls; Section 10, by no means as extravagantly rich as the other three but, situated between the old town and the harbour and united with the adjacent quayside Section 18 (La Loge) in defence of commercial interests, considerably more prosperous and salubrious than nearby Section 9 or, even more so, Section 11, in the heart of the old town itself. These Sections in particular would be inclined to do all they could to attract rich merchants to their meetings and, once they were there, to protect them from outside attack.

Moreover the question of taxation again came to the fore. The principal tax-collector, Peyre-Ferry, was an ardent Jacobin. On 21 May he reported that 925,000 *livres* of the 1791 tax of 1.36 millions had not yet been paid.[3] Some weeks earlier he had circulated a 'last call' to tax payers which aroused the indignation of the sectionaries. It stated that taxes came in quickly when French armies were victorious; but, since Dumouriez' treason and the Vendée revolt, his bureau was deserted. He summoned rich citizens:

[1] ABR, L1972, Section 6, 2 June 1793.   [2] ABR, L1974, n.d.
[3] ABR, L1987, P. Peyre-Ferry's tax-statement, 21 May 1793.

Avez-vous fondé l'espoir que la République serait renversée et que vous vous soustrairiez par là à l'acquit de vos impositions? Sachez que vous serez les premiers sacrifiés.[1]

Such language, said the sectionaries, would cause a civil war of the poor against the rich: some asked that the Sections should take over the task of tax collection. A *cahier* containing replies to requests for the reduction of tax assessments of individual citizens shows that under the Jacobins most assessments were maintained whereas, under the rule of the Sections (in June and July), the great majority of the assessments challenged were reduced.[2] The impression that well-off citizens welcomed the supremacy of the Sections for the prospect of tax reductions is confirmed by other, admittedly fragmentary, indications. Thus at Ansouis, in the Vaucluse, the Section appointed commissioners to go through tax lists to repair injustices.[3] The universal declamation against Jacobin forced loans suggests a similar preoccupation.

It is not easy to judge whether attacks on the Sections as being under the domination of the rich were justified or not. It is difficult to make real comparisons of the social composition of the sectionaries before and after the watershed of April–May 1793, because the minutes of the Sections – where they exist for the necessary period – rarely give enough information. Where some sort of comparison is possible, it seems that many of those who led the Sections – were officials, made speeches and motions – before April 1793 continued to do so afterwards. They were *bourgeois*, lawyers, school-teachers, merchants 'of the second class', and members of the liberal professions. Throughout 1791 and later, people of a fairly humble social status – masons, cobblers, bakers, tanners, warehouse-porters and the like – formed a substantial proportion of total membership.[4] This

---

[1] ABR, L1987; Section 1, 12 May 1793, reviews, in scandalised terms, Peyre-Ferry's 'Dernier avis aux contribuables' from which this quotation comes.

[2] A. Comm., 2G1, *Premier cahier des réponses aux pétitions relatives au quart de revenu*, (Feb.–Aug. 1793).

[3] ABR, L1974, Section of Ansouis appointed commission, 11 June 1793.

[4] For instance, ABR, L1932, Section 1, 19 June 1791 – *menuisiers, emballeurs, cordonniers, serruriers*; L1941, Section 8, 19 June 1791, numerous *cordonniers*, some *portefaix, tonneliers*, etc.; L1940, Section 7, 19 June 1791,

did not change, as far as can be seen, with the federalist revolt. Bearing this in mind – and the fact that there was a large population of wage-earners, unskilled workers who are rarely present on sectionary lists – it is obvious that the Sections found most useful those men who could draft a cogent petition and make a good show in welcoming deputations of sister-Sections and from neighbouring towns. This was the case for the year or so in which the Sections played a significant part in town politics and could not easily be changed. The Sections, in repudiating the 'dictatorship' of the Club, had appealed to doctrines of direct democracy, appeals which, however specious one may suspect them to have been, may have attracted men of low social rank into their assemblies. Declamations against anarchy may have had this effect, at a time when commerce and industry were languishing. The fact that, apart from one or two instances, there is virtually no evidence that rich merchants were playing an active part in sectionary politics; that, on the contrary, the Sections followed the Club in deploring the selfish indifference and laziness of the rich, can be taken with references in their registers to the large number of *ouvriers* in their meetings[1] to suggest that one should not exaggerate the extent to which these assemblies were inundated by the capitalists and merchants of Marseilles. Rather, the middle-ranking group of articulate and educated individuals – to be found in all Sections, despite considerable differences as to the social composition of the total population of individual Sections[2] – continued to form the bulk of those who formulated and executed the policy-decisions of these assemblies. Only in the last days of the revolt, when the problem of food supplies came to the fore, can one detect the timid emergence of eminent merchants (Samatan, Hugues, etc.) from the shadows into the lurid sunset of the federalist revolt. Moreover those merchants who were punished

---

cordonniers, fripiers, maçons, etc.; L1943, Section 12, 20 June 1791 – *tanneurs, chapeliers, cordonniers* . . .

[1] For instance, ABR, L1936, Section 4, 19 Apr.; one of the reasons Bayle and Boisset wanted fewer meetings of the Sections was because such meetings 'tired' the workers. A. Nat., AF II 90⁶⁶⁴, *Compte rendu* of Bayle and Boisset; see also, ABR, L1936, Section 4, 21 Apr. 1793.

[2] Evidence of the lists of active citizens in June 1791. Comparison of these lists with lists of 1793 (spring, till April) and with names mentioned for subsequent months.

for their contribution to federalism were accused of having given financial aid rather than active participation.[1] A royalist merchant, Jean-Joseph Abeille, long after the collapse of federalism, lamented the absence of 'les hommes distingués par leurs lumières, leurs vertus et leurs fortunes' from the movement.[2]

The implication of merchants in the revolt cannot be measured merely by counting their attendance in the Sections: that they felt themselves to have been implicated is indicated by the exodus of merchants, *marchands, courtiers* and manufacturers after the fall of the Sections, as the republican army advanced towards the city.[3] The very real sense in which the prosperity of the whole city could be said to depend on the merchants being allowed to get on with their jobs must also be taken into account when arguing that the Sections – without considerable participation by merchants – pursued policies which favoured or at least did not harm mercantile interests. Traditionally, the merchant of Marseilles was not a political animal: but his intervention in politics did not have to be direct to be influential.

There was certainly considerable economic and social disruption in Marseilles at this period[4] and this was doubtless important in determining participation in and attitudes to the revolt of the Sections. The price of meat and wine rose to a peak in March. Bread was at 5 *sous* and some bakers are said to have been closing their shops. Prices remained high throughout this period, and though, in the spring and summer of 1793, famine conditions did not prevail, they did threaten and it was only by hasty expedients that Marseilles was fed. Trade was disrupted by the presence of British fleets in the Mediterranean, April 1793 seeing the virtual ending of the long-distance trade.

[1] Except Laurent-François Tarteiron (see below, p. 304), and half a dozen rather less eminent merchants.

[2] J. J. A. Abeille, *Notes et pièces officielles relatives aux événements de Marseille et de Toulon en 1793* (Paris, 1815).

[3] See *Histoire de la Provence*, p. 429, for the extent – considerable – of commercial emigration from the district of Marseilles: and see below, pp. 293 ff.

[4] The facts as to the economic situation of Marseilles at this time are taken from Charles Carrière, 'Le problème des grains et farines à Marseille pendant la période du maximum, 4 mai 1793–4 nivôse an iii', *Extrait des Mémoires et documents*, No. xiii (Paris, 1958); and 'Les entrées de navires dans le port de Marseille pendant la Révolution', *Provence historique, tome* 7, 1957, pp. 200–25.

Carrière speaks of the year after 1 April 1793 as being 'l'année terrible' of Marseilles' trade. The high price of bread was linked with the collapse of trade, since Marseilles usually imported corn to feed her own population and the population of the hinterland.

Industry and artisanal trades such as shoemaking were hit by a lack of raw materials and by the emigration of notable manufacturers and the flight of capital – the soap, sulphur, tanning and textile industries were all suffering. Unemployment ensued, but no wage increases sufficient to offset higher prices. May 1793 seems to have seen a revival of labour troubles, with strikes fomented by *compagnonnages* of shoemakers.[1] The abolition of corporations had left workers unprotected: the *portefaix* lamented that their charitable funds were being combined with those of other former corporations – their funds were running down, yet the number of unfortunate workers was increasing.[2] Whether this economic distress was reflected in political life is difficult to see. But the way was certainly prepared for popular acquiescence in the triumph of the Sections.

Many *gens aisés*, like Barbaroux, blamed the struggles in Paris and Marseilles for the neglect of measures to protect trade, blamed inflation on the profligate issue of *assignats*, and commercial disruption on the Jacobins, whose threats of forced loans would not encourage traders to disclose their wealth by making it circulate. The fall of Mourraille and Seytres added to the confusion. Those who were unemployed would have no loyalty to the Club which, its enemies skilfully put about, had caused all the disruption by driving the rich merchants from Marseilles or terrorising them into inactivity. The Sections, by stressing the need for law and order and by demanding an end to attacks on the rich, who alone could restore trade and prosperity, might win over not only the rich but all those who suffered from the economic crisis, while the Sections' collections for the poor, inadequate as they were, did show a measure of concern.[3] Such propaganda, such activity might well make the Club's attempts at a counter-attack abortive.

---

[1] A. Comm., 21136, report to a *bureau* of General Committee of meetings of *ouvriers cordonniers* to form coalition to get wage increase, 14 May 1793.

[2] A. Comm., 214, petition of *portefaix*, n.d.

[3] ABR, L1946, Section 21, 9 Apr. 1793; L1943, Section 12, 11 May 1793, etc.

Attacks on the Sections were indeed frequent, often concentrating on their social composition, describing them as full of rich 'egoists' and capitalists.[1] Typical is the proclamation issued by Bayle and Boisset at Montélimar on 14 May,[2] accusing the Marseillais of having bowed their heads, without resistance, to 'l'orgueilleuse opulence', of having accepted chains of gold from those 'pour qui l'égoïsme est un dieu et l'égalité un supplice'. The ghost of the monarchy walked in silence through the city streets. Other letters attacked the capitalists and rich merchants for refusing to contribute to the war-effort and, taking advantage of some avowed irregularities in the levying of money, reversing the whole course of the Revolution.[3]

But no real counter-attack was launched. The Central Committee of the Club had become isolated from the rank and file clubists and had aroused antagonism against extremism not only from men who had hitherto taken no part in politics, but also among moderate clubists. Isoard wrote later that he alone, in face of the desertion of many of the clubists, had continued the hopeless struggle.[4] Many prominent Marseillais – Pierre Laugier, Mauger Manneville, Antoine Maurin, Bertrand d'Apt among them – who had learned lessons of militancy in the Club, now practised them in the Sections.

Now attacks were launched at the very basis of the Club's position. Section 7 voted that the Club was not a *corps constitué* and that the clubists could easily make their views known in the Sections,[5] while Section 12 declared that clubs had no legal existence.[6] A pamphlet explained that the Club – full of criminals who had fled from their own countries – had duped the people who however had suddenly woken up and joined the Sections.[7] Soon the Sections voted that no political assembly

[1] ABR, L1980, Club of Marseilles to Jacobin Club of Paris, 13 May 1793.

[2] A. Nat., AF II 90⁶⁶⁴, *Compte rendu* of Bayle and Boisset; also ABR, L1947, Section 23, 19 May 1793.

[3] Letters of Baille and Beauvais, *Représentants en mission* at Toulon, A. Nat., AF II 90⁶⁶⁴; also ABR, L2076, *La Société populaire de Toulon au peuple marseillais*, 23 May 1793; L1960, letter of B. Vence, 18 May 1793.

[4] ABR, L2076, *Discours prononcé par un membre de la Société populaire de Marseille*, n.d.; *La Vie politique de François Isoard*, n.d. (*nivôse* II).

[5] ABR, L1940, Section 7, 6 May 1793.

[6] ABR, L1943, Section 12, 7 May 1793.

[7] ABR, L2011 ᵇⁱˢ; *Les Clubs et les Sections: Les Sections sauvent la Liberté, les Clubs la tuent*, n.d.

should meet when they were in session,[1] and since the Sections were in permanent assembly, this implied the elimination of the Club.

By 12 May, the Club had purged itself of some of its more extreme members,[2] but some ardent Jacobins continued the struggle, though with increasing desperation and a sense of isolation in a hostile or indifferent city which believed that the Club no longer had a recognised rôle in the revolutionary struggle – to educate the masses or to keep a check on the abuses of the *hommes en place*. Such tasks were now assumed, not by a dictatorial secret committee, but by the whole city in democratic and open assembly. If there were respectable citizens in the Club – and this was sometimes admitted by the Sections – let them join the rest of the city in throwing off the tyranny of a handful of 'intrigants'. The clubs were seen as relics of an earlier, more turbulent age; like castle keeps they gave shelter to bands of dissolute and unruly adventurers who made sorties of pillage and of rapine that kept the countryside in a state of terror. Therefore these adventurers were arrested.

The arrest of the leading clubists completely emasculated that society and, at one fell swoop, brought an end to effective Jacobin resistance. The General Committee proclaimed that, by these arrests, it had forestalled a new Saint Bartholemew's Massacre, after which the persecutors had intended to seize the property of the murdered.[3]

Men deserted the Club, which disavowed its earlier policies and its earlier leaders.[4] Those who changed opinions claimed that they had been misled by all the Jacobin journals which were read to the exclusion of those of the Girondins.[5] But the final closing of the Club came after news of the events of 29 May at Lyons aroused fears that in Marseilles too the Club – thought

---

[1] ABR, L1940, Section 7, 15 May 1793 – endorsed by the majority of the Sections.

[2] ABR, L1937, Section 4, 12 May 1793; L1947, Section 23, 12 May 1793.

[3] See above, p. 91; and ABR, L3100, *Le Comité général au Tribunal populaire.* . . . 1 July 1793; ABR, L1976, draft proclamation of General Committee, 15 May 1793.

[4] See, for instance, Bib. Mun., Marseilles, proclamation of Club, 25 May 1793.

[5] ABR, L1966, Section 19, 21 May 1793.

to be full of arms – might provoke a bloody battle. On 3 June therefore the Club was closed by deputies of the Sections, who took possession of its belongings.[1] Even before this happened, many clubists, responding with great alacrity to the invitations of the presidents of their Sections, had surrendered their Club cards.[2]

A proclamation of the General Committee set the seal on this episode in the history of Marseilles. It condemned the Club for imposing its will on the Administrations and for influencing elections; for using its affiliations throughout France to provoke sudden and frightening outbursts of violence which spread to every corner of the country, thus subjecting the majority of citizens to 'une minorité toujours active, surveillante et audacieuse'.[3]

The fall of the Club seems to have left the bulk of the Marseillais indifferent – only the *fédérés* of 10 August protested, complaining that their flag had been used in the ceremony consecrating the closure of the Club.[4] This was a significant but almost isolated incident – though protests came from Jacobin clubs throughout Provence and from clubists who had fled to Paris.[5]

[1] ABR, L1946, Section 21, 3 June; L1943, Section 12; L1936, Section 4; L1947, Section 23 – all 3 June 1793.
[2] ABR, L1940, Section 7, 3 June 1793, etc.
[3] ABR, L2076, *Le Comité général au nom de ses commettants*, 4 June 1793.
[4] ABR, L1935, Section 2, 6 June 1793.
[5] And see below, pp. 124 ff., for the oppositional politics of Section 11.

CHAPTER FIVE

The Régime of the Sections and the Struggle against the Convention

How were the Sections to use their newly acquired power? For their ideals of peace and order, for the unity and the indivisibility of the Republic, for individual liberty, freedom of speech, freedom from the fear of terror? No doubt most of the sectionaries were sincere in upholding these ideals and tried to put them into practice. Perhaps the men who used these ideals to protect their lives and fortunes from Jacobinism were self-interested; but, initially, at any rate, the bulk of the Marseillais followed the leadership of the sectionaries, even if only because they were, as one sectionary put it, 'fatigués de marcher de révolution en révolution'. Thus, either from idealism – a liberal belief in the supreme need to uphold individual liberty in face of monarchical despotism at one extreme, popular insurrection at the other – or from self-interest, or from a mixture of the two, most people either tolerated or supported the new régime.

Unfortunately for the ideal, however, reality was infinitely harsher than most sectionaries anticipated. Left to themselves, they might have developed a stable, calm society – though their constant tendency to equate 'busyness', talking, committee work, oratory, exhortation, with actual achievement suggests that even then they might have been ineffective. Confronted with a threatening situation outside Marseilles, however, they proved incapable of sustaining the energy which had brought them to power. They were forced to abandon their own ideals and to resort to measures against their opponents which were not very different from those used by the Jacobins. Taking a negative view of the Revolution – one born of fatigue – and a static view, they tended to leave decisive action to two groups of men whom they abhorred – the Jacobins and the royalists. Having little constructive to offer, they were outmanœuvred by those who had a cause for which they were willing to make personal sacrifices. Men who had come into political life, or into power, to avoid making such sacrifices found themselves ineffectual against more determined opponents. Nor in general were the Marseillais very creative revolutionaries – or counter-revolutionaries – producing few original leaders or ideas. And this lack of character in individual leaders – what for instance is there to say about Peloux and Castelanet, chiefs of the General Committee? – applied equally to the rank and file of the movement. There can be no such vivid picture of the 'ideal sectionary' – a self-effacing individual – as has been made of the 'typical' *sans-culotte*. Certainly they had little time to evolve an ethos of their own; but, even so, their collective and individual anonymity is somewhat disappointing.

Having had such an easy passage to power in Marseilles, they tended to underestimate the storms which would assail them when they tried to navigate outside the sheltered waters of their home port. While the Republic itself was battered by tempests, the sectionaries tried to build a fool's paradise of peace and comfort, whose flimsy walls would soon be blown down by the gales from outside, unleashed on Marseilles by the events of 2 June. Marseilles could not accept the 2 June, for this implied rebuilding the Club of Marseilles, releasing the 'anarchists', 'plotters' and 'murderers' from Fort Saint-Jean and opening their own purses for the benefit of the Montagnards. So, confident as ever that what was adopted by Marseilles should be adopted in the Republic as a whole, they did not shrink from embarking on a policy directly opposed to that proclaimed by the Convention. Already therefore one of their ideals – 'La République une et indivisible' – had been shattered. Not, of course, by the Marseillais, but by the Convention itself.

Consolidation of power at home: expansion outside the city – this was the programme of the Sections which, convinced that Paris had been plunged by the 2 June into a blood-bath, seized hold of every authority in Marseilles, first in June by electing provisional members to these bodies, and then in July by calling an electoral assembly which by mid-July gave the Sections complete control over all aspects of policy in Marseilles. All opinion was henceforth expressed through the Sections.[1]

To win the department to the cause of the Sections, more envoys were sent out to propagate their principles, while many deputations came from outlying areas to relate how, at Tarascon, Manosque, Lourmarin or Velaux, Jacobin municipalities had been turned out, Sections had been established and clubs closed, denunciations received against clubists, terrorists disarmed and the manifestoes and addresses of Marseilles promulgated.[2]

As yet, the authority of the Convention had not been challenged by the Marseillais. But, in some of their addresses to that assembly, notably those demanding the death of the king, the vehemence of the accusations levied against individual deputies or groups showed that the Marseillais were not prepared to accept servilely dictation from Paris.[3] The long-standing belief that the Convention neglected their city's interests was combined with the conviction that the Convention was wasting its time in useless debates. The campaign against the *appelants* likewise provoked opinions which did not flatter the legislators, while the actions of Bayle and Boisset discredited the Convention which had invested them with such wide powers. To many citizens, whatever their political beliefs, their mission seemed all too reminiscent of those of the *Intendants*, of Caraman and Bournissac. The Sections attacked the grant of unlimited powers to the *Représentants* and hoped that their acts – especially the 'despotic' suppression of the Popular Tribunal – would be disavowed by the Convention.

Deputies of the Sections went to the Convention to win a vote of confidence for their policies and a repudiation of those of Bayle and Boisset, and of Robespierre, Danton and Marat. The reports of these deputies described the situation of Paris in May 1793,[4] – the mass of *Conventionnels*, without energy or talent,

[1] ABR, L1964, General Committee, 12 June 1793; L943, District Administration, 2 July 1793; L278, Electoral Assembly of the Bouches-du-Rhône, 10 July 1793.

[2] ABR, L1959, deputy of Section 8 from Tarascon, 14 June 1793, to his Section at Marseilles; L1938, Section 5, 11 July 1793, etc.

[3] See above, pp. 60 ff.

[4] ABR, L1968, *Rapport fait aux trente-deux Sections . . . de Marseille par leurs commissaires députés à la Convention nationale*, 7 July 1793.

allowed themselves to be used by the despotic deputies who sat on the left, and by the occupants of the tribune and the Paris mob; the Montagnards encouraged mob violence in order to intimidate their opponents in the Convention. The capital was full of lies concerning Marseilles – rumours that the sectionaries wore the *cocarde blanche*, that patriots were massacred in the streets, that the Sections were in league with the Vendeans, that they had sent men, money and ships to the enemies of France, that they were trying to re-establish the monarchy in the Midi and were to give the crown to Barbaroux. In the Sections of Paris, the Marseillais were surrounded by men whose moustaches were still stained with the blood of 2 September. However, the insurrections of 31 May and 2 June prevented full consideration of the situation at Marseilles and caused the dispersal of the deputies of the Sections, who returned home to report on the anarchy which had engulfed the capital.

Already, on 27 May, the Municipality had summoned the Convention to execute Marat and to leave Paris for a town where the deputies could prepare, in freedom and security, a just constitution.[1] Five days later, the General Committee issued an address against Marat, urging the (Girondin) Convention to appeal frankly for aid from Marseilles, if it felt unable to defeat the Montagne,[2] while Section 23 heard, on 28 May, what were perhaps the first discussions of the possible formation of a 'force départementale' to expel the Montagne from the Convention.[3]

On 2 June, the unpurged Department, in a letter to the Committee of Public Safety, expressed Marseilles' frustration at the various failures of the government.[4] It complained of the lack of arms with which to defeat the foreign enemies of the Revolution, and of the complete neglect of Toulon. It said that Marseilles' commerce was non-existent, with serious results for the Midi as a whole and for the citizens of Marseilles in particular. Paris was blamed for allowing enemy fleets control of

[1] ABR, L1031, *Adresse de la Municipalité de Marseille à la Convention nationale*, 27 May 1793.

[2] ABR, L1969, Committee General, 1 June 1793, endorsing a petition of Section 23 against Marat, 21 May 1793.

[3] ABR, L1947, Section 23, 28 May 1793.

[4] ABR, L128, Dept. Admin., to Committee of Public Safety, 2 June 1793.

the Mediterranean, without making any effort to protect French merchantmen. The administrators (by no means all sympathetic to the Sections) spoke of the contempt which their just demands had received from Paris and of a plan to abandon the Midi to the enemies of the Republic. They asked the Convention,

> Pourquoi animer continuellement le peuple contre les riches et accomplir par là la fable de celui qui tua la poule aux œufs d'or?

The rich, fleeing from a reign of terror, had been forced to emigrate or send their capital abroad and this reduced industry to inactivity and deprived the poor of work. Such grievances united the majority of townspeople behind the Sections when, after 2 June, they could point to the troubles in the capital and blame the Montagnards.

News from other towns confirmed their determination to resist the new masters of the Convention. On 17 May, in Section 2, an address from Bordeaux had been read, pledging the Bordelais to send half their National Guard to Paris if their deputies were not protected from insult.[1] News of the battle at Lyons on 29 May arrived on 2 June and, on 6 June, a deputation from the Sections of Lyons was welcomed.[2] Letters from Barbaroux – 'Je soulèverai la France entière contre les brigands' – and from Rebecquy and Gensonné likewise aroused indignation against the Convention.[3]

This indignation was expressed most forcefully by the reestablishment of the Popular Tribunal, a decision which, taken by the General Committee on 6 June, contravened the decree of 15 May suppressing the Tribunal, established without legislative consent. This decree was well known in Marseilles so the judges had laid down their functions on 27 May. But the Sections – except Section 11 – refused to accept their decision,[4] though the Department, District and Municipality declined to

[1] ABR, L1934, Section 2, 19 May 1793.
[2] ABR, L1944, Section 16, 2 June 1793; L1947, Section 23, 6 June 1793.
[3] ABR, L1944, Section 16, 17 June and 22 June; L1935, Section 2, 23 June 1793; A. Nat., AF II 45³⁵⁵, *Correspondance de Charles Barbaroux*.
[4] ABR, L1944, Section 16, 27 May; L1940, Section 6, 27 May 1793, etc.

attend the re-installation of the Tribunal, on 9 June.[1] The Tribunal's reputation soon spread into the department; even towns such as Aix accepted its jurisdiction gratefully and sent evidence to be used against the clubists. The Criminal Tribunal was repudiated, its members having been elected as a result of pressure from the terrorists.[2] On 3 July, Louis Barthélemy, clubist and member of the Department, was condemned to death for extorting money and for trying to rally the clubists after their defeat at Marseilles.[3] On 28 July, Abeille, Grimaud and Bazin were sentenced to death and members of the Jacobin municipality of Salon who had aided Abeille and his colleagues were imprisoned for arbitrary arrests and monetary exactions.[4] From the point of view of the Sections, the Tribunal punished those who had not hesitated to use brutal methods to advance their cause: to the clubists, it was a 'tribunal de sang', outlawed by the Convention, and its acts were just as arbitrary as those of the so-called anarchists. The Tribunal was sustained by a complex infrastructure of sectionary *comités de surveillance* which provided it with both suspects and evidence.

Despite knowledge of a law of 19 June which outlawed members of the Tribunal – and even those who testified before it[5] – the Tribunal was maintained, a member of Section 19 denouncing a Convention which had allowed those implicated in the September Massacres to go free, while outlawing judges whose sole concern was to protect the innocent. The decree was burnt – Section 24 outlawed the Convention for passing it.[6]

But to the sectionaries, Barthélemy and Abeille were not sacrificed to a sterile lust for vengeance but in order that a coherent and humanitarian view of the Revolution should prevail against that of Paris. Thus the General Committee co-ordinated demands that the authority of the Convention should be repudiated, by producing, on 12 June, its *Manifeste*:

[1] ABR, L3100, proclamation of General Committee, 8 June; L46, Dept. Admin., 9 June 1793; L3100, *procès-verbal* of re-installation of Popular Tribunal, 9 June 1793.
[2] ABR, L3100, General Committee of the Sections of Aix, to Popular Tribunal, 25 June 1793.
[3] ABR, L3100. Judgement of Popular Tribunal, 3 July 1793.
[4] ABR, L3106. Judgement of Popular Tribunal, 28 July 1793.
[5] ABR, L3100.
[6] ABR, L2006, Section 19, 23 June; L1933, Section 1, 28 June 1793.

Marseille aux Républicains français,[1] justifying the revolt of the Sections. It declared that the departments whose deputies had been arrested considered themselves unrepresented in the Convention. The anarchists in Paris and Marseilles wished to put the corrupt Égalité on the throne of France; but Marseilles declared itself 'en état légal de résistance à l'oppression' and refused to obey the laws of the Convention until the arrested deputies were restored to their places. The Sections invited 'les gens de bien que Paris renferme encore dans son sein' to help the departmental coalition to defeat the 'factieux'. Forces were to be levied by the departments to march to Paris; for the Marseillais, who wished to end the Revolution which they had begun, had already ordered the levy of their contingent and appealed to others to do likewise. The flags of the Departmental Army were to bear the motto 'République une et indivisible; Respect aux Personnes et aux Propriétés'. This mixture of idealism and self-interest satisfied everyone in Marseilles except out-and-out Jacobins. The promise that the Departmental Army would 'end' the Revolution would certainly reassure the commercial aristocracy of Marseilles, while those who hated the monarchy would respond to the denunciation of Orléans. The Manifesto was sent to all the departments of France.[2]

Moreover, the Constitution and the decree of 26 June, giving administrators three days to retract oaths taken against the legislative body, failed in their purpose of reconciling the federalists to the new régime – and, in any case, they were not published. Deputations from Lyons, Nîmes and Bordeaux confirmed the Marseillais in their resolve.[3]

On 16–17 June, a meeting of the Three Administrations and

[1] ABR, L3120, papers of Revolutionary Tribunal, dossier of Antoine Boeuf.

[2] It seems that the Manifesto was enthusiastically received by the Sections of Provence. Those of Aix, besides recalling that the Parisians were provided with bread at *3 sous* at the expense of the whole Republic, attacked the Jacobins for passing laws against morality, the social order and against the closest links of marriage and legitimate fatherhood (ABR, L1974, *Acte d'adhésion*, 18 June). Everywhere the pledge to defend property was welcomed; those countrymen, it was asserted, who had thrown off the yoke of feudalism would not bow down before the anarchists (ABR, L1975, declaration of the inhabitants of Villelaure in the Vaucluse, 16 June 1793).

[3] ABR, L1947, Section 23, 6 June; L1972, General Committee, 9 June; L1944, Section 16, 12 June 1793.

the Sections accepted the Manifesto and swore an oath not to recognise decrees of the Convention voted since 31 May, to recognise the Popular Tribunal, to defend the 'République une et indivisible' and to respect lives and property.[1] As a result of this decision, the Department, which received from Paris copies of the decrees of the Convention, did not send them to the subordinate authorities and so decrees after 31 May – including the Jacobin Constitution – were not officially published at Marseilles.[2] Also, the oath not to recognise the Convention was imposed on all men who entered public office and so no office-holder could avoid swearing to uphold the aims of the Sections.[3]

The levying of a departmental army was voted by the General Committee on 10 June,[4] to crush the 'anarchists' of Paris, free the Convention from oppression and re-establish 'la représentation nationale dans son intégralité'.[5] At first, 512 men were to be sent from the National Guard of Marseilles, financed, provisionally by public funds, and then by voluntary subscription.[6] Recruiting of volunteers was brisk but 'Maratists' were excluded: no doubt many jobless men went, and some who had previously marched in the battalions of Marseilles.[7]

On 26 June deputies from the Hautes-Alpes, the Gard, and the Gironde attended a meeting of the General Committee which decided to hold a convention at Bourges, to which each department would send two deputies, and to set up seven secondary centres to organise the levying of armies which were to converge on Paris – Marseilles, Lyons, Toulouse, Bordeaux, Rennes, Strasbourg and Rouen were the towns chosen.[8] An electoral assembly chose men for Bourges, while others were appointed to debate the formation of a 'Commission centrale'

[1] ABR, L48, Three Administrations, 16–17 June 1793.

[2] ABR, L46, Dept. Admin., 18 June 1793.

[3] There was even a plan to make *every* citizen of Marseilles swear a personal oath of loyalty. ABR, L1938, Section 5, 27 July 1793.

[4] ABR, L1946, Section 21, 7 June; L1972, General Committee, 10 June 1793.

[5] ABR, L1990. Proclamation of General Committee, n.d. Adopted by Section 9, 20 June 1793.

[6] ABR, L1995, Section 5, 11 June 1793.

[7] ABR, L1947, Section 23; L1944, Section 16, 12 June and 17 June; *Journal de Marseille, feuille* of 25 June 1793.

[8] ABR, L1967, General Committee, 26 June 1793.

to be established in a town of the Midi to co-ordinate measures of self-defence. Thus the whole of the Midi was to become a unified centre of resistance against the Montagnards of the north of France.[1]

The Departmental Army had left Marseilles and, after a little resistance, had occupied Avignon by the second week of July, under Rousselet, an ex-army officer.[2] A small force had been detached from the Army of the Alps and was marching to meet it.[3] But, as yet, resistance served merely to intensify the hatred the sectionaries felt for their opponents, and though cracks soon appeared in the featureless façade of sectionary unity, final collapse was postponed by a series of desperate half-measures for some two months. As a response to the decree of 19 June, Section 4 voted to declare traitor anyone who spoke in favour of the Convention or of its decrees.[4] Decrees came to be known in Marseilles by means of the newspapers, and though the Department did debate whether to accept the Constitution, it decided, on the warning of the General Committee, not to submit it to the discussion of the people – and so the people, though 'sovereign', were to have no opportunity to discuss matters which vitally concerned them.[5] But the mere fact that the Department had considered publishing the Constitution made its members suspect in the eyes of the Sections – who replaced them by their own nominees.[6]

Even worse from the Sections' point of view was a decision by the District Administration to retract the oath sworn against the Convention and to pledge their allegiance to that body as the unique centre of the Republic one and indivisible.[7] They too however were soon replaced by nominees of the Sections.

[1] ABR, L278, Electoral Assembly of the Bouches-du-Rhône, sessions of 12, 13 and 18 July 1793.

[2] ABR, L1994. Proclamation of Rousselet from Avignon, 7 July 1793.

[3] Formed partly of Allobroges, a legion of whom was levied by François-Amédée Doppet (authorised by Legislative Assembly, 31 July 1792); based on Grenoble, composed of Savoyards, Piedmontese and Swiss; helped to unite Savoy with France; joined Army of Alps. See F. A. Doppet, *Mémoires politiques et militaires* (Paris, 1824), pp. 55 ff.

[4] ABR, L1948, Section 28, 23 June; L1971, Section 4, 24 June 1793.

[5] ABR, L46, Dept. Admin., 1 and 2 July 1793.

[6] ABR, L46, Dept. Admin., 3 July 1793 (installation of provisional Dept. Admin.).

[7] ABR, L943, District Administration, 3 July 1793.

The Electoral Assembly, which replaced all the administrators and judges of Marseilles and the department, was whole-heartedly devoted to the Sections, accusing Paris of usurping the rights of France and of discrediting liberty by the means used to obtain it, demanding a consultation of all the Sections of France to decide between the policies of Paris and the Convention and those of Marseilles and the Sections.[1] But such a consultation was denied by the General Committee to the people of Marseilles; for the General Committee was as tyrannical as the Committee of Public Safety which it so abhorred. Anyone who spoke in favour of the Constitution or of decrees voted after 31 May was declared a traitor;[2] and men appeared before the courts for violating this decree.[3]

Also, Avignon had been occupied as a result of being threatened with bombardment and soon many of its citizens were to be massacred by the soldiers of the Departmental Army.[4] At Arles, the Marseillais disarmed those who opposed their views and repulsed a flotilla which arrived from Toulon to bring help to the patriots. Throughout the department, agents of the Sections were destroying the clubs and dispersing legally elected municipalities (sometimes accused of having failed to solve the problem of food supplies), while in Marseilles many of the leaders of the Club remained in prison without trial. The General Committee had ruthlessly replaced administrators who refused to bow to its will.

Resistance to the Sections had forced them to have recourse to these arbitrary measures. Such resistance included the army of Carteaux, propaganda from the Convention and alleged Jacobin plots within the city. Marseilles was in much the same position as the Republic as a whole – faced with both external and internal enemies – and, like the leaders of the Republic, those of Marseilles abandoned liberal principles for measures of severity. The Sections had their *Comités de salut public*, their *Tribunaux révolutionnaires*, *Représentants en mission*, their central-

---

[1] ABR, L278, *Déclaration de l'assemblée électorale du Département des Bouches-du-Rhône à tous les Français*, 13 July 1793.

[2] ABR, L1938, Section 5, 11 July 1793.

[3] See below, p. 123.

[4] ABR, L3121, papers of the Revolutionary Tribunal of the Bouches-du-Rhône, dossier Rousselet; also L3112, trial of Rousselet by Revolutionary Tribunal, 11, 12, 16 Sept. 1793.

isation of government; and they were, in theory at least, soon to have their *levée en masse*.

For, besides the external threat, domestic opposition had revealed itself in various unruly manifestations in the Sections, showing that Jacobinism was not quite dead and warranted a constant watchfulness on the part of the Sections – *visites domiciliaires* to the homes of people who had behaved in a surly manner in sectionary assemblies, nocturnal patrols to break up meetings which the Jacobins were said to be holding fairly frequently in and around Marseilles, the summoning to their assemblies of trustworthy but lazy 'egoists', as well as the disarmament and arrest of real, tangible Jacobins and the weeding out of Maratists from the companies of the National Guard.[1] Yet despite elaborate precautions, the harmony of their meetings was frequently broken by unrepentant clubists who met in the Café François to commiserate with each other over the reign of peace and order established by their enemies. In Section 2 – normally very go-ahead in initiating sectionary measures — a minority made a great row on 10 June in favour of the old Municipality and Department,[2] while on the same day a deputation from all the Sections had to go to Section 11 to persuade it to renounce its factiousness – its refusal to re-install the Popular Tribunal and a demand for the suppression of the General Committee – a factiousness which, it was said, had spread to two other, no doubt adjacent, Sections.[3] Section 11 – des Prêcheurs – did seem to be the stronghold of Jacobin feeling. At the heart of the old town, inhabited by some of the poorest people in the city, it could easily be aware of feelings in the turbulent streets of the old town. Perhaps however there was no real economic or social basis to this *frondeur* spirit, for it was not the only poor Section, nor did it refuse approval of many decisions which would appear violently anti-Jacobin.

But references to tumult in other Sections abound in June, and especially in July. On 13 June for instance more than fifty members of Section 19 – also situated in the old town, in the

[1] ABR, L1947, Section 23, 14 June 1793; L1972, General Committee decided that *chasseurs* of Section 21 to be disbanded as Maratist, 14 July 1793; L2011*ter*, Municipality forbade all nocturnal meetings, 3 July 1793, etc.   [2] ABR, L1935, Section 2, 10 June 1793.

[3] ABR, L1939, Section 6; L1943, Section 12, 10 June 1793.

area around the cathedral – were forced to ask for asylum in Section 16; while Section 3 (a fairly well-off one in the newer district), Section 4 (usually advanced in anti-Jacobin motions), Section 6 (one of the richest of the new town and likewise heavily committed to the sectionary cause) and Section 9 (one of the poorest of the *vieille ville*) were all said, on several occasions in July, to be in an uproar.[1] Section 14, situated in the dingiest region of the old town, went as far as, for a few days, refusing men for the Departmental Army and recalling those who had already marched.[2] Reports also blamed deserters from the Departmental Army for causing trouble in the Sections.[3]

Such disturbances culminated on 21 July in a riot in which some four hundred people advanced on the building where the General Committee met, crying 'Nous sommes les sans-culottes' and demanding the release of the Jacobin prisoners.[4] They were easily dispersed but a Military Tribunal and a Committee of Public Security were set up to defeat dissension. The Military Tribunal, composed of elected representatives of each Section, was to judge – within twenty-four hours and with no provision for appeal – all those implicated in a 'plot' to divide the Sections one from another, to destroy the General Committee, release the prisoners, help Carteaux's army enter Marseilles and there revive former scenes of terror and massacre.[5]

With the Departmental Army – which at its largest probably numbered some 3500 men[6] – retreating from Avignon, all men between the ages of eighteen and forty-five (widowers and childless) were called up at Marseilles.[7] But resistance was stubborn, especially in outlying areas, where several riots occurred.[8] The General Committee appealed to the Sections in

[1] ABR, L1944, Section 16, 13 June; L1938, Section 5, 2, 3 July, etc.; L1939, Section 6, 6, 7, 11 July, etc.; L1947, Section 23, 3, 10 July, etc.

[2] ABR, L1947, Section 23, 21 July 1793.

[3] ABR, L1938, Section 5, 18 July – troubles in Section 22.

[4] ABR, L1976, official account of *émeute*. See also *Journal de Marseille*, *feuille* of 25 July 1793.

[5] ABR, L1976, proclamation of *Comité de sûreté publique*, 25 July 1793; L1935, Section 2, 25 July 1793.

[6] S. Vialla, *Marseille révolutionnaire*, p. 419.

[7] ABR, L48, Three Administrations, 23 July 1793.

[8] ABR, L128, Dept. Admin., to Croze (envoy at Dept. Army at Aix), 26 July 1793. There are indications that those whose immobilism had

the countryside to provide 'les volontaires propriétaires' to defend persons and properties:[1] but property-owners seem to have been indifferent to the army's fate. A propaganda offensive was waged against Carteaux in order to stiffen resistance to the 'horde of brigands' advancing to put Marseilles to flame and sword and to put Orléans on the throne.[2] Villeneuve, a royalist *émigré*, replaced Rousselet as commander of the Departmental Army[3] but the flight from Avignon was scarcely halted. Deserters increasingly spread alarming news in Marseilles:[4] financial means were lacking, levies were slow in forming.[5]

On 4 August, the Three Administrations desperately urged their army to do its utmost to keep the road from Arles open so that corn could still be sent to Marseilles.[6] The problem of foodstuffs added to the preoccupations of the Sections, as an acute threat of dearth reinforced the more constant problem of high prices. No longer could the Sections confine themselves to blaming the Convention for the *maximum*, the excessive issue of *assignats*;[7] nor could they rely on such piecemeal expedients as alms collection and subscriptions from the rich. A *Bureau des comestibles* had been set up on 8 June, as a response to warnings that the 'méchants' blamed the high price of soap, oil, sugar, coffee, vegetables, etc. on the negligence of the Sections.[8] The General Committee pointed to industry paralysed by the cost and shortage of raw materials and by the almost complete destruction of luxury trades which had made money pass from hand to hand in abundance, to the requisition of these materials for the armies, and to the distrust which foreign traders showed for the *assignat*. Public misery increased each day; for the wages

---

defeated the clubists – 'tout ce qui est propriétaire et bourgeois' – likewise refused to come to the aid of 'Les sections en danger'. ABR, L1911, envoys of Aix at Forcalquier, 1 Aug. 1793.

[1] ABR, L1914, General Committee to Sections of the countryside (n.d.).

[2] A. Comm., *Affiches*, 25 July; ABR, L1937, Section 4, 28 July; L1935, Section 2, 27 July; A. Comm., *Affiches*, 28 July; ABR, L1995, General Committee, proclamation, 27 July; A. Comm., *Affiches*, 29 July 1793.

[3] Scipion-Joseph-Alexandre de Villeneuve-Tourettes, *maréchal-de-camp*.

[4] ABR, L1947, Section 23, 27 July 1793.

[5] ABR, L1944, Section 16, 29 July; L1947, Section 23, 31 July 1793.

[6] ABR, L48, Three Administrations, 4 Aug. 1793.

[7] ABR, L1936, Section 4, 14 Mar. 1793, etc.

[8] ABR, L1981*bis*, Section 14, 5 June 1793.

of many workers did not satisfy their basic needs – and their basic *rights* to work and bread. The Sections asked the administrators to provide public works and to take measures to revive industry, while the General Committee opened a subscription, the proceeds of which were to be used to reduce the price of oil, soap, leather and so on.[1]

In fact, during this period of the collapse of foreign trade and the decay of industry, the *Bureau des subsistances* – set up by the Municipality in September 1792, financed by the Convention and an interest-free loan to which the merchants contributed over two million *livres* – was able to provide 400 *charges* of grain a day. This was the average daily consumption of Marseilles and was attained despite the fact that arrivals by sea had virtually ceased. But, for men hit by the adverse economic conditions, the price was high – 5 *sous* for a pound of bread from 4 March to 21 August, and then an extra *sou*. Though there was never a situation of famine, fears on this score were understandably intense.[2]

Thus the *Bureau des comestibles*, established on 8 June, co-ordinated the work hitherto done by individual Sections – making lists of needy citizens, organising collections for them, buying foodstuffs for redistribution at lower than cost price. Its main work was to appeal to the rich to donate generously, to make censuses of the available supplies of wine, meat, leather and other commodities.[3] But its activity did not silence complaints of 'l'augmentation des denrées' and troubles in the town were linked with the crisis in supplying the city with food.

Of course the Sections suffered from being in power at a most difficult time – when the naval blockade was biting deep and in the dangerous period before the harvest was gathered in. Moreover on 8 July the Committee of Public Safety ordered the naval forces at Toulon to intercept ships destined for Marseilles.[4] The Sections sent out agents to supervise the purchase

[1] Bib. Nat., *Un recueil de l'Arlésien Mège*, (*1788–1816*), *Documents pour l'histoire du fédéralisme marseillais*, Committee General, proclamation of 8 June 1793.

[2] Charles Carrière, 'Les entrées de navires dans le port de Marseille . . .', *Provence historique, tome* 7, 1957; 'Le problème des grains et farines à Marseille', pp. 165 ff.

[3] ABR, L2009, first meeting, 9 June 1793; L1981*bis*, passim.

[4] A. Comm., 33H33: the admiral in charge refused, however.

of foodstuffs but they ran into many difficulties.[1] They reported that the crop in the Arles region was good and at first hoped that the 'political regeneration' operated by the Sections would guarantee the free circulation of corn. But, aware of food riots directed against the sectionary authorities of several towns and villages,[2] they counselled that it would be unwise to buy too lavishly and so encourage further price rises. Landowners did not want to sell for *assignats* and, even if they did, they demanded exorbitant sums. Those entrusted with the purchase of corn for Marseilles even hoped to buy at prices enforced by the *maximum*, in principle execrated by the Sections. The Departmental Army had requisitioned carts and horses, so transport was difficult, especially as a republican naval squadron blocked the sea route from the Rhône to Marseilles.

It is not surprising, therefore, that trouble occurred within the city. A riot, on 2 August, on the Place de la Linche, a square overlooking the Vieux-Port from the flank of the old town, was attributed to popular anger at high prices.[3] But Arles fell and the only way by which Marseilles could get corn from inland France had been cut off long before the year's harvest had been gathered.

The Departmental Army had largely disintegrated, harried by Carteaux's Allobroges. Disaffection increased in the city, one observer writing on 28 July that the majority of Marseillais were prevented from accepting the Constitution only by the rich who feared the release of the clubists from prison,[4] while a letter from Poultier, written from Avignon on 6 August, reported that the people of Marseilles had begun to murmur its wish that the Constitution should be accepted and that the Departmental Army – composed of *émigrés* and young men who had been forced to march – was about to break up.[5] Whether the increased discontent was caused by doubters joining the

---

[1] A. Comm., 46F13: extensive correspondence between *Comité des subsistances* and its agents.

[2] ABR, L1974, riot of 6 June at Aix; L1975, *émeute* of 15 June at L'Isle-sur-le-Sorgue in the Vaucluse.

[3] ABR, L485, Military Tribunal, judgement of Marie Lacroix, 9 Aug. 1793.

[4] A. Nat., D XLII 4, J. Berard to Admin. of District of Briançon, 28 July 1793.

[5] *Moniteur*, XVII, p. 380, No. 226 of 14 Aug.; Convention, 12 Aug. 1793. Letter of *Représentant*, François-Martin Poultier.

winning side or by Jacobins taking courage and coming out into the open, is not obvious. Men were being punished by the Military Tribunal for saying that Carteaux's army was composed not of brigands but of patriots;[1] that decrees favourable to the people should not be withheld; for demanding the recall of the Departmental Army and for complaining of the inaction of the Sections as regards foodstuffs.[2] On 9 August, the Military Tribunal sent a woman to prison for having taken part in the riot of 2 August – 'un attroupement de femmes . . . sous prétexte de réclamer contre l'excessive cherté des denrées'.[3] One man was denounced for affirming that the Constitution would soon be accepted at Marseilles and others were accused of 'regretting' the Club and of favouring the entrance of Carteaux into Marseilles.[4]

To combat such disorder, measures were taken to speed up the working of the Popular Tribunal,[5] measures of terrorism were advocated against deserters,[6] a *levée en masse* was proclaimed on 19 August,[7] and attempts were made to get landowners to provide their surpluses of corn for the municipal granaries.[8] Basile Samatan lent the Municipality 160,000 *livres* to buy corn, stocks of which were nearly exhausted. The announcement of a future rise in prices (with consumers partly compensated by municipal subsidy) caused landowners and merchants to hold on to their stocks till they could benefit from the higher price.[9] The Sections also complained that rich citizens were exporting their corn in order to take advantage of the higher prices (up to 9, 10 or even 12 *sous*) in the interior of Provence. But on 18 August the vice-president of Section 5 said that only a successful stand by the Departmental Army

[1] ABR, L1942, Section 8's *comité de surveillance*.

[2] A. Comm., *Affiches*, Military Tribunal, judgements of 30 July, 3 Aug. 1793, etc.

[3] ABR, L485, Military Tribunal, judgement of Marie Lacroix, 9 Aug. 1793.

[4] ABR, L3101, committee of surveillance of Section 1, 25 July 1793; ABR, L1942, secret committee of Section 8; L1939, Section 6, 13 Aug. 1793.

[5] ABR, L48, Three Administrations, 27 July 1793.

[6] ABR, L1996, Section 2, 17 Aug.; Section 24, 28 July 1793.

[7] ABR, L48, Three Administrations, 19 Aug. 1793.

[8] ABR, L48, Three Administrations, 10 Aug. 1793.

[9] ABR, L48, 10 Aug.; A. Comm., *Affiches, Conseil général provisoire*, 17 Aug. 1793; 46F13, correspondence of *Bureau des subsistances*; also 46F12.

could save Marseilles from famine, since the Spanish and British controlled the sea routes.[1]

On 11 August however the Departmental Army had been shattered by a detachment of Carteaux's army reinforced by peasants, and was now falling back on Aix.[2] At Marseilles a Committee of General Security, of five members with unlimited powers, was set up and more repressive measures, including disarmament, were enforced.[3] As a final confession of the bankruptcy of their ideas, a religious procession was held on 18 August 'pour désarmer contre nous la colère céleste si justement méritée'; but this death-bed repentance proved highly unsuccessful in terms of actual results achieved.[4] All those who did not agree with the policies of the Sections were ordered to leave the city or be judged within twenty-four hours.[5] Eight men from Aix were hurriedly executed after judgement of the Popular Tribunal – for complicity in the murder of prisoners at Aix in February.[6] In all, some nineteen men had been executed by judgement of this Tribunal. But most of the arrested Jacobins remained in prison, so Section 4 demanded a purge of the prisoners, followed by a *levée en masse*.[7] New verbal attacks launched against Carteaux were however, like the other measures voted, of little avail.

As Carteaux's army approached, Section 11 rebelled against a proposal of Section 23 to send a petition to the commanders of the allied fleets to obtain free passage of grain convoys from Italy for the Marseillais.[8] The bulk of the Sections seem to have adhered to this petition, often with great enthusiasm.[9] Section 11 protested and urged its fellow-Sections to try to come to terms with Carteaux rather than with foreign enemies;[10] but a

[1] ABR, L1938, Section 5, 18 Aug. 1793.

[2] A. Comm., 2I32, Castelanet to Municipality, 13 Aug. 1793.

[3] ABR, L48, Three Administrations, 14 Aug. 1793; L1933, Section 1, 19 Aug. 1793, etc.

[4] ABR, L1938, Section 5, 18 Aug. 1793, etc.

[5] ABR, L1933, Section 1, 20 Aug. 1793.

[6] ABR, L1972, General Committee, meeting of 20 Aug.; L1938, Section 5, 20 Aug. 1793.

[7] ABR, L2011, Section 4, 21 Aug. 1793.

[8] ABR, L1938, Section 5, 19 Aug. 1793.

[9] ABR, L1944, Section 16, 20 Aug.; L1939, Section 6, 20 Aug.; L1938, Section 5, 19 Aug. 1793, etc.

[10] ABR, L2003, Section 11 – whose register has not survived – 20 Aug. 1793.

ship put out, with envoys of the Sections on board, to discuss with Admiral Hood the possibility of allowing free entrance of merchant ships into Marseilles.

Section 23 was one of the wealthiest of the Sections and had on numerous occasions distinguished itself by the vehemence of its principles. Backed up especially by Sections 5 and 6, both full of rich merchants who would have the fullest knowledge of the position as regards food supplies – but also by less affluent districts – Section 23 was combated by the most popular of the districts of Marseilles, supported by the adjacent Sections of the old town – 9, 12, 13 and 14 – all characterised by an exceptionally high percentage of the labouring classes, men who before all others, one would have thought, would be alarmed by the depletion of Marseilles' food stocks. But Section 11 especially had a record of pro-Jacobin manifestations, opposing the destruction of the Club and the Jacobin administrations, resisting the re-installation of the Popular Tribunal and demanding the promulgation of the Constitution. At the very outset of the Revolution, it had sheltered meetings which attacked the tax-farms with particular vehemence. According to Barère's report of 16 *germinal* II (5 Apr. 1794), Section 11's loyalty to the Jacobins exposed it to persecution by other Sections as regards the sharing of work and food, deprivations which, Barère said, merely sharpened the revolutionary spirit of the patriots.[1] Certainly opposition continued, for Section 11 opposed demands for the summary punishment of deserters from the Departmental Army and rejected, on 1 August, the plan of Section 1 to quicken the procedure of the Popular Tribunal and to reduce safeguards for the accused.[2] One of the acts by which this Section called attention to itself does suggest that its rebelliousness derived from social causes; for early in June it had spread the rumour that Section 18 – outpost of bourgeois and merchants – had proposed to disarm 'les ouvriers'.[3] But one would be unwise to ascribe too much to social and economic causes; for other Sections – 7, 16, for instance, not at all affluent – did not share Section 11's spirit of resistance.

[1] British Museum, F655(5). See also F656(11), *Pétition de la Section Onze de Marseille.*
[2] ABR, L1996; L2006, 1 Aug. 1793.
[3] ABR, L2000, Section 18, 5 June 1793.

Nor must the rôle of individual members in swaying a Section be underestimated. Geographical considerations may have played a part; for the massive church of Les Prêcheurs, in the midst of a labyrinth of narrow streets, and on the side of the town nearest to the approaching republican army, offered an ideal fastness from which to defy the last desperate offensive of the sectionaries. Moreover, once the standard of rebellion had been raised, the patriots of Section 11 (perhaps only a small minority) were joined by others, first from neighbouring districts and then from further afield, to the number of several thousand according to one estimate.

Thus Section 11 assembled its company of the National Guard in defiance of the majority of the other Sections – though Sections 9, 12, 13 and 14 rallied to the demand that the Constitution should be accepted and the town delivered to Carteaux. The Sections loyal to the General Committee and the Municipality attacked those which had rallied to Section 11 and, for a time, fired mortar bombs into the church of Les Prêcheurs in which the patriots took refuge. Some twenty people of one side or the other were said to have been killed.[1] On the evening of the 24th, however, Villeneuve arrived from the Departmental Army to tell Marseilles that he had been routed at Septèmes, just to the north of the city. The leading sectionaries abandoned Marseilles and fled to Toulon.

*   *   *

There is little doubt that *in extremis* the Sections of Marseilles, with the exception of Section 11 and its allies, had preferred to have recourse to the royalists and the enemies of the Republic rather than concede defeat at the hands of the Jacobins.

In the eyes of the victorious Montagnards, this merely aggravated their crimes.

---

[1] For the confused chronology of these events, see *Moniteur*, xvii, p. 632, No. 256 of 13 Sept.; Convention of 11 Sept. 1793: *Précis des événements qui ont eu lieu à Marseille, les 23 et 24 août*; A. Nat., D XLII 4, Proclamation of Admiral Hood, 23 August 1793: see also Jean-Joseph-André Abeille, *Notes et pièces officielles relatives aux événements de Marseille et de Toulon en 1793* (Paris, 1815).

CHAPTER SIX

Marseilles under the Montagnards

(a) BACKGROUND TO REPRESSION

Carteaux entered Marseilles on 25 August.[1] Immediately the work of establishing *le gouvernement révolutionnaire* began, under the control of the *Représentants* who had accompanied the army.[2] Many of the people who had controlled the destiny of Marseilles in the last few months had fled to Toulon; others were in hiding in the city or its neighbourhood. The patriots of Marseilles were released from prison. An effort was made to restore the situation which had existed before the sectionary revolt and to use this situation as a base on which to build the edifice of the revolutionary government. One of the most important organs of this government was the Revolutionary Tribunal, which was the principal instrument for the Jacobins' attempt to cut out from the life of Marseilles and the department the cancer of federalism.

[1] Most of the details in this chapter are taken, as far as printed sources are concerned, from A. Aulard, *Recueil des actes du Comité de salut public* (Paris, 1899–1951). In the dispatches from Marseilles and Toulon, the essentials of the narrative may be followed. Edmond Poupé, *Lettres de Barras et de Fréron en mission dans le Midi* (Draguignan, 1910) is also invaluable. The registers of the deliberations of the administrations provide the backbone of the documentary evidence. The documents of the Club of Marseilles have not been preserved *in extenso*.

[2] Antoine-Louis Albitte, Christophe Saliceti, André Pomme (dit l'Américain), Joseph-Christophe Charbonnier, Pierre-Claude Nioche, Jean-François Escudier and Thomas-Antoine Gasparin, as well as Barras and Fréron, were all active in Marseilles in late August and September. The presence of some of these deputies – of Nioche and Escudier (who accompanied Carteaux) and of Charbonnier (sent to the Bouches-du-Rhône on 7 September) is known primarily because they signed various *arrêtés* in company with their more prominent (or disputatious) colleagues. For most of them therefore the evidence is too fragmentary to provide coherent pictures of their characters and policies.

The release of the patriots, the restoration of the Club and the former Jacobin Administrations (elected in the autumn of 1792),[1] the publication of decrees passed since 31 May 1793, the acceptance by Marseilles of the Montagnard Constitution,[2] the establishment of the Revolutionary Tribunal,[3] a general disarmament,[4] the purging of the National Guard, the levying of men to march to recapture Toulon from the federalists and the British and Spanish,[5] the enforcement of the law of 23 August on conscription,[6] two levies, each of four million *livres*, on the trading community of Marseilles[7] – all these acts marked a powerful effort by the *Représentants* and the agents of the Committees of the Convention to weld the fortunes of Marseilles to those of the Republic as a whole. Many of those who had taken the oath against the Convention retracted it soon after the arrival of Carteaux.[8] The acceptance of the Constitution saw attempts to draw a veil over past events, to pretend that they had never occurred; but it also expressed the hope of many Marseillais that their time of troubles was over and that the Convention would thereby be persuaded to be lenient in its punishment of those who had rebelled against it. 'Cette acceptation a été le baptême républicain d'une ville qui s'était souillée du crime de fédéralisme'.[9] Marseilles (Montagnard Marseilles, that is), torn between pride in her past services to the Revolution and shame at recent crimes, entered a period in which she alternately exalted and humiliated herself, a period moreover in which, because of the presence of the

[1] ABR, L3012, *arrêté* of Saliceti, Albitte and Gasparin, 26 Aug. 1793.

[2] ABR, L944, District Admin., 2 Sept. 1793; A. Nat. F I^cIII B.-du-Rh. 8, address of Municipality, to the Convention, 19 Sept. 1793.

[3] See below, pp. 143 ff.

[4] A. Comm., *Affiches*, 28 Aug. 1793, municipal proclamation.

[5] ABR, L120, *arrêté* of Albitte, Gasparin, Saliceti, 31 Aug. 1793, etc. The register L120 contains the majority of surviving *arrêtés* of the *Représentants*. Also L3012, L3013, L3109-L3111, L3127, etc.

[6] ABR, L120, *arrêté* of Fréron, Barras, 28 *vendémiaire* II (19 Oct. 1793).

[7] A. Comm., *Affiches*, 29 Aug. 1793, *Avis de la Municipalité aux commerçants*: also 2G31 and 2G32.

[8] ABR, L47, Register of Deliberations of Dept. Admin., 28 Aug. 1793, etc.

[9] See ABR, L944, District Administration, 2 Sept. 1793. A. Nat., F I^cIII B.-du-Rh. 8 for the address of the Municipality to the Convention, 17 Sept. 1793, from which this quotation is taken.

Représentants[1] within her walls, she was no longer mistress of her own destiny.

The *Représentants* had to learn whom they could trust and who had been contaminated by participation in recent events. They recognised that Marseilles had always contained some patriots – as did the Committee of Public Safety, which sent agents to point out these men. They recognised that many Marseillais had been misled and so they rearmed the patriots and paid indemnities to those who had suffered for the Montagnard cause. These patriots were needed against Toulon.[2]

The patriots of Marseilles took advantage of this attitude of the *Représentants* and a proclamation of the Municipality stated that Marseilles as a whole had been misled.[3] The patriots who had been imprisoned by the federalists demanded consideration from the *Conventionnels* – and a more than routine part in the running of their town's affairs. Ricord *fils* stressed Section 11's rôle in preparing the way for the final victory of Carteaux: he referred to the townspeople as 'trompés' and demanded the rigorous punishment of those – the rich – responsible for misleading them.[4] The patriots wished to prove to France that some Marseillais had always upheld their city's reputation for revolutionary zeal and that Marseilles as a whole was uncontaminated by the disease of federalism and could resume its place as the leader of the Revolution in the Midi. 'Marseille régénérée' was their slogan and ideal – and they wished to attain this ideal without outside direction. To provide their city with a task to rekindle its ardour, the picture of Toulon in the hands of the British was evoked. This succeeded in bolstering

[1] Some of whom were strangers to Marseilles – if not to the Midi as a whole – Albitte from the Seine-Inférieure, Nioche from the Indre; Pomme, although originally from Arles, had spent ten years in America and represented La Guyane; others, however, came from the neighbouring department of the Var – Escudier, Charbonnier, and Barras – while Saliceti came from Corsica; Gasparin was a member of the deputation of the Bouches-du-Rhône, but he was plagued with ill-health and died at his home at Orange on 11 Nov. 1793. Later, Jean-François Ricord, representing the Var, and Augustin Robespierre, deputy of Paris, likewise seemed to pay more attention to the admittedly more pressing task of reducing Toulon than to pacifying Marseilles.

[2] Aulard, VI 180; ABR, L79, Dept. Admin., 11 Sept. and 4 Oct. 1793, etc.
[3] A. Comm., *Affiches*, 28 Aug. 1793.
[4] ABR, L47, Dept. Admin., 29 Aug. 1793.

Marseilles' sense of revolutionary superiority and, once more, Marseilles was summoned to bring its neighbours up to its own elevated revolutionary standards – Toulon was now what Aix, Arles and Avignon had once been.

At the Convention, the patriots and patriotism of Marseilles found their champions. On 17 *fructidor* I (3 Sept. 1793) Granet the *Conventionnel* pleaded that Barère should expedite his report on Section 11, 'pourqu'enfin justice soit rendue à cette minorité imposante'. Granet attacked the 'unjust anger' of Barras and Fréron, 'qui ont englobé dans leurs mesures outrées l'innocent avec le coupable'.[1] The entrance of Barras and Fréron on the scene led to more acrimonious relations between the various *Représentants* and the Jacobins of Marseilles.

Barras and Fréron were at Marseilles from 3 to 6 September, from 12 October to 3 November, and from 19 November till 10 December and for about a month after 12 January 1794. However they were mainly concerned with the Alpes-Maritimes and the Var but especially with Toulon.[2]

Whereas Barras and Fréron alleged that Marseilles, if left to itself, would admit the British fleet,[3] Albitte wrote that republican laws were beginning to command respect and patriotism was reviving;[4] he counselled more moderation in the execution of decrees against suspects – if all the guilty were punished, three quarters of the population would disappear; for almost all citizens had, from fear or error or weakness, played a rôle in the federalist revolt. He suggested an amnesty in favour of the weak and the misled; for, he said, repression of the ringleaders was not incompatible with pacification and reconciliation for the bulk of the Marseillais.[5] The Committee of Public Safety agreed

[1] A. Nat., AF II 90⁶⁶⁶.

[2] Poupé. The *Introduction* gives an account of the movements of Barras and Fréron, who were occupied in the Basses- and Hautes-Alpes and the Var since being sent from the Convention on 9 Mar. 1793. The *amour-propre* of these two deputies, making them demand exclusive credit for any improvement in the situation in the Midi, soon led them into conflict with their colleagues. Anyway, there were far too many *Représentants* at Marseilles, with inadequately defined powers, for harmony to prevail among them.

[3] Aulard, VI 183. Barras and Fréron at Cotignac (in the Var), 29 Aug. 1793; Aulard, VI, p. 320, Barras from Marseilles, 6 Sept. 1793.

[4] Aulard, VI 393–4. Albitte from Marseilles, 9 Sept. 1793.

[5] Aulard, VI 456. Albitte from Marseilles, 12 Sept. 1793.

that 'l'homme qui n'a été qu'égaré' should not be confounded with the 'scélérats'.[1]

Barras and Fréron, however, emphasised that 'LA TERREUR EST A L'ORDRE DU JOUR'.[2] The two *Représentants* threw themselves with great energy into their task – 'sauver Marseille et raser Toulon' – and soon the revolutionary laws received vigorous enforcement.[3] Arsenals and workshops were organised for war production, all manner of workers requisitioned, some drafted towards Toulon, others employed in destroying the buildings where the Sections had met; iron and lead and copper was stripped from churches and châteaux; the ashes of the comtes de Provence thrown into the common cemetery; dungeons and castles demolished; shirts requisitioned from rich citizens and goods taken from the stocks of condemned merchants to satisfy the needs of the *Représentants*, their wives and retinues; naval construction was organised; theatrical representations patronised; gambling suppressed. Decrees were passed against prostitution – though the Municipality softened that of Barras and Fréron by making, in this sphere as in the field of more overtly political crimes, a distinction between those 'plus faibles peut-être que coupables' who sinned momentarily and the more persevering offenders.[4] A census was undertaken to facilitate the distribution of food. A festival marked the final overthrow of feudalism by burning remaining feudal titles. Money was distributed to patriots who had suffered under the sectionaries.[5] Attempts were made to enforce payment by the rich of the tax of 3 September 1793, steeply progressive in its incidence.[6]

However, dissension appeared among the *Représentants*, with Barras and Fréron attacking Albitte for his 'invincible répugnance pour les grandes mesures'. Fréron implied that Albitte let the occasion for thorough repression escape when Carteaux

[1] Aulard, VI 458, Committee of Public Safety, n.d.

[2] Aulard, VII 404, note 1, *arrêté* of Barras and Fréron, Marseilles, 12 Oct. 1793.

[3] See especially Poupé, passim.

[4] See H. Mireur, *La Prostitution à Marseille* (Marseilles, 1882).

[5] ABR, L120, *arrêté* of Barras, Fréron, Servière, Pomme (14 Oct. 1793): the rich were to pay for provisional monetary help to patriots.

[6] A. Comm., *Affiches*, municipal proclamation, 12 *brumaire* II (2 Nov. 1793).

entered Marseilles – and promised that he would not do the same when Toulon fell.[1] In particular, Albitte let the merchants escape. 'Il a toujours dit alors qu'il ne fallait pas rendre la révolution odieuse.' 'Le fédéralisme n'est qu'endormi', wrote Fréron.[2]

On 14 *brumaire* II (4 Nov. 1793) the Convention decreed Marseilles in a state of siege and charged the *Représentants* with preventing the aristocrats – even in the guise of clubists – from usurping the powers of the Convention and from reviving federalism.[3]

A General Assembly of over seventy clubs from the Midi, which had been formed at Valence in September, had transferred its activities to Marseilles and aroused, among the delegates of the Convention, the most lively apprehensions of a new outbreak of federalism. Its purpose was to hasten the enforcement of revolutionary measures throughout the Midi and to give the effort against Toulon all possible support.[4] This annoyed the *Représentants* who considered that they alone had the right to initiate policy in the areas under their authority. The clubs enjoyed a prominent position in the structure of revolutionary government; but they tended to abuse this position by unruly actions; and, though the clubists of Marseilles did co-operate with the *Représentants*, some of the General Assembly's deliberations caused disquiet. Thus envoys were to be sent to Paris by the Assembly to demand 'de grandes mesures' to consummate the victory of freedom in the Midi – a mission which might seem to suggest a certain inadequacy on the part of the *Représentants*. The Assembly sent envoys to the army before Toulon to enquire about the condition and morale of the troops and the patriotism of the generals. Though the *Représentants* authorised such measures it was, no doubt, to judge from their dispatches, *à contre-cœur*. Moreover, the General Assembly voted to send deputies to the Drôme, the Vaucluse

---

[1] Poupé, p. 47, letter to Bayle and Granet, 23 *brumaire* II (13 Nov. 1793).

[2] Aulard, VII 532 ff., Fréron and Barras, from Marseilles, 20 Oct. 1793.

[3] Aulard, VIII 222, Committee of Public Safety, 14 *brumaire* II (4 Nov. 1793).

[4] See *Moniteur*, XVIII 391, No. 52 of 22 *brumaire* II (12 Nov. 1793), Jacobin Club session, 19 *brumaire* II (9 Nov. 1793), and ABR, L2076, *Précis des opérations des Sociétés populaires ... à Marseille*, an incomplete *compte rendu* of the debates of the General Assembly of the Clubs of the Midi.

and the Hautes- and Basses-Alpes, and it invited the Convention to authorise each year the clubs of each department to
appoint a committee to watch over the actions of the departmental authorities. The Convention was to authorise the
sending of one member of each club to annual general assemblies of the clubs of France to be held two months after the
convocation of each legislative assembly. This was obviously
designed to bring pressure to bear on the legislators. The clubs'
levy of an *armée révolutionnaire* – the *Légion de la Montagne*, about
2200 strong,[1] – also caused much friction with Barras and
Fréron, who tried to withhold their authorisation for as long as
possible. On matters of food supply, the clubs took a radical
line, at least in comparison with indigenous Marseilles standards
in this question. They criticised the Convention for failing to
produce a 'general law', and for relying on palliatives, laws of
circumstance. In time of crisis, French land and industry were
to be 'd'immenses manufactures nationales, dont la nation est
usufruitière et dont les propriétaires ne sont que des agents'.
The price of bread was to be fixed in proportion to wages. They
looked forward to the effects which the laws of inheritance
would have in dividing up landed property, thus affording land
to the poorer rural classes: but, in short-term emergencies,
revenues were to be 'mis en communauté', and the revenue of
the rich was to subsidise the bread of the *journaliers*, or wage-
earners.[2] Though the exceptional nature of these plans was
underlined, their radical and comprehensive nature makes
them unique, as far as we know, in the history of the Revolution
at Marseilles, where they seem to have aroused no great echo.
Again, however, they were part of a radical criticism of the
Convention at a time when disturbances at Paris were alarming
the deputies. It was certainly with great relief – as appears from
their correspondence – when, on 2 *frimaire* II (22 Nov. 1793),

[1] R. C. Cobb, *Les Armées révolutionnaires*, 2 vols. (Paris, 1961–3) pp. 52–3
and 232–3.
[2] Certainly, the fragmentary nature of the evidence here makes it
difficult to assess the real significance of these projects. See A. Comm.,
2114, for the most explicit criticism of 'toutes les assemblées nationales' on
the question of food supplies. Also A. Cochin and C. Charpentier, *Les
Actes du gouvernement révolutionnaire*, 3 vols. (Paris, 1920–35) I 244, and D.
Guérin, *La Lutte des classes sous la Première République, 1793–1799*, 2nd ed.
(Paris, 1968) I 187.

Barras and Fréron were at last able to sign the act of dissolution of the General Assembly.

On 14 October, Pomme had denounced the agitators of Marseilles – 'L'intrigue y prend le masque du patriotisme . . . le fédéralisme n'est qu'à demi vaincu, il est prêt à se lever avec plus de force'. The administrators of Marseilles 'paraissent toujours vouloir se soustraire à l'action qui doit partir du centre du gouvernement'.[1] Moreover, a letter of 16 October to the Committee of Public Safety attacked the 'excessive patriotism' which, making the 'Reign of Liberty' as hateful as the 'Rule of Despotism', had already given rise to the federalist revolt. The author of this letter, one Cazal, demanded strict control by the deputies of the Convention, and denounced three leaders of the Club – Chompré, Ricord *fils* and Maillet *cadet* – as men 'sans mœurs' who terrorised the city.[2]

In mid-*frimaire* II (early December 1793), came a trial of strength between the Jacobins of Marseilles and the *Représentants*, who had proclaimed Marseilles in a state of siege in order to strengthen their control over the forces of public order in the city (13 *frimaire* II; 3 Dec. 1793). A proclamation of Barras, Fréron, Ricord and Robespierre *jeune* denounced those who attacked the authority of the Convention and its agents – 'On ne veut voir que Marseille dans toute la République'. Because the Municipality had resisted their orders to send two battalions of *sans-culottes* to Toulon and had tried to stir up the people by making a sudden reduction in the price of bread (though food supplies were now the responsibility of the military authorities), it was replaced by a *Commission municipale* nominated by the *Représentants* and including an important complement of non-Marseillais.[3]

In a letter to Moïse Bayle,[4] Barras said that the so-called

[1] A. Nat., AF II 185¹⁵²⁰, Pomme *l'Américain*, from Marseilles, 14 Oct. 1793. He left Marseilles a month later, having been sent to the Midi on 6 Aug. 1793.

[2] A. Nat., AF II 58⁴²⁷, Cazal to the Committee of Public Safety, 16 Oct. 1793.

[3] ABR, L1210 ᵇⁱˢ, *Journal Républicain de Marseille*, No. 30 of 16 *frimaire* II (6 Dec. 1793), and No. 32 of 20 *frimaire* II (10 Dec. 1793), and A. Nat., AF II 90⁶⁶³, *arrêté* of Fréron, Barras, Robespierre *jeune*, and Ricord at Marseilles, 15 *frimaire* II (5 Dec. 1793).

[4] Poupé, pp. 55 ff., Barras to Moïse Bayle, 14 *frimaire* II (4 Dec. 1793).

patriots had used the declaration of the state of siege as a pretext to impose their will on the delegates of the Convention, had tried to raise the port workers and to gain support from the peasants of the *terroir*. The Club humiliated the military commander who enforced the declaration and the Municipality resisted the orders of the *Représentants*. These were acts of federalism, more serious in that they had delayed the departure of the proconsuls for the siege of Toulon.

The affairs of Marseilles were debated in the Convention. The *Représentants* wrote of the perfidy of the Marseillais and accused them of wishing to resurrect federalism by their opposition to the agents of the Convention. 'On parle de République une et indivisible et le fédéralisme est enraciné dans les cœurs'.[1] On 22 *frimaire* II (12 Dec. 1793), Barère made a report on the situation at Marseilles. Marseilles, he said, showed a greater love of independence than of liberty; only the deeds of Section 11 showed that there had been patriots there during the federalist revolt. The 'marche fédéraliste' of an assembly of clubs had forced the Convention to declare the city in a state of siege. In approving Barère's report, the Convention charged its deputies at Marseilles to arrest all those who disobeyed their orders.[2]

Marseilles was therefore once more on trial. Fréron wrote to Bayle that the city had never been able to tolerate a superior authority – the 'intrigants' were attacking the *Représentants* as 'modérés' but any attempt to restrain the extremists of the clubs would be denounced as despotic. He accused the clubists of trying to massacre all the prisoners and the *Représentants*

---

[1] *Moniteur*, xviii, 647, Convention, 22 *frimaire* II (12 Dec. 1793). Written at Marseilles by Barras, Fréron, Robespierre *jeune* and Ricord, 14 *frimaire* II (4 Dec. 1793). The two latter deputies, Augustin Robespierre, deputy of Paris, and Jean-François Ricord, ex-mayor of Grasse and deputy of the Var, were sent by a decree of 15 and 19 July 1793 to the Army of Italy. Like most of the other deputies in Provence, they were principally occupied with Toulon, staying at Marseilles for very short periods, often showing little appreciation of the situation in the civil port. Ricord spent much of his time at Nice, and also had gone to Lyons to get men for the army against Toulon. Ricord was especially bitter in his denunciations of the Marseillais, who, in return, accused him of surrounding himself with aristocrats, etc. Later implicated in the Babeuf and Malet conspiracies.

[2] AF II 91⁶⁶⁸, *Rapport au nom du Comité de salut public par B. Barère*.

themselves. The patriots, he said, who because of their imprisonment under the Sections had won a hold over the Marseillais, committed many arbitrary acts, indiscriminate arrests, attempted massacres, sale of *certificats de civisme*, abuses in the management of *biens nationaux* and so on. Maillet *cadet* was denounced for leading the Club's resistance to the *Représentants*, and Marseilles was denounced for its 'esprit d'égoïsme, d'intérêt, de cupidité, de fédéralisme, d'isolement, de domination. . . .' Fréron wished to get rid of clubists like Isoard, Maillet *cadet* and Joseph Giraud – who were in the Revolution for their own profit.[1]

In the absence of records of the Club, it is impossible to know whether the detailed accusations of Fréron and his colleagues were accurate. Both sides, the local Jacobins and the *Représentants*, used any and every accusation, however stereotyped, against their opponents, because they clashed on the fundamental problem of who was to control the revolutionary government at Marseilles. Barras and Fréron wanted to win a reputation for being stern, energetic and just; and convinced that, had they been in control of Marseilles from the end of August, that city would have given no more trouble, they darkened the Marseillais in order to highlight their own actions as 'sauveurs du Midi'. The local patriots, proud to have suffered in the cause of the Revolution, were equally head-strong and demanded control of their city's destiny; but the agents of the central government – a centralising government which was stifling all initiative from below – were unsympathetic to their demands.

'Marseille est à jamais incurable', said Fréron in justifying two important measures taken by himself, Barras, Saliceti and Ricord.[2] One *arrêté*, recalling that Marseilles was the first town of the Midi to have rebelled against the Convention and had recently rebelled once more, decreed that the city should be called, provisionally, 'Sans Nom': and that the haunts of the

---

[1] Poupé, pp. 58 ff., Barras to Moïse Bayle, from Ollioules (in the Var), 20 *frimaire* II (10 Dec. 1793); pp. 61 ff., Fréron to Moïse Bayle, from Marseilles, 22 *frimaire* II (12 Dec. 1793); pp. 66 ff., Fréron to Moïse Bayle, from Marseilles, 22 *frimaire* II (12 Dec. 1793).

[2] See Poupé, pp. 120 ff., Fréron to Moïse Bayle, from Toulon, 16 *nivôse* II (5 Jan. 1794).

federalist Sections should be demolished.[1] Another *arrêté*, likewise of 17 *nivôse* II (6 Jan. 1794), quashed the Revolutionary Tribunal of Marseilles for alleged judicial irregularities in dealing with those implicated in the federalist revolt, in particular for allowing the richest merchants to go free, even though their wealth had sustained the Sections.[2] Already, in fact on 22 *frimaire* II (12 Dec. 1793), Fréron, in accusing the clubists of projecting a prison massacre, underlined the fact that the prisons were full of cobblers and journeymen, while the 'big boars' had been released 'parce qu'apparemment ils avaient financé'.[3] Fréron particularly lamented the release of Payan and Samatan – freed by the Municipality – on the pretext that they alone, by virtue of their commercial relations with Africa and the Levant, could furnish the city with corn. The president and public prosecutor of the Revolutionary Tribunal – Maillet *cadet* and Joseph Giraud – were arrested and sent before the Revolutionary Tribunal of Paris. Their Tribunal was replaced by a Military Commission, whose judges, nominated by the *Représentants*, were not Marseillais: the Commission's president was Leroi *dit* Brutus, a Parisian. Within a few weeks Fréron was able to write exultantly that both Samatan and Payan had been executed and that more merchants were to suffer the same fate the next day.

> C'est à eux que nous nous attachons, car ce sont là les véritables auteurs de la rébellion du Midi: mais c'était à eux qu'on avait résolu à épargner.[4]

Fréron had already confessed that he would like to see Maillet and Giraud – and other prominent clubists – sent away from Marseilles.[5] But now the disease went deeper: Marseilles had infected the whole Midi, was responsible for the revolt of Lyons and Bordeaux and the treason of Toulon. Now Fréron stated:

---

[1] A. Nat., AF II 90⁶⁶³, *arrêté* of Barras, Fréron, Saliceti, Ricord at Toulon, 17 *nivôse* II (6 Jan. 1794).

[2] A. Nat., AF II 90⁶⁶³, *arrêté* of Barras, Fréron, Saliceti, Ricord at Toulon, 17 *nivôse* II (6 Jan. 1794). For these 'judicial' allegations, see below, pp. 324–9.

[3] Poupé, pp. 69 ff., Fréron to Moïse Bayle.

[4] Poupé, p. 148, Fréron to Bayle, 6 *pluviôse* II (7 Jan. 1794).

[5] Poupé, pp. 66 ff., Fréron to Moïse Bayle from Marseilles, 22 *frimaire* II (12 Dec. 1793).

Je crois que Marseille est incurable à jamais, à moins d'une
déportation de tous les habitants et une transfusion des
hommes du Nord. . . .[1]

The Committee of Public Safety, in a letter of 4 *pluviôse* II
(23 Jan. 1794), while agreeing with the aims of Barras and
Fréron, who were now in sole control at Marseilles, expressed
reservations as to their specific acts, advising that the name of
Marseilles should be retained, for it recalled the past services of
that city to the Revolution. This letter was in a certain sense an
apology for Marseilles, recalling the 10 August, Section 11 and
the Marseillais who had fought at Toulon.[2] In an accompanying
note, the Committee wrote that 'c'est la masse à Marseille qui
est patriote; lors de la contre-révolution elle n'était qu'égarée.'[3]
Maignet, sent on a mission to the Vaucluse and the Bouches-du-
Rhône, was given the task of persuading Barras and Fréron to
comply with the advice of the Committee.[4]

Barras and Fréron stood fast and their comments on the
Marseillais became more scathing:

Marseille est la cause originelle, primordiale de presque tous
les maux intérieurs qui ont affligé la patrie. . . . Marseille

[1] Poupé, pp. 120 ff., Fréron to Moïse Bayle, from Toulon, 16 *nivôse* II
(5 Jan. 1794).
[2] Aulard, x 400, Committee of Public Safety, to Barras and Fréron, 4
pluviôse II (5 Jan. 1794).
[3] Bibliothèque Municipale of Clermont-Ferrand, MS. 357. (Committee
of Public Safety to Maignet, n.d.).
[4] Aulard, x 517, Committee of Public Safety, to Maignet, 10 *pluviôse* II
(29 Jan. 1794). Étienne-Christophe Maignet, native and deputy of the
Puy-de-Dôme; member of the Legislative Assembly and Convention;
after a mission to the Moselle, was on 21 August added to the *Représentants*
accompanying the Army of the Alps against Lyons, where he pursued a
fairly moderate policy. A decree of 9 *nivôse* II (29 Dec. 1793) sent him to
organise revolutionary government in the Bouches-du-Rhône and the
Vaucluse. At Marseilles, had eight secretaries in his house engaged in
copying his numerous *arrêtés* and letters; organised bread-rationing in
Marseilles in the dark days of late *pluviôse*-early *ventôse*. Faithful servant of
Robespierre (publishing 'decrees of *ventôse*'); enthusiastic towards religion
of the Supreme Being); concerned with purging administrations (cleaning
up sale of *biens nationaux*, arrest of notorious ultra-terrorist Jourdan Coupe-
Tête), took his principles to excess in the Vaucluse; but at Marseilles
showed good sense and sobriety. Did not indulge in vainglorious declamations. Above all, demanded information before he took important decisions.

courbera sa tête orgueilleuse sous le niveau de la Loi ou elle disparaîtra du sol de la République.[1]

In a letter of 6 *pluviôse* II (25 Jan. 1794) Fréron complained to Bayle that Laurent Granet had written to his brother, the *Conventionnel*, to complain of the *arrêté* which deprived Marseilles of its name and that agitators of the Club had gone to Paris to intrigue against them.[2] Barras, who had received the letter asking the *Représentants* to modify their *arrêté* of 17 *nivôse*, wrote to Bayle upbraiding him for intervening on behalf of Marseilles.[3] Barras and Fréron then wrote to the Committee of Public Safety insisting that it was Marseilles which had begun the counter-revolution of the Midi. They said that

l'importance que l'on mit à conserver le nom de Marseille serait peut-être la raison la plus puissante pour le changer. Le Marseillais, par sa nature, se regarde comme un peuple à part. La situation géographique, les montagnes, les fleuves qui le séparent du reste de la France, son langage particulier, tout alimente cette opinion fédéraliste . . . ils voudraient des lois pour eux seuls; ils ne voient que Marseille; Marseille est leur patrie. La France n'est rien.

Marseilles was responsible for the treason of Toulon. It was said that the bulk of the Marseillais were patriot but only bad faith could disguise the fact that the warehouse-porters, sailors and workers in the port were just as 'egoist' and aristocratic as the merchants themselves.[4]

However, Marseilles had found its champions. Moïse Bayle sprang to the defence of his adopted town and decried the *arrêté* which deprived Marseilles of its name – 'Peut-on envélopper dans la même proscription le patriote avec l'aristocrate?' He revealed that he had told the Committee of Public Safety of his opposition to the *arrêté* and had prevailed upon it to send

---

[1] A. Nat., AF II 90⁶⁶², proclamation of Barras and Fréron, Marseilles, 3 *pluviôse* II (22 Jan. 1794).

[2] Poupé, pp. 144 ff., Fréron to Moïse Bayle, from Sans Nom, 6 *pluviôse* II (25 Jan. 1794).

[3] Poupé, p. 151, Barras to Moïse Bayle, from Fox-Amphoux in the Var, 13 *pluviôse* II (1 Feb. 1794).

[4] Poupé, pp. 154 ff., Barras and Fréron to Committee of Public Safety, from Marseilles, 14 *pluviôse* II (2 Feb. 1794).

letters advising Barras and Fréron to suspend its execution. He maintained that only the merchants, lawyers and some 'abused' citizens had been implicated in the counter-revolution. How could a city which had defied Julius Caesar, the Goths, the Constable of Bourbon, the Emperor Charles V and Louis XIV bow its head permanently under the federalists?[1]

Maignet had arrived in Marseilles. He showed the greatest possible inclination to co-operate with the local patriots and his prudence and sagacity helped enormously to calm down the acrimonious disputes which had embittered relations between the townsmen and his predecessors; for he generally sought a consensus of local patriotic opinion before coming to a well-deliberated decision.[2]

With great tact, he criticised his predecessors for wishing to punish all Marseillais indiscriminately, for humiliating Marseilles – even to the extent of being prepared to demolish the Maison Commune, where Section 18 had met. The Marseillais 'réclament la justice qui gradue les peines, qui ne les fait peser que sur la tête des vrais coupables'. He wanted the punishment of those who had openly resisted Barras and Fréron in early December, but he also asked the Convention to restore Marseilles' name so that its citizens would be put under an obligation of loyalty and gratitude to the Convention and its agents. He criticised the Military Commission for its inevitable lack of knowledge of local circumstances.[3]

The advice of Maignet was decisive; for, on 24 *pluviôse* II (12 Feb. 1794), as a result of his representations, the Convention decreed that Marseilles would keep its name.[4] For Barras and Fréron this meant the triumph of calumny and intrigue. They did not regard their humiliating defeat lightly but harboured resentment for a long time to come.

With the slogan, 'Mort aux conspirateurs, mais protection

---

[1] ABR, L2076, *Lettre de Moïse Bayle, Représentant du peuple, à son collègue Barère*, Paris, 11 *pluviôse* II (30 Jan. 1794).

[2] See, for instance, ABR, L129, his letter of 17 *pluviôse* II (5 Feb. 1794) to the Departmental Administration.

[3] See Aulard, x 762, note 3. Letter from Maignet to Fréron, 18 *pluviôse* II (6 Feb. 1794); Aulard, x 762 ff., Maignet to Committee of Public Safety, 19 *pluviôse* II (7 Feb. 1794); Aulard, xi 32 ff., Maignet to Committee of Public Safety, 21 *pluviôse* II (9 Feb. 1794).

[4] Aulard, xi 93, Convention, 24 *pluviôse* II (12 Feb. 1794).

aux patriotes. Point de confusion dans le châtiment',[1] Maignet criticised the Club for being too often the theatre of vindictive quarrels which forced law-abiding citizens to desert it; for having failed to instruct the people, and thus helping to cause the tragic events which had split Marseilles. Able to steer a satisfactory course between indulgence and extremism, Maignet, by his firmness, checked the excesses of the patriots and harnessed their energy to work with him in the service of the Revolution as a whole. Constantly at Marseilles (Barras and Fréron were more often at Toulon) he was better able to work with the patriots while his analysis of the federalist revolt further reveals how he could do this:

> Tant que la révolution n'a porté que sur ce qu'on appelait les deux premiers ordres, tant que le riche négociant a cru pouvoir remplacer le noble, le parlementaire, et dominer à son tour le peuple, on l'a vu se jeter avec empressement dans la révolution et en pousser le char avec rapidité; il se proposait bien d'en arrêter la course au moment où il verrait que ses intérêts pourraient être froissés. Mais quand il s'est aperçu que, majestueux dans sa marche, il écrasait de son poids tout ce qui s'éloignait du but où l'égalité l'appelait, on a vu ces protées mercantiles singer les talons rouges, se relever avec autant d'afféterie que nos ci-devants, nous parler de leurs propriétés avec autant de philanthropie et de bonne foi que les autres en avaient mis à nous parler de leurs privilèges. . . . Marseille, comme toutes les villes de commerce, renfermait une foule d'hommes riches. Leur luxe insultait aux mœurs et les avait corrompues; il ne faut pas s'étonner si ces hommes qui avaient en leur pouvoir d'immenses trésors ont trouvé tant de partisans, même dans la classe précieuse du peuple.[2]

The people – ignorant because of the policy of the *Ancien régime* and the failings of the Club – had been easily misled. Maignet, who had read the documents which cast light on the federalist revolt, blamed the revolt on the moneyed classes.

[1] See Aulard, XI 132 ff., Maignet to Committee of Public Safety, 25 *pluviôse* II (13 Feb. 1794).

[2] A. Nat., F⁷4435, speech of Maignet at Club of Marseilles, 1 *ventôse* II (19 Feb. 1794).

He was able to win the respect and co-operation of the patriots, whom he divested of the bulk of the blame for the counter-revolution, by his hard work in all fields of revolutionary activity and by actions which showed his concern for the welfare of the Marseillais. It was he who, in co-operation with Club and Municipality, organised rigid bread rationing and, for eight days in *ventôse*, confined the Marseillais to biscuits. He reduced the number of men in the garrison, whose soldiers had frequently insulted the townspeople, obtained the replacement of Lapoype, military commander, for having failed to stop his soldiers' insolence,[1] and rejected a plan of Bonaparte to rebuild the walls of the citadels of Louis XIV which dominated the town.[2] The restoration of Marseilles' name helped to improve the morale of its citizens. Throughout *ventôse* Maignet referred to this improvement and spoke of the good order which now reigned.[3] Maillet and Giraud, released by the Revolutionary Tribunal of Paris, returned and resumed their posts,[4] while other patriots, imprisoned by Barras and Fréron, were set free, measures of police – including disarmament – were revoked, the Maison Commune was saved[5] and a fête organised to mark the return of harmony to the city.

Thus, on 12 *germinal* II (1 Apr. 1794), Maignet felt able to leave Marseilles for Avignon, leaving the machinery of revolutionary government in the hands of the local Jacobins. His confidence received the Convention's approval when, four days later, Barère made a report which, celebrating the restoration of calm at Marseilles, expressed what he hoped would be an

---

[1] For Maignet's activities see, in the British Museum, the printed collection of his *arrêtés*, F.80* (3–5); A. Nat., F⁷4435; ABR, L120, etc. and the correspondence in the Bibliothèque Municipale of Clermont-Ferrand. For his dealings with the garrison and Lapoype see A. Nat., F⁷4435, *arrêté* of 3 *ventôse* II (21 Feb. 1794); Bib. Mun. of Clermont-Ferrand, MS. 359, Maignet to Committee of Public Safety, 7 *ventôse* II (25 Feb. 1794); Aulard, XI 545, Maignet to Committee of Public Safety, 14 *ventôse* II (4 Mar. 1794).

[2] A. Nat., F⁷4435, Maignet to Committee of Public Safety, 28 *pluviôse* II (16 Feb. 1794).

[3] Aulard, XI 406 ff., Maignet to Committee of Public Safety, 7 *ventôse* II (25 Feb. 1794); pp. 470 ff., letter of 10 *ventôse* II (28 Feb. 1794); pp. 686 ff., letter of 23 *ventôse* II (13 Mar. 1794).

[4] ABR, L1009, *arrêté* of 11 *ventôse* II (29 Feb. 1794).

[5] ABR, 100E32, *arrêté* of 13 *ventôse* II (3 Mar. 1794).

epitaph on the federalist revolt at Marseilles, by recalling the unique position of that town, which,

> Placée en face du grand canal de navigation de la République, appelée presque seule au commerce de l'ancien monde, devrait tous les jours tourner ses regards vers le centre de la France, au lieu de les porter sans cesse vers la mer et les pays étrangers. . . .
>
> Que Marseille se rattache donc invariablement aux principes d'unité et d'indivisibilité qui nous distinguent de tous les autres peuples, de toutes les autres constitutions. Ne vaut-il pas mieux d'être Français que Marseillais? Appartenir à un État immense et fertile, qu'à une plage aride? A un grand continent qu'à des mers orageuses? . . .[1]

(b) INSTRUMENTS OF REPRESSION

Thus throughout the autumn of 1793 Marseilles as a whole was on trial for federalism. Finally the attitude, held most strongly by Barras and Fréron, which saw in every Marseillais a former federalist – and probably a future one too – had been repudiated by the Convention and by Maignet. The Convention had never subscribed to the view that the Marseillais, by their very nature, were vowed to federalism. It had always – despite much discouraging evidence – preserved its faith in the patriots of Marseilles. But if it desired the recognition of the services which the patriots had rendered to the Revolution, it was likewise determined that the 'authors' of the counter-revolution which had threatened to disintegrate the Republic should be ruthlessly punished. This determination was shared by the *Représentants en mission* who came to Marseilles with the army of Carteaux.

On 26 August, Gasparin, Albitte and Saliceti decreed that the Criminal Tribunal of the Bouches-du-Rhône should, according to the laws of April 1793 – which attributed revolutionary jurisdiction to such tribunals – begin trying those implicated in the federalist revolt, under its new title of *Le*

[1] A. Nat., AF II 44³⁴⁶, *Rapport fait par. . . . Barère*, session of Convention, 16 *germinal* II (5 Apr. 1794).

Tribunal criminel révolutionnaire du département des Bouches-du-Rhône.[1]

Its president, Augustin Maillet *cadet*, a 36-year-old school-teacher, *maître-ès-arts*, native of the Basses-Alpes, had been an ardent patriot from the early years of the Revolution, holding office as J.P. and *notable* of the Commune of Marseilles. Elected in November 1792 president of the Criminal Tribunal, he filled this post till imprisoned by the federalists. He seems always to have taken his duties extremely seriously: when elected J.P., he shut himself away to study the legislation of the Revolution.[2] The son of a *notaire royal*, he and his brother seem to have been of very 'mediocre' wealth, living a rather austere and restricted life.[3] However he was always very conscious of his dignity as a magistrate. There is little indication that he affected exaggerated airs of 'sans-culottism': in fact, when he related how, after being elected J.P., he was besieged by 'une foule de gens de tout état' who aspired to the office of his secretary, he appears rather distant from the populace:

> tantôt c'était un doreur, tantôt un marchand d'indiennes; il n'était pas jusqu'à des artisans qui savent à peine mettre leur seing qui ne voulussent devenir greffier.'

In political matters, he was an orthodox Jacobin. His writings as a clubist show him preoccupied with the political struggle against the counter-revolution, especially against the Girondins: he does not seem to have been much preoccupied with social questions. He was sent on numerous missions — to the Army of the Midi in July 1792[4] and to Lyons in March 1793[5] – and maintained himself in the vanguard of revolutionary opinion, haranguing the *fédérés* going off to the 10 August, deploring the presence at Lyons of hordes of *émigrés* and counter-revolutionaries, attacking the *appelants* and playing a full part in preparing

---

[1] ABR, L3012, *arrêté* of 26 Aug. 1793; L3012, *arrêté* of Gasparin, Escudier and Saliceti, 29 Aug. 1793.

[2] A. Comm., 2I18, petition of the Maillet brothers to the District Tribunal.

[3] See A. Comm., 2G9, quittances for patriotic subsidy, Aug. 1789.

[4] A. Comm., 1D3, General Council of the Commune, 23 July 1792.

[5] *Jnal. Dépts. Mérid.*, LXXII and LXXIII, for his visit to Lyons in August 1792; *Jnal. Dépts. Mérid.*, CLXVI, for his mission in March 1793.

the measures of terrorism in April–May 1793 (*Comité central, Comité de défense générale*, levy of 6000 men, etc.). One of the first to see that the Sections, in attacking the Savons, were putting the Revolution on trial, he was consequently confined in prison from 18 May to 25 August.

During his period as president of the Revolutionary Tribunal, he was still active in the Club. His rôle in the events of mid-*frimaire* led to his arrest by Barras and Fréron and to the replacement of the Revolutionary Tribunal by a Military Commission. Giraud, the public prosecutor, and Maillet were sent before the Revolutionary Tribunal of Paris, which acquitted them. The testimony of several members of the Convention – including Moïse Bayle, Laurent Servière, Granet, Bernard Laurens, Escudier, Pellissier and Jean-Baptiste Leblanc – and of agents of the *pouvoir exécutif*, secured their acquittal. They were triumphantly received at the Convention, the Jacobin Club and the Cordeliers and sent back to Marseilles to resume their functions.[1]

Joseph Giraud, originally from Arles, had occupied the post of *commissaire du pouvoir exécutif* before being elected, in November 1792, public prosecutor. Like Maillet, we know little of him besides what appears in the records of the Club, where he was active in the spring of 1793, embracing, like Maillet, the most vehement of Montagnard policies – banishment or death of the Bourbons, expulsion of the *appelants*, measures of *défense générale* to be taken by the clubs of the Midi. Therefore, it was not surprising that he was arrested by the General Committee of the Sections. In *frimaire* II, Giraud, with Maillet, led the Club against the policies of the *Représentants*. His acquittal by the Revolutionary Tribunal of Paris enabled him to return to his functions at Marseilles.

Étienne Chompré, a school-teacher, occupied a less important position on the Tribunal, yet, in the early years of the Revolution as a municipal officer throughout 1790 and 1791, he had been prominent in the Revolution. He had been imprisoned during the period of Bournissac's persecution of the

---

[1] A. Nat., W329, *Tribunal révolutionnaire* of Paris, Case 545 – other witnesses included *comédiens* attached to theatres at Paris and Marseilles, and members of the *Armée révolutionnaire* of Paris. See also *Moniteur*, XIX, p. 588, No. 161 of 11 *ventôse* II (1 Mar. 1794).

patriots.[1] He had then become *greffier* of the Criminal Tribunal, until in June 1793 he was arrested by the sectionaries. Like Maillet *cadet* and Giraud, he had been active in the Club, especially in its campaign against the Rolandins. (It was his idea to send the address of 17 March 1793, demanding the recall of the *appelants*, and he was one of the clubists who wrote it.)

If we know very little of the three principal members of the Revolutionary Tribunal, we know next to nothing of the men who acted as ordinary judges – Étienne Bompard, *oratorien* and merchant who had been a member of the Departmental Administration in the winter of 1792–3 and who had opposed such measures of the Sections as the re-installation of the Popular Tribunal on 9 June and the refusal to debate the Constitution; Antoine Riquier, who for a time acted as public prosecutor in Giraud's absence, and then as his assistant and who enjoyed an unsavoury reputation as a bankrupt. Jacques-François Brogy and Michel-François Leclerc *fils*, who were among the agents of the Club so bitterly denounced by the Sections, and Mathieu Maurin and François-Joseph Rouedy are even more obscure.

The first session of the Revolutionary Tribunal took place on 28 August.[2] On 1 *pluviôse* II (20 Jan. 1794) the *arrêté* of Barras and Fréron suppressing the Tribunal was put into effect and a Criminal Tribunal was later set up at Aix. Crimes against the Revolution were to be judged by the Military Commission, staffed by judges from Paris.[3] After the acquittal of Maillet and Giraud, however, Maignet, by an *arrêté* of 23 *ventôse* II (13 Mar. 1794), restored the Revolutionary Tribunal. Maillet and Giraud were to resume their posts on their return from Paris.[4] Until the session of 21 *germinal* II (10 Apr. 1794), Bompard acted as president and Riquier as public prosecutor. From 25 *ventôse* II (15 Mar. 1794) to 5 *floréal* II (24 Apr. 1794) the

---

[1] See above, pp. 23–5.

[2] The main documents concerning the Revolutionary Tribunal are in the ABR, L3112 to L3127 – *procès-verbaux* of its sessions, lists of the accused, denunciations, justifications, etc.

[3] The surviving papers of the *Commission militaire* of Marseilles are to be found in ABR, L3128–30.

[4] ABR, L3127, *arrêté* of Maignet, 23 *ventôse* II (13 Mar. 1794).

Revolutionary Tribunal continued its near-daily sessions. On receipt of the law of 27 *germinal* II (16 Apr. 1794), ordering the transference to Paris of all prisoners charged with crimes against the Revolution, the Tribunal suspended its sessions.

In the two periods of its activity, 975 people appeared before it to undergo interrogation: of these, 97 (10 per cent) were not finally judged, but were 'renvoyé', sent back to the prisons for more information to be obtained regarding their cases. Four hundred and seventy-six (48·8 per cent) of the accused were acquitted and released; 289 (29·6 per cent) were condemned to death; 67 (6·9 per cent) were given prison sentences (including one batch of 39 soldiers); 44 (4·5 per cent) were to be detained as a precautionary measure in a *maison de réclusion* 'jusqu'à la paix'. One person was sentenced to deportation. William Castle, a sailor from Kent, was acquitted of the charge of piracy, but was interned as a prisoner of war. Some were fined even though released;[1] but apart from eleven cases, the sums were inconsiderable.

Leaving aside 61 soldiers from a wandering band judged together from 11 to 15 *frimaire* II (1–5 Dec. 1793), the birthplaces of the accused can be seen from the following table, divided according to sentences imposed:

TABLE I

Place of Birth

Sentence Imposed	Marseilles	Bouches-du-Rhône	Provence	France	Abroad	Unidentified	Totals
Death	71	138	31	37	4	1	282
Freed	124	194	71	62	10	—	461
Réclusion	13	21	5	3	2	—	44
Prison	3	21	2	1	1	—	28
P.o.W.	—	—	—	—	1	—	1
Deportation	—	—	1	—	—	—	1
Renvoi	29	35	19	10	3	1	97
Totals	240	409	129	113	21	2	914

Thus 26·3 per cent of the accused (61 soldiers excepted) were born in Marseilles; 44·7 per cent in the Bouches-du-Rhône

[1] See below, pp. 312 ff.

(excluding Marseilles);[1] 14·1 per cent in Provence,[2] exclusive of the Bouches-du-Rhône; 12·4 per cent in the non-Provençal departments of France:[3] and 2·3 per cent abroad.[4] If the 61 soldiers are added, 24·7 per cent of all the accused (975) were born in Marseilles, 42·8 per cent in the Bouches-du-Rhône, 13·9 per cent in Provence and – since most of the soldiers came from the Midi of France – 16 per cent in the French departments, while 2·4 per cent were born abroad.

Excluding the soldiers once more – they were not judged for crimes connected with the federalist revolt – whereas 30·9 per cent of all sentences were capital, 32·7 per cent of those born in the French departments and 33·7 per cent of those from the Bouches-du-Rhône were condemned to death. In fact, these latter, 44·7 per cent of those judged, received 48·9 per cent of the death sentences. This contrasts – albeit slightly – with the situation of those born in Marseilles (26·3 per cent), who received 25·2 per cent of the death sentences: similarly, with 29·6 per cent of their number condemned to death, the Marseillais were marginally below the average of all the accused. Acquittals amounted to 50·4 per cent of the Tribunal's judgements: again the Marseillais were slightly favoured – 51·7 per cent were freed, compared with only 47·4 per cent of their fellows from the department. In fact, those born in the Bouches-

---

[1] The largest contingents were from Aubagne, 60 (the town's population n 1793 was about 8000); Aix, 25 (population around 25,000); Tarascon, 39 (population 13,000); Arles, 22 (population 25,000); Éguilles, 20 (N.W. of Aix, population 2800); Martigues 17, (population 7000); Cassis, 14 (population 2000); Berre (population 1800) and Saint-Chamas (population 3270), 13 each; Roquevaire, 12 (N.E. of Marseilles, population 3080) ; Salon (population 5800) and Velaux, (W. of Aix, population 1060), 11 each. All other localities were represented by ten or fewer individuals. The population figures, rounded, are taken from ABR, L1982, census of July 1793.

[2] Thirty-one were born in the Basses-Alpes, 13 in the Hautes-Alpes, 11 in the Alpes-Maritimes, 6 in the Drôme, 40 in the Var, 27 in the Vaucluse and one person came from an unidentified locality.

[3] The largest numbers came from the following localities: from the Hérault, 13; Lyons, 9; the Gard and Paris, 9 each; the Isère, 6; the Jura, 5. Thirty-five other departments provided contingents of 3 or below, while some of the accused were described as coming from the 'former' provinces – Dauphiné, Quercy, etc.

[4] Five were born in Spain, 4 in the Italian States, 4 in the Swiss Cantons, 4 in the West Indies; one each came from Saxony, Flanders, England and Constantinople.

du-Rhône received only 42·1 per cent of the acquittals compared to 48·9 per cent of the death sentences. Sentences of prison and *réclusion*, taken together, were more severe for those born in the department than in the city.

Perhaps more revealing indications regarding the Tribunal's work are provided by figures concerning the place of domicile of the accused. These are again divided according to sentence.

TABLE 2

Sentence Imposed	Marseilles	Bouches-du-Rhône	Provence	France	Abroad	Totals
Death	116	151	11	4	—	282
Freed	235	195	19	11	1	461
Réclusion	23	20	1	—	—	44
Prison	6	21	1	—	—	28
P.o.W.	—	—	—	—	1	1
Deportation	—	1	—	—	—	1
Renvoi	57	35	3	1	1	97
Totals	437	423	35	16	3	914

Thus 47·8 per cent of the accused resided in Marseilles; 46·3 per cent in the Bouches-du-Rhône;[1] 3·8 per cent in the rest of Provence; 1·75 per cent in the rest of France. The following table shows the provenance (according to birthplace) of those resident in Marseilles and the Bouches-du-Rhône:

TABLE 3

Place of Birth

Place of Residence	Marseilles	Bouches-du-Rhône	Provence	France	Abroad	Unidentified	Totals
Marseilles	226	39	76	79	17	—	437
Bouches-du-Rhône	12	361	29	18	1	2	423

The large influx of people into Marseilles is clearly established.

As appeared from the figures regarding places of birth, it seems that Marseillais (of whatever vintage) were favoured at the expense of the residents of the department. With 47·8 per cent of those accused, they received only 41·1 per cent of the

[1] Aubagne, with 65 of the accused, provided the largest contingent: Aix followed with 39, Tarascon with 38, Arles with 27, Éguilles with 23, Berre with 18, Salon and Velaux with 15 each, Cassis and Sénas with 14, Saint-Chamas and La Ciotat with 13 each.

TABLE 4

THE AGES OF THOSE JUDGED BY THE TRIBUNAL

Age	Death	Freed	Réclusion	Prison	Sentence P.o.W.	Deportation	Renvoi	Total
−15	0	5 1·1%		1			7	5 0·6%
16–20	0	29 6·3%		2			6	37 4·1%
21–25	11 3·9%	41 8·9%	4	3			10	65 7·1%
26–30	16 5·7%	58 12·6%	5	3	1		10	92 10·1%
31–35	21 7·4%	49 10·7%	2	5			7	85 9·4%
36–40	36 12·8%	53 11·5%	4	3			11	105 11·3%
41–45	55 19·5%	48 10·4%	3	1			15	120 13·2%
46–50	38 13·5%	50 10·9%	5	4			14	109 12·0%
51–55	30 10·6%	38 8·3%	5	2			3	91 10·0%
56–60	25 8·9%	27 5·9%	4	2		1	4	61 6·7%
61–65	26 9·2%	29 6·3%	5	1			7	67 7·4%
66–70	17 6·0%	18 3·9%	5					48 5·3%
71–75	6 2·1%	12 2·6%	1					19 2·2%
76–80		3 0·7%						3 0·3%
81+	1 0·4%							1 0·1%
	282	460	43	27	1	1	94	908

death sentences but 51 per cent of the acquittals, whereas the *départementaux*, with 46·3 per cent of those judged, received 53·5 per cent of the death sentences and only 42·3 per cent of the acquittals. Correspondingly, whereas 30·9 per cent of all sentences were death sentences, only 26·5 per cent of the Marseillais were sentenced to death, the corresponding figure for the inhabitants of the Bouches-du-Rhône being 35·7 per cent. With regard to acquittals, the Tribunal was less generous to the men and women of the department – whereas 50·4 per cent of all sentences were acquittals, only 46·1 per cent of the residents of the department were freed, while 53·8 per cent of the Marseillais were acquitted. Again, prison sentences were proportionately much lighter on the Marseillais.

Within the department, there were many variations in the intensity of the repression – often having little obvious correlation with population figures, perhaps depending on the zeal of local *comités de surveillance*, or the somewhat chaotic order in which suspects were sent from the localities or extracted from the prisons. Arles, with 27 persons judged, and a population of some 25,000 had 15 persons condemned to death; Aubagne, population 8000, had 65 persons judged, of whom 15 were condemned to death. Arles had witnessed bloody struggles between revolutionaries and the aristocratic-clerical' chiffonnistes'.

Information regarding the age of each of the accused – except for the soldiers, all fairly young, and six men for whom we do not have this information – is tabulated in Table 4 and Fig. 1. From these, it appears that the Tribunal showed particular harshness towards men in the 41–45 year age group, whereas it was relatively lenient towards younger offenders. Mature office-holders formed a sizeable proportion of the former category, misled soldiers of the Departmental Army being numerous in the younger age groups.

As for the intensity of the repression, this varied considerably from day to day and from week to week. Often the figures were swollen by batches of men – such as those of the sixty-one soldiers judged on 15 *frimaire* II (5 Dec. 1793), or the group of sailors freed on 11 *germinal* II (31 Mar. 1794); the latter group included a family with children fourteen, eleven and nine years old who were 'judged' with their elders. Thus a detailed statistical account is perhaps misleading. What can be gained from a statistical analysis of the judgements is that the repression was more intense in the period after the re-installation of the Tribunal than during the earlier period.

Figs. 2 and 3, plotting death sentences and acquittals, show that, as far as numbers are concerned, the Tribunal worked at a markedly increasing tempo till the very end of its existence.

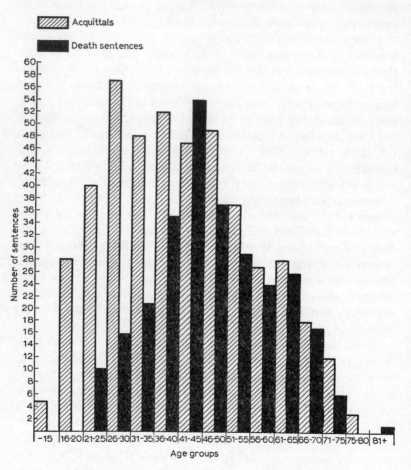

Fig. 1. The ages of those judged by the Tribunal (death sentences and acquittals)

But though the early weeks are characterised by a smaller number of judgements, this does not necessarily reflect on the zeal of the judges, for among the people condemned to death in this period were many of the most important, and articulate, sectionaries. It is during this period that the debates between president and accused are most lengthy, most thorough and most interesting. The greater intensity of the repression after the re-installation of the Tribunal may be accounted for in several different ways – until Maillet and Giraud returned from Paris, Bompard and Riquier were in charge and may have speeded up the functioning of the Tribunal; they may have been alarmed that their colleagues should have been sent to Paris because of alleged sloth. Maignet may have been influential here, though there is no indication that he did breathe down the necks of the judges; it may simply have been that the machinery of repression was working more smoothly now – the suspects had been rounded up and imprisoned, the registers of the Sections had been scrutinised for incriminating documents, denunciations had been collected, the Tribunal had established its own routine, the skill of the judges had been sharpened by experience and they perhaps thought themselves more skilful in seeing through the lame excuses of some evident sectionary. Perhaps, on the other hand, they were exhausted by their daily task and wished to get it over more summarily – though there is little evidence of this in the accounts of the interrogations. Perhaps the sessions lasted longer. When Maillet and Giraud returned, they kept up the hard work of Riquier and Bompard. As the summer approached one can detect also a certain concern as to the conditions in the overcrowded prisons.[1] Thus the

---

[1] ABR, L1726, letter of Riquier, 'adjoint à l'accusateur public', of 18 *germinal* II (7 Apr. 1794), announcing that, when the prisons of Marseilles were emptied, the Tribunal would travel around the Department. The Tribunal was to expedite its task – 'Les prisonniers y sont entassés et les devoirs de l'humanité exigent que le citoyen soit respecté jusqu'au moment de son jugement'. See L1727 for petitions complaining of the state of the prisons of Aix. But though prison conditions were no doubt horrible, medical reports were not catastrophic. Even the royalist Lautard, himself a prisoner, wrote that there was no serious disease in Sainte-Claire: in fact in the winter of 1793 the prisoners heard rumours that plague had struck the Old Town – Lautard, I, 350. Certainly the prisoners of Marseilles were not scenes of holocausts of disease, as were those at Nantes for example.

FIG. 2. The Incidence of the Repression: Death Sentences and Acquitt

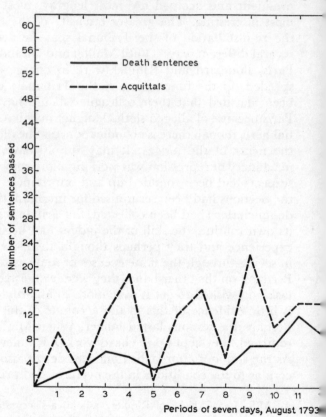

Periods of seven days, August 1793

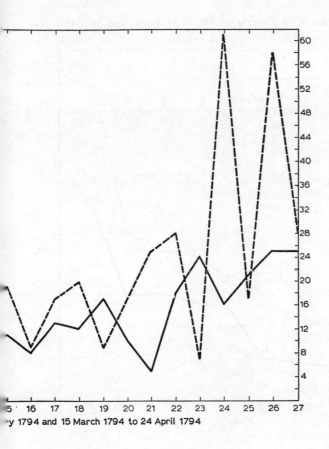

5 16 17 18 19 20 21 22 23 24 25 26 27
y 1794 and 15 March 1794 to 24 April 1794

Fig. 3. The Incidence of the Repression. Death Sentences and Acquittals (2).

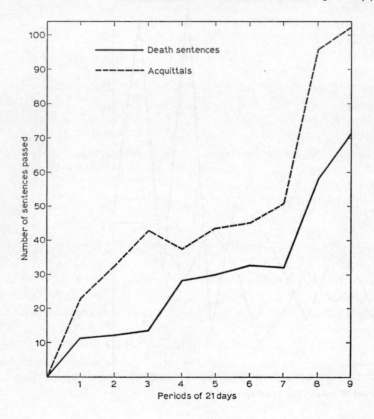

established fact that the intensity of the repression increased during *ventôse*, *germinal* and in the early days of *floréal* can be explained by a number of hypotheses – for none of which is there conclusive evidence.

Men of every social class and of every profession appeared before the Revolutionary Tribunal.[1] By far the two largest groups of people were the ninety-one who called themselves 'cultivateurs' and the ninety-three who took the title 'propriétaires'. But these groupings were very ill-defined, and indeed, as the terms 'propriétaire-cultivateur' and 'cultivateur-propriétaire' suggest, merged into each other. Also, those called 'propriétaires' were often described as 'bourgeois'; those called 'cultivateurs' were often termed 'ménagers'. Only one person who appeared before the Tribunal was called a 'paysan'. Obviously some of the men described as *propriétaires* were very rich, as can be seen from the estimates of the value of the estates of those executed after judgement of the Tribunal – estates, in many cases, both urban and rural.[2] From Gantel-Guitton, who owned most of one of the rural quarters of Marseilles,[3] to some of the more humble countrymen, the whole range of wealth was represented in the men called *propriétaires* and *cultivateurs*. There was little in common between the many young men of the countryside who had been drafted into the Departmental Army and the wealthy men whose estates dominated Saint-Chamas, Éguilles, Eyragues[4] or the outskirts of Marseilles. In the city itself, some of the *négociants* were among the most wealthy of those judged by the Tribunal.[5] The inventories of the possessions of Basile Samatan, Jean-Pierre Reynier, Laurent-François

---

[1] See Appendix, pp. 346–50.

[2] See Paul Moulin, *Département des Bouches-du-Rhône, Documents relatifs à la vente des biens nationaux*, 4 vols. (Marseilles, 1908–1911) 1 525, 557; 4 182, for the vast properties of Joseph-Louis Caussigny (*ci-devant* Valbelle), condemned to death, 21 *germinal* II (10 Apr. 1794); 2 514; 3 448, 590, for those of François Cler, 'agriculteur-propriétaire' of Saint-Chamas, condemned to death, 18 *germinal* II (7 Apr. 1794); 2 404, for those of Jean-François Olivier, 'agriculteur-propriétaire' living at Éguilles, condemned to death, 11 Nov. 1793, etc.

[3] Nicolas-Jean-Joachim Gantel-Guitton, *propriétaire* of Marseilles; Moulin, 3 115; and ABR, *Série Q*, (*Biens des émigrés et des condamnés*), 4Q204. And see below, pp. 212–14.

[4] For these 'rural bourgeois', see below, pp. 204 ff.

[5] For the merchants, see below, pp. 301 ff.

Tarteiron or Pierre Timon-David reveal a style of living of a splendour unsurpassed at Marseilles: they had superbly furnished houses in town and vast and beautiful estates in the country.[1] Thirty-three *négociants* were judged by the Tribunal: only eight of these were freed. Some of the *fabricants* – there were only sixteen of them – were quite well-off, as were the exchange brokers (*courtiers*). Lawyers, too, might be wealthy, as might *bourgeois*, but here again we have a varied category, ranging from ex-nobles of great fortunes[2] to modest *rentiers* crippled by revolutionary inflation. There were many men who belonged to the middle ranks of society – the more modest *négociants* and *hommes de loi*, the bulk of *courtiers, marchands, avoués, capitaines marins, notaires*. Lautard's description of the prisons as full of artisans[3] is given some substance by the list of the accused. Only a few people called themselves 'garçons' or 'ouvriers'. Eighty-seven women, including a former nun, were judged – sixty-two were freed: where professions (their own or their husbands') are given, they were overwhelmingly 'populaires'. Thirty priests were judged: they met with great severity; twenty-two were condemned to death.[4]

The Military Commission judged 218 people, 123 were sentenced to death, 1 person was imprisoned, 94 were fined. As Barras and Fréron had intended, in its ten sessions from 4 *pluviôse* II (23 Jan. 1794) to 19 *ventôse* II (9 Mar. 1794) it was very severe to merchants, 22 of whom were sentenced to death. Twelve *marchands* of various description likewise received the death penalty, as did 11 *propriétaires* and 5 *curés*. By contrast, no *cultivateurs* were executed after its judgements. Certainly several of the most prominent merchants of Marseilles – Jacques Seimandy, Joseph Hugues *l'aîné*, Basile Samatan and Jean Payan – were sent by it to the guillotine. At the preliminary interrogation, the president always asked about the 'fortune' of the accused. Unfortunately, the professions of those freed are not always stated; but the comments 'pauvre' and 'peu aisé'

---

[1] ABR, *Série* Q. For Samatan, 4Q236; for Reynier, 4Q231; for Tarteiron, 4Q241; for Timon-David, 4Q242.

[2] For Joseph-Marie Barrigue, of Marseilles, and others in this category, see below, pp. 208 ff.

[3] Lautard, p. 304.

[4] For the priests, see below, p. 236 ff.

occur frequently on the dossiers of the *bourgeois*, clerks, cobblers, masons, and cultivators set free. In only one aspect is the Commission's documentation more complete than that of the Tribunal: we know the Sections in which all but one of the *condamnés à mort* resided. Of 85 Marseillais, 17 lived in Section 18, in which the Bourse was situated, a Section described by Maillet *cadet* as dominated by counter-revolutionary lawyers; both categories – merchants and lawyers – were represented among the accused, but most numerous were *marchands*. The most important *négociants* came from Sections 1, 2 and 5.[1] However, because of the otherwise fragmentary nature of the surviving documents, no firm impression can be gained of the work of this Commission. It seems that the types of accusation which confronted those who appeared before it were similar to charges described more fully in the pages of the Revolutionary Tribunal.

*   *   *

Thus four hundred and twelve persons were condemned to death at Marseilles during the Terror. The city had no revolutionary tribunal during the period of the 'Great Terror' which preceded *thermidor*; and the Marseillais sent to Orange were saved by the fall of Robespierre. It is difficult to ascertain how many people were held in prison during this period – Lautard gives the figure of 1500 for the end of 1793. Writing to the Committee of Public Safety on 21 *pluviôse* II (9 Feb. 1794), Maignet confirmed Lautard's figure, but after further examination was surprised to find only 615 persons in the principal *maisons d'arrêt*.[2] G. Martinet, as a result of his studies of the Year III, estimates at 1200 the number of prisoners at Marseilles in *thermidor* (July–Aug. 1794).[3] Such figures hardly reflect the perpetual movement of prisoners – 1096 were judged by the Military Commission and Revolutionary Tribunal – but they

[1] A list of 1234 suspects – or possibly prisoners – contains 118 from Section 18; 102 from Section 6; 82 from Section 9; 80 from Section 8; 77 from Section 5; 69 from Section 1 and 64 from Section 2. A. Comm., 2143.

[2] Lautard, 1, pp. 304 ff.; for Maignet, A. Nat., F⁷4435, letters of 21 and 25 *pluviôse* II (9 and 14 Feb. 1794), to Committee of Public Safety.

[3] G. Martinet, 'La vie politique à Marseille en 1795 et 1796', *Provence historique*, tome 16, Apr.–June 1966, p. 154.

do afford indications as to the extent of the Terror's impact at Marseilles.

(c) LAWS OF REPRESSION

The grounds for the judgement of the men who appeared before the Revolutionary Tribunal – and the Military Commission – are to be found in the *Code pénal* of 25 September 1791[1] and in subsequent revolutionary legislation. These laws were read out in court as the verdicts and sentences were pronounced, in order to demonstrate to the condemned men and to the audience that the Tribunal's justice was based on legislation. Sections of the *Code pénal* stipulated that crimes involving armed conflict on behalf of France's enemies, both internal and external, were punishable by the death penalty, especially if such crimes threatened the security of the Legislative Assembly or any of its members. Later laws, in response to given situations, extended and tightened up the provisions of the *Code pénal*. The fundamental law was that of 19 March 1793, against those implicated in riots and revolts which took place during recruiting. These men were to be tried without recourse to the usual safeguards of the criminal tribunals, without juries. Those who took part in such revolts and had borne arms were to be punished by the death penalty imposed by the criminal tribunals of each department; they were to be judged within twenty-four hours. Besides priests, former nobles and *seigneurs, émigrés,* the agents and domestics of these people, and foreigners and public officials, all those men who provoked revolts, who served in them with rank or who committed murder or pillage were liable to the death penalty.[2] On 10 April, the Convention declared that those who worked for a monarchical restoration were guilty of a counter-revolutionary crime and were to be judged according to the law of 19 March.[3] By a law of 7 June 1793, anyone found guilty of

---

[1] *Loi contenant le Code pénal, Donnée à Paris, le 6 Octobre 1791 (Décret de l'Assemblée nationale du 25 Septembre 1791).* From *Procès-verbal de l'Assemblée Nationale,* vol. 72.

[2] *Procès-verbal de la Convention Nationale, Tome Huitième,* pp. 88 ff., law of 19 Mar. 1793. See also *Tome Onzième,* p. 197, law of 10 May 1793, stating that only the leaders of revolts were to be punished by death.

[3] *Procès-verbal de la Convention Nationale, Tome Neuvième,* p. 194, law of 10 Apr. 1793.

crimes not covered by the *Code pénal* or subsequent laws, and whose presence in France would constitute a danger to the Republic, was to be deported for life or for a period of years.[1] On 5 July, a further law clarified that of 19 March and defined the leaders of revolts as

> Les membres des comités de régie et administration formés, soit pour leur direction, soit pour leur vêtement, l'armement, équipement et les subsistances des révoltés, ceux qui signent les passeports, ceux qui enrôlent; seront pareillement réputés chefs des dites émeutes et révoltes, les prêtres, les ci-devant-nobles, les ci-devant seigneurs, les émigrés, les administrateurs, les officiers municipaux, les juges, les hommes de loi qui auront pris part dans les dites émeutes et révoltes; en conséquence, ils seront, comme les chefs eux-mêmes, punis de mort.[2]

This law, together with that of 19 March, was most frequently cited by the Revolutionary Tribunal.

September 1793 saw another burst of legislation concerning suspects: a law of 4 September ordered the representatives of the Convention to punish those implicated in the revolt of Marseilles,[3] while the famous law of suspects of 17 September was likewise applied to the situation in the Midi. Suspects were to be arrested and could be kept in prison even if they had been acquitted of specific accusations. By virtue of this law, the Revolutionary Tribunal was to send forty-four to 'réclusion'.[4] This law was intensified by one of 8 *ventôse* II (26 Feb. 1794), stating that people acknowledged as enemies of the Revolution were to be imprisoned till peace, then banished for life.[5]

Several laws concerned above all Marseilles – that of 19 June outlawing the judges and witnesses of the Popular Tribunal, for instance.[6]

The agents of the Convention did all they could to see that this revolutionary legislation was enforced. By an *arrêté* of

[1] *Tome Treizième*, pp. 131–2, law of 7 June 1793.
[2] *Tome Quinzième*, p. 157, law of 5 July 1793.
[3] Aulard, VI, p. 272.
[4] *Procès-verbal de la Convention, Tome Vingt et unième*, pp. 33–5, Law of Suspects, 17 Sept. 1793.
[5] *Tome Trente-deuxième*, p. 292.
[6] *Tome Quatorzième*, pp. 118–19, law of 19 June 1793.

27 August 1793, the Department was authorised by the *Repré-sentants* to arrest all persons whose principles appeared danger-ous to the consolidation of the republican system,[1] while on 24 September the Department ordered the arrest of all people publicly suspected of aristocracy and *incivisme*.[2] In *brumaire* II (Oct.–Nov. 1793) it appointed men to go through the registers of the administrative organs and send their findings to the public prosecutor.[3]

Maignet gave much attention to the rounding-up of suspects, though like Barras and Fréron and their colleagues, he did not intervene in the administration of justice, which continued fairly independently of the activity of the *Représentants* (except when they quashed the Revolutionary Tribunal). First he attacked those who agitated for an amnesty.[4] He assiduously sought – in the registers of the Sections and administrative bodies – information on the counter-revolution and demanded lists of those who had occupied offices during the rebellion.

Thus a heavy barrage of laws and *arrêtés* was directed against those implicated in the federalist revolt and the *comités de surveillance* had ample scope for their activities. Denunciations were numerous. But despite the abuses which must have occurred in this field of repression, the Revolutionary Tribunal, by its dependence upon the laws of the Convention and by the indefatigable activity of the public prosecutor in seeking out documentary proof of alleged crimes, was able, as far as can be seen from the verbatim reports of its trials, to exercise a rigorous examination of the evidence presented to it. The fact that judgement on nearly one hundred of those interrogated was postponed until more information was available regarding their alleged offences suggests a high level of thoroughness on the part of the judges. The quick dismissal of a large number of baseless allegations suggests that being designated a suspect by the *comités de surveillance* was not the equivalent of being sen-tenced to death.

---

[1] ABR, L120, *arrêté* of Saliceti, Albitte, Gasparin, Escudier; Marseilles, 27 Aug. 1793.

[2] ABR, L81, Dept. Admin., 24 Sept. 1793.

[3] ABR, L47, Dept. Admin., 4 and 18 *brumaire* II (25 Oct. and 8 Nov. 1793).

[4] A. Nat., AF II 91⁶⁶⁹, *arrêté* of Maignet, Marseilles, 21 *pluviôse* II (9 Feb. 1794).

Disquiet was, however, strong in Marseilles during this period, as arrests multiplied and more and more buildings were converted, hastily, into prisons. According to the patriots, 'aristocrats' spread rumours that every man who had ever aided the counter-revolutionaries was to be punished. These rumours were designed to 'discredit' the revolutionary government. The agents of the government were therefore to tell the people that only 'les conspirateurs notoirement connus' would be executed – for the punishment of the weak and the blind would stain the Montagne's triumph.[1] Maignet consistently upheld this view, complaining that the conspirators, in order to shield themselves, alleged that the guillotine was aimed at men who had momentarily been led astray, whereas, he pledged, only those who had persevered in their errors were to be given exemplary justice.[2]

This was undoubtedly the ideal of justice to which the Revolutionary Tribunal aspired. Only a detailed consideration of its judgements will show whether it came anywhere near realising its aspirations.

[1] ABR, L47, Dept. Admin., speech of Ricord *fils*, 15 Sept. 1793.
[2] A. Nat., AF II 9⁶⁷⁰. Proclamation of Maignet, Marseilles, 16 *ventôse* II (6 Mar. 1793), to the people of the Vaucluse.

CHAPTER SEVEN
Some Leading Sectionaries

The dossiers of some of the men who appeared before the Revolutionary Tribunal are sufficiently well-stocked to give a fairly full picture of their activities during the federalist revolt.

The proceedings in court[1] opened with the establishment of the identity of the accused; then the public prosecutor defined the alleged crimes, whereupon the president conducted an interrogation of each of the accused. During the interrogation, witnesses might be called both for the defence and for the prosecution. The Tribunal met in public, so sometimes men and women from the audience came forward to support or contradict the assertions of the accused. Sometimes also the president ordered that documents, collected by the secretary and by the public prosecutor, should be read out. This was most frequently done to prove detailed accusations but *attestations* were also read out in favour of the defendant. The committees of surveillance of Marseilles and the towns of the Bouches-du-Rhône collected much of this material and sent it to Giraud or Chompré. These documents, grouped around the minutes of each day's session, form each suspect's dossier. Étienne Chompré wrote a word-by-word account of the questions and answers, of the confrontation between confirmed Jacobin and alleged federalist. In many cases, the president quickly accepted the innocence of a defendant and passed rapidly on to the next man. In other instances, however, the Tribunal saw a real and impassioned debate between two conflicting views of the

[1] See the written verbatim accounts of the trials of the Revolutionary Tribunal, ABR, L3112 to L3119; for the few sessions for which no such accounts exist, see the printed series, L3023, L3024, L3025. This printed series sometimes gives more explicit indications as to the motives of the judges in coming to a particular verdict. There are also two bundles of letters, petitions, denunciations, etc., regarding the men who appeared before the Tribunal – L3120, L3121, (arranged by alphabetical order according to the name of the accused).

Revolution. Such cases however were rare. After the interrogation the public prosecutor summed up, the judges deliberated *à haute voix*, with the president speaking last, judgement and sentence were passed and the texts of the appropriate laws read out.

Those who had the most thorough interrogations were men who had occupied the most prominent positions in the Sections, and in the administrations dominated by the Sections, men who had taken the initiatives which had led to the federalist revolt, men who had drawn up the pamphlets justifying the Sections' policies, who had supervised the day-to-day running of the Sections' affairs. They were men who could give an articulate account of their actions and attitudes. Though their favourite line of defence was first to assert that they had not been responsible for their actions, that they had been forced or misled into counter-revolution, that they had been passive instruments of forces beyond their control, the president, seeing their signatures at the foot of the deliberations of the Sections, quickly brushed aside these reticences and subjected them to a more searching cross-examination.

Such men formed a small minority of those tried by the Revolutionary Tribunal: some fifty or sixty might be assigned – rather arbitrarily – to this category of men whose dossiers are fuller than those of their less eminent colleagues. A few case histories give a good impression of the ideas of these men, of the arguments with which they defended themselves, of the services they thought would earn them the clemency of the Tribunal and, finally, of the attitude of the Jacobins to the federalists and their acts.

One of the most important of these men was Antoine Maurin, a 42-year-old lawyer from Arles, who appeared before the Revolutionary Tribunal on 9 December 1793.[1] He was subjected to a powerful denunciation by the public prosecutor:

Maurin, ci-devant procureur général syndic du département des Bouches-du-Rhône, a fait servir ses talents, sa place, son influence à accréditer la contre-révolution. Il s'est

[1] ABR, L3114; 19, 21, 22 *frimaire* II (9, 11 and 12 Dec. 1793), Antoine Maurin. For most of this material, see the documents in his dossier, unless otherwise indicated.

montré l'appui des meneurs sectionnaires. Il s'est donné dans plusieurs circonstances pour un instigateur soufflé par les ennemis du peuple.

After having thus implied that Maurin sinned as much by weakness of character as by positive counter-revolutionary action, Giraud, in a speech which may be taken as typical of those with which the accused were confronted, went on to give details of Maurin's record as a public official:

Il a reconnu l'autorité usurpatrice du comité général. Il a fonctionné dans les assemblées générales, où se trouvaient des gens méconnus par la loi. Il a autorisé la désorganisation de toutes les autorités du département, qui étaient sous sa surveillance. Il a correspondu avec les administrations de plusieurs départements en révolte. Il n'a pas su mourir à son poste comme il avait dit en prêtant le serment ... il a reconnu les députés envoyés par les départements contre-révolutionnaires. Il a requis d'arrêter la publication des décrets de la Convention; il a requis de ne plus les expédier aux autorités subordonnées ... Il a requis la détention criminelle des représentants du peuple. Il a requis de prêter le serment de méconnaître la Convention, d'adhérer au Manifeste de rébellion marseillaise ... Il s'est montré lâche diffamateur des clubistes à qui il avait juré estime et cordialité. Sa conscience l'a troublé et ne lui a fait voir d'autre salut que la fuite.

As *procureur général syndic*, it had been Maurin's duty to explain the constitutional and legal positions regarding matters and projects debated by the Departmental Administration and he had thus held a position of great responsibility during the revolt of the Sections. Appointed by the electoral assembly of the autumn of 1792, he did not owe his position to the Sections; it was as a public official that it had been his duty to see that the laws of the Republic were made known in the Bouches-du-Rhône and were obeyed, and also to see that the proper hierarchy of administrative organs was maintained and that the decisions of the Departmental Administration were enforced. Before a decision was reached in the Departmental Administration, it was the duty of the *procureur général syndic* to summarise the arguments of previous speakers, try to reconcile them with each other, and, more importantly, with the law, before recommending a course of action for the Department to take. In many cases, therefore, resolution on his part might have been decisive in swaying the Department towards legality, towards in other words, resisting the pressure the Sections brought to bear against the legal authorities. And, as Maillet pointed out frequently, the example of administrative bodies was very important in determining the attitude of the people as a whole.

Maurin denied that he had positively supported the revolt of the Sections. He had indeed sworn the oath against the Convention, an oath which he described as 'le blasphème national qui nous fut arraché en la trop mémorable séance de Saint-Jaume et que mon cœur exécrait'. Unfortunately, however, he had retracted only after the army of Carteaux had occupied Marseilles; and so Maillet rebuked him by saying that if he had been a patriot, he would have retracted his oath immediately, as several of his colleagues had done. Maurin confessed that several of his colleagues had indeed retracted the oath next day and that, if he had not, it was because he was fearful of being persecuted for his past record of patriotism. Much of his plea regarding his past services to the Revolution was indeed true. He had been sent by Bayle and Boisset with other clubists to Aix, to investigate reports that patriots had been arrested and imprisoned there. Leaving Marseilles on 18 April 1793, they released the patriots at Aix, imprisoned the 'aristocrats' who had oppressed them, disarmed suspects and so on. It was at this time that, to punish the aristocrats of Aix, Bayle and Boisset had ordered the suppression of the town's Sections.[1]

Unfortunately for Maurin, Maillet, his one-time colleague, was not predisposed (because of his own stand against the sectionaries and his acceptance of suffering under their régime) to accept this excuse as justifying Maurin's action.

When confronted with various deliberations which he had signed – notably that of 18 June, when he demanded that the Department should not order the publication or even the mention of the decrees of the Convention – Maurin had no defence to offer but to affirm that no one in Marseilles was

[1] A. Nat., AF II 90⁶⁶⁴, *Compte rendu*. . . . of Bayle and Boisset.

unaware of the force which the Department was threatened with at that juncture and to blame some of his colleagues for pushing the Department in a counter-revolutionary direction. He explained that even if the texts of the decrees of the Department mentioned the *procureur général syndic* as having spoken, this was merely a ruse to persuade the people that the decisions of one or two men had been given the approval of men who had not in fact spoken. He appealed to Étienne Bompard, a member of the Revolutionary Tribunal who had been next to him in the Department, to testify that this was true but Bompard, no doubt aware that he too had signed various decrees which, though soon retracted, had tended towards counter-revolution, did not intervene. Anyway, Bompard had in fact protested on several occasions at the way the Sections imposed their will on an impotent Department – for instance, when the Popular Tribunal, with the connivance of the Department, had begun to judge various members of the Departmental Administration. And, moreover, he had demanded that the Constitution be read.[1] Maillet therefore asked Maurin why he had not likewise made known his views on such matters. Maurin could only reply by referring to his pusillanimity. This fear had also prevented Maurin from intervening on behalf of the imprisoned patriots for he had not had the courage to require the execution of a law ordering the transference of these prisoners from Marseilles to still-loyal Toulon, a law whose object was to save the prisoners from the Popular Tribunal. Another reason for his failure to enforce this law was explained to the Tribunal — circumstances were such at that time that it was prudent for an administrator to be on guard against false examples of the Constitution, circulated by the counter-revolutionaries of Marseilles in order to mislead the people. This excuse misfired; for Maillet observed caustically that if he had opened the Constitution, he would have found, besides the foundations of a republican régime, the preservation of the clubs. Such a constitution could not have been the work of aristocrats; and, if the people had been allowed to see it, they would have recognised measures designed for their benefit. But Maurin continued to say that he had had no chance to oppose the levying of the

---

[1] For Bompard's protests see ABR, L46, Dept. Admin., 9 June, 30 June 1793. For Maurin's rejection of the Constitution, see 2 July 1793.

Departmental Army and the closing of the Club; and when he was forced to admit that he had signed an address to the Convention calling the patriots 'brigands', he pleaded that he had done so, 'a knife at his throat'. For his part in the revolt of the Sections, he was condemned to death. The judgement made special mention of the Department's *arrêté* of 19 June, which ordered the transfer of Bô and Antiboul from Aix to the prisons of Marseilles to be held there until the deputies held at Paris were freed.

Other documents included the minutes of the assembly which first took the oath against the Convention and refused to transfer the Jacobin prisoners to Toulon, the deliberation of 2 July that the Constitution should not be published and so on. Finally an unsigned petition of 29 August 1793, written by members of the Departmental Administration to which Maurin had belonged, expressed the difficulties which had faced administrators confronted with the revolt of the Sections, underlining the hazards which would have accompanied any open defiance of the will of the Sections;

> 'Représentants,' [it pleaded] 'jugez quelle devait être notre position; nos amis livrés à leurs bourreaux, la plus affreuse perspective offerte à nos yeux, l'impossibilité de quitter un poste qui nous devenait toujours plus odieux, tel était le tableau déchirant qui frappait sans cesse nos regards.'

The petitions were perhaps exaggerated but it had required decisive resolution and courage to defy the mounting power of the Sections, especially if that involved, at the very least, losing one's position in the administration or, at the worst, being sentenced to death by the Popular Tribunal – Louis Barthélemy had been a member of the Departmental Administration yet had been condemned to death by that Tribunal. Moreover, since many of the aims of the Sections had been laudable – the preservation of order and so on – members of the Administrations were initially tempted to go along with them, hoping that they could reconcile their duty to their fellow-citizens at Marseilles with their duty to the law and the Revolution. But such a choice was never proposed to the administrators in clear-cut terms and in the confusion many would be willing to go along with the actions of their friends and colleagues in

Marseilles, rather than defy them in the name of far-off abstractions like 'the Law, the Constitution and the Revolution', abstractions which had perhaps brought them little personal satisfaction or benefit. Uncertainty as to what was really happening in Paris contributed to the difficulty of making a firm stand against the Sections.

Maurin in particular had seemed one of the most zealous servants of the Revolution in Marseilles – that is, he had been a leading member of the Jacobin Club[1] – and from this had stemmed his mission to Aix; his membership – proposed by Maillet *cadet* – of the notorious Central Committee of the Club; his membership of its Constitutional Committee; his presence, as clubist, at the meetings of 16 and 17 March which decided to set up a revolutionary tribunal; and his position as vice-president of the Club during the latter part of April.

But Maurin deplored the arbitrary acts which were frequent throughout the Bouches-du-Rhône in the early part of 1793. On 27 April, therefore, he had spoken eloquently in favour of a decree designed to prohibit the levying of taxes without the Department's consent.[2] Thereafter Maurin threw in his lot with the Sections, demanding the recall of the levy of 6000 men, proclaiming the 'bon esprit' which reigned in the Sections (4 May), adhering on 10 May to the Sections' proclamation that they were in legal resistance to oppression, agreeing that the Department should pay the *commissaires* which the Sections were sending through the countryside to round up the clubists. Nevertheless Maurin refused to attend the re-installation of the Popular Tribunal on 9 June – though he wanted a petition to be sent to the Convention to recognise the Tribunal – and had voted to send the laws of 12 and 15 May to its judges. But throughout June and July he played a full part in the revolt against the Convention. The career of Maurin therefore seems typical of those of men who, no doubt devoted to their conception of the Republic and the Revolution, gradually slipped into

---

[1] For Maurin's activities as clubist see *Jnal. Dépts. Mérid.*, CXLIX, CLVI, CLXXVI; ABR, L48, Three Authorities, 16 and 17 Mar. 1793 – Maurin attended, as a member of the Club, the meetings which voted the creation of a Revolutionary Tribunal.

[2] ABR, L1986, Dept. Admin., *arrêté* of 27 Apr. 1793. The register of the deliberations of the Dept. Admin., L46, contains most of Maurin's acts as *procureur général syndic*.

a movement which ended in acts likely to reverse the Revolution and to dismember the Republic.

Many of those who appeared before the Tribunal had held office in towns other than Marseilles – in Aix, Arles, Saint-Rémy, Tarascon etc. Marseilles, and, to a lesser extent, Aix and Arles, had dominated the department and drawn the villages along the path of counter-revolution, and leading sectionaries from the villages co-operated with those of Marseilles, Aix and Arles. Of these sectionaries, Joseph-François Bertet was one of the most articulate to appear before the Tribunal.[1] He described himself as an *homme de loi*, a designation which may cover a multitude of social positions, but which, when taken with the fact that he came from the tiny village of Bouc,[2] a few miles south of Aix, suggests that he was perhaps one of the best educated and most influential members of his village community. That this was so is confirmed by the explanation he gave for having accepted a post in the electoral assembly under the Sections of Marseilles – he had been appointed to that assembly by the commune of Bouc, which had chosen him for countless other deputations because he had won – and certainly deserved – the full confidence of that commune. Bertet continued to stress that he had been more concerned with making himself useful to his fellow-villagers than with the legalities of the electoral assembly – for instance, accused of dominating the 'so-called' Popular Society of Bouc, he affirmed that he had persuaded the clubists to set up a granary which enabled the citizens to eat bread at 6 and 7 *sous* when surrounding communes had to pay 10 and 11.

But he weakened this aspect of his defence by pleading that a small village like Bouc could not withstand the influence of a town the size of Marseilles – a town which, for four years, had dominated the department and forced others to obey. Another argument was produced by Bertet, one which was frequently heard, and disregarded, by the judges of the Tribunal: he said that he had served the Sections in the offices which he had been forced to fill at Marseilles, in the hope of doing good or of opposing the advance of counter-revolution. When this hope faded, he added,

[1] ABR, L3113, 1 and 2 Oct. 1793, Joseph-François Bertet.
[2] Bouc-Bel-Air, *arrondissement* of Aix, *canton* of Gardanne.

je me suis mis moi-même dans une espèce d'état d'arrestation, pendant quarante heures de suite, sans manger ni dormir, me dévouant à la mort, en espérant de faire entendre ma justification.

To mitigate the fact that he had served in the Departmental Administration elected by the Sections, he pleaded that in that post he had done all he could to help the patriots, especially those who – including several members of the Tribunal that judged him – had been imprisoned in Marseilles, and claimed that he had obtained the release of several patriots imprisoned by the despotism of the General Committee. But he had also accepted the post of public prosecutor, whose task it had been to levy charges against those patriots still in prison.

One action which he did admit to have taken, was, in his quality of administrator of the Department, to have ordered the payment of money to Peloux and Castelanet, fleeing from the victorious Carteaux. This he justified by saying that he had feared that the departmental chests might be pillaged during the troubles occasioned by the revolt of Section 11 and the arrival of Carteaux; but the president did not accept this explanation, accusing him of favorising their flight in wasting on them 'l'argent qui était la sueur du peuple'.

Another act of Bertet's – and one which should have redounded to his credit – was to have, according to him, given copies of the Constitution to those who asked for them; but unfortunately, in saying this, he admitted having convoked a meeting of the Three Administrations which, according to the minutes read out by the Tribunal, had also appointed Villeneuve, a *ci-devant émigré*, as commander of the Departmental Army.

As public prosecutor, he admitted to having attended two judgements – though he said that he had intervened in a way which favoured the plaintiffs – but a document shows him acting as a liaison officer between the Popular Tribunal and the General Committee;[1] while the minutes of the Three Administrations show him, as member of the Department, co-operating in the work of the counter-revolutionary authorities throughout August.[2]

[1] ABR, L3100, Criminal Tribunal, 3 Aug. 1793.
[2] ABR, L48, Three Administrations, 4 Aug., 8 Aug. 1793, etc.

In the face of this documentary evidence, Bertet was condemned to death – not only had he used his position in Bouc to play a leading rôle within the village, but he had also served the federalists on a much more important stage. Little wonder then that, when the tables were turned, he should have suffered the severest penalty.

He was not the only non-Marseillais who attracted the special attention of the Revolutionary Tribunal – which, in a few cases, extended its authority beyond the department. Another public official (and a prisoner whom Barras and Fréron were determined to see sentenced to death) was Joseph Imberty,[1] who had held the office of *procureur général syndic* in the Departmental Administration of the Basses-Alpes.

The two *Représentants* sent him from the Basses-Alpes to Marseilles for the promptest possible judgement. In these circumstances, it would have been difficult for the Tribunal to have acquitted Imberty, even if he had been able to put up a good defence. As it was, however, the proof against him was clearly established.

The public prosecutor denounced him as having defied decrees of the Convention which called him to the bar, as the principal instigator of the troubles of his department and as having abused his position by misleading the people into supporting the rebels of Marseilles.

At first, Imberty denied knowledge of the decree which ordered him to the bar of the Convention but, forced to admit that he had taken flight in August, he thereby admitted to a feeling of guilt as to his past actions. Nevertheless he affirmed that, in his posts, he had done all he could to preserve peace and harmony in the Basses-Alpes. The president did not accept this, accusing him of treating the *commissaires* sent to the departments – and especially Barras and Fréron – as monsters and brigands. But Imberty claimed, in mitigation, the right of every republican 'dire avec franchise ce qu'il croit utile à sa patrie et dénoncer tout ce qui tend à en troubler l'harmonie'.

Another defence open to men who could not deny that they had held important offices during the period of the counter-revolution was seized by Imberty when he claimed that he had

[1] ABR, L3113, 22 Oct. 1793, Joseph Imberty. Also L3023, 22 Oct. 1793.

done all he could to get the Constitution accepted in his department and when he maintained that the department had not
ceased to recognise the Convention, had accepted its laws, and
had published them within its area. If he had advocated the
acceptance of the Constitution merely as a means whereby new
electoral assemblies were to be called to replace the Convention,
this was because, the Constitution once enforced, a new era of
peace and concord would dawn, and the Convention's task be
fulfilled – it was not designed to get rid of a body which he
considered illegal and incompetent, even though some of its
actions in June and July might have given the impression that
the Convention was not free and that freedom itself was in
peril. Again Imberty finished his argument by saying that

> J'observe enfin, qu'un des plus grands droits de la Constitu-
> tion et des droits de l'homme est de pouvoir librement
> exprimer sa pensée et ses craintes sur les dangers de la patrie.

So direct and firm an appeal to the rights of free speech as
defined in the Constitution of 1793 and in the Declaration of
Rights was fairly infrequent during the hearings of the court.
But of course Imberty was an experienced administrator, whose
office had given him every opportunity to formulate views on
public issues and to explain to his colleagues the legal implications of proposed acts; and he was therefore better placed than
some of the more timid and ignorant people who appeared
before the Tribunal to demand his rights.

Witnesses were called against him. To the accusation that he
had seized patriots at Manosque to send them before the
Popular Tribunal, he replied that he had always maintained

> qu'on ne devait poursuivre contre qui que ce soit pour tout
> ce qui était relatif à la Révolution

a doctrine which obviously invalidated his own trial before the
Revolutionary Tribunal, and the punishment of all classes of
revolutionary 'suspects'. But Imberty also asked to be allowed
to call as witness a man who was present in the audience. This
man said that Imberty had used this belief in clemency and
understanding not for suspects who plotted against the Revolution, but against aristocrats who persecuted the patriots.

The president thereupon changed the subject. By what right had he convoked, in his quality of *procureur général syndic*, without express permission of the Convention, the primary assemblies of his department? What right had he to order the formation of a departmental army which was to march to Paris? Imberty replied that it had been thought necessary to call the primary assemblies in order to ascertain the opinions of the inhabitants of the Basses-Alpes on the insurrection of 31 May. This was to convict himself completely and irrevocably; for Imberty here defined the most essential meaning of 'federalism' – to give one's locality the right or the opportunity to call in question an action decided upon by the supreme authority of the Republic. Once the insurrection of 31 May had been consecrated by the vote of the majority of the Convention on 2 June, only an act of open defiance, of evident federalism, could call it in question.

Not surprisingly, therefore, Imberty was found guilty and sentenced to death, by virtue of the law of 5 July 1793 against those who actively took part in revolts against the Convention. And, attached to the judgement of Imberty, are several documents which provided the bases for the charge and for the conviction.

One was an address of the Department of the Basses-Alpes, issued at Digne on 21 June 1793, and signed by, among others, Imberty. This was a document similar to the Manifesto of Marseilles, deploring the assault which the Parisians had made on the National Sovereignty and exhorting the citizens to rise in defence of their persons and properties against, not only cannibals such as Barras and Fréron, but against an *armée révolutionnaire*, 6000 strong, levied by the Convention. In defiance, a departmental army was to be formed and primary assemblies to be called. A similar appeal to resist oppression was launched by Imberty from his post as president of the Committee of Public Safety of the Basses-Alpes. This one intensified the attack upon Barras and Fréron:

> Les trésors de la nation, fruits précieux de la sueur du peuple, sont largement prodigués à corrompre l'esprit public –

six million *livres*, destined for this purpose, had been seized in the baggage of the two *Conventionnels*. The Constitution was to be accepted as the surest, promptest way to replace, by a legislature worthy of confidence, a Convention which had fully forfeited the people's faith. Finally, the Revolutionary Tribunal made use of another address of the Committee of Public Safety of the Basses-Alpes, of 14 July 1793, which, directed towards the soldiers of the Third Battalion of the same department, summoned them not to obey any requisition which might be made to them by the vile envoys of Marat and company to oppose the brave Marseillais who were marching to defend the National Sovereignty. But, unfortunately for Imberty and his colleagues, the battalion refused to obey the exhortations of the 'Vendeans of the Midi' to march against their brothers – 'nous sommes les soldats de la République', they affirmed.

These documents fully implicated Imberty in the federalist movement. Moreover, a letter from him, dated 20 June 1793, assailed Barras and Fréron for preaching (as Bayle and Boisset were accused of doing at Marseilles) that the people should rise *en masse* to exterminate priests, nobles and the overweening bourgeoisie.[1] Thus the Tribunal found itself able to confirm the judgement of Barras and Fréron that he had, the first in his department, raised the standard of revolt and had preached and organised a crusade against the Convention.

Imberty gives the impression of having been a 'mature' counter-revolutionary, whose convictions were perhaps strengthened through experience of office and maturity of years. A vastly different impression emerges from the answers Jean-Baptiste Vence gave to the Tribunal.

Jean-Baptiste Vence was to Marseilles what Barbaroux was to the Republic as a whole. Aged 22, describing himself as a 'négociant', he appeared before the Revolutionary Tribunal on 11 September.[2] Brought up at Lyons, he arrived at Marseilles at the dawn of the Revolution and embraced – with enthusiasm – the party of liberty. He had been expelled successively from Palermo and from England for expressing his admiration for the Revolution. Returning to France with the intention of going on board a ship which his uncle was fitting out to fight the British, at Toulon, waiting to embark, his Section in Marseilles appointed him member of the deputation taking the Address of the Sections of Marseilles to the Convention.

    [1] ABR, L363.
    [2] ABR, L3112; 11, 12 Sept., 1793, Jean-Baptiste Vence.

Alors je n'avais jamais encore parlé dans ma section, et je ne fus nommé que parce qu'on crut que j'avais plus qu'un autre le moyen de faire le voyage. Je regardais cette commission effectivement comme une promenade et je partis.

On his return to Marseilles he became, reluctantly, a member of the Departmental Administration. Then, having spoken a few times at the Department, he won a reputation as an orator and was elected deputy to Bourges. Vence denied accepting this appointment, saying that the whole plan was abandoned when the Departmental Army was chased from Avignon. To rally the army, he was sent to stiffen the soldiers' resistance by offering them more pay. At the army, he became aware of the need to re-establish relations with the Convention. From then on, he took no part in political life; but, strongly affected by a sense of his country's plight, he fell ill from chagrin.

The president was principally concerned to prove that Vence had occupied his posts knowing that they involved him in a counter-revolutionary movement – a knowledge which Vence denied. The only reason he could think of for having been chosen to go to the army was because he had a strong voice and was, therefore, thought suitable to speak to soldiers. As for his election as deputy to Bourges, he denied having accepted the place and affirmed that he had not known the reason for calling an assembly, but said that he had the suspicion that it was to encourage the Convention to give France a constitution – once this had been formulated, the commission was annulled. Maillet was not prepared to accept this excuse, pointing out that Vence, in his quality of provisional member of the Department, knew the Constitution and it was because this document was favourable to the people that he refused to publish it throughout the department. On the contrary, affirmed Vence, – he claimed that he had seen only a few extracts of the Constitution in the newspapers and had done his best to circulate these among his friends since he thought that only by its acceptance could peace be restored; but since the prevailing opinion was against its acceptance, he had been unable to proselytise his fellow-citizens. As to Vence's claim that the assembly at Bourges might be used to force the Convention to produce a constitution, Maillet dismissed this by observing that the best means to obtain this result was by petition – a way left open to all individuals in the French Republic. Moreover, Vence had taken the oath not to recognise the Convention and its decrees – including any constitution it might produce after 31 May – and, anyway, he had accepted his nomination to Bourges long after copies of the Constitution had arrived in Marseilles.

Maillet then quoted a speech of Vence which repudiated the authority of the Convention and in addition attacked the Jacobin Clubs of Marseilles and Paris. Maillet remarked,

> Quand vous auriez parlé des clubs, leurs principes étaient favorables au peuple. Vous avez suivi le système des Bouillé, des Lafayette, des Brunswick, des Dumouriez, des Cobourg, de tous ces tyrans coalisés qui croyaient ne pouvoir nous redonner des fers que par l'anéantissement des clubs, qui sont les sentinelles vigilantes de la liberté du peuple.

Vence replied that he had referred only to the Cordeliers at Paris, but Maillet, ardent clubist, rejected this interpretation.

Two other charges against Vence were that he had been a member of the *Comité de sûreté générale* and had contributed to the fall of Toulon to the allied powers. To neither accusation could Vence find a reply which satisfied the Tribunal – he had joined the Marseillais who fled to Toulon when Carteaux entered Marseilles but denied that he had helped deliver Toulon to France's enemies.

In fact, there could be little doubt that Vence deserved the death penalty, since he had indeed played a prominent part in the revolt of the Sections. It is clear that he showed not the slightest hesitation in accepting his nomination to the assembly at Bourges[1] and that he did all he could, in the closing stages of the Sections' régime, to rally the men of the Departmental Army and to halt their long retreat from Avignon.[2] A speech before the Three Authorities, and before deputies of the Gard, the Hautes-Alpes and the Gironde,[3] shows him attacking members of the Convention who were implicated in the

---

[1] ABR, L46, Dept. Admin., 13 July 1793.
[2] A. Comm., *Affiches*, 28 July 1793, and 29 July 1793 – two proclamations to the Departmental Army.
[3] ABR, L48, Three Authorities, 7 July 1793.

Massacres of September, denouncing the creation of a new department centred on Avignon, attacking intriguers who tried to destroy the harmonious relations between the Sections of Marseilles, praising the Departmental Army and the departmental coalition, and describing the men of Carteaux as brigands. The proclamation of 29 July to the Departmental Army likewise condemned the policies of the Convention, policies which had led to disaster on the frontiers and civil war at home. In these two documents, the zeal of Vence for 'the cause of Marseilles' shines through and leaves no doubt as to his enthusiastic devotion to the policies of the Sections. Moreover it was his reports (his and those of his colleagues on the deputation to Paris) which had finally strengthened the resolve of the Sections to raise the standard of revolt against the Convention.[1] Thus Vence, at the end of his examination by the Revolutionary Tribunal, was true to his principles when he declared that he had never considered the revolution of the Sections as counter-revolutionary. In saying this, of course, he made inevitable his conviction; for he seems to have thrown himself into the cause of the Sections with the same zeal and youthful idealism as the 'patriots of '89' showed in embracing the Revolution.

The men whose cases have been reviewed above were convicted of having served the counter-revolution from positions in the *autorités constituées*. More numerous however were those who had sat in the committees which the Sections established to give them control of the legal authorities. Men who had served in the 'general committees' were considered to have committed the most serious crime, whereas some men who had served in *comités de bienfaisance* were treated with indulgence by the Tribunal: for such committees had not been founded for the sole purpose of advancing the cause of the counter-revolution. But the mere presence of men in the general committees was often accepted as proof of counter-revolutionary intent.

One of the most important members of the General Committee of the Sections of Marseilles was Paul-Raimbaud Bussac, *maître de langues*, who appeared before the Tribunal on 7 October.[2] He was denounced by the public prosecutor

[1] ABR, L1944, Section 16, 22 May, 2 July, 5 July 1793.
[2] ABR, L3113, 7 Oct. 1793, Paul-Raimbaud Bussac.

comme ayant été vice-président du comité général des 32 sections de Marseille; comme journaliste à gage des sections disséminant avec audace les principes qui dirigeaient les ennemis de la patrie, ayant des correspondances suivies avec les meneurs placés à différentes distances, pour réunir toutes les trames du complot fédéraliste.

Bussac confessed to having been a member of the General Committee from its formation, almost to the end of its life-span. On 21 August however he had been dismissed for reasons which he asked the Tribunal to take into consideration. He claimed that he had been dismissed for opposing the disarmament of Section 11 and for protesting against any negotiations with the British and the Spanish, even for the sake of obtaining food supplies for Marseilles –

J'osai . . . soutenir . . . que de vrais républicains savaient mourir de faim, comme d'un coup de canon. . . . Le lende- main, veille de l'arrivée du général Carteaux à Marseille, je fus averti que j'allais être arrêté au nom du comité de salut public; ainsi je me trouvai en but entre les deux partis, sort ordinaire des gens qui ne veulent que le bien dans les révolutions.

The president however accused Bussac of having served the counter-revolutionaries for four months and of abandoning their cause only when he saw Carteaux's army approaching – 'Tel est le sort des traîtres, d'être méprisés et chassés des deux partis'.

In vain Bussac advanced the argument that, had he been a traitor, he would have fled to Toulon with the rest of the committee: the president could overwhelm him by an account of the policies he had helped to formulate during his vice-presidency of that committee –

N'est-ce pas être contre-révolutionnaire que d'avoir été pendant trois mois et demi, un des membres les plus pré- pondérants d'un comité qui avait usurpé tous les pouvoirs, qui avait fait détruire toutes les autorités constituées, qui avait juré de ne plus reconnaître la Convention, qui avait fait un manifeste contre elle, qui voulait la faire remplacer par une commission nationale à Bourges, qui avait fait marcher contre elle une force armée, qui avait fait arrêter et incarcérer des représentants du peuple; qui avait formé des liaisons liberticides avec Toulon, qui s'est donné aux Anglais . . . enfin qui avait allumé la guerre civile dans tous les départements méridionaux; qui non seulement entretenait et alimentait les révoltés mais qui forçait encore le bon peuple de Marseille à se joindre à cette troupe de révoltés?

Indeed, this attack by Maillet was fully justified by facts which were to be found in the registers of the Popular Tribunal and the Sections. As early as 6 May, Bussac had been appointed by Section 4 to go to debate means to set up a committee to co-ordinate the work of the Sections; and, from the very first, he had been a member of the committee whose establishment had been the first step taken to consolidate the sectionary revolt.[1] At the same period, he had proposed the creation of a journal of the Sections, and had been appointed to carry this project into effect.[2] This he did, with the aid of collaborators, and produced a paper which justified every aspect of the Sections' revolt.[3] As vice-president of the General Committee, he had played a prominent part in the arrest of the clubists[4] and had demanded the recall of the 6000 men levied by Bayle and Boisset and the dispersal of the clubist committee of Salon.[5] He had also signed the deliberation of the General Committee of 8 June which, starting by attacking the disorders in the Convention, refused to recognise the decree of 15 May which suppressed the Popular Tribunal, and voted that the Tribunal should be re-established.[6] On 10 June, he was appointed by the General Committee to debate measures designed to levy a Departmental Army and to establish a departmental coalition in conjunction with deputies from Nîmes, Aix and Lyons, then on mission at Marseilles.[7] Two days later, he signed the

---

[1] ABR, L1936, Section 4, 6 May 1793.

[2] ABR, L1937, Section 4, 14 May 1793.

[3] Bib. Mun. of Marseilles; *Fonds de Provence*, 1881, *Résumé des procès-verbaux des délibérations des Sections de la Commune de Marseille*.

[4] ABR, L1937, Section 4, 16 May 1793.

[5] ABR, L1976, General Committee to Dept. Admin., 14 May 1793. Also letter to Dept. Admin. of 13 May 1793.

[6] ABR, L3100, General Committee, 8 June 1793.

[7] ABR, L1972, General Committee, 10 June 1793.

proclamation of the General Committee declaring that the Municipality had lost the confidence of the people and should be replaced by delegates of the Sections,[1] while, on 2 July, he consummated the Sections' overthrow of the legally-established authorities of Marseilles by voting in favour of the convocation of an electoral assembly destined to form a new Departmental Administration and to elect members for the replacement-Convention at Bourges.[2] He also signed the deliberation of the Three Authorities setting up, on 22 July, a *Comité de sûreté publique* to consolidate the repressive power of the Sections following the *émeute* of 21 July against the General Committee.[3] Finally, on 28 July, he denounced those who hailed the soldiers of Carteaux as brothers, describing the horrors of pillage and rapine which Carteaux' army had committed on its path of devastation towards Marseilles.[4] On 21 August however, a deputation from the General Committee denounced Bussac to his Section; he had been sent to Section 11 to try to persuade it to abandon its opposition to the plans of many of the other Sections to negotiate with the Spanish and the British; on this deputation he had expressed views in contradiction to those held by the General Committee. Section 4 ousted him from that committee.[5] Thus, Bussac's career during the Sections – in outline at least – was clear; till near the end of their régime, he had, as Maillet said, supported those acts which tended most to undermine the unity of the Republic and the fact that for so long and so consistently he had served in a patently counter-revolutionary organ indicated that he had observed with pleasure the general course of Marseilles' political life in the summer of 1793; for even his argument that the committee was a passive tool in the hands of the Sections could not demolish the fact that, had he disapproved of the acts of the Sections, he had been free to withdraw from the committee at any stage in its life.

Bussac, in a classic statement, denied that the General Committee's acts had been counter-revolutionary,

[1] ABR, L1964, General Committee, 12 June 1793.
[2] ABR, L1961, Section 4, adhered to proposal of General Committee of 2 July 1793.
[3] ABR, L48, Three Administrations, 22 July 1793.
[4] ABR, L1937, Section 4, 28 July 1793.
[5] ABR, L1937, Section 4, 21 Aug. 1793.

Dans la force départementale, je n'ai jamais vu qu'une force faite pour assurer les délibérations de la Convention, et non pour la détruire . . . sa liberté ayant cessé un moment, j'ai toujours dû la croire sous l'oppression . . . la force départementale n'était pas dirigée contre la Convention, mais contre la force armée parisienne qui opprimait la Convention, qui détruisait par là la représentation et insultait à tous les départements.

Bussac affirmed that two members of the Convention – Bô and Antiboul – imprisoned in Marseilles, had themselves, though members of the dominant party, confessed that the Convention had not been free on 2 June.

Il est possible que ces 32 membres soient coupables mais comme leurs crimes n'ont point été constatés par une procédure authentique et légale, le Comité a pu très innocemment regarder l'intégrité de la Convention comme violée. . . . Telle a été du moins ma constante manière de le voir.

The president asked whether he shared the views of the thirty-two deputies: in reply Bussac answered that he knew of no lawful proceedings directed against them. Thereupon the public prosecutor intervened to the effect that, by this reply, Bussac had declared himself of counter-revolutionary opinion and that he should therefore be declared an outlaw, according to the law of 27 March 1793. This the Tribunal did forthwith. This was an unprecedented step for it to take: it was unprecedented because no other defendant was so bold a champion of the principles of the Sections.

Quite the reverse was François-Hyacinthe Bertrand, an *homme de loi* born at Apt and living at Marseilles, who was accused by the acting public prosecutor of having been a leading member of the General Committee of Marseilles, 'après avoir joué quelque temps le patriote'.[1] This was denied by Bertrand but one of the foremost clubists, Guillaume Carles, affirmed that the accused had helped draft the Sections' abusive address to the Convention and, after having been well rewarded by the Club for previous services, had become the most bitter

---

[1] ABR, L3117, 2 and 8 *germinal* II (22 and 28 Mar. 1794), François-Hyacinthe Bertrand.

enemy of that society. After other witnesses had repeated this testimony, Bertrand was condemned to death.

According to his justification, he had voted for the death of Capet and had gone to the Sections only when threatened with punishment; he had defended Bayle and Boisset and opposed the destruction of the Club; he had attacked Barbaroux and Rebecquy, encouraged patriots to refuse to march against the Convention, urged them most of all to rally and to launch a third revolution, against the aristocracy of wealth. Finally he had preached the Constitution, attacked priests who invited the peasants to join the procession of the Virgin and had always devoted himself to the defence of the poor – 'son amour pour le peuple l'a toujours tenu dans la pauvreté'. (In fact, lists of confiscated property show him to have owned at least three houses in Marseilles, two *bastides* and other assorted property in the *terroir*.)[1] Bertrand provided himself with certificates from many patriots who asserted that he had protected them from oppression under the Sections, that he had denounced the rich and those who closed the Club and that he had – at considerable sacrifice to his interests – refused to do business at Marseilles until that city recognised the Convention. The committee of surveillance of the club of Apt testified that Bertrand had defended the interests of the clubists, while

> son dévouement à la Constitution lui a même fait oublier le respect filial et l'amour fraternel en se décidant à se séparer d'avec son père [et] sa sœur égarés par le fanatisme.

Other documents show him rejecting an arbiter in a lawsuit because of his 'aristocracy'.[2]

As a lawyer, Bertrand obviously did not intend to let his own case go unstated for he drew up yet another petition which may be regarded as the *profession de foi* of an ideal *sans-culotte*. Bertrand, it said, had never denounced the patriots but had been a vigilant sentinel against the abuses and rapines of the rich. In November 1792, when he had criticised some of the *commissaires* of the Club for arbitrary exactions, he had been acting in the true interests of the Club. He had done everything

[1] ABR, 4Q177; A. Comm., 2G5 – petition for reduction of taxation.
[2] ABR, L3120.

– dared everything – against the privileged, in favour of the people, and in support of the poor. He declared that

> quoique son intention fût d'agir avec prudence, il ne marcherait pas moins à grands pas vers la fin de la révolution, et qu'il briserait tous les obstacles que les aristocrates tentaient d'y apporter. Ce fut à ces fins qu'il fit la motion d'inviter toutes les sociétés de la République à demander à cœur et à cris un décret qui mit en masse tous les revenus des riches au-dessus de leurs nécessaires, pour le soutien de la République, le soulagement du peuple et l'entretien des généreux défenseurs de la patrie.

He summoned his judges to remember that he had always advocated that the aristocracy of the former Chamber of Commerce should be abolished, for 'Il n'avait . . . rien de bon à espérer de ces riches messieurs'. He had not been a member of the 'usurping' General Committee. Moreover

> Bertrand fut dénoncé par Poitevin, hydrographe, comme clubiste outré, déclamant toujours contre la destruction du lieu de ses séances, contre les riches et leurs propriétés, calomniant Barbaroux et Rebecquy . . . enfin comme un perturbateur du repos public en soulevant les citoyens pour ne pas marcher dans l'armée départementale.

He had been subjected to 'visites domiciliaires', at which the sectionaries had tried to disarm him: he had denounced the General Committee, saying that

> il faut se réunir plus que jamais et faire une troisième révolution dans Marseille. . . . Dès que la Constitution parut dans les papiers publics, Bertrand en instruisait les cultivateurs de son quartier. Lorsqu'il y eut convocation aux curés, prêtres et marguilliers des quartiers de se rendre à la procession hypocrite, il défanatisa les esprits et personne n'y vint.

At Section 11, he preached his ideal to his fellow-patriots, who, thereafter,

> voyaient clairement que les riches ne se faisaient aucune difficulté pour assassiner le peuple, afin de conserver leur dominion.

A final profession of faith came from his pen – he wrote to the president

> tu verras par mes écrits, que j'ai toujours voulu être pauvre. Salut et fraternité au nom de Marat, qui était mon philosophe favori en 1791 et qui l'a toujours été.[1]

Last among the *pièces justificatives* was a printed *affiche*[2] telling of the proposed creation of a 'Bureau de facilité pour les étrangers' which was to help foreigners of all nations in matters concerning successions and bankruptcies: it was specially designed for the poor, for those who had a 'certificate of poverty' from the Club. All other clubs were invited to set up similar bureaux throughout France, 'afin de déraciner les rapines qui s'y font par les gens d'affaires'.

Thus at least one aspect of Bertrand's services to the poor was documented. Also to his credit were the certificates from those patriots whom he had protected. And even the acting public prosecutor admitted that he had once been a 'patriote' – even if he implied that he had only pretended to be one. Little definite proof had been given that Bertrand had sat in the General Committee, though it is certain that a man of his surname took part in some of the most counter-revolutionary debates of that committee, and was, indeed, a secretary. Two sessions, 2 and 8 *germinal* (22 and 28 Mar. 1794), had been needed before the Tribunal satisfied itself as to his guilt. Patriots testified to his denunciations of the rich and his defence of the clubists, though on the other hand the denunciations of Guillaume Carles and François Galibert, staunch clubists and friends and colleagues of Maillet, and the acting president, Brogy, would have had great weight with the president. Perhaps Bertrand had been a 'patriot' up to the autumn of 1792 when, together with men like Pierre Laugier and Louis Meyfrédy (as well as Barbaroux and Rebecquy), he had become alarmed at the excesses of the clubists. It is significant that one of the few trustworthy details we have of his activities concerns his denunciation of the agents of the Club in November 1792, agents who had tried to extract money from him. From this first criticism of the Club, it may be that he became more

---

[1] ABR, L3109, Bertrand to president and judges of Revolutionary Tribunal, two petitions.   [2] ABR, L3109. The plan is dated 1790.

and more sympathetic towards the aims of the Sections, while yet showing a personal loyalty to old friends of his 'patriotic' years, who suffered most openly under the régime of the Sections. His petitions obviously suggested otherwise but one might say that, in them, he paints a portrait 'too good to be true'.

Whereas Bussac and Hyacinthe Bertrand – and several others who were condemned by the Tribunal – had served in the General Committees of the Sections, a larger number of men had served as presidents or secretaries of the individual Sections. Sometimes their deeds were amply documented in the surviving registers, so in many cases the Revolutionary Tribunal had little difficulty in securing convictions.

Thus Antoine-Joseph-Blaise Colombon, a former lawyer from Marseilles, aged 50, appeared before the Tribunal to explain why, despite possessing talent and education, he had presided over Section 18 – a Section perverted by counter-revolutionary lawyers; why he had recognised and obeyed illegal authorities without enlightening the people about the errors into which they had been plunged; why, after having helped elect a committee of finances dealing with monetary matters which were the preserve of the legislators, he had been appointed *suppléant* to Bourges.[1]

Asked if it was during his period as president of Section 18 that the Municipality was changed, he replied – 'avec la meilleure foi du monde' – that so many things had happened so quickly that he could not remember. Anyway, the president was 'un être passif', accepting majority decisions, though he had openly suggested that the Sections were exceeding their powers. To this, the president of the Tribunal replied,

> Quand on ne peut pas empêcher le mal, si l'on est républicain, l'on se retire et l'on n'y participe pas.

Colombon replied that

> Des républicains persistaient à rester dans la section. Je pensais comme eux, que l'on pourrait revenir à la raison, et je tenais bon, comme eux, en blâmant ouvertement tout ce qui se faisait de mal.

[1] ABR, L3115, 18 *nivôse* II (7 Jan. 1794) Antoine-Joseph-Blaise Colombon.

In a further effort to reduce his responsibility, Colombon had recourse to the excuse that he had signed many deliberations without noticing their content. But he did not succeed in parrying one of the initial questions of Maillet,

> Pourquoi, vous qui êtes éclairé et qui saviez que tous les changements étaient illégaux, sanctionniez-vous par votre signature toutes ces délibérations liberticides?

Maillet mentioned a decision of Section 6, taken on 13 July, to set up a committee of finances to take measures against 'la dilapidation que l'abus de notre papier-monnaie ne rend que trop facile'. Colombon, as president of Section 18, gave his consent to this motion, – a motion which implied one of the most powerful of the Sections' grievances against the Convention, that by issuing too many *assignats* it helped produce inflation. Another deliberation cited was a motion, passed by Section 18, to disarm men who had no fixed address. The Jacobins had spread the rumour that this was intended to disarm the working classes, so Section 18 had to explain that it had no intention of depriving 'les ouvriers' of their arms and, with them, of their political rights. Instead, those to be disarmed were defined as 'les gens sans aveu' – unruly people, vagabonds and robbers who had no fixed address – in contrast to workers who only lacked a fixed address in the sense that they often lived in lodging-houses in the city. Maillet refused to accept the second interpretation of this motion, and maintained that

> cette intention décèle la contre-révolution, puisqu'en attaquant la classe des ouvriers, on les dégoûtait, on les irritait, et on marchait par là droit au plan concerté de tout détruire.

There were, however, many other deliberations, not quoted by Maillet, which might have served just as well to convict him – as when he demanded the arrest of the members of the District who had retracted their oath against the Convention; when he agreed that the expenses of envoys of the Sections should be paid out of public funds and, on another occasion, that those who fled from the Departmental Army and spread bad news in Marseilles should be arrested and imprisoned by a special tribunal.[1]

More important than some of these deliberations was his election as *suppléant* to the assembly of Bourges – no evidence could be found to back his claim that he had formally refused the post.

Finally, he was accused of having had, when arrested, several incriminating documents in his possession. Among these was the famous proclamation of Admiral Hood; others included the laws of 27 March and 5 July against suspects – the latter specifically aimed at people who took part in the rebellion in the provinces. Colombon's abject attempts to destroy the papers, when he was being arrested, implied that he feared that an unfavourable conclusion would be drawn from his possession of them. But it was his service to the counter-revolutionary cause as president of Section 18 which earned him the death penalty.

Other presidents of Sections appeared before the Tribunal. Thus the public prosecutor outlined the career of Jean-Louis Tronc,[2] a 55-year-old *peseur public*, of Marseilles, the ex-president of the opulent Section 6 which, under his aegis, had voted to send its cannon to the Departmental Army, to give a further 30 *sous* a day to men who joined the army, had elected a member to the Military Tribunal, had outlawed the members of the Convention and those who approved the suppression of the Popular Tribunal. Tronc himself had 'vomited' insults against Barras and Fréron, threatened a citizen with a king and had proposed that the *émigrés* should be allowed to return and had been elected *suppléant* to the Popular Tribunal.

This formidable indictment, showing how thoroughly Giraud had scrutinised the documents which threw light on Tronc's activity in the Sections, was supplemented by witnesses called to testify against him. Their accusations were varied – that he had rejoiced at news that the *émigrés* were to return and had

---

[1] See, in particular, ABR, L1961, General Committee, 2 July 1793; L1963, Section 18 adhered to demand of Section 16 of 6 July 1793 to arrest 'parjures' of District; L1996, as president of Section 18, adhered to proposal of Section 24, of 25 July 1793, on fate of deserters from Departmental Army. See also documents, under Colombon's name, in L3120.

[2] ABR, L3113, 28 Oct., 1793, Jean-Louis Tronc.

said that those who refused to march against Carteaux were cowards and should be compelled to go by force; that he had called Carteaux 'Cartouche'; that he had said that all patriots should be imprisoned so that the 'honnêtes gens' could at last speak openly. According to one witness, Tronc had a voice which declaimed with terrible strength against all patriots, calling them men bathed in blood; he had said that Barras, Fréron and their like should not be spared for they spared no one. Again, he was alleged to have exulted that, whereas formerly the 'honnêtes gens' who left their homes in the morning could not be sure of returning home peacefully in the evening, now, under the Sections, the 'honnêtes gens' were in power and should maintain themselves there 'en criant toujours aux brigands'.

Tronc answered some of the accusations as they were made – that he had never demanded the recall of the *émigrés*; that, if his son had marched against Carteaux, 'C'est malgré moi qu'il a ainsi marché'; that he had rejoiced, not at the persecution of patriots, but at the end of the time of hangings. Likewise he denied the views attributed to him in the first question of the president, 'Ne dîtes-vous pas que c'étaient des poules aux œufs d'or qu'il fallait conserver?' He denied having said, during the trial of Capet, that despite all the intriguers could do, France would always have a king, or having voted to declare traitors those who voted against supporting the Popular Tribunal. Another question of the president confirmed the impression that Maillet regarded him as typical of the 'honnêtes gens' of the Sections; for he asked if it was not under Tronc's presidency that it was decided to oblige the rich to keep rifles in their houses, whereas the poor, who had no money to buy arms, would be at their mercy. But this was also denied.

Unfortunately for Tronc, the signature of the president of Section 6 appeared frequently in the papers of the Sections and in the remains of the register of Section 6. Elected president on 25 June, Tronc served throughout July.[1] Immediately, he received deputies from the Gard, the Hautes-Alpes and the Gironde and discussed means to speed the formation of the departmental coalition. Previously he had been vice-president and had signed an address which asked why the rich should be

[1] ABR, L1939, Section 6, 25 June, 26 June etc., 1793.

attacked since they were the 'benefactors of humanity' and likewise attacked the Club for preparing a massacre: Bayle and Boisset were denounced for provoking civil war and levying a private army, for closing the Sections of Aix and so on.[1] As regards the arming of men during the régime of the Sections, he had voted, just after the closure of the Club, to rearm 'les intègres ouvriers' so as to use them against the Jacobins who took the destruction of the Club as a pretext for subversion.[2] Then, in mid-July, he supported a plan by Section 5 to make the rich buy arms and to serve in the National Guard.[3] Coming at a time when the *émeutiers* of 21 July were trying to overthrow the General Committee, such a deliberation was certain to be regarded by Maillet and the Jacobins as a means to arm the rich against the poor. This impression could only partly be altered in Tronc's favour by his proposal that the Sections should set up a *Comité de secours* to make collections from the rich to help the poor, and his support of the plan to set up a *Comité de bienfaisance* to distribute cheap food to the populace.[4] Moreover, he had demanded that the procedure of the Popular Tribunal should be speeded up, a demand which had had as its object the quick punishment of men who, like Maillet and Giraud, were then held in prison by the sectionaries.[5] Likewise during his period as president, the Section elected judges for the Military Tribunal.

Thus even if the Tribunal did not press home to the full some of its charges – that he had accepted a place as *suppléant* in the Popular Tribunal, for instance, – enough evidence was forthcoming to show that Tronc had co-operated to the full in the activities of the Sections; and it was for this that he suffered the death penalty.

Colombon and Tronc were only two of the presidents of Sections who were executed on judgement of the Tribunal. But many others escaped to Toulon or remained undetected in Marseilles and the towns and villages of the Bouches-du-Rhône. Certainly many more escaped than were brought to trial.

---

[1] ABR, L1972, proclamation of General Committee, 2 June 1793.
[2] ABR, L2000, proposal of Section 9, 5 June 1793.
[3] ABR, L2000, proposal of Section 5, 19 July 1793.
[4] ABR, L2009, proposal of Section 4, 28 May 1793.
[5] ABR, L2006, Popular Tribunal, proposal of Section 1, 1 Aug. 1793.

In fact, besides judges of the Popular and Military Tribunals and men employed on commissions by the Sections,[1] 219 men were sentenced who had occupied posts under the Sections. Of these, 55 had been members of 'General Committees' – 47 were condemned to death, 3 freed, 1 sentenced to *réclusion* and 1 to prison (3 cases were not terminated). Those condemned to death included 8 men who described themselves as *propriétaires*, 5 *hommes de loi* (and 2 *notaires*), 4 *négociants*; and 5 *prêtres* (and a *vicaire*). If we include a few members of the liberal professions (a doctor, a surgeon, etc.), it would seem that members of the bourgeoisie played a big part in these committees, though there were also many artisans and shopkeepers. A further 24 men were sentenced as presidents of individual Sections, and 21 as secretaries. Of the presidents, 17 were condemned to death, only 3 were freed: of the secretaries, however, 6 received the death sentence, while 7 were freed. Again, lawyers, landowners and priests were well represented among those condemned to death. Members of various sectionary sub-committees accounted for 23 more cases, with 8 condemnations to death and 8 freed: often the distinction here was between members of *Comités de surveillance* and those of less political committees, dealing with charitable matters or food supplies. A further 13 men had had other posts under the Sections – illegally-appointed justices of the peace or their 'assessors', 4 members of an illegal Tribunal of Commerce at Marseilles etc., – 8 were condemned to death and 3 freed. Moreover, 7 men were condemned to death (none freed) as illegal electors; 10 members of non-municipal administrative bodies (Department, District etc.) were sentenced to death, while a person who was appointed but never attended was released. A further 65 of the accused had held municipal office under the Sections: of these, 45 were condemned to death, including no fewer than 12 *propriétaires* and 4 *bourgeois*, 4 *notaires*, and 3 *médecins*. Among the 12 municipal officers released were 5 *cultivateurs* and 6 *ménagers*.

In total, of the 219 office-holders judged, 147 were condemned to death, 12 to *réclusion*, 1 to deportation, 13 to prison; the trials of 9 reached no definite conclusion, while 37 were released.

Of the 147 condemned to death, the largest social group was

[1] See below, pp. 252 ff. and 260 ff.

formed by 27 *propriétaires*, who might no doubt be augmented by the several men who described themselves as 'agriculteur-propriétaire,' 'agriculteur-bourgeois' or 'propriétaire-cultivateur'. Various categories of lawyers formed the second largest group, whose core was provided by 8 *hommes de loi* and 8 *notaires*. Other numerically important groups were the 13 *négociants* and 9 *cultivateurs* while 9 *prêtres*, together with a *vicaire* and a 'propriétaire ci-devant curé' formed an imposing clerical contingent. Even though many of the remainder were artisans, shopkeepers or workers, there were also quite a few members of the non-legal professions (5 doctors, 3 surgeons, 3 ship's captains and so on).

Of the 37 who were released, 9 were *cultivateurs* and 6 *ménagers*. No other profession had more than two representatives, the majority being artisans and shopkeepers, with one or two merchants, lawyers and property-owners.

Such figures,[1] not surprisingly perhaps, tend to fit in with the picture of the Sections given by the interrogations of the Tribunal; for the president frequently showed that he regarded the sectionary offices as staffed by men of some social standing. For example, he observed to a *bourgeois* who had been a provisional municipal officer of Marseilles under the Sections,

> Vous voyez qu'au commencement de la contre-révolution on avait semé le bruit, qu'il n'avait que des ouvriers, des ignorants en place, que cependant la loi s'observait et lorsqu'on y eut placé des négociants, des bourgeois, qu'on supposait des gens éclairés, toutes les lois ont été méconnues.

The accused, Jean-Alexandre Artaud, remarked that in his municipality there had been as many 'citoyens artisans' as in the previous one: but the president did not believe him.[2] Similarly, as regards the towns and villages throughout Provence, the judges thought of the administrations and Sections as staffed by men who combined education with a measure

---

[1] Note that these figures are likely to be lower than the reality since some of the accused no doubt held office under the Sections without this becoming known to their judges. Note also that where – as in numerous cases – one man held several offices, only the most important (as defined by the Tribunal) has been counted.

[2] ABR, L3113, 24 Oct. 1793, Jean-Alexandre Artaud.

of affluence. Some of the peasants who appeared before the Tribunal said that they had been led – misled – by school-teachers, lawyers, and *bourgeois* on municipalities and sectionary committees. And the final judgement sheets, placarded for all to see, showed that the judges accepted this excuse in several cases.[1] One peasant told how he had been elected to office by other peasants 'pour empêcher les Messieurs de faire ce qu'ils voudraient.'[2]

It does seem that many men were coerced or misled into serving the Sections. Sometimes they took up posts from a sense of civic responsibility, to keep the administration going, to manage a hospital, to continue the register of births, marriages and deaths, to act as judges of commerce so that trade could continue smoothly, to organise food supplies. Sometimes they hoped to be of use to patriots (though the Tribunal denied that they could help the patriots by becoming counter-revolutionaries). The Tribunal, in fact, showed only qualified sympathy to those who pleaded ignorance:

> J'y étais un morceau de bois. . . . j'étais un vrai mouton et beaucoup d'autres comme moi. . . . je n'ai pas d'autre motif de défense que de dire que j'étais mené bêtement. . . . j'étais là comme un imbécile

– such men were guilty of failing to exert themselves against the Sections and this was sometimes as serious a crime as active participation. Many of these excuses stem from the despair of men who saw little chance of escape.

> Il a été malheureux pour nous qu'on ait jeté les yeux sur nous

said Augustin-Denis Carle.[3] But Carle was a notary and should therefore have known what was happening.

Others claimed that they had been given their office because

---

[1] This is seen very clearly in the case of Lazare Girard, carpenter of the small village of Fontvieille, near Arles: his Section was run by a school-teacher who dominated the 'gens du travail' who formed the bulk of membership. Though Girard had been secretary of the Section, he was released. ABR, L3113, 22 Oct. 1793, and L3023.

[2] ABR, L3113, 12 Oct. 1793, Jean Rey, *cultivateur*.

[3] ABR, L3113, 6 Nov. 1793; L3115, 2 and 3 *nivôse* II (22 and 23 Dec. 1793), Augustin-Denis Carle.

they were the oldest men in the commune or the best educated. Even wealth might be used as a motive of justification: Pierre Decroi, a banker, was so obviously rich that it was impossible to deny it – and indeed the acting public prosecutor expressly stated that 'Decroi pouvait par sa fortune être utile aux sans-culottes' – so he emphasised the usefulness of his work as treasurer of the *caisse des comestibles* even though he had been appointed by the sectionaries. He had imported corn, though by refraining from sending money abroad he had lost three-quarters of his fortune.[1]

Only a few people resolutely stood by their decision to serve in the Sections or tried to justify themselves on general grounds, though a few said they had been following the will of the majority and defended the Sections' right, as 'sovereign', to elect administrative bodies. Jean-Baptiste-François Nicolas explained his acceptance of a post in the Popular Tribunal by saying

> j'ai cru ne devoir pas m'écarter des ordres du peuple souverain immédiat, de la loi du plus fort et j'ai cédé à la grande majorité.[2]

In fact one has only to look at the proclamations issued by the Sections in the early weeks of their revolt to see why some at least of their members accepted office – to restore peace to a troubled country, and to replace old administrators, who owed their places to 'la crainte de la lanterne', by freely and demo-cratically-elected citizen-administrators. Such a movement, according to some, would be nation-wide: thus the General Committee of the Sections of Marseilles had received a pam-phlet saying that

> le salut public [demanded] impérieusement de ne pas trop retarder l'organisation d'un gouvernement provisoire digne d'être accepté par la coalition des sections de la République, afin de terrasser ces hommes pétris de tous les crimes qui, dans ces temps, désolent l'humanité.[3]

---

[1] ABR, L3119, 5 *floréal* II (24 Apr. 1794), Pierre Decroi. The Tribunal came to no decision and it was its last session.

[2] ABR, L3112, 28 Sept. 1793, Jean-Baptiste-François Nicolas.

[3] ABR, L3115, 22 *nivôse* II (11 Jan. 1794), deliberation of Section I, 22 June 1793.

Until this reign of justice was established, however, a period of upheaval was inevitable. Not surprisingly, the Jacobins, ousted from their posts in the spring of 1793, considered that this upheaval was more anarchical than their 'actes arbitraires': they had been elected constitutionally in the autumn of 1792 and no legitimate authority had ordered new elections. Thus those who displaced the legally-elected administrators were most severely dealt with by the Tribunal. Those who accepted office acquiesced in and benefited from 'la désorganisation'; they encouraged those they administered to follow their example of disobedience to the laws. Office-holding under the Sections therefore tended towards the dissolution of the Republic.[1]

Thus, as we have seen, the prominent members of the Sections were struck down by the judgement of the Tribunal. And the pleas of those who claimed that the laws were aimed only at those who had led the revolt were rejected out of hand. Louis-Pascal-Marie Sard, a lawyer, put forward this plea, that 'les subalternes' should not be punished on account of the deeds of the 'chefs'; but he did so in vain.[2] Others were equally unsuccessful in saying that, since they had not taken part in any counter-revolutionary deeds, they should not be punished for the mere membership of a post in the Sections. If they had been patriots, they would not have been chosen for office – this was Maillet's retort to such a plea. For the Tribunal, the mere presence in any obviously counter-revolutionary authority was proof that a man had actively advanced the projects of the Sections. Any authority which supported the levying of the Departmental Army was counter-revolutionary. Since all the Sections of the Bouches-du-Rhône accepted the Manifesto of Marseilles, since every member of the department's administrations swore the oath against the Convention, members of these organs fell clearly under the provisions of the law of 5 July 1793 and were punished by death as leaders and instigators of rebellion, unless the Tribunal allowed mitigating circumstances.

A very few office-holders justified their acceptance of posts

---

[1] See ABR, L484, Revolutionary Tribunal, 8 *nivôse* II (28 Dec. 1793). Public prosecutor vs. Pierre-Simon Ginoux (or Gignoux).

[2] ABR, L3109, Louis-Pascal-Marie Sard, to the judges of the Revolutionary Tribunal; condemned to death, 13 Sept. 1793, L3112.

by pleading that they were so hard-pressed for jobs that they could not be too particular as regards political allegiance. One such man was Jean-François Amalric, a warehouse-porter, who had been employed to take chests of money to the Departmental Army. He was also appointed *garde-magasin* – to guard the food of the poor, as he put it. He seems to have suffered for his strength of arms, for he had led the gang of men which smashed the furnishings of the Club. However, Amalric pleaded that he had been dying of hunger and only with great difficulty obtained the post of *garde-magasin*. Unfortunately, however, he had also served in the General Committee and for this he was executed.[1]

The Tribunal very rarely accepted the excuse of poverty and necessity. On the other hand, the fact that thirty-seven people were released after it had been established that they had served in counter-revolutionary bodies shows that excuses of ignorance and ineffectiveness were sometimes accepted. Provided the Tribunal was convinced that an accused man had been politically harmless – had indeed been a 'fifth wheel', to use one quite popular excuse, had indeed gone to sleep or spent all his time looking at maps of geography – then such a man might be released. After his experience in prison, and before the judges, he was unlikely to cause further trouble.

[1] ABR, L3112, 25 and 30 Sept. 1793, Jean-François Amalric; and L3023.

CHAPTER EIGHT

Crimes, Justifications, Judgements

'Je ne sais pas ce que c'est qu'un
aristocrate.'[1]

(a) ARISTOCRATS

In the eyes of the Revolutionary Tribunal, 'aristocracy' was
the counter-revolutionary crime *par excellence*. 'Do you wish to
recognise an aristocrat?', asked the journal of the Club in
October 1793.[2]

> Ne croyez pas qu'il n'existe que dans la caste noble et jadis
> privilégiée. C'est là, sans contredit, que réside l'aristocratie
> par excellence, mais non pas exclusivement. Vous ne sauriez
> croire combien d'aristocrates on rencontre parmi les valets
> des ci-devants et les domestiques des bourgeois. On serait
> tenté de croire que cette classe prolétaire idolâtre le servage,
> et que l'habitude de marcher à quatre pattes dans les anti-
> chambres ne lui permet plus de se tenir debout. Cherchez
> donc les aristocrates partout, parce qu'il y a des aristocrates
> dans toutes les classes; les uns par principe, par orgueil;
> les autres par intérêt, par préjugé, par routine moutonnière
> et tous par méchanceté.

At Marseilles, a man who, not frequenting the Sections before
May 1793, often appeared thereafter, was to be considered an
aristocrat.

> Vous l'auriez vu jadis chamarré d'or, si c'est un riche élégant
> ou soigné dans sa mise; et pendant ce trimestre de contre-

---

[1] ABR, L3118, Joseph Molliès, *ferblantier*, condemned to death, 27
germinal II (16 Apr. 1794).

[2] ABR, L1210 *bis*, *Journal Républicain de Marseille*, No. 6.

révolution, il a paru sous les vêtements les plus modestes. Il
aura fait rapiécer son habit neuf; il l'aura frippé tout
exprès, pour avoir l'air de l'homme simple ou peu aisé. . . .
Il vous contera dix fois ce qu'il a payé pour ses impositions
et pour les offrandes patriotiques; il aura toujours ses
quittances à la main.

Then followed a definition of 'l'égoïste' who

n'aime que lui et ne s'agit que pour lui. . . . En un mot. . . .
vous trouverez, qu'il réunit toutes les qualités de marbre:
DUR, FROID et POLI.

To the Revolutionary Tribunal, the aristocrat and the egoist –
with their most pure examples, the noble and the rich bourgeois
– merged into each other to form a creature who was the most
insidious and dangerous enemy of the Revolution. Some of those
who appeared before the Tribunal were, or had been, nobles
or *seigneurs*, but these were a small minority of those who were
accused of 'aristocracy'.

Thus Elzéard Artaud, a property-owner (*propriétaire*) of
Éguilles, was accused by Giraud of exhibiting aristocratic
tendencies:

sous les dehors de la simplicité, il a toujours caché des
sentiments aristocrates, tirant vanité de se lier avec les riches
entachés plutôt qu'avec les cultivateurs patriotes.

Aristocratic leanings were, above all, anti-patriotic, so anyone
who seemed to the Tribunal to be 'against the cause of the
people' found himself charged with 'aristocracy'. Obviously
such an offence did not have a great deal to do with the former
nobility – there was no question of Artaud being of noble
origin, no question, in the deeds imputed to him, of specifically
feudal or noble crimes. Instead, he was accused of having been
president of his Section, of having disarmed the patriots of his
town, and of having spoken in favour of the régime of the
Sections. As a landowner, and a fairly wealthy one, he was no
doubt a member of the class of 'riches entachés' who, in the
eyes of the Tribunal at least, dominated the villages around
Marseilles. (Incidentally, during the course of his examination,

Artaud gave a definition of an 'aristocrat' of Éguilles as 'un de ceux qui n'allaient pas à l'église'.)[1]

As for Jean Brunet,[2] a stone-cutter (*tailleur de pierres*) of Marseilles, he had shown himself, said Giraud, very zealous in his Section.

> Il a plus d'une fois donné raison aux ennemis du bien public. Il n'a pas voulu user envers eux cette défiance salutaire que souvent on lui dit d'avoir; il a été un des plus séduits de sa section. Il a compromis l'honneur et la vie d'un véritable républicain. Il a paru dans ce cas faire moins d'estime d'un ouvrier patriote que d'un prétendu honnête homme aristocrate.

Thus Brunet, while not being accused of being an aristocrat nor even of showing aristocratic leanings, was nevertheless denounced for showing sympathy to aristocrats. Again, aristocracy is used as a vague term to cover any feelings or opinions which were directed against the patriots, and, in particular, the distinction between 'un ouvrier patriote' and 'un honnête homme aristocrate' suggests that 'aristocracy' was a sin to which the well-to-do were most prone.

That this is so is also suggested by the accusation[3] against two women, Thérèse Furrier and Louise-Élisabeth Fabrègue, both of Berre, who

> ont toujours été aristocrates. Toutes les deux ont fait parler d'elles par leur acharnement contre les patriotes de l'un et de l'autre sexe. Toutes les deux se prétendent bourgeoises. Toutes les deux ont dit qu'elles ne voulaient pas s'encanailler.

But they both denied the accusation.

Though nobles might be poor, aristocrats were generally thought of as 'gens aisés'. Madame Furrier must have been fairly well-off, for she had been subjected to demands for forced loans. One citizen declared himself too poor to be an aristocrat,[4] while another, Jean Sicard, a *cultivateur*, affirmed

---

[1] ABR, L3115, 3 *nivôse* II (23 Dec. 1793), Elzéard Artaud. See Moulin, *La Vente des biens nationaux*, 2, pp. 403 and 412, for his lands at Éguilles.

[2] ABR, L3115, 17 *nivôse* II (6 Jan. 1794), Jean Brunet.

[3] ABR, L3115, 23 *nivôse* II (12 Jan. 1794), Thérèse Furrier, *femme* Billon, and Louise-Élisabeth Fabrègue, *femme* Bigaudy.

[4] ABR, L3118, 23 *germinal* II (12 Apr. 1794), François Pradel, a young *ouvrier en bas*.

that he was not a member of 'le parti des bourgeois aristo-crates'.[1]

Those who defended the interests of the *honnêtes gens* were also qualified as aristocrats. Thus Joseph Cossul, a *colporteur-propriétaire* of Berre, was denounced for having helped to

> fortifier le parti des prétendus honnêtes gens. Il s'est toujours montré sensible aux perfides caresses des aristocrates et insensible aux malheurs et aux besoins du peuple, dont il est membre.[2]

Obviously, the Tribunal considered that many of the 'people' had been misled by the aristocrats and had therefore ceased to serve the 'popular' cause. Like Claude Malarin, a *tourneur* of Tarascon, who was described as 'vendu à l'aristo-cratie', they oppressed the patriots by disarming them, arresting them and imprisoning them;[3] and since the patriots were always assumed to be on the side of the 'people', it was normal that the Tribunal should consider the aristocrats and their lackeys as enemies of the people, as men who feared, above all, 'l'égalité'. In this sense, the *aristocrates* were the opposite of the *sans-culottes*, and men accused of being 'tous pour les aristo-crates, nuls pour les sans culottes' were considered as the chief enemies of the Republic. Thus Nicolas Pascal, a doctor from La Seyne, was attacked by a witness as

> un scélérat, un aristocrate des plus gros, qui a été un chef de parti et a perdu notre pays. Les pauvres étaient persécutés par lui. Quand il sentit remuer l'esprit des patriotes, il se réfugia à La Seyne. . . .

In the judgement condemning him to death, Pascal was described as so obviously an aristocrat that he had constantly upheld a distinction between *assignats* and metallic money, a crime considered anti-popular in the extreme and usually attributed to hoarders and rich bourgeois merchants and tradesmen. To wash himself of the charge of aristocracy, Pascal claimed that he had shown his love for the poor by offering his poor patients free medical attention. On the other hand, his

---

[1] ABR, L3113, 29 *brumaire* II (19 Nov. 1793), Jean Sicard.
[2] ABR, L3114, 25 *frimaire* II (15 Dec. 1793), Joseph Cossul.
[3] ABR, L3115, 27 *nivôse* II (16 Jan. 1794), Claude Malarin.

alleged friendship with the former *Intendant* must only have confirmed, in the Tribunal's view, his reputation for aristocracy.[1]

One of the most comprehensive indictments of an aristocrat was levied against Joseph Perrinet:

> Joseph Perrinet de Salon est homme de loi, ses lumières et ses connaissances ont été ou nulles ou nuisibles à la révolution. Il s'est toujours trouvé depuis quatre ans dans les mouvements aristocratiques. Il a toujours été mêlé dans les réclamations anti-civiques des bourgeois de sa commune . . . il n'a paru humain que pour ses intérêts; il n'a été généreux que pour la contre-révolution.[2]

Similarly, Jean-Joseph Truchemant of Sénas, who was described as a *marchand propriétaire*, was denounced for having repudiated the Convention and declared openly that

> il soutiendrait la noblesse jusqu'à la dernière goutte de son sang et que, quand le pauvre n'aurait plus de bled, il mangerait du foin.

Like that of Malarin and Perrinet, Truchemant's 'aristocracy' consisted in the alleged indifference of a well-to-do property-owner for the interests of the poor. He was even accused of taking his aristocratic principles so far as to refuse to sow corn on his land.[3]

Those who served the aristocrats, and whose lowly social position made them almost immune to the charge of being 'aristocrats' themselves, were also thought guilty of aristocracy. Thus Joseph Guillermy, a mason of Aubagne, who had frequented the parties and banquets held at a former château, had shown his true colours when he rallied to the 'honnêtes gens' who led the counter-revolution.[4] A salt-trader, Jacques Colombet of Tarascon, was sent to prison as one of the subaltern agents which the counter-revolutionaries planted in each

---

[1] ABR, L3118, 16 *germinal* II (5 Apr. 1794), Nicolas Pascal – he was also the owner of extensive property at Allauch in the *canton* of Marseilles.

[2] ABR, L3024, 11 *nivôse* II (31 Dec. 1793), Joseph Perrinet.

[3] ABR, L3024, 5 *nivôse* II (25 Dec. 1793), Jean-Joseph Truchemant, from Sénas (*arrond.*, Arles; *canton*, Orgon).

[4] ABR, L3115, 19 and 28 *nivôse* II (8 and 17 Jan. 1794), Joseph Guillermy.

locality to mislead the peasants.[1] Often it seems that the concept of aristocracy was quite independent of the social position of the person on whom this description was bestowed. Thus even a *garçon confiseur*, Pierre Brest, was denounced as an aristocrat –

> quand il voyait un patriote, [il] lui disait: 'Retire-toi, que tu me fais ombrage!' C'est un aristocrate enragé.[2]

It seems that what was important was not one's social position, but one's political attitudes: Brest had denounced the whole battalion of the 10 August. A question put to Jean-Baptiste Rouquet, a *cultivateur* of Éguilles, also suggests this. He was asked by the president

> Pourquoi avez-vous dit à l'ouverture des sections que vous aviez été patriote, mais que vous cessiez de l'être, et que vous aimiez mieux être aristocrate?

Here also it was alleged opposition to the republicans which involved him in charges of aristocracy, though the Tribunal went on to more specific accusations of subservience to priests and nobles.[3] Louis Goiran, a blacksmith of Auriol, was accused of being

> noté d'aristocratie depuis le commencement de la révolution. Il a été le serviteur vil et bas des nobles et des prêtres.

In fact, he had been the agent of a member of the *Parlement* of Aix.[4]

But underlying these charges of aristocracy was the judges' belief that material interests were involved. Precisely because of their lowly social status, many of those denounced as aristocrats or as servants of the aristocrats were considered to have betrayed the Revolution – with all its achievements on behalf of the lower classes – for the hope of reward, often of a material nature, from men whose wealth and power was in some cases bequeathed by the *Ancien régime*, in others, augmented by the Revolution itself. The public prosecutor revealed this

---

[1] ABR, L3115, 27 *nivôse* II (16 Jan. 1794), Jacques Colombet.
[2] ABR, L3118, 26 *germinal* II (15 Apr. 1794), Pierre Brest of Marseilles.
[3] ABR, L3115, 2 and 3 *nivôse* II (22, 23 Dec. 1793), Jean-Baptiste Rouquet.
[4] ABR, L3114, 24 *frimaire* II (14 Dec. 1793), and L3110, denunciation of *Comité de surveillance* of Auriol. Louis Goiran was condemned to death.

clearly when he denounced François Pradel, an *ouvrier en bas*, as

> le partisan des aristocrates. Il a voulu par de sales injures attaquer la Convention et la nouvelle Constitution. Il s'est étudié à jeter du ridicule sur l'armée de la République. . . . il vantait la fortune, l'honnêteté et les ressources des honnêtes gens contre-révolutionnaires. Il ne donnait d'autre qualification aux patriotes que celle de brigands et de scélérats.

From an *exposé* of Pradel's 'political' attitudes, the public prosecutor moved naturally to a denunciation of his social expectations.[1] Many other peasants and workers were denounced for putting their trust in the powerful and wealthy. Four peasants, of whom one was the *fermier* of the former *seigneur* from La Roque-d'Anthéron, a small village on the Durance, had become servants of the aristocrats:

> Les promesses des soi-disant honnêtes gens leur ont fait oublier les bienfaits de la Révolution populaire.[2]

Others were accused of saying that the peasants could only gain by the triumph of the 'honnêtes gens'.

The Sections, and the administrations under their control, were seen as dominated by aristocrats: any more popular participation was mere window-dressing or deception. They pursued anti-Montagnard policies not so much because they were thought to be staffed by nobles, priests, and *émigrés* as because those of Marseilles were thought of as controlled by merchants, capitalists and lawyers and those of the surrounding towns and villages by the 'aristocratie bourgeoise', 'la bourgeoisie villageoise',[3] 'les honnêtes gens'.

In fact, perhaps paradoxically, the real core of the aristocracy lay in the ranks of the bourgeoisie. To make the extremely common allegation that suspects flattered the rich bourgeois of their localities was to brand them as lackeys of the aristocracy. As we shall see, many former nobles had become virtually

---

[1] ABR, L3118, 23 *germinal* II (12 Apr. 1794), François Pradel.

[2] ABR, L3114, 29 *frimaire* II (19 Dec. 1793), Antoine Feraud was the *fermier*: all four were freed.

[3] A term used, for example, in the trial of Jean-Joseph Vellin, ABR, L3118, 15 *germinal* II (4 Apr. 1794).

indistinguishable from bourgeois *propriétaires*. But the accusation of serving the bourgeois was much more frequent than that of showing devotion to the *ci-devants* (and even the danger of many of the nobles, as far as the Revolution was concerned, lay in their wealth, which should have been, but rarely was, used for the benefit of the Revolution). Certainly some of the rural bourgeoisie were seen as clearly linked with the former nobles as *fermiers* and agents. Nicolas Pascal, a doctor of La Seyne in the Var, had been *subdélégué* of the *Intendant* and a friend of some of the most reactionary *Parlementaires* of Aix. Yet the bourgeoisie was a power in its own right. Using Moulin's work on the sale of *biens nationaux* in the Bouches-du-Rhône,[1] at least thirty-five inhabitants of the smaller towns of the department, (excluding, that is, Marseilles, Aix and Arles), can be identified, among those judged by the Tribunal, as belonging to the rural or small-town bourgeoisie. These men seem to have met with unique severity when they came before the Tribunal: at least thirty were executed. They include many who described themselves as *propriétaires*; others are *bourgeois*, *marchands* dealing in various commodities; former priests; doctors and surgeons; *hommes de loi* and *notaires*; retired merchant captains; *négociants*. It would seem that some of those who described themselves as *cultivateurs* came into this category. This is suggested by the frequency of the terms *propriétaire cultivateur* and *cultivateur propriétaire* and by the use of the phrase '*ménager bourgeois*' by some poor peasants (*travailleurs*) designating those who managed a sectionary committee.[2] Undoubtedly, many *ménagers* joined the bourgeois in denouncing forced loans levied principally on 'les bourgeois', as at Salon. It was no doubt customary to play down one's social status when standing before the judges; but the lists of confiscated property sometimes show that a 'cultivateur' might own extensive land.

Though of diverse professions, or of no real profession at all,

[1] Moulin, of course, deals with only one *département*, while the Tribunal judged men from the whole of Provence: hence it may be assumed that the figure of thirty-five substantial property-owners is not the total of all those in this category who came before the Tribunal. Also Moulin's work is rather incomplete and does not afford indications of more than the minimum wealth of those people who do appear in it.

[2] ABR, L3113, trial of Étienne Goirant etc., 8 Oct. 1793.

these men all owned land of substantial value and often drew their wealth from varied sources: they owned land of varying description – *terres labourables*, meadows (not too common usually in Provence), orchards, gardens, vineyards, marshy areas for fishing – often they possessed urban property as well as *bastides* and farms in the countryside; frequently they drew money from the ownership of mills and inns or small industrial premises.[1] To the Tribunal, it was the possession of landed revenue which characterised this class of suspects, as was seen when the president asked some women,

> n'avez-vous pas dit qu'il fallait qu'il n'y eût que les soi-disant honnêtes gens, c'est-à-dire les riches possédant-biens, qui devaient occuper des places?[2]

These men, in the eyes of their judges, were contemptuous of 'the peasant': they showed 'tout l'orgueil de la bourgeoisie villageoise'.[3] The judges saw the conflict within rural society as basically two-sided, between the rich and the poor. When a lawyer said that, though retired, he still gave advice freely and referred to a certain beneficiary of his counsel, the president asked if this person was 'du nombre des personnes pauvres ou du nombre des riches'. The lawyer replied that the man concerned 'ne tient pas à la classe des riches sans être absolument dans celle des pauvres'. Other suspects, however, joined the judges in seeing the Revolution as a struggle – or the culminating phase in a long struggle – between rich and poor – 'J'ai toujours détesté les riches parce qu'ils ont toujours été les tyrans des pauvres'.[4]

Sometimes, however, evidence of more specific relationships between rich and poor emerged, as when the president asked a *cultivateur* of Éguilles, 'Pourquoi étiez-vous du parti des aristocrates?', to hear the reply, 'Cela m'était indifférent: ils me faisaient travailler et je servais tout le monde.'[5] On

[1] Honoré Bens, a 'cultivateur-ménager' of Aubagne, owned a 'fabrique de tuiles' (Moulin, 2, p. 183); François Gourel, *notaire* of Berre, had a 'halle servant pour le tirage des cocons' (Moulin, 2, p. 276).

[2] ABR, L3113, 26 Oct. 1793; Thérèse Comte, etc.

[3] ABR, L3118, 15 *germinal* II (4 Apr. 1794), Jean-Joseph Vellin.

[4] ABR, L3117, 11 *germinal* II (31 Mar. 1794), Joseph Chabert, *marchand mercier*.

[5] ABR, L3115, 2 *nivôse* II (22 Dec. 1793), Michel Artaud.

occasions, also, authors of denunciations or witnesses before the Tribunal testifying against members of the rural bourgeoisie, were challenged by the accused: 'Imbert est un de mes ouvriers. Je lui ai refusé un prix: il me dénonça.'[1] Whatever economic links bound the poor to the rich, however, the judges were firmly of the belief that, by serving the bourgeois, an accused man could never have good intentions towards the patriots. Such a man – once more – was a perfect aristocrat.

Many typically aristocratic crimes revealed a desire to return to the *Ancien régime*, with all its privileges, a wish to restore the monarchy, and, in general, a detestation of equality. A desire to 'stop the Revolution' was seen as the distinguishing trait of the aristocrat. It was this attempt to put the clock back – 'faire rétrograder la Révolution' – which characterised both aristocrats and sectionaries.

From the wide Montagnard definition of aristocracy, the world of the nobility, or of the ex-nobility, 'les ci-devants', seemed rather remote and restricted – certainly the number of nobles who appeared before the Tribunal was small in comparison with the number of aristocrats. Moreover it is sometimes difficult to find, in examining the records of the trials of many of the nobles, factors which set them apart from the bulk of those accused of counter-revolution. This makes it difficult to be precise about the number of nobles judged. Some were denounced as nobles, even condemned as nobles, while denying all past affiliation to that Order. And their formulations regarding their position seem to have, quite naturally, further blurred matters. In thirty-one cases, the accused was either alleged to have been a member of the nobility or has been identified as a noble. A batch of five prisoners was sent from Arles, accused of no crimes, arrested solely because they were nobles:[2] generally, however, it was difficult for the judges to be certain about the past allegiance of their *prévenus*.

Of the thirty-one persons cited above, eighteen described themselves as *propriétaires*, three as *bourgeois*; there were two priests and a *vicaire*; a *négociant*, a *commerçant*, a retired sea captain, a naval officer, a former councillor of the *Parlement* of

[1] ABR, L3117, 8 *germinal* II (28 Mar. 1794), Pierre Michel.
[2] ABR, L499, report of their arrival at the prisons of the Palais de Justice, (Oct. 1793).

Provence, a woman (one of the *propriétaires* was a woman, too), and a *maréchal-de-camp*. Eighteen were condemned to death; five to detention as suspects; five were freed; judgement on three was postponed.

Perhaps the most important of the nobles was Étienne-François-Antoine-Baudil-Senchon Bournissac, a 64-year-old *maréchal-de-camp* who had been in charge of the provostal trials in the early days of the Revolution.[1] Despite the fact that he pleaded that he had not shed one drop of blood when he was judge, that he had done his duty according to the laws of the epoch, that he had led a quiet life after going to 'Ville-Affranchie' and then when residing outside that city's walls, that he had given bread to the patriots of Lyons when they were starving at the end of the siege – despite all these alleged services to the Republic, Bournissac was condemned to death as a 'ci-devant seigneur noble convaincu d'aristocratie'. His condemnation was a foregone conclusion.[2] His interrogation is chiefly interesting in establishing that several other nobles of Marseilles – some, like Bournissac, prominent under the *Ancien régime* and in the persecution of the patriots in 1789, (Demandolx of the *Sénéchaussée*, for example) – had taken refuge at Lyons.[3]

Of these nobles, three others appeared before the Tribunal. Joseph-Louis Caussigny *dit* Valbelle, of Aix, was of an extremely ancient family. He owned the château at Meyrargues, north of Aix, with a paper manufactory and a lucrative *auberge* (land worth nearly 350,000 *livres* was restored to his family). He also had houses in Marseilles. He was condemned to death for his period of residence at Lyons.[4] Joseph-Marie de Barrigue de Fontanier, former *conseiller* of the *Parlement* of Provence, was sentenced to *réclusion* for the same offence.[5] Again, he seems to have been very wealthy, owning numerous houses in the most opulent area of Marseilles, together with at least five rural

---

[1] See above, pp. 24–5.   [2] ABR, L3115, 6 *nivôse* II (26 Dec. 1793).

[3] See below, pp. 292–3.

[4] ABR, L3118, 21 *germinal* II (10 Apr. 1794). For his fortune see Moulin, 3, p. 424, and ABR, 4Q185: Meyrargues is north of Aix.

[5] ABR, L3113, 11 Oct. 1793. For his fortune, see Moulin, 3, p. 66, and F. Spannel, 'Les éléments de la fortune des grands notables marseillais', p. 121. He was assessed for 5000 *livres* for the first 'loan', 15,000 for the second – A. Comm., 2G31, 2G32.

properties on the outskirts of the city. Quite heavily taxed by the forced loans of the autumn of 1793, he nevertheless emerged from the Revolution with much of his property intact. An avowed *conseiller* of the *Parlement* of Aix had likewisebeen at Lyons – Antoine-Hippolyte L'Hermitte. In his defence, he claimed that his father, knowing his inclination for the daughter of a *laboureur*, forced him to go to Lyons.

J'ai reconnu les lois, [he said] et leur stabilité au point d'adopter mon enfant fils d'un honnête laboureur et je l'ai reconnu.

However, he too was sentenced to death.[1]

François L'Évêque also belonged to a *robe* family – his father had been president of the *Chambre des comptes*. He described himself as a *propriétaire* but Giraud qualified him as 'sans profession . . . un homme inutile'. He was found guilty of having served in the Departmental Army. Since the age of ten, he said, he had been in prison: only the Revolution had brought freedom. He had never been seen talking to an aristocrat or a *ci-devant*.[2] But his armed service secured his execution.

Charles Clapiers *dit* Colongue, of Gémenos, was another ex-noble of ancient lineage, who called himself a *propriétaire*.[3] He was condemned to death after witnesses had spoken of his attempts to get patriots murdered or disarmed and after denunciators had described his opposition to a forced loan and his efforts to raise the peasants against the Convention and, in his capacity of commander of the National Guard at Gémenos under the Sections, to make men march against Carteaux. He was owner of a fief with château at Gémenos and his rural property included a tile 'factory' and a 'mine de plâtre de très bonne qualité'. Clapiers' case is similar to that of Tourel d'Alméran, *seigneur de terre*, former *commissaire des guerres*, likewise condemned to death for regretting the demise of the *Ancien régime* and stirring the peasants to rebellion.[4]

---

[1] ABR, L3118, 25 *germinal* II (14 Apr. 1794).

[2] ABR, L3115, 6 *nivôse* II, 26 Dec. 1793, François L'Évêque.

[3] ABR, L3117, 5 *germinal* II (25 Mar. 1794), Charles Clapiers *dit* Colongue, from Gémenos (*arrond.*, Marseilles; *canton*, Aubagne). For his fortune, Moulin, 2, p. 497, etc., and ABR, 4Q189.

[4] François-Honoré Tourel d'Alméran, judged 2 *germinal* II (22 Mar. 1794); ABR L, 3117. He was a relative of the moderate *Conventionnel* Durand-Maillane.

Clapiers and Tourel d'Alméran were rural nobles. Joseph-Louis Saint-Jacques was a landowner on the outskirts of Marseilles: he was described alternatively as a *propriétaire* or as a *bourgeois* with 24,000 *livres* of *rentes* who at his interrogation affirmed enigmatically, 'Je ne suis pas noble et j'ai voulu cesser de l'être.' No real crime was imputed to him – or to his son – so judgement was postponed until more information could be found.[1] Another noble from Marseilles, Jean-Baptiste Marin, was also described as a *bourgeois* – 'riche de 100,000'. His assurances that, though born noble, he had always given as much as he could to the Revolution, combined with his absence of a counter-revolutionary record, obtained his release. He had been a naval officer under the *Ancien régime* but gave no sea-service to the Sections. Moreover, the terms of his indictment – 'il n'a jamais aimé la Révolution, ayant toujours manifesté des principes contraires au bien du peuple, lui qui pouvait beaucoup par ses talents et ses richesses' – while being forbidding in a ritual sort of way suggests that the public prosecutor's *a priori* prejudice against nobles, while real, was not so marked as to deny the very possibility that a noble might serve the Revolution.[2]

Several nobles had indeed served France in the commercial field. François-Ignace Bonnecorse, formerly a ship's captain of Marseilles, was condemned to death for discrediting the *assignats* and for more general expressions of contempt for the Revolution.[3] He came to Marseilles during the Sections and returned to his lands at Les Baux to spread counter-revolution there: he had thus violated the decree ordering *étrangers* out of counter-revolutionary cities. Nobles such as Bonnecorse were dangerous to the patriots because they often had extensive and widely-scattered possessions, linking town and country: they were always, together with the merchants of Marseilles and members of the rural bourgeoisie, suspected of holding

---

[1] ABR, L3130, interrogation before Military Commission: L3118, 26 *germinal* II (15 Apr. 1794), Joseph-Louis and Pierre-Louis Saint-Jacques. They too preserved much of their landed property at La Capelette – F. Spannel, p. 121.

[2] ABR, L3118, 26 *germinal* II (15 Apr. 1794), Jean-Baptiste-Philippe Marin. He certainly contributed to the two forced loans of Aug.–Sept. 1793, though his total assessment is not known.

[3] ABR, L3118, 17 *germinal* II (6 Apr. 1794), François-Ignace Bonnecorse.

royalist meetings in their *bastides*, or giving shelter there to dangerous fugitives.

Of two other ex-nobles engaged in trade, Joseph-François Deguin was given the more sympathetic hearing by the Tribunal.[1] The judgement sheet in fact accepts his account of his life:

> Deguin a dérogé à la noblesse éteinte depuis l'âge de quatorze ans, a navigué pendant 33 ans sur les vaisseaux marchands; qu'il s'est retiré paisiblement de toute affaire, refusant places et emplois, désapprouvant très fort le système sectionnaire. . . . que si l'on n'eût pas refusé au club d'Aubagne ce qu'on appelait les messieurs, il en eût été, puisqu'il y tenait de cœur.

Deguin said that he forfeited his nobility at the age of fourteen because he had no money. The Tribunal, in freeing him, adopted tones of paternal concern which it usually bestowed only on ignorant peasants misled by aristocrats.

A much more wealthy mercantile noble – though he described himself as a mere *commerçant* – was Joseph-Marie-Honoré Rostan, who lived in a fine house in the rue Solon, and who owned a whole *îlo* (block) of Marseilles, comprising two soap-factories, warehouses and dwelling houses, whose stocks included Black Sea wool, coffee and sugar. He told his judges,

> Je ne sais si je suis noble, j'ai fait gloire d'être commerçant. . . . je ne me suis pas aperçu si j'étais noble; j'ai toujours, étant attaché au commerce, fait des actes qui me rendaient incapable de la soutenir. Je ne crois pas que cette noblesse a été achetée.

There was a mercantile-noble dynasty of de Rostan at Marseilles but obviously the connection between this family and the accused was problematical. He was condemned to death – as a noble, however, – because he had been a member of the General Committee of the Sections of Marseilles.[2] Two brothers of the Mestre family – originally a trading family

---

[1] ABR, L3113, 5 Nov. 1793 and L3023; Joseph-François Deguin de Paule.

[2] ABR, L3118, 27 *germinal* II (16 Apr. 1794), Joseph-Marie-Honoré Rostan.

which attained nobility and owned the *seigneurie* of Les Ayga-
lades in the *terroir* of Marseilles – likewise repudiated noble
connections. The accusation was not pressed; they were fined
40,000 *livres* (one described himself as 'riche de 600,000') and
freed, convicted of 'nullity' in the Revolution.[1] (Another noble
who had done nothing energetic against the Revolution was
Pierre Francheschi, a priest, but perhaps because of his clerical
status and because he was not so rich as the Mestre brothers,
he was sent to a *maison de réclusion*, 'convaincu de parfaite
nullité dans la révolution').[2]

François-Marie Rasque was described as a *bourgeois* from
Draguignan (in the Var), but he admitted to having been a
noble. The motive for suspicion was that he had in his possession
a medal of the Emperor. The president suggested,

> Votre attachement à vos parchemins ne devait pas vous
> faire aimer la révolution?

But Rasque replied,

> Je ne me suis mêlé de rien, que de prier Dieu pour tout le
> monde.

Maillet suggested, 'Excepté pour la prospérité de la République'; but Rasque prayed for that too. The questions Maillet
put suggested the sort of crime he expected from a noble – had
he not tried to mislead the inhabitants of the countryside?
Had he any relatives who had emigrated? As for the medal,
Rasque bought it because it was beautiful and cheap: he had
not resumed his military career because of his rheumatism. The
Tribunal accepted his explanation as regards the medal but
sent him to *réclusion* as a suspect – because he was a noble.[3]

Perhaps the most 'feudal' of the noble plaintiffs was Nicolas-
Jean-Joachim Gantel-Guitton, a 50-year-old 'propriétaire' –
who was very rich – who was condemned to death for having
deposed against patriots before the Popular Tribunal. He was
described as

---

[1] ABR, L3116, 29 *ventôse* II (19 Mar. 1794), Jean-François-Melchior
and Pierre-Joachim-Melchior Mestre.
[2] ABR, L3118, 15 *germinal* II (4 Apr. 1794), Pierre Francheschi.
[3] ABR, L3113, 6 Oct. 1793, François-Marie Rasque.

propriétaire ci-devant, se disant seigneur de Mazargues, terroir de Marseille, que son père et lui avaient usurpé.

A rather gratuitous observation on the judgement sheet informed the people of Marseilles that this Guitton – or at least his father – had, without consultation, aligned the village of Mazargues, knocked down and put up houses, on each storey of which he imposed a *cens*; had diverted the local water-supply into a reservoir outside the village, at the end of his estate, and thereby forced the villagers to come a quarter of a league to get water.[1]

Again, this was originally a trading family, attaining nobility by the purchase of an office of *secrétaire du roi*. The father of the guillotined man had been mayor of Marseilles from 1779–82. He had been bitterly denounced in a *cahier* and in a letter sent to Necker in April 1789 by the deputies of Mazargues, who outlined the seignorial burden imposed upon them: a *tasque* of 25 per cent on all grains, olives and vegetables, 20 per cent on grapes; restrictions on harvesting; abuses practised by the *fermier* of the seignorial oven; abuses of seignorial justice; fields devastated by the lord's game; the extension of all these burdens to land for which Gantel-Guitton had no title.[2] In September 1790, the last *seigneur*'s son (the accused), had asked the Municipality to enforce the payment of these dues by his peasants and the Commune had indeed urged them to do so.[3] During 1790, however, the château of Mazargues had been devastated by the patriots and its *seigneur* had fled to Lyons. His son had been in trouble several times – his *fermiers* for singing anti-patriotic songs, he himself, arrested by demand of the Club, subjected to a fine of 20,000 *livres* in March 1793[4] and in November 1793 to another fine, this time of 30,000 *livres*, for having applauded a man who smashed the bust of

[1] ABR, L484, 8 *nivôse* II (28 Dec. 1793); L3114, 2 *frimaire* II (22 Nov. 1793); L3123, *Liste des condamnés par jugement du Tribunal révolutionnaire*; Nicolas-Jean-Joachim Gantel-Guitton.

[2] J. Fournier, p. 328, n. 1.

[3] A. Comm. 1I173, complaint of Nicolas-Jean-Joachim Gantel-Guitton, 4 Sept. 1790; Commune's instruction to *curé* of Mazargues, 23 Sept. 1790.

[4] A. Comm., 4D6, Municipality reported this to the Sections, 25 Mar. 1793; the report gave no reasons for the fine. His arrest was demanded by the Club, A. Comm., 1D3, deputations to the Municipality, 20 Mar. 1793.

Brutus during the destruction of the Club.[1] Taken with a contribution of 36,000 *livres* for the forced loans of August–September 1793, these fines must have made inroads on his fortune.[2] But besides the *seigneurie* of Mazargues, his family owned large amounts of land elsewhere in the *terroir*, as well as houses in the most fashionable and lucrative area of town.[3]

Gantel-Guitton's consistent record of anti-revolutionary sentiment was exceptional. Most nobles were condemned for having welcomed the counter-revolution as an opportunity to give expression to latent viewpoints: rarely were they accused of offences which implied that they had played a prominent part in the events which led to the establishment of the régime of the Sections. Rather, the Tribunal seems to have visualised them as having led retired lives in the months preceding the summer of 1793, living the lives of landowners and gentlemen of leisure in their *hôtels* or *campagnes*, coming into the open – timidly – only when the Sections had firmly gained power. Thus the public prosecutor said, of the Saint-Jacques, father and son, that, as nobles, 'ils ont vu éclore avec plaisir la contre-révolution',[4] and he described Jean-François Seigneuret *père* of Arles (yet another *ci-devant* disguised as a *propriétaire*) as a man who was, at all times, the secret enemy of freedom and especially of equality and who profited from the triumph of the 'honnêtes gens' to denounce the patriots.[5] A description of the 68-year-old Joseph-Ayminy Mablanc appearing on the town square of Tarascon with a pitchfork in his hands as the legal municipality was being expelled hardly gives the impression of dynamic participation in the counter-revolution.[6]

The fact that the hostility of these nobles towards the Revolution had lain dormant for many months – and one of the causes of that hostility – is shown in a denunciation which

---

[1] A. Comm., 2114, judgement of *Tribunal de police municipale*, 25 *brumaire* II (15 Nov. 1793).

[2] A. Comm., 2G31 and 2G32.

[3] ABR, 4Q199, 4Q204, 4Q216 and Moulin, 3, 115 and 209.

[4] ABR, L3118, 26 *germinal* II (15 Apr. 1794), Joseph-Louis Saint-Jacques, *père*; and Pierre-Louis Saint-Jacques, *fils*.

[5] ABR, L3119, 5 *floréal* II (24 Apr. 1794), Jean-François Seigneuret, condemned to death, with his son.

[6] ABR, L3115, 27 *nivôse* II (16 Jan. 1794), Joseph-Ayminy Mablanc, condemned to *réclusion*.

'François de Seigneuret' made to the Sections of Aubagne in July 1793; in March 1792, he had been forced to pay a loan levied by the municipality of Aubagne. Obviously the nobles – and the bourgeois from whom the Tribunal scarcely distinguished them – were alienated from the Revolution by the demands it made upon their pocket.

A good example of the 'bourgeois noble' was François-Xavier Garnier, *propriétaire* of Cassis.[1] He was mayor during the Sections and, as such, recognised the Popular Tribunal and welcomed the Manifesto of Marseilles. Owner of extensive residential property at Marseilles,[2] he was too important a person for the revolutionary municipality of Cassis to contain. In 1791, this municipality complained to Marseilles of his arrogance towards them:

> ce ne peut être que parce que nous n'avons pas fléchi le genou devant l'idole d'or, ou parce qu'il était ci-devant un de ces ci-devant nobles qui tiraient plus de vanité de la noblesse que ceux qui la tenaient de l'épée depuis des siècles.[3]

The municipality, which wanted Garnier accepted as an active citizen at Marseilles (where he was said to have had 600,000 *livres* of revenue), not at Cassis, appealed to the authorities to make him, and rich citizens like him, respect town councillors. In fact, however, he was declared a citizen of Cassis and was thereby enabled to dominate that commune during the counter-revolution. He was condemned to death on 5 January 1794.

The nobles who stood before the Tribunal were a mixed bunch. The crimes they were accused of were often much the same as those attributed to members of other Orders: one was a judge of the Military Tribunal;[4] another denounced patriots;[5] a third was a member of the General Committee of the Sections

---

[1] ABR, L3122, 16 *nivôse* II (5 Jan. 1794), François-Xavier Garnier.

[2] ABR, 4Q199, 4Q203, 4Q238.

[3] A. Comm., 3G19, letter of municipality of Cassis, 16 Dec. 1791.

[4] ABR, L3113, 3 *frimaire* II (23 Nov. 1793); Jean-Pierre Gérard-Reissolet, a former naval officer, condemned to death.

[5] ABR, L3118, 22 *germinal* II (11 Apr. 1794), François Pont le Roi, *propriétaire*, condemned to death.

of Salon;[1] a fourth, member of the similar General Committee of Marseilles;[2] another, finally, was condemned to death as a member of the provisional municipality of the same city.[3] There seems little indication that the Tribunal, and the agents in the *Comités de surveillance* who worked for it, made any determined effort to round up nobles merely because of their nobility.[4] Indeed, the fact that an accused man was a noble often came to light, if at all, only accidentally during the cross-examination. In the eyes of the Tribunal, the fact of nobility was an added motive for suspicion, but was not, in itself, a sufficient reason for condemnation to any fate more serious than detention till time of peace. In most cases nobles, by 1793, were scarcely distinguishable from the bourgeoisie, and the term 'propriétaire' designated 'gens aisés' of both noble and non-noble origins.

Finally, the Revolutionary Tribunal was suspicious of men who showed an unseemly devotion to the old noble caste – thus the public prosecutor's denunciation of Joseph-Scipion Martin, a cook of Lambesc –

> Il fréquentait les aristocrates de Lambesc et des environs. Il a été saisi dans un ci-devant château où sa liaison avec le propriétaire l'avait conduit.

When Martin said that he was at the château, not to plot with its owner, but merely to cook for him, the Tribunal released him, observing that

> Martin allait travailler de son métier de cuisinier dans un château sans avoir rien de commun avec les aristocrates . . . qu'il ne pouvait être lié des aristocrates après avoir été trente-six mois dans les prisons d'Aix, accusé de la chasse, sans avoir jamais pu se venger.[5]

[1] ABR, L3114, 22 *frimaire* II (12 Dec. 1793), Jean-Joachim Gail, *vicaire* at Salon, condemned to death.

[2] ABR, L3113, 25 *brumaire* II (15 Nov. 1793), Jean-Louis-Joseph Boyer, *propriétaire*, condemned to death.

[3] ABR, L3113, 24 Oct. 1793, Jean-Alexandre Artaud, condemned to death.

[4] Besides a report of the arrival of five nobles from the Arles region (ABR, L499), there were reports of widespread arrests of nobles on 18–19 *thermidor* II (5–6 Aug. 1794); ABR, L594–6.

[5] ABR, L3113, 9 Nov. 1793, and L3023, Joseph-Scipion Martin, of Lambesc (*arrond.*, Aix; *chef-lieu de canton*).

Likewise Antoine Guien, a cultivator of La Fare, accused of being an 'agent' of a *ci-devant*, was acquitted when it was established that he was only his head-valet.[1] A man who was more compromised by his position in relation to a former noble was Jean-Baptiste Blachet, a carter of Saint-Paul-de-la-Durance. According to the public prosecutor, Blachet

> était fermier d'un ci-devant : il a secondé toute l'atrocité de ce tyran seigneurial. Il a mesuré du crédit que lui donnait son titre. Il n'a rien fait pour faire oublier son injustice ; on ne peut pas dire de lui qu'il ait volontairement corrigé les persécutions dont il était l'instrument.

With so unfavourable an introduction, it was a proof of Blachet's skill in defending himself – as well as of the Tribunal's impartiality – that he obtained acquittal.[2] Others were accused of expressing regret for the passing of the nobility : one man said that the Order should be restored, if the people were to be able to eat once more.[3] On the whole, however, such expressions of regret were scarce.

(b) ARISTOCRATS AND THE ANCIEN RÉGIME

Naturally enough, men who expressed regret at the passing of the old order were branded by the Montagnards as aristocrats. Those who had demanded the restoration of the monarchy were destined for a severe punishment, while those who, in compounding these crimes with treasonable negotiations with the enemies of France, had thrown in their lot with both the domestic and foreign enemies of the Revolution were justified in trembling when they were summoned from the prisons. To the Tribunal, the leaders of the Sections had tried to reverse the Revolution, had tried to undo the results achieved by the 10 August and the 21 January. Thus, anyone accused of counter-revolution was understood to have desired a return to

---

[1] ABR, L3115, 29 *nivôse* II (18 Jan. 1794), Antoine Guien of La Fare-les-Oliviers (*arrond.*, Aix; *canton*, Berre).

[2] ABR, L3114, 22 *frimaire* II (12 Dec. 1793), Jean-Baptiste Blachet. See also L1730, case of one Antoine Beisson (not judged by the Tribunal), arrested because, as an artist, he had accepted noble patronage.

[3] ABR, L3118, 23 *germinal* II (12 Apr. 1794), Jean-Baptiste Rousseau.

the *Ancien régime*, or, at the very least, to the balmy years of 1789–91.

> Dragon ne s'était jamais décidé en faveur de la révolution, ainsi que Chegarry. Ils se sont montrés complaisants et zélés dans la contre-révolution. Ils ont contribué à faire revivre le régime monarchique de 1789.

Antonin Chegarry, a merchant (*négociant*), Jean-Joachim Dragon, a former merchant, and Honoré-Philippe Magnan, a draper, all of Marseilles,[1] had accepted places as judges in the Tribunal of Commerce. As members of the commercial aristocracy of Marseilles, they had accepted these places – of professional rather than political importance – without thinking in terms of revolution or counter-revolution. The president however claimed that the decrees abolishing corporations prohibited the assembly of the body of merchants and manufacturers to elect judges of commerce. And indeed the deliberation of the Sections which called for the election of new judges expressly set aside the law which decreed that these should be elected by the electoral assembly of the department and substituted a corporation of the town's mercantile élite. The deliberation likewise repudiated judges elected under the law's provisions, dismissing them as tools of the Jacobins. 'Vous voyez combien on était amoureux de cette constitution de '89' said Maillet, finishing his cross-examination.

Another person charged with maintaining his allegiance to the régime of 1789 was Siffren Boulouvard *père*, a merchant of Arles, accused, in his quality of ex-Constituent, of unseemly loyalty to the 'Constitution of 1789'. However, Boulouvard explained,

> J'ai été le partisan de la Constitution de '89 parce que j'y ai coopéré, mais je ne l'ai été que jusqu'au moment où il a fallu cesser de l'être.

The Tribunal was of the opinion that Boulouvard,[2] like Chegarry, Dragon, and Magnan, deserved the death penalty for excessive loyalty to an imperfect constitution which the

---

[1] ABR, L3115, 22 *nivôse* II (11 Jan. 1794), Antonin Chegarry, Jean-Joachim Dragon, Honoré-Philippe Magnan.

[2] ABR, L3113; 18, 19 Oct. 1793, Siffren Boulouvard.

sectionaries – it appeared – wished to hold up against the sublime, Jacobin, Constitution of 1793. Certainly Boulouvard had committed all possible counter-revolutionary crimes in the name of the 'Constitution of 1789'.

These cases showed the obvious need to be up-to-date in the Revolution, especially since any desire to return even to the early months of 1792 implied a desire to restore the monarchy. Pierre Resquier, a school-teacher of Marseilles, was accused of having attacked the Club:

> il a autorisé [said Giraud] sa motion feuillantine, de toutes les maximes dangereuses qui appuyaient la constitution de 1789, se déclarant par là l'ami et le partisan chaud d'un retour criminel à la royauté.[1]

Thus faith in the so-called constitution of 1789 implied allegiance to the monarchy and to those forces, both French and foreign, who were pledged to achieve this restoration.

Pierre-Antoine Favet, a priest, got into trouble for having distributed a book, printed in 1791, which contained prayers for the king[2] while Joseph-Marie Rostan, a rich merchant who, according to his story, had been made captain of a company of *sans-culottes* in 1790, found himself accused of desiring a restoration because he had, in 1790, drunk the health of the Nation, the Law and the King – 'C'était alors le cri général', he explained.

The consequences of failing to advance with the Revolution could be grave therefore. To use terms of the *Ancien régime* was a proof that one had not yet been weaned from allegiance to a bygone age. Only by getting rid of one's *croix* and *brevet* as a *chevalier de Saint-Louis* could one prove that the change from service to tyranny to love of the Revolution had been sincere.[3] Otherwise condemnation was inevitable; for such men, in the words of Maillet, did more harm than spring hail by their opinion. Service in the armies of the *Ancien régime* was likely to predispose the Tribunal against an accused – one man who had

---

[1] ABR, L3114; 23, 24 *frimaire* II (13, 14 Dec. 1793), Pierre Resquier.

[2] ABR, L3113, 12 Nov. 1793 and L3114, 6 *frimaire* II (26 Nov. 1793), Pierre-Antoine Favet.

[3] ABR, L3117, 2 *germinal* II (22 Mar. 1794), François-Honoré Tourel d'Alméran.

served in the bodyguard of Louis Capet found it very difficult to prove his devotion to the Revolution.[1]

But not all those who were accused of desiring a return to the state of France before the Jacobin revolution had confined themselves to vague expressions of regret at the passing of a vanished order, nor were they accused of merely platonic longings. Some had given rise to graver suspicions, suspicions not based entirely on hypothetical links with institutions of the *Ancien régime*, links often more theoretical than real.

The most common of these causes of suspicion concerned those accused of having urged the restoration of the monarchy, though men who did demand a king, master or dictator had been outlawed by the Sections. Thus Ange-Henry Ferroul, a notary's clerk from Marseilles, was denounced because he had complained of the high price of foodstuffs, which he blamed on the *assignats*.[2] According to him, Rebecquy had been right to vote for the appeal to the people, 'un atelier ne pouvant rester sans chef, il nous fallait un maître'. Ferroul was sent to prison for expressing an opinion held by other members of the Sections.[3]

With the troubles which afflicted the Revolution from the spring of 1793 and with the difficulties encountered by the Sections in their attempt to provide a stable and prosperous alternative to Jacobinism, the convinced royalists had emerged from their hide-outs to take part in a chorus – as yet small and ineffective – demanding the return of the monarchy. As Carteaux approached from the north, this chorus may have grown in volume. Certainly the most evident manifestation of this feeling – the negotiations with the allied fleets – came at this time. Moreover, since the main object of the Sections' attacks was the Convention which had executed the king, inevitably some people considered that, if they were to condemn some of the actions of the Convention, they should condemn one of the most important acts of all, the execution of Louis XVI.

Yet Mitre-Roche Froment was one of the very few people

[1] ABR, L3115, 25 *nivôse* II (14 Jan. 1794), Jules-André-Joseph Colin.

[2] ABR, L1813^bis, denunciation against Ange-Henry Ferroul, before Committee of Surveillance of Marseilles, 26 *frimaire* II (16 Dec. 1793).

[3] ABR, L3118, 25 *germinal* II (14 Apr. 1794), Ange-Henry Ferroul.

sentenced to death for having demanded the return of the monarchy.[1] According to a witness, Froment, a priest from Auriol, had said that without a king France would never enjoy peace nor would her affairs prosper – both points of view commonly expressed by defenders of the royalist cause:

> Il n'y avait que des coquins et des gueux qui ne voulaient pas de roi.[2]

Going from words to deeds, Étienne Blanc, a lawyer and president of Fuveau's Section, was accused of having voted to restore the royal arms in a former chapel.[3]

The most eminent servant of the Sections to be accused of having monarchical principles was Rousselet, chief of the Departmental Army, who was alleged to have prophesied that France would soon have a king – French, British, Spanish, Prussian or Imperial.[4] On the whole, however, accusations of monarchism were generally combined with other allegations, allegations more capable of material proof. It does not seem that royalist sentiment was frequently expressed during the period of the Sections, or expressed with any great conviction. Most often, the views attributed to the accused are vague expressions of discontent rather than pledges which betray a fierce allegiance to the idea of the monarchy or to the person of a king.

Only those of the accused who had been captured at Toulon, when the city fell to the republican troops, had been deeply implicated in a royalist revolt, and, to a lesser extent, those who had negotiated with Admiral Hood in the attempt to obtain the raising of the Mediterranean blockade. The latter negotiations implicated the Sections in the crimes of treason and of royalism, since the British admiral demanded, as a condition of ordering a relaxation of the blockade, the free entrance of his ships into the Vieux-Port and the proclamation of Louis XVII. However, despite the fact that the republicans, on their entry into Marseilles, made determined efforts to get their hands on those envoys who had been sent to the allied fleets, these men

---

[1] ABR, L3113, 16 Oct. 1793, Mitre-Roche Froment.

[2] ABR, L3114, 22 *frimaire* II (12 Dec. 1793), Louis Tournatori.

[3] ABR, L3114, 26 *frimaire* II (16 Dec. 1793), Étienne-Joseph Blanc, of Fuveau, (*arrond.*, Aix; *canton*, Trets).

[4] ABR, L3112; 11, 12, 16 Sept. 1793; and L3121; Jean-Marie Rousselet.

eluded their grasp and so the men who had co-operated with the royalists and their allies at Toulon were almost alone in representing those who had carried their royalist principles to their furthest conclusion. Here the Tribunal had to decide whether the accused had co-operated willingly with the enemies of the Republic or whether they had tried to escape from Toulon to join the republicans. Thus Charles Audibert, a young soldier, had been caught in Toulon when the city was occupied by the royalists and foreigners; but he was acquitted by the Tribunal because he had escaped after the entry of the enemies of France but before the proclamation of the king.[1] Some of those who had been at Toulon were able to prove that they had braved great dangers in order to escape – by swimming out from the port, by seizing small boats and escaping from under the guns of the allied men-of-war.

Most of those who stayed at Toulon were sailors, a batch of whom was freed on 31 March 1794, after affirming that they had not served under the British and Spanish nor cried 'Vive le roi', nor worn the white cockade.[2] A further group of sailors was more indulgently treated in the early days of October since they had left Toulon long before the town was captured by the republicans. They had escaped from a vessel in the port, a man-of-war whose officers had co-operated with the enemy. The sailors were contemptuous of their officers; when asked if their leaders had opposed the enemy fleets, they replied that, on the contrary, the officers had abandoned them and had gone on shore. On the other hand, the crews had been determined to fight.[3]

Among those most irrevocably implicated in the treason of Toulon were two municipal officers of La Seyne, a small port near Toulon, François Trabut, a shoemaker, and Jean Hermitte, a carpenter, who were denounced as having given the most authentic proof of the commitment of the Toulonnais to the rebellion by signing a passport dated from the reign of Louis XVII. Both claimed that they had acted under threat of *force majeure*. When the allied troops landed, they tore up the tree of liberty and, sabre and pistol in their hands, forced the

---

[1] ABR, L3116, 28 *ventôse* II (18 Mar. 1794), Charles Audibert.
[2] ABR, L3117, 11 *germinal* II (31 Mar. 1794).
[3] ABR, L3113, 4 Oct. 1793.

unfortunate municipal officers to do their will. They claimed that when the Toulonnais wanted men from La Seyne to help them repulse the army of Carteaux, three or four hundred workers came from the arsenal of Toulon and forced them to send men to the great port. Of the men of La Seyne who went there, Trabut and Hermitte explained that they were workers who were dying of hunger and who were given food by the foreigners, who forced them to come to Toulon to collect it and work in the arsenal for them. The municipal officers signed some three hundred passports for these men, passports dated the first year of the reign of Louis XVII. They were condemned to death by virtue of a law of 10 April 1793, which covered all those accused of working for a royalist restoration.[1]

Some Marseillais were accused of having played a part in the surrender of Toulon to the coalition powers. Jean-Baptiste Vence was denounced in general terms for having, as member of a sectionary committee of Marseilles, led a movement which, in the eyes of the Tribunal, tended inevitably to royalism and treason.[2] But most of those who might have been charged with this offence had committed their crimes in Toulon itself and had fled before this city fell to the republicans.

However a few citizens were accused of having wished to deliver Marseilles to the British, of having preferred the British to the Allobroges. But on the whole these accusations were not driven home and rarely provided the basis of a conviction.

(c) ARISTOCRATS MISLEAD PATRIOTS

> Il n'est rien que les sectionnaires n'aient mis en usage pour perdre . . . la classe ignorante des agriculteurs –

Thus the members of the Commune of Graveson excused the misdeeds of the poor inhabitants of their village.[3] Certainly, in the eyes of the Revolutionary Tribunal, the *cultivateurs* were the group of people most vulnerable to the propaganda of

---

[1] ABR, L3113, 14 Oct. 1793; François Trabut and Jean Hermitte.

[2] ABR, L3112; 11, 12 Sept. 1793; and see above, pp. 176–9.

[3] ABR, L3118, 16 *germinal* II (5 Apr. 1794), petition for one Jacques Petit, to the Military Commission, from the *sans-culottes* of Graveson (*arrond.*, Arles; *canton* of Châteaurenard-Provence). Petit was described in a way which no doubt fitted others who appeared before the Tribunal.

the counter-revolutionaries; and so, when dealing with the in-habitants of the countryside, the Tribunal followed the views of a petitioner who said that it was not the cultivators who had perpetrated counter-revolutionary crimes but the bourgeois, in alliance with the rich sectionaries of Aix and Marseilles. This view was Jacobin dogma.

In more general terms however, the misleading of citizens was held by the Tribunal to be a serious crime. Those who spread the propaganda of the Sections were severely punished for it. Here the division between guilty and not-guilty was based on the criterion of knowledge and intelligence – men of a sufficiently elevated social position, or of a sufficiently well-educated profession, being considered by the Tribunal to have been aware of the issues involved in the struggle between the Sections and the Jacobins. People who could neither read nor write – and these were numerous in the lower ranks of the suspects[1] – were often considered by the Tribunal as not wholly responsible for their actions. The Jacobin tendency to find a plot in every act of opposition to their plans came to the aid of the less well-endowed among the suspects; for, it was assumed by the Jacobins, these men and women had been misled by the better informed counter-revolutionaries, misled, in other words, by the *bourgeois*, the lawyers, the priests and the merchants. 'Misleading the people' was one of the most common crimes encountered by the Tribunal.

Practically all the people who held offices were accused of having misled the people whom they governed – their proclama-tions defending the principles of the Sections, their *arrêtés* defining the policies of the Sections, their oaths and their manifestos, their journals and their registers – all these docu-

---

[1] How numerous, it is impossible to say. The poorer, ill-educated men and women often got their neighbours, or lawyers or employers to write out their petitions. The formula at the end of each judgement sheet – 'ont signé ceux qui ont su et pu' – shows that men, often having just been sentenced to the guillotine, were not always capable of signing even if they knew how. Even the signing of their name does not show that they were literate in any meaningful sense. Moreover the question of the knowledge of French by the lower classes is raised by the case of Dominique Lieutaud, a *cultivateur* of Martigues (ABR, L3113, 8 Oct. 1793), who did not know French. No mention of how this difficulty was overcome during the interrogation was made – the *procès-verbal* continues in French.

ments served to seduce the people from their true allegiance to the Convention and its laws. These men had failed to fulfil an administrator's sacred duty – the duty of informing and instructing his fellow-citizens.[1] For this reason, therefore, while being indulgent towards those who could genuinely plead that

un acte d'ignorance de ma part ne peut être un crime, la faute est à celui qui doit m'éclairer,[2]

the Tribunal was severe on those who had failed to 'enlighten' the people. The Tribunal assumed that, unless proof was provided to the contrary, those who had held office had by that very fact been in a position to instruct the people. In some cases office-holders were obviously justified in pleading ignorance – for the supply of literate people being very limited, especially in outlying areas, ignorant and inexperienced people were more or less press-ganged into office. This was admitted even by the public prosecutor, who said, of one of the accused, that, not knowing how to read or write, he had had the weakness to accept a post in his Section. Pleas of ignorance (general ignorance, as opposed to ignorance of a specific law of the Convention) were extremely frequent and the Tribunal had to be on its guard to reject the pleas which had no basis in fact.

Je ne suis pas instruit comme bien d'autres et c'est là mon malheur et j'ai été trompé,

was a stock excuse, to which the Tribunal might well reply

Laissez faire cette réponse à un illettré et non pas à vous qui savez toute la marche de la Révolution.[3]

In order to forestall such excuses, the public prosecutor often drew attention, from the very beginning, to the state of education of the accused:

Constans a reçu une éducation propre à l'éclairer sur les conséquences contre-révolutionnaires; malgré ses lumières,

[1] These accusations were levied at almost all those who held office in the Sections. See, for example, ABR, L3115, 17 *nivôse* II (6 Jan. 1794) Ambroise Le Roi.

[2] ABR, L3113, 4 Nov. 1793, Philippe-Mathieu Gajot.

[3] ABR, L3115, 6 *nivôse* II (26 Dec. 1793), François L'Évêque, a *propriétaire*.

il a accepté la place de procureur provisoire de la commune de Saint-Rémy.[1]

Those who abused their education to mislead the people were very severely treated. Several priests were accused of ascending the pulpit to preach the doctrine of the counter-revolutionaries and to read out their pamphlets, while bishop Charles-Benoît Roux had led his priests' campaign to seduce the people.[2] An innkeeper was accused of stimulating counter-revolutionary opinions in the people who came to his hostelry:[3] notaries were frequently denounced for abusing the confidence of their fellow-citizens – as were other lawyers, *bourgeois*, shopkeepers, property-owners, merchants and tradesmen.

Other men were accused of tearing down patriotic posters. Those who opposed the reading of the Constitution were in the forefront of the plot to keep the people ignorant, while men like Antoine Maurin, general procurator syndic of the Department, who belonged to organs which decided not to circulate the laws of the Convention throughout the Bouches-du-Rhône, were likewise at the centre of this plot.[4]

Riches and talents often went together in the eyes of the Tribunal; they were a combination which, in the right hands, might have done much to propagate the principles of the Revolution; but, as it was, these commodities had remained fallow in the slothful minds and heavy pockets of men who were, at the very least, indifferent to the Revolution. Worse, every commodity which might have been used to aid the Revolution had, it seemed to the Tribunal, been exploited to abuse its principles. One man had used the charms of his daughter to entice passers-by into the meetings of the Sections. Old men had not used their experience to defend the principles of the Revolution but to defame them. Above all, however, it was education which had been abused and perverted by the counter-revolutionaries – education, a privilege which implied duties as well as rights, which set some men apart from the bulk of

---

[1] ABR, L3114, 1 *frimaire* II (21 Nov. 1793), Joseph-Dominique Constans, *citoyen*.

[2] ABR, L3118, 15 *germinal* II (4 Apr. 1794), Charles-Benoît Roux. See below, pp. 236–8, for the case of the bishop.

[3] ABR, L3116, 27 *ventôse* II (17 Mar. 1794), Vincent Andoul, of Saint-Chamas.   [4] See above, pp. 165 ff.

their fellow-citizens and gave them great power over them, an instrument of power and domination which, in the hands of men whose hands were clean and whose hearts were pure could make effective all the most generous principles of the Revolution. Instead, it had been used in the service of perverted and selfish men and so, in the eyes of the revolutionaries, the good name of education itself had sometimes seemed compromised.

Certainly some of these privileged people did claim to have tried to inform the poor and the ignorant. Hyacinthe Bertrand, and many others, claimed that they had expounded the Constitution to their fellow-citizens,[1] while Pierre Borrely, a priest of Aix, claimed that he went through the villages opening the eyes of the peasants who had been blinded as to their real interests.[2] On the whole, however, these professions were not taken very seriously by the Tribunal.

Naturally, since the judges concentrated their attacks on men who had misled the people, they admitted the existence of a class of people who had been misled, men and women who, pleading ignorance as an excuse for their actions, often won the indulgence of the judges. Those who had been seduced into joining the Departmental Army were invariably released.[3]

La classe du peuple crédule, simple, laborieux . . . était comme moi dans l'impuissance de se plaindre. . . .

explained one of the accused.[4]

Il est pauvre travailleur, chargé d'une famille . . . il peut avoir été trompé mais il n'a pas été corrompu.

This plea came from Joseph Coste, a mason,[5] – it was that of a large number of people whom the Tribunal recognised as having offended out of ignorance, rather than from any deep-seated counter-revolutionary design.

There were many references to the poor, ignorant people of the countryside, misguided by the educated and well-to-do

[1] See above, pp. 183–7.
[2] ABR, L3115, 26 *ventôse* II (16 Mar. 1794), Pierre Borrely.
[3] See below, pp. 283–6.
[4] Claude Chabra, in a petition to the Military Commission, ABR, L3129.
[5] ABR, L3129, petition of Joseph Coste of Aubagne (*arrond.*, Marseilles; *chef-lieu de canton*).

inhabitants of the country towns and the owners of the large *campagnes* which abounded near Marseilles. Jean-Baptiste Berenger, a former *curé* of Peypin, was speaking on behalf of his parishioners as well as for himself, when he explained that, in his small commune, they were 'privés de lumière' and were inundated by the deliberations and orders of the Sections of Aix and Marseilles. They, too, should not be punished for deeds which had been forced upon them. In this case, however, the Tribunal seems to have decided that the accused was not as unfortunate as he pretended and sentenced him to death for acts of rebellion.[1] Perhaps in the sophistication of their arguments, some disproved their own assertions of ignorance – after all, in defence of their own lives, they were tempted to use as cogent arguments as possible. Such men also were no doubt well aware that they were using formulae which, if carefully employed, would win the clemency of the Tribunal.

Many an accused was denounced as 'l'ennemi de la société des cultivateurs' or for frequenting the company of 'les riches entachés plutôt qu'avec les cultivateurs patriotes'; or for persuading the cultivators that either the *Ancien régime* or the rule of the Sections was preferable to the domination of the Jacobins. The *curé* of Salon, André Reyne, was just one of those condemned to death for having

> abusé de ses talents pour exciter ou apaiser à son gré la classe des cultivateurs.[2]

Also, several cases came to light where men were accused of abusing their 'title' of cultivator in order the better to mislead their fellow-citizens. Thus François Mouisson de Jacques, a *cultivateur* of Salon, was accused of having persecuted patriots,

> abusant de son titre de cultivateur pour corrompre la classe des gens simples et peu éclairés. . . . il a été l'agent bien connu des bourgeois contre-révolutionnaires de Salon.

Since Mouisson had deposed at the Popular Tribunal, he was condemned to death.[3] In the light of such cases, the revolu-

---

[1] ABR, L3117, 4 *germinal* II (24 Mar. 1794), Jean-Baptiste Berenger of Peypin (*arrond.*, Marseilles; *canton*, Roquevaire).

[2] ABR, L3114, 4 *frimaire* II (24 Nov. 1793), André Reyne.

[3] ABR, L3113, 25 *brumaire* II (15 Nov. 1793), François Mouisson de Jacques.

tionary judges were understandably sceptical when faced with petitions asking for exceptional clemency for the cultivators. From Arles for instance came a petition giving the names of many people who had been arrested as suspects, indicating

> Que tous ces citoyens sont cultivateurs, artisans, tous enfin ne vivent que du travail de leur main, la plupart chargés de famille, réduits à l'aumône, et leurs femmes et leurs enfants dans la dernière extrémité.[1]

Another petition, from Berre on behalf of Le Noir *dit* Francour, said that the accused was

> un motionnaire ardent, absolument dévoué à la section, mais l'état misérable dans lequel il se trouve et sa qualité de cultivateur réclament votre indulgence.[2]

From Salon came a petition speaking of

> des cultivateurs et des femmes sans expérience qu'un curé scélérat. . . . menaçait des tourments d'une autre vie.[3]

Such petitions were common enough. That they were sometimes effective in gaining clemency is shown by the case of the men defended in the petition from Graveson quoted at the start of this section – they were all released, despite the fact that they had held office in the counter-revolution.[4] In short, therefore, the Tribunal showed itself disposed to agree with a petitioner who explained that

> les gens de la campagne croient plus de lumières à ceux des villes. Ils ne sont guère en état de discerner le danger. . . .[5]

To the Jacobins, the rural population was really an unknown quantity, which assumed importance only as an instrument of more active and more influential groups of men. It was a large

[1] ABR, L3109, n.d.

[2] ABR, L3111, from Berre-l'Étang (*arrond.*, Aix; *chef-lieu de canton*). For Le Noir *dit* Francour, 2 *nivôse* II (22 Dec. 1793).

[3] ABR, L3109, committee of surveillance of Salon, 6 *frimaire* II (26 Nov. 1793).

[4] ABR, L3118, 16 and 26 *germinal* II (5 and 15 Apr. 1794), Jean Chabert, etc.

[5] ABR, L3113, 8 Nov. 1793, Antoine-Balthasar Lecomte, retired merchant-captain of Aubagne.

and somnolent population which was to be exploited both by the Jacobins and by their enemies; for both parties in the struggles which racked the Bouches-du-Rhône used the rural population for their own ends, to be pacified or provoked according to the needs of the moment. The cultivators were half feared and half patronised by both the sectionaries and the Jacobins; for both factions were based most actively in the towns and had little knowledge of the people of the countryside. To them, the country people were like a great and docile animal which, generally trusting by nature and needing protection, might suddenly turn surly and use its great strength and weight to dash the fruits of the Revolution from out of their hands.

(d) THE TRIBUNAL AND THE POOR

Giraud wrote to the committee of surveillance of Berre:

> Je m'imagine bien que vous ne prendrez pas les coupables imbéciles et ignorants au lieu de saisir les coupables adroits et éclairés; ce n'est pas le cultivateur qui a commencé la contre-révolution mais bien les bourgeois et les fermiers. . . .
> Il faut punir seulement ceux qui savaient ce qu'ils faisaient.[1]

It was, therefore, in the interests of the accused, either to claim that they were poor and ignorant, or, if this was patently not the case, to describe their humanitarian principles, their works of charity, their sense of fraternity with the poor and unfortunate.

'N'étiez-vous pas bigotte?' asked the president of Louise Fabrègue, *femme* Bigaudy.

> Nennie, citoyen, je suis veuve, pauvre, travaille de ville, et ne peux prendre aucun parti. J'étais amie avec les pauvres comme avec les riches et me faisais avec tout le monde.

She had been accused of having adopted the tones of the bourgeois, but evidently the Tribunal decided that she was a woman 'of the people' and so ordered her release.[2] Antoine Gérard, a public official of Aix, advanced in his defence the

---

[1] ABR, L1754, 26 Oct. 1793.
[2] ABR, L3115, 23 *nivôse* II (12 Jan. 1794), Louise-Élisabeth Fabrègue, *femme* Bigaudy.

fact that, as he said, he was the only *huissier* who frequented the *sans-culottes*.[1] Simpleness of life was always a recommendation in the eyes of the Tribunal.

Né pauvre, je me suis accoutumé à rester dans une médiocrité qui m'était naturelle. J'ai travaillé quarante ans sans relâche dans cette commune et par mes peines et mon travail je me suis amassé un bien-être. Je vivais tranquille et heureux, entouré de ma famille que je chéris et qui prenait soin des infirmités qu'un travail dur et pénible m'a occasionné.

Perhaps this picture was too clearly painted to the tastes of the Tribunal, for Marc Aillaud, a 61-year-old *fabricant tanneur* was fined the stiff sum of 60,000 *livres* for his indifference to the Revolution.[2]

De plus, son inclination l'a toujours porté à secourir les malheureux. . . . faisant du bien en secret aux pauvres et aux amis de la société . . . il a constamment été attaché aux intérêts du peuple dont il se glorifie d'être membre. . . . J'ai donné aux pauvres. . . . je crois avoir fait mon devoir, en donnant pour les pauvres, veuves, et les enfants pour lesquels demandait la société des secours. . . . je partageais tout avec les pauvres. . . . loin d'avoir été persécuteur des pauvres, je les ai toujours aimés; j'ai rempli ma profession [de médecin] au point de traiter gratis les pauvres de tous les partis. . . . dans tous les temps il a coopéré à tous les actes de bienfaisance envers les pauvres –

these, and many similar phrases, show that the comparatively well-off men and women who came before the Tribunal thought it a good policy to mention their works of charity. But the Tribunal, thinking that charity was merely a duty and a privilege of the rich, was often deaf to such professions of *bienfaisance*.

Some of the accused volunteered more particulars of their services. Honoré Liane described himself as head of a bonnet-making establishment which provided a livelihood for some three to four hundred of the poorest people. But, although also

[1] ABR, L3115, 24 *nivôse* II (13 Jan. 1794), Antoine Gérard.
[2] ABR, L3116, 29 *ventôse* II (19 Mar. 1794), and L3118, 19 *germinal* II (8 Apr. 1794), Marc Aillaud.

a good husband and father, he had, unfortunately for his freedom, been instrumental in the imprisonment of patriots, and for this he was sent to prison.[1] Jacques Grenier, a wealthy merchant of Marseilles, accused of being 'useless' to the Revolution, claimed that he had always cared for the poor and for his numerous family; that he had imported foodstuffs to provide cheaply for the poor.[2] Dufort-Julien, a landowner and *bourgeois* of Marseilles, described how he had distributed bread to the poor and how he had always led a regular and irreproachable life. More to the point, he had been one of the first to protest against the abuses of the *fermes* – abuses which pushed up the cost of food and raw materials in the city.[3] Another plaintiff, a landowner, said that he did all he could to give work to the rural poor, by keeping his land in cultivation, whereas other property-owners kept it fallow or uncultivated. Likewise, Mathieu Étienne, a dealer in leather, demonstrated his patriotism and his love of the poor by saying that he had imported plenty of leather and other raw materials without making excessive profits.[4] But when Antoine Peyras, a landowner of Aix, claimed that he had made good use of his goods by giving employment to the *cultivateurs* – 'il en a fait travailler pendant trois ans environ cent cinquante' – he might well have branded himself as one of those bourgeois so distrusted by the Tribunal.[5]

Some other men had been on committees whose job it had been to collect money for the poor; but sometimes they were sent to prison for having accepted such sectionary posts. Basile Samatan and Hugues *l'aîné* had furnished money for their city to buy corn but were executed by the Military Commission. Samatan, at his trial before the Revolutionary Tribunal, did not mention his services in procuring corn for the city.[6] Pierre Decroi had been treasurer of the *Bureau des comestibles*: described

---

[1] ABR, L3118, 21 *germinal* II (10 Apr. 1794), Honoré Liane.

[2] ABR, L3118, 28 *germinal* II (17 Apr. 1794), Jacques Grenier.

[3] ABR, L3119, 1 *floréal* II (20 Apr. 1794), Jean-Pierre Dufort-Julien.

[4] ABR, L3118, 28 *germinal* II (17 Apr. 1794), Mathieu Étienne.

[5] ABR, L3122, 5 *nivôse* II (17 Apr. 1794), Antoine Peyras.

[6] ABR, L3114; 19, 21 *frimaire* II (9, 11 Dec. 1793), Basile Samatan – condemned to death by the Military Commission on 4 *pluviôse* II (23 Jan. 1794). Hugues *l'aîné* was condemned to death by the Military Commission on 8 *ventôse* II (26 Feb. 1794).

as 'riche de 400,000 l.' he was not judged by the Tribunal before it ended its sessions.[1]

Generally, however, men were assigned to one of the two categories of social and anti-social citizens more on the basis of their speeches or general attitude than on the grounds that they had accepted such and such a post. The merchants of Marseilles were thought of as the most blatant egoists and it therefore became necessary for men who were cross-examined by the Revolutionary Tribunal to dissociate themselves from that hated class. Undoubtedly Hyacinthe Bertrand, a lawyer from Apt, took this line as far as it could go, describing himself as 'la sentinelle vigilante contre les riches', as having demanded that the rich should be deprived of all revenues save those absolutely necessary to keep them from poverty, and as having urged the people to effect a third revolution against the rich.[2] Also a letter to Crudère *père*, detained in prison in *ventôse* II (Feb.–Mar. 1794), expressed the hope that his detention was due only to

> votre titre de négociant, classe contre laquelle on ne peut se dissimuler qu'il n'existe une juste prévention. . . .[3]

The *négociants* were likewise slighted in a petition of Basile-Hilarion Terris, who claimed that, as an advocate, he had defended the interests of the sailors of the privateer 'Le Club de Marseille' in defence of their prizes which the shipowners claimed for themselves.[4] Finally, Nicolas Clastrier, captain in the merchant marine, claimed that he had been dismissed from his job by the shipowners, whose lack of loyalty to the Revolution was notorious at Marseilles.[5]

Inevitably the accused, knowing the Tribunal's views or prejudices, may well have exaggerated their antipathy towards the rich and their sympathies for the poor –

> Tu verras par mes écrits, que j'ai toujours voulu être pauvre,

---

[1] ABR, L3119, 5 *floréal* II (24 Apr. 1794), Pierre Decroi.

[2] ABR, L3117, 2 and 8 *germinal* II (22 and 28 Mar. 1794), François-Hyacinthe Bertrand.

[3] ABR, L3129, Military Commission, dossier of Jean-François Crudère, *père*.

[4] ABR, L3130, Military Commission, dossier of Basile-Hilarion Terris, or Terry.   [5] ABR, L3112, 26 Sept. 1793, Nicolas Clastrier.

wrote Hyacinthe Bertrand to the Tribunal.[1] Some of the professions were too fulsome to be entirely convincing.

Pleas of vague philanthropic intentions towards the poor hardly convinced the Tribunal:

> J'ai prêché pour la révolution et j'ai toujours aimé le peuple. Mon père était bourgeois et aimait la campagne et les cultivateurs. . . . j'ai un penchant pour le paysan. . . . j'ai toujours vécu avec tout le monde et surtout avec les paysans et les sans-culottes du village.

Such phrases were used by – and useful to – men who were conscious of their status and of their position in society – not by men who really did live as peasants or workers. They were the words of Augustin-Denis Carle, a notary of Éguilles, and of Antoine Colomb, a notary of Aubagne – men whose profession lifted them above the peasants and shopkeepers of their villages.[2]

In other words, many of those who protested their fellow-feelings for the poor, formed part of the category of 'gens aisés' so bitterly denounced by the Jacobins and so constantly sought out by the Revolutionary Tribunal. All their self-justifications implied an awareness of the gap between the rich and the poor, both in Marseilles and in the surrounding villages and country-side.

Whereas a poor citizen – or one deemed to be poor by some rough and ready criterion adopted by the judges – might be freed unless he had contributed in some overtly political way to the régime of the Sections, those who fell into the ill-defined category of the rich were viewed with suspicion and even if they had shown no active participation in the counter-revolution were sometimes condemned for indifference or 'nullity'.[3] The Tribunal's judgement sheets, on the other hand, spoke lyrically of the private virtues and political nullity of poor people who were so ignorant or hard-working that they were barred from any political rôle.

---

[1] See above, pp. 183–7.

[2] ABR, L3113, 6 Nov. 1793 and L3115, 3 *nivôse* II (23 Dec. 1793), Augustin-Denis Carle; and L3113, 5 Nov. 1793, Antoine Colomb.

[3] See below, pp. 312–15.

Ermieu n'a été de rien à Éguilles . . . il était trop vieux pour se mêler de quelque chose.

Jean Ermieu, a peasant, was freed.[1]

Gille, ménager d'Arles, ne s'est mêlé de rien, que s'il n'a pas fait du bien, il n'a fait aucun mal, parce qu'il n'a rien entendu à toutes les affaires du temps et n'a voulu se mêler que de sa campagne.[2]

Gille also was released. Such men had only to suggest that they lived an honest family life – in the bourgeois sense of the term – to be sent back to their villages, no doubt cured of any temptation to meddle in politics.

To the Jacobins, though, the Revolution was 'populaire'. In an *arrêté* of 19 *frimaire* II (9 Dec. 1793) Barras, Fréron and Robespierre *jeune* observed that the Convention had voted money for the solution of the problem of *mendicité* but that the 'sectionary aristocracy' had diverted this money, using it against the Republic. They accused hoarders and egoists of trying to sabotage the food supplies of Marseilles, of throwing men out of work by stopping all industrial and commercial activity.[3] So the *Représentants* set up a *Commission de bienfaisance* to succour the poor. What effect this commission had is uncertain. On 14 *ventôse* II (4 March 1794) a municipal proclamation declared that half the *maximum* valuation of requisitioned goods should go to the poor but whether this resulted in any action is again doubtful.[4]

Nevertheless the Revolutionary Tribunal did show some measure of clemency to the poor and at least some of those who claimed that they had been forced to accept posts in the Sections because they had no money for bread gained their freedom from the Tribunal, if it seemed fairly obvious that they were speaking the truth and if they had not persisted in their crimes.

J'ai vu dans une bannière que la République française protège les malheureux et la vieillesse. Je suis âgé de 74 ans. Je ne puis plus travailler pour nourrir ma femme.

[1] ABR, L3023, 5 Nov. 1793, Jean Ermieu.
[2] ABR, L3024, 12 Nov. 1793, Jean-François Gille.
[3] A. Comm., 11743.
[4] A. Comm., 3D1, municipal proclamation approved by Maignet and by Buonarroti, *commissaire national*.

This was written by Joseph Chabert, a former draper, who gained his liberty.

Even to such people, the Revolution was a time of hardship and harshness – Chabert, in his seventies, had had to spend several months in harrowing conditions in the jails of Marseilles.[1] At least, however, the Revolutionary Tribunal tried to show some sympathy to the more unfortunate among the accused. For many of them this was small comfort; but it was comfort none the less, especially welcome when many of them must have given up hope of seeing their homes again. A sentimental benevolence towards the poor and the unfortunate – similar in kind to that manifested by the bourgeois who claimed that they 'liked the poor' – had, in this case at least, very real benefits to bestow upon those most in need of bounty.

This emphasis on a conflict between aristocrats and patriots lies underneath many of the attitudes of the Tribunal. For instance, besides the Jacobins, another group of men claimed to help the poor, to enlighten them, to administer to their needs. How had the priests performed these tasks? Unfortunately, the Tribunal found that many of them, instead of embracing the popular cause, had rejected the most Christian gospel of the Jacobins in favour of the wiles of the aristocrats.

(e) THE PRIESTS

Thirty clerics appeared before the Tribunal and one woman who was described as a former member of a religious order, who was condemned to *réclusion* for having drawn a State pension without taking the State oath.[2] Of the male members of the clergy, the most eminent was Charles-Benoît Roux, constitutional bishop of the Bouches-du-Rhône.[3] He was accused of having co-operated with federalism –

> Loin d'instruire ses prétendus brébis il leur a donné l'exemple de la révolte en prêtant à la tête de son clergé le serment de ne pas reconnaître la Convention.

[1] ABR, L3117, 11 *germinal* II (31 Mar. 1794), Joseph Chabert.

[2] ABR, L3119, 5 *floréal* II (24 Apr. 1794), Anne-Jeanne Pauquet.

[3] ABR, L3118, 15 *germinal* II (4 Apr. 1794), Charles-Benoît Roux. And L3123, on a list of those convicted by the Revolutionary Tribunal.

Bompard taxed him with accepting the pay but not the laws of the nation. A witness was called who said that Roux had doubted whether Marseilles, in June 1793, was in counter-revolution, unless it was to restore public order. The witness backed up Roux' claim to have done all he could to intervene with the Popular Tribunal to save members of his flock; but, for his pains, Roux was told by Bompard that he had thereby recognised the outlawed Popular Tribunal. He was also blamed for waiting till 30 *brumaire* II (20 Nov. 1793) before resigning, instead of having resigned rather than take the oath against the Convention. In an observation, as he was condemned to death, it was noted that he had been the first and last bishop of the Bouches-du-Rhône and that

il a montré jusqu'à son dernier moment un dévouement parfait à l'assemblée constituante et aux prérogatives de l'épiscopat.

The documents forming the basis of the charges against him suggest that Roux was condemned more for his allegiance to the principles of the Constituent Assembly, than for his devotion to episcopal privileges. It was the ambiguity of his position as 'constitutional' bishop which was the cause of his downfall. In a letter to the *Amis de la Constitution* of Marseilles, in May 1791, he wrote that

le conseil que nous donne le sage quand il nous dit que les lèvres du ministre de la religion doivent être l'organe de la loi et son cœur le dépositaire de la vérité sera toujours la règle de ma conduite.

Roux professed to see himself as the voice of the law and therefore made it his duty not only to preach obedience to the Christian gospel and to the Catholic Church, but also obedience to the laws of the State. His civic duties included saying mass at the ceremonies of State and thus he was summoned to celebrate mass when, on 14 July 1793, the sectionaries of Aix swore the oath against the Convention. Roux was therefore in the same position as any other State functionary; he was regarded by the municipality and the Sections of Aix as an important figure who had to use the prestige of his office and his influence over the people to add dignity to a purely secular function. Perhaps he considered that he could best serve his congregation by continuing in office even under an illegal régime. Certainly he tried to intervene with the Popular Tribunal to obtain the release of some of his priests but received only a smart rebuff, a warning to keep himself out of matters of public security, to confine his solicitude to the care of souls. Yet these authorities which thus rebuked him were those which had summoned him to celebrate mass to bolster their own schemes, thus involving him in the political struggle which raged in his diocese.

The letter of resignation of Bishop Roux, written by him at Aix on 30 *brumaire* II (20 Nov. 1793), clearly shows that he was weary of such struggles, especially at a time when, as he put it, the prolongation of his mission might appear suspect. It seems that Roux had been a mild benevolent man, who had felt out of place in the turbulent strife of his diocese, a man who would, perhaps, have been more at home in 1791 than in 1793.

Some of his clergy, on the other hand, had had no hesitation in throwing themselves heart and soul into the struggles of these months. Marcellin Angalier, a priest of Lambesc, had been president of the committee of surveillance of the Sections of Lambesc, had denounced patriots to the Sections of Marseilles and had voted to seize the goods of the legal municipal officers who had been ejected.[1] Jean-Pierre Pidoux, a priest of Aix, had been a member of the committee of the Sections of that town. He claimed that

> les ci-devants se méfiaient de moi, on me regardait comme leur bête noire, parce que j'allais dire la messe ayant prêté le serment.

Pidoux had been one of the most ardent apologists of such revolutionary legislation as the Declaration of the Rights of Man; he had been a specially severe denouncer of the wealth of many of the clergy and so welcomed the Revolution, by which

> la religion, avilie par le luxe de ses principaux ministres, est ramenée à sa sainteté primitive.

---

[1] ABR, L3113, 8 Nov. 1793, Marcellin Angalier, condemned to death. From Lambesc (*arrond.*, Aix; *chief-lieu de canton*).

Unfortunately however his post in the Sections of Aix deprived him of the indulgence of the Tribunal.[1]

Jean-Baptiste-Laurent Aube, a *vicaire* of La Ciotat, had likewise occupied a post in the Sections of his town. Moreover, according to Giraud, he had urged counter-revolutionary propaganda from the pulpit –

> C'est un de ces prêtres qui employaient avec succès les armes du fanatisme et qui savaient gagner les esprits, surtout des femmes.

He had read from the pulpit a letter from Danton to Dubois-Crancé, which the Sections of Marseilles had circulated as showing the bloodthirsty principles of the Jacobins.[2] The dangerously exposed position of the country priests was underlined here, for they were obliged, if they were to keep their salaries and their churches, to act as organs for the prevailing faction.

But it was a *curé* of Marseilles – of the parish of Saint-Étienne – who had perhaps the most active counter-revolutionary career.[3] Pierre-Antoine Allemand was denounced for having

> abusé de la profession de son culte pour égarer les esprits faibles et ignorants. Il s'est fait gloire de les maîtriser à son gré, garantissant leur appui aux prétendus honnêtes gens. Il a mêlé dans ses moyens de séduction de l'argent, du fanatisme et des promesses de pardon. . . . il a rendu grâce au ciel, qu'il outrageait impudemment, à la nouvelle de la fermeture de la société populaire. . . . il a oublié ce qu'il devait aux maximes de son culte, aux principes de la révolution, aux intérêts de la vérité, à l'ignorance des sans-culottes, et à la fidélité de son serment. Il a été caressé, prôné, consulté par les meneurs contre-révolutionnaires.

As president of Section 13, Allemand had certainly distinguished himself in the counter-revolution. It seems that he had been a member of the Popular Tribunal in its early days.[4]

[1] ABR, L3113, 8 Nov. 1793, Jean-Pierre Pidoux.

[2] ABR, L3114, 28 *frimaire* II (18 Dec. 1793), Jean-Baptiste-Laurent Aube. And L3123, on a list of those convicted by the Revolutionary Tribunal.

[3] ABR, L3024, 11 *nivôse* II (31 Dec. 1793), Pierre-Antoine Allemand.

[4] ABR, L3100, Popular Tribunal, address of 1 Oct. 1792.

He had been among the first to demand the creation of a
general committee of the Sections of Marseilles;[1] and from the
end of April onwards he signed, as president of Section 13,
almost all the deliberations of the Sections of Marseilles – to re-
install the Popular Tribunal, to speed up its activity, to send
addresses to attack Marat and to defend Barbaroux, to fine
those who did not attend the Sections, to call the assembly of
Bourges, to levy the Departmental Army. Thus the Revolutionary Tribunal spoke truly when it declared that Allemand had
led astray the whole of Section 13.

All the priests whose careers we have glanced at were
executed by judgement of the Revolutionary Tribunal. Several
others suffered the same fate for denouncing patriots and so on.
Others took the oath against the Convention, seized patriots,
urged their parishioners to repudiate the Convention, sat on the
committees of their Sections. Mitre-Roche Froment, denounced
by a fellow-priest, was condemned to death for having preached
royalism in the sacristy of his church.[2] Pierre-Louis Ricaud,
prêtre-vicaire de l'évêque, had been a member of the committee
of the Sections of Aix.[3] André Reyne, *curé* of Salon, had,
according to Giraud,

> occasionné presque tout le désordre à Salon, en usant du
> fanatisme et de l'ascendant qu'il avait pris sur les femmes.

He had been the object of most of the denunciations of Grimaud,
Bazin and Abeille, who had accused him and the bourgeois and
aristocrats of Salon of stirring up civil war; he had been forced
by them to flee to Montpellier and had been declared an
émigré. He returned when the Sections of Marseilles dominated
the department and played a prominent part in establishing
Sections at Salon and in ejecting the Jacobin municipality.[4]
Dominique Cayras, a priest of Marseilles, had been a member
of the General Committee of Marseilles.[5] Finally, of all the

[1] ABR, L1950, Pierre-Antoine Allemand 'adhering' on behalf of Section
13 to a petition of Section 23 of 29 Apr. 1793.

[2] ABR, L3113, 16 Oct. 1793, Mitre-Roche Froment of Auriol (*arrond.*,
Marseilles; *canton*, Roquevaire).

[3] ABR, L3114, 1 *nivôse* II (21 Dec. 1793), Pierre-Louis Ricaud.

[4] ABR, L3114, 4 *frimaire* II (24 Nov. 1793), André Reyne.

[5] ABR, L3113, 7 Oct. 1793, Jean-Louis-Dominique Cayras.

priests who were condemned to death, Jean-Joseph Franchicour, from Aix, was the only one who had been deported – in
July 1792 – for failing to take the oaths; he had gone to Genoa,
but had returned to Marseilles in August 1793 and was
condemned as an *émigré*.[1]

Judgement on other priests was less severe. Toussaint-André
Beaumont, *curé* of Cuges, was freed, although he had been
president of that village's Section, for he had been well loved
by the villagers for preserving their peace and quiet against the
Marseillais.[2] In other cases, judgement was deferred. In most
cases, the priests were accused of stirring up the people against
patriots and against the Republic.

Thus the offences attributed to the priests were much the
same as those for which suspects of other professions were
punished, and in many cases little reference was made by the
Tribunal to specifically priestly characteristics of their crimes.
Men like Allemand had played as full a part in the sectionary
movement as the *abbé* Bausset had done in the Jacobin cause.[3]
Some of the priests convicted had left the priesthood and had
assumed other occupations or had retired. All of them, however, were distinguished from the majority of their fellow-
citizens by their education and their experience at haranguing
men. It was probably for this reason that so high a proportion
of them had occupied positions of importance,[4] especially in
the villages of the department. The opinion of these villages was
often modelled on the opinions of their priest. Both the sectionaries and the Jacobins knew this, as is suggested, for instance,
by a proclamation addressed by the Club on 28 *vendémiaire* II
(19 Oct. 1793) to the *curés des campagnes*,[5] saying that while
religious instruction was voluntary, political and civic instruction, by the priests, was obligatory. The sectionaries had tried
to exploit for their own purposes the hold the priests had over

[1] ABR, L3113, 8 Nov. 1793, Jean-Joseph Franchicour. And see below,
pp. 296–7.

[2] ABR, L3113, 11 Oct. 1793, Toussaint-André Beaumont of Cuges-les-
Pins (*arrond.*, Marseilles; *canton*, Aubagne).

[3] Or Leydet, *curé* of Auriol, imprisoned by the sectionaries; or the
Jacobin Boutin, former *capucin*, *curé* at Marseilles. Several of the most
active clubists of Marseilles had been priests.

[4] And see above, p. 192, reference to clerical office-holders during the
Sections.   [5] ABR, L2076.

the minds of their parishioners: the Jacobins realised this and thought that in many cases the sectionaries had won the priests over to their cause and the priests had won the people. Throughout its career the Tribunal had been much concerned with those who had 'misled the people' and, in the priests, it considered that it had found those most clearly responsible for the prostitution of the people's natural goodness. Thus, before the Tribunal, priests received punishment which was perhaps proportionately more severe than that meted out to any other group of people. Of twenty-five priests whose trial was terminated, twenty-two were condemned to death.

Men and women appeared before the Tribunal charged with serving religious 'fanaticism' rather than the Revolution. To the Tribunal, which agreed with Fréron's dictum that 'La Constitution française doit être l'unique évangile',[1] there was a difference between religion and fanaticism. Priests who had been active counter-revolutionaries had been unfaithful not only to the principles of the Revolution, but also to those of their religion; for fanaticism was the use of religious principles and influence to resist the advance of Jacobinism; true religion, on the other hand, consisted of the use of such principles to aid the popular revolution. To a certain extent, the division between fanatics and the genuinely religious was drawn between, on the one hand, the refractory priests and their supporters, and, on the other, the constitutional priests and their congregations.[2] However, as the cases described above show, the constitutional priests, who formed the vast majority of those condemned to death by the Tribunal, were very often convicted of fanaticism. Indeed the priests *en place* were often more dangerous to the Jacobins than were the non-jurors who for the most part had been deprived of their churches and congregations. Thus, whereas the constitutional priests were often fanatics, the non-jurors were always fanatics; they were fanatics by definition.

The fact that only one non-juror priest was judged by the

---

[1] ABR, L945, Fréron, 28 *brumaire* II (18 Nov. 1793).

[2] Only 38 per cent of the priests of Marseilles were jurors – and some of those retracted: comparative figures – 50 per cent for the Bouches-du-Rhône as a whole; 84 per cent for the Basses-Alpes and 96 per cent for the Var. *Histoire de la Provence*, pp. 409–10.

Tribunal – and it is doubtful whether he was still active – suggests that most of them had been deported, as the authorities of Marseilles had tried to get rid of them once and for all in the summer of 1792. Also, those who remained – and it seems that only one, the *abbé* Gabriel Reimonet, stayed in Marseilles throughout the Terror[1] – would have lain low during the autumn of 1793 and evaded capture. Some priests conducted services in the hills and caves around Séon, Les Pennes and Roves;[2] but the fact that so many people were charged with 'regretting' their old priests suggests that these priests had, in fact, disappeared from most parishes or had finally taken the constitutional oath. On the other hand, some 150 priests renounced their priesthood in Marseilles, mostly in *ventôse*, and *germinal* II, perhaps partly as a result of the work of the Revolutionary Tribunal and the Military Commission but almost certainly attributable to the policy of Maignet.[3] In *germinal* II, the District of Marseilles stated categorically that no priest continued in exercise.[4]

However justified the District's confidence, the Tribunal seemed to fear that some non-jurors still remained hidden by those who stood before it. Women, especially, were asked if they longed for the return of the refractory priests but some replied that, on the contrary, they had placed their money in the lands of the clergy.[5] Some of the accused, however, stressed that, though not fanatics, they still practised their religion.[6]

[1] Casimir Bousquet, *Notice historique sur l'église Saint-Théodore* (Marseilles, 1856).

[2] F. Verany, *Monographie de la Chartreuse de Marseille* (Marseilles, 1860) p. 142.

[3] ABR, L945, registers of the District Administration, which received these abdications. Also villages are seen petitioning to change their churches into Temples de la Raison. The whole question has now been dealt with by M. Vovelle, 'Prêtres abdicataires et déchristianisation en Provence', *Actes du 89e Congrès national des Sociétés savantes, Lyon, 1964* (Paris, 1964) pp. 62–98.   [4] ABR, L1035.

[5] ABR, L3113, 3 Nov. 1793, Marie Martin.

[6] See also ABR, L1289 *bis*, (*police générale*), reports on 'l'esprit public': question – 'Le mouvement sublime du peuple contre la superstition a-t-il trouvé des obstacles à son développement?' Answer of Vernègues, 'Ce mouvement n'est pas arrivé jusqu'à nous, il n'est connu ici que par des oui-dire.' (21 *pluviôse* II). L1290 – Saint-Chamas replied by giving the names of 49 'fanatics'.

In most cases, the Tribunal did not press too hard the charge of fanaticism, being resigned to the fact that many citizens – and the women especially – were still devoted to their priest. As for the distinction between refractory and constitutional priests, many of the accused pretended not to recognise it or to be indifferent to it – 'J'ai été à la messe tous les jours sans m'embarrasser qui la disait.'[1] Sometimes however, the fanaticism of a suspect was looked at more closely for, in some cases, fanaticism seemed to the judges to be too aggressive to be left alone – as when juror priests were threatened, a woman doing her washing on a feast day was arrested, or a man plotted with a 'ci-devant grand vicaire' to win back his locality for fanaticism. To be the brother of a fanatical priest was to be suspect oneself. More seriously, Jean-Joseph Barlatier, a *marchand* of Istres, was accused of hiding a refractory priest in his house, and holding a religious ceremony to celebrate the election of an anti-Jacobin municipality. This priest maintained that the church was schismatic and that a 'constitutional mass' was worthless: but these accusations were not mentioned during Barlatier's trial.[2]

Jean Duperret, a property-owner of Marseilles, was confronted with the most serious charge of 'personal fanaticism' to come before the Tribunal, since it was alleged that, instead of helping the Revolution, he stayed at home reading 'les ouvrages pestiférés de la contre-révolution et du fanatisme'.[3] Hoping to make himself useful to the 'honnêtes gens', he circulated these dangerous brochures – which, as the president pointed out, included a papal letter excommunicating them all, and a book of Catholic maxims to be used by the faithful in periods of schism and persecution. Despite Duperret's plea that these were old brochures which he had forgotten about, he was condemned to death.

Pierre-Antoine Favet, a printer of Marseilles, was also incriminated by the possession of religious documents. According to Giraud, he circulated a book entitled *Manière de réciter le chapelet à l'usage des dévots et des dévotes* from the church of Notre-Dame de la Garde,

[1] ABR, L3113, 9 Nov. 1793, Pierre Castinel.
[2] ABR, L3114, 8 *frimaire* II (28 Nov. 1793), Jean-Joseph Barlatier.
[3] ABR, L3118, 23 *germinal* II (12 Apr. 1794), Jean Duperret.

dans lequel livre il se trouve des prières en faveur d'un pape qui ne les mérite pas, en faveur d'un roi qui a été guillotiné. . . . Cette distribution s'est faite dans le moment où les ennemis de la chose publique unissaient l'aristocratie au fanatisme religieux pour pervertir entièrement l'esprit civique.

But when Favet half-convinced the Tribunal that the book had been published in 1791 and that the last distribution of it had been in the same year, and when he pointed out that all other Roman Catholic books were being openly sold in Marseilles unchanged, he was given his freedom after paying a small fine.[1]

Only a few other people were accused of minor religious offences. Some who attended, at Marseilles, the Sections' procession in honour of the Virgin were rebuked. Many of these cases were trivial however. But from the serious cases heard by the Tribunal comes the confirmation of impressions given by other incidents in the revolutionary history of Marseilles. Throughout the Revolution, the patriots had been jealous and fearful of clerical influence exercised over the lower classes. Moreover the revolutionaries often suggested that religion was, for many clerics, only a mask for material interests which were ultimately to be defended by political intrigue. One example of the Jacobin distrust of clerical influence derives from the difficulties which ensued at Marseilles after the Convention had deprived the Church of its control over *l'état civil*. It was alleged that the local clergy, acting on instructions from the bishop, continued to keep registers of births, marriages and deaths. At a town meeting on 20 January 1793, this practice was denounced as divisive, preparing the way for civil war and massacre. A town councillor expressed great alarm at the temporal ambitions of the clergy – 'ils sont aujourd'hui si jaloux de se trouver à la tête d'une quantité de disciples éprouvés et comptés'. The Municipality instructed the clergy to surrender such registers.[2] Control over the *état*

---

[1] ABR, L3113, 2 Nov. 1793; and L3114, 6 *frimaire* II (26 Nov. 1793), Pierre-Antoine Favet.

[2] A. Comm., 1D3, meeting of Municipality, 20 Jan. 1793; 4D6, letter of Municipality to *curés*, 6 Feb. 1793.

civil was seen as vitally important for the consolidation of the principles of the Revolution – for example, Maignet, by an *arrêté* of 29 *pluviôse* II (17 Feb. 1794), ordered that all acts of *état civil* registered under the Sections were to be renewed.[1]

Another aspect of the Church's power – its control over education – had alarmed the patriots of Marseilles, who were determined (though rather belatedly as far as positive measures were concerned) to use education as a weapon against both fanaticism and despotism, as a political instrument to win the allegiance of the masses. Thus, on 31 March 1794, the Municipality took steps to enforce the decree of 29 *frimaire* II (19 Dec. 1793), which provided for the establishment of free public primary education (whose teaching texts were to be the laws and works of the legislators of France).[2] This plan must have received a measure of realisation at Marseilles, because on 6 June the Municipality complained of the activities of those parents for whom 'une conformité d'éducation est un supplice' and ordered the closure of schools where any teacher 'oserait encore se permettre d'enseigner et de donner des leçons particulières ou dangereuses (en cela seul, qu'elles diffèrent de celles que reçoivent les enfants d'une classe moins fortunée)'.[3]

Since this whole scheme of education was expressly directed against fanaticism, it seems that distrust of the clergy's insidious influence sometimes converged with the Jacobins' suspicion of the corrupting power of money. Both money and fanaticism perverted the natural goodness of the people. Often, priests were denounced as the servants of the bourgeois in the countryside – in fact, the *curé* of Salon was denounced as a bourgeois.[4] The subaltern agents of the counter-revolution were denounced fairly indiscriminately as the servants of nobles, priests, bourgeois, and 'honnêtes gens'.

Thus, from evidence taken from both within and without the confines of the dossiers of the Revolutionary Tribunal, it appears that much of the Jacobins' antagonism to the priests was of a political nature. There is little evidence that the

[1] A. Comm., 3D1.

[2] A. Comm., 3D1, *Organisation des écoles primaires*, municipal proclamation of 11 *germinal* II (31 Mar. 1794).

[3] A. Comm., 3D1, municipal proclamation of 18 *prairial* II (6 June 1794).   [4] See above, p. 57.

Jacobins of Marseilles were fervently atheistical 'dechristian-isers': many of the most blatant acts of dechristianisation at Marseilles were due to outsiders[1] – notably Maignet – and were of a fairly late date, as if in emulation of activities at Paris or in other provincial centres. Not till 13 March 1794 was the statue of the virgin of Notre-Dame de la Garde melted down; not till 1 April 1794 did Maignet inaugurate the *Temple de la Raison* at Marseilles in the church of Section 11, Les Prêcheurs. The wave of abdications from the priesthood seems to have been three or four months later than at Paris or the more advanced provincial areas.[2]

It seems therefore that many of the anti-religious activities of the revolutionaries – including the condemnation of priests by the Revolutionary Tribunal and Military Commission[3] – were directed against the 'aristocracy' of the clergy. To the Jacobins, most priests were aristocrats in clerical disguise.

Thus aristocrats had established their dominion over the Bouches-du-Rhône for four months in the summer of 1793. It had been, in the eyes of the Revolutionary Tribunal, an anti-popular régime, a régime based on deceit, on privilege, on contempt for the honest people of Provence. It was main-tained in power, however, not merely by abusing the ignorance, the open-hearted credulity of the people, but also by acts of violence and, in some cases, by armed force, only superficially decked out with trappings of legality.

---

[1] This impression may be partly determined by the paucity of records from the Club, Committee of Surveillance, Municipality (etc.) of Marseilles.

[2] Moreover, some measures against religious observance – notably protests at the celebration of Sundays by shopkeepers and especially peasants – seem to have had distinct economic undertones. The Club of Marseilles stated that 'les instructions politiques et civiques' given out by priests should give renewed vigour to work in the fields (ABR, L2076, *La Société républicaine de Marseille aux curés des campagnes*, 19 Oct. 1793), a preoccupation echoed by other documents (Sunday observance, 'Préjudice encore (*floréal* II) essentiellement aux travaux des campagnes'). Note also that the citizens of Séon, in the *terroir* of Marseilles, offered their church to the military for use as a barracks. This act, acclaimed by the Municipality, (6 *germinal* II 26 Mar. 1794), as heralding the extinction of fanaticism at Séon, is put into sharper perspective by a petition of the citizens of Séon, complaining that a company of soldiers was quartered in their country houses. A. Comm., 4D8.   [3] Which condemned nine clerics to death.

CHAPTER NINE

Virulent Counter-Revolution

(a) THE SECTIONS

Those who had attended the Sections were inevitably considered as suspects by the Revolutionary Tribunal; but even more suspect were those who had attempted to set up Sections or to persuade or coerce citizens into attending them; and, naturally, the *commissaires* sent by the Sections of Marseilles to establish similar organs in the towns and villages of the department were regarded as the most blameworthy of all agents of rebellion.[1] But other citizens, many of whom had held no special commission from the Sections, were punished for helping in their establishment and activity.

Those who defended the legitimacy of the Sections were held to have insulted the Convention by setting up inferior bodies as equal in sovereignty to the supreme legislative authority in France.

On nous faisait croire que les sections étaient souveraines

was a cry of despair and resentment repeated by many of those who had succumbed to the propaganda emanating from the Sections. In their struggle with the Club, in their rejection of the authority first of Bayle and Boisset and, subsequently, of the Convention, the Sections had advanced pretensions to sovereignty.[2] Since the Convention had been enslaved by mobs whose will had repudiated the legally-expressed desires of many of the departments of France – and the majority of them for a short while in June – the Sections of Marseilles considered that the supreme power in the State returned to the people from whence it came. Since, in their view, the Convention had dissolved itself, it was the Sections, as *Assemblées primaires*, on whom the task of electing a new assembly devolved. All those who had accepted posts in the Sections, who had taken part in the

---

[1] See below, pp. 252 ff.　　　　　　　[2] See above, pp. 88–9.

electoral assemblies held under the auspices of the Sections had *de facto* accepted this doctrine. When they later came to stand before the Revolutionary Tribunal, a few of them tried to justify their actions by defending the Sections' claims to sovereignty.

The terms they used were identical to those contained in the pamphlets of April and May 1793. Generally the accused affirmed that the Sections constituted the 'people' and that they therefore had the right to elect all members of the established authorities, including an assembly to replace the Convention. Thus Jean-Baptiste Nicolas said that he remained as a judge of the Popular Tribunal because the sovereign people had elected him in the Sections. To this, the president replied

> Je vous observe que le peuple en masse est souverain, qu'aucune portion du peuple ne peut exercer cette souveraineté séparément, qu'il a délégué ses pouvoirs à ses représentants pour lui donner des lois.[1]

This was the orthodox Jacobin view. It was a valid interpretation of the constitution if it was not admitted that it had been the force of the mob which, in the insurrection of 31 May and 2 June, violated the Convention; and, in fact, some of the accused claimed that they had supported the interpretation of the president.

On the whole though, few of those who defended the Sections before the Tribunal appealed to general principles: few men were accused of having provided a theoretical justification for the seizure of power by the Sections. Most of the accused defended – or had defended – the Sections for having brought to an end the reign of anarchy in Marseilles, and this they did in terms similar to those employed in the pamphlets written during the struggle between the Sections and the Club. Even here however, the Tribunal did not deal with many people whose primary crime had been to have defended in words the deeds and pretensions of the Sections. When Paul Bussac appeared before the Tribunal his activities on behalf of the Sections as a propagandist-journalist were indeed mentioned; but it was upon his actions as a member of the General Committee that the Tribunal concentrated;[2] for it concerned

---

[1] ABR, L3112, 28 Sept. 1793, Jean-Baptiste-François Nicolas.

[2] ABR, L3113, 7 Oct. 1793, Paul-Raimbaud Bussac, *maître des langues*.

itself principally with those who had served the Sections in deeds rather than in words.

It was therefore those who held offices in the Sections and those who attended them who were most frequently dealt with by the Tribunal. Those who recruited for the Sections were similarly taken to task. Toussaint Beaumont, *curé* of Cuges, told the Tribunal that the village of Allauch had been disarmed because it refused to open a Section – at Cuges, Beaumont had been president of the Section, but he pleaded that the Section was merely the club under a different name. This excuse was accepted by the Tribunal and Beaumont was acquitted of the very serious charge of having established a Section in his village.[1] On the other hand, the notorious *curé* of Salon, André Reyne, was sentenced to death as 'l'auteur principal de l'ouverture des Sections à Salon'.[2] Inhabitants of villages and small towns who had co-operated willingly with the *commissaires* of Aix and Marseilles in the opening of Sections, were thus severely punished.

Those who visited the Sections frequently found it necessary to explain away this aspect of their activity. Guillaume Vallette was lucky with his description of himself as seated in the corner of Section 7, laughing and scoffing at their work and predicting their fall within two months.[3] Louise Fabrègue, from Berre, went only twice:

> un soir que la section fut ouverte, qu'on fit un feu, et qu'on chantait une chanson et une autre fois qu'on disait qu'il était venu des commissaires. Ils tardèrent trop: je m'en allais pour avoir soin de ma vieille tante.[4]

Finally, Charles-Pierre Brack, employed in the customs, affirmed unrepentently that

> J'ai paru dans ma section comme tout citoyen d'après la loi qui ordonne que les sections sont permanentes tant que la patrie est en danger.[5]

---

[1] ABR, L3113, 11 Oct. 1793, Toussaint Beaumont.

[2] ABR, L3114, 4 *frimaire* II (24 Nov. 1793), André Reyne.

[3] ABR, L3118, 28 *germinal* II (17 Apr. 1794), Guillaume Vallette.

[4] ABR, L3115, 23 *nivôse* II (12 Jan. 1794), Louise-Élisabeth Fabrègue, *femme* Bigaudy.

[5] ABR, L3109, petition; L3113, 17 Oct. 1793, Charles-Pierre Brack, who was released.

The most common excuse for attendance was that force had been used against them and this excuse was given validity by the existence of summonses sent out by the Sections to those who had failed to respond to invitations to attend their meetings. These summonses declared that those who did not come to the Sections would be regarded as indifferent to the work they were doing and would bring upon themselves 'quelque chose de fâcheux', preparatory to denunciation to the General Committee.[1]

Thus the petitions of those who claimed that, had they not frequented the Sections, they would have been deprived of their political rights, were in a large part justified. Since the Sections regularly had recourse to measures of coercion and threats, it is not surprising that men went into the Sections (and perhaps increased their membership) without caring much for what was going on there – men such as Étienne Arnaud, a cooper, who after serving in a *corsaire* returned to Marseilles in the summer of 1793, after three months absence. He was told that if he did not go to the Sections he would be regarded as a suspect. So he went:

> Je n'entendais parler que de respecter les personnes et les propriétés et d'aller au secours d'une république une et indivisible.[2]

Some of the men and women who came before the Tribunal had their own explanations of why they did not go to the Sections, of how they avoided going. According to their stories – obviously not always true – they feigned illness or deafness, they pretended that they were more stupid than they really were, and so on. Often their occupations prevented them from going, but other reasons were not lacking –

> Femme, je m'en occupe de mon ménage et non de la politique.
> Accablé d'infirmités je suis retiré à la campagne.
> On a eu beau heurter à ma porte. Je ne paraissais pas. Je faisais le sourd. La section était vis-à-vis.

---

[1] ABR, L3116, 29 *ventôse* II (19 Mar. 1794), dossier of Pierre-Henri Peylard, letter from Section 23, 28 July 1793.

[2] ABR, L3130, interrogation by Military Commission, 1 *ventôse* II (19 Feb. 1794).

Je ne restais pas à la section et je n'ai jamais fait de motion.
J'allais passer toutes les soirées chez ma maîtresse.

Often, hard work in the fields kept the *cultivateurs* away from
the Sections, while sometimes a family of seven or eight children
had the same effect. Thérèse Gibouin described herself as

une pauvre blanchisseuse qui ne me suis mêlée de rien . . .
j'ai ma vie à gagner et n'ai pas mon temps à perdre.[1]

Most of these humble people were released by the Tribunal:

Bernard, livré à son état et abattu de fatigues le soir, a peu
connu sa section et n'a pas fréquenté le club antipolitique à
son regret.

So Bernard, a blacksmith, was released.[2]

The judges regarded the Sections as instruments of the rich,
who might at most choose some peasants, illiterate and bur-
dened with work, to preserve a front of popular participation.
This picture was confirmed by some of the evidence heard by
the Tribunal. François Gourel, a *notaire* of Berre, apologised
when he offered an attestation signed by only one witness: all
the other members of his Section who knew how to write had
fled because they occupied illegal posts.[3] Other stray indications
give the same impression. When Mathieu Cypriot, a pulley-
maker (*poulieur*) of Marseilles, was asked why he went to the
Section, he replied, 'J'y allais pour tirer paiement de mon
bourgeois qui y était toujours.'[4]

(b) ENVOYS OF THE SECTIONS

Those who had served the Sections of Marseilles and Aix
outside the bounds of these towns formed a fairly large proportion of those who appeared before the Tribunal charged with
carrying out the tasks of the Sections. In general, they did much

---

[1] ABR, L3113, 5 Nov. 1793, Thérèse Gibouin.

[2] ABR, L3113, 26 Oct. 1793, Balthasar Bernard.

[3] ABR, L3113, Gourel was condemned to death, 25 *brumaire* II (15 Nov. 1793).

[4] ABR, L3118, freed 16 *germinal* II (5 Apr. 1794); but this phrase comes
from his interrogation by the Military Commission.

the same work as those who remained at Marseilles but had more scope for individual enterprise. They set up Sections, quashed Jacobin municipalities, closed the clubs, helped levy men and money for the Departmental Army, promulgated the proclamations and ordinances of the Sections of Aix and Marseilles, ordered the disarmament of local Jacobins and so on. They were commonly referred to by the public prosecutor as 'les commissaires désorganisateurs'. Though they had virtually the same tasks as the *commissaires* of the clubs, who had gone out in the early months of 1793, and though they carried out these tasks in much the same way as the Jacobins, they claimed that, far from being destructive, their activities were designed to bring to the department the same benefits of peace and order which the revolt of the Sections had restored in Marseilles and in Aix.

Twenty-one men were judged by the Tribunal for being envoys of the Sections – apart from sectionary office-holders who had been sent out on commission. Of these twenty-one, eighteen were condemned to death; not one was freed. Mostly they seem to have been artisans, customs employees, small tradesmen – rather than the *bourgeois*, lawyers, and *propriétaires* who served the Sections in a more sedentary capacity.

One of the most active of these envoys was Jean-Jacques Caillol, owner of a sailing-boat. His sphere of action had been the valley of the Rhône. There, according to Giraud, he had helped the counter-revolutionaries of Arles to repulse a flotilla of naval ships sent from Toulon to support the patriots. Caillol admitted having been sent on 28 May to Arles and to Tarascon, and to having been away from Marseilles for six weeks. His letters from these towns to the General Committee of Marseilles were read out to the Tribunal.

'On me menait comme un enfant', he explained. He had asked the Sections of Saint-Rémy to send men from their National Guard to help repulse the patriots of Arles and their allies: he had arrested two citizens going from Grenoble to Toulon on the affairs of the Convention. He wrote to the General Committee of Marseilles asking for control of the men of the Departmental Army who were passing through Arles, and this he obtained. Thus the Tribunal had collected enough documents to establish, without chance of refutation, the guilt

of Caillol, and therefore the death penalty imposed upon him
could not have been unexpected.[1]

François Philippier, a timber-merchant of Marseilles, had
performed a similar mission on behalf of his Section. At Toulon

> il a mangé avec tous les habits galonnés soit de terre soit de
> mer . . . il a bien gagné dans le crime l'argent qu'on lui a
> donné.

As in the trial of Caillol, Philippier was confronted with the
letters which he had written when on mission. His answers
were all in a tone of despair which betrayed that he knew that
he did not have a chance of escaping with his life. He made no
attempt to deny the accuracy of the allegations of the president,
instead, he contented himself with repeating 'on m'a envoyé
comme on envoie une boule'. His activities in Section 16 were,
however, conspicuously detailed in the pages of the register.
On 29 May he had left Marseilles to visit the communes to set
up Sections in the department; on 18 July he had been sent to
the Sections of Toulon, which had recently followed the
rebellious example of those of Marseilles. His letters from
Toulon were extremely incriminating, for he denounced the
Montagnards for trying to send out the fleet from Toulon in an
ill-equipped condition, so that it would fall into the hands of the
coalition powers, and he rejoiced at the arrest of the deputies
Pierre Baille and Beauvais and expressed the hope that Barras
and Fréron were also taken. Thus, as with Caillol, there could
be no doubt as to his guilt and he was condemned to death.[2]

Often the *commissaires* acted as the real authorities when they
stayed for a short time in the villages. Thus many of the
inhabitants of the communes through which they passed were
accused of having collaborated with them – of having pointed
out to them patriots to be arrested and taken to Marseilles, of
having gone to Aix or Marseilles to ask that *commissaires* be
sent to overthrow the Jacobins, of aiding them disarm the
patriots and so on. Many villagers pleaded that they had been

---

[1] ABR, L3114, 1 *frimaire* II (21 Nov. 1793) Jean-Jacques Caillol; and
L1990, letters from *commissaires* to General Committee.

[2] ABR, L3118, 29 *germinal* II (18 Apr. 1794), François Philippier and
L1944, Section 16, 29 May 1793, etc.; L2003, letters from Toulon to
General Committee, 17 and 21 July 1793.

forced to set up Sections by the *commissaires* from Marseilles or
had done so only to obtain corn from Marseilles.[1] This city,
especially, had a reputation for sending out its National Guard
to bring into line recalcitrant communes and if Aix and Arles
could be dragooned into submission to the will of Marseilles,
how much more hopeless was it for Éguilles, Forcalquier or
Ventabren to resist.[2] No doubt the later *commissaires* were at
first described as 'ces anges tutélaires' but they too came to
demand money, to levy men to fight in Marseilles' battalions.
Not only the dispossessed Jacobins, therefore, resented the
commissaires of Marseilles and Aix. Nor would it be true to see
every village in the Bouches-du-Rhône as the scene of tumul-
tuous skirmishes between Jacobins and 'aristocrats'. Many
villages slept in conditions of perfect lethargy, changing the
name 'club' into that of 'section', but keeping the same men in
office in both institutions, showing great activity when the
Marseillais were present, but soon reverting to their own ways
of sloth and indifference.

'Marseille nous a forcé la main comme à toutes les communes'
was a plea which was tempting to make, especially since its
commissaires came not only with force to back them up, but with
propaganda also – the Manifesto was designed for this purpose
and served admirably to 'lead astray' the inhabitants of the
countryside – 'On nous faisait entendre que 66 départements
étaient pour le fédéralisme. . . .' This propaganda had a great
effect since, as one countryman remarked, the people of the
villages were accustomed to believe that those of the town were
better informed.[3]

Those who called in the *commissaires* of Marseilles were,
however, held to be the chief culprits by the judges of the
Revolutionary Tribunal and were denounced accordingly,
whereas those who had obviously been imposed upon were
treated with leniency.

[1] ABR, L3115; Jean-Joseph-François Camoin, *notaire* of Les Camoin, in
the *terroir*, said that they set up a Section to obtain corn from Marseilles.
(28 *nivôse* II, 17 Jan. 1794).

[2] That there was some resistance, see above, p. 122. Also, one envoy
from Marseilles, François Blanchard, *marchand*, sent back reports that the
peasants of Mornas (in the Vaucluse) resisted the establishment of Sections.
ABR, L3115, 25 *nivôse* II (14 Jan. 1794).

[3] ABR, L3113, 11 Oct. 1793, Toussaint-André Beaumont.

Thus the Revolutionary Tribunal followed, in its treatment of the *commissaires* of Marseilles and Aix, and their allies, the principles which marked its treatment of sectionary office-holders. In other words, it attempted to distinguish between the leaders and the led.

(c) SECTIONS AND CLUBS

Since the Club of Marseilles, and the clubs of the other towns in Provence, were the centres of bitter fighting between Jacobins and their enemies, it is natural that many of those who appeared before the Tribunal were accused of offences which had been directed against the clubs and against their members. Those who could prove that they had been members of a club were sure to gain the indulgence of the Tribunal, provided that during the reign of the Sections they had not been too eager to renounce that membership or to repudiate the principles of the Jacobins. The most unfortunate men were those who had served the clubs in 1789–92 but who had, in 1793, turned against them.

> Après avoir été longtemps membre de la Société populaire, il l'a hautement calomniée, il a dit que les clubistes étaient des intrigants.

This was a dire accusation, for which Jean-Joseph Gaillard, a property-owner, was fined 4000 *livres*.[1] It was quite a common one, however, in various forms. Thus Jean-Baptiste Blanc, a *ménager* of Jouques, had assumed the disguise of 'un homme simple' but had been secretly ashamed of belonging to a club and had welcomed the Sections.[2] On the other hand, Pierre Garnier had been a keen member of the Club of Marseilles; however, he changed suddenly and became a rabid sectionary.[3] Such accusations confirm the impression that many sectionary activists had been prominent in the clubs.[4]

A large number of people were accused of saying that the

---

[1] ABR, L3116, 29 *ventôse* II (19 Mar. 1794), Jean-Joseph Gaillard.

[2] ABR, L3113, 11 Nov. 1793, Jean-Baptiste Blanc. (Jouques is in the *arrond.* of Aix; *canton* of Peyrolles.)

[3] ABR, L3118, *renvoi*, 28 *germinal* II (17 Apr. 1794), Pierre Garnier.

[4] See above, p. 80.

clubists were a horde of brigands, who continually plotted massacre and pillage, who terrorised the legal administrations and broadcast anarchist principles throughout the Republic. A man accused of being an opponent of the clubists voted to throw them out of their hall – and said that it would have to be disinfected before the 'honnêtes gens' could use it. If he had the misfortune to belong to a club, he quickly burnt his membership card. When he heard of the Club's closure, 'il a rendu grâce au ciel, qu'il outrageait impudemment'. Or perhaps, as *veuve* Garrely was said to have done, she draped her house in black in mock mourning for the demise of 'la maison de Lucifer'.[1] Perhaps he – or she – was present at the closing of the club. Then the public prosecutor would say,

> on l'a vu assister à la destruction du club, on l'a vu grimacer aristocratiquement le long des rues à l'enterrement de cette même société. Il faisait signe aux fenêtres de battre les mains.[2]

If, like Louis Barthélemy, he had been a member of the general committee of the Sections of Aubagne, he would have taken part in a motion to proceed to the rooms of the club, to burn everything found there, pull down the *tribune*, burn the debris and cap everything by a firework display.[3] He may even have taken part, actively, in the destruction of the club, and have 'renversé de ses mains sacrilèges la tribune de la liberté' – as did Jean-François Amalric, who presided over the meeting of warehouse-porters which decided to break up the Club.[4]

On the other hand, many claimed that they had done something to prevent the closing of the clubs and had spoken against men who wanted to close them. One man advanced the fact that, far from having destroyed the club of Auriol, he had saved the Declaration of the Rights of Man from the blaze.

Those who disarmed clubists or took part in *visites domiciliaires* were severely punished. It was ironic that a movement which

---

[1] ABR, L3114; 19, 21 *frimaire* II (9, 11 Nov. 1793), Catherine Blanc, *veuve* Garelly.

[2] ABR, L3118, 29 *germinal* II (18 Apr. 1794), Claude Jogaud.

[3] ABR, L3119, 5 *floréal* II (24 Apr. 1794), dossier of Marie-Roch Barthélemy.

[4] ABR, L3112; 25, 30 Sept. 1793, Jean-François Amalric.

started ostensibly as a revolt against such measures should have
had widespread recourse to them; and Giraud made much of
this, dwelling on the brutality with which these operations were
effected and on the blatant discrepancy between principles
and practice. Another indignity imposed on patriots was the
destruction of their trees of liberty, objects of emulation and
symbols of revolutionary virility. For the aristocrats, the felling
or destruction of these 'trees' (some painted against house-
walls) presaged the decapitation of the patriots.

Even those who slandered the patriots appeared before the
Tribunal, though such men had often contributed to the
counter-revolution in more substantial ways. Jérôme Mathieu,
an 'écrivain public' of Marseilles, was accused by Giraud of
having spoken at his Section

> avec le ton de véhémence contre-révolutionnaire de vider les
> prisons, d'engraisser l'échafaud, et d'éteindre au plutôt la
> race des clubistes.

Asked if he had made a motion to slaughter the patriots who
were in prison – patriots who included Maillet and Giraud –
he replied that he had merely wished to leave a strong guard
on the prisons while the sectionaries went off to fight Carteaux.
But the president persisted in affirming that Mathieu had
urged his fellow-sectionaries to massacre the prisoners.[1] And
indeed, a motion which might well have been interpreted in
this way had been made in the Sections – 'to empty the prisons'
– as the army of Carteaux approached Marseilles.[2] Mathieu
had a long record of counter-revolutionary crimes – he had, it
seems, attacked the patriots of Section 11, and he admitted
having escorted patriots to the guillotine. He was therefore
condemned to death by the Tribunal.

Another proposed prison massacre, this time at Tarascon,
was referred to by the president when he asked Antoine
Imbert if he had not suggested the slaughter of the prisoners
in the château, to make room for more. But this accusation
was not proved and Imbert was released. Other anti-Jacobin
pronouncements were varied – suggestions that Marat's
murderer should be rewarded or even made queen; that the

[1] ABR, L3115, 17 *nivôse* II (6 Jan. 1794), Jérôme Mathieu *dit* Bertrand.
[2] See above, p. 124.

people should be made to eat hay and so on. Those who denounced Bayle and Boisset, who said that the patriots wished to put Orléans on the throne, who described the disarmament of 19 March as the prelude to a massacre of 6000 'honnêtes gens' were severely punished. One man was accused of denouncing the whole battalion of the 10 August and of having remarked (with Jacobin callousness), 'Demain il y aura du gibier à la guillotine'.[1]

Women were accused of this type of offence more often than any other except 'fanaticism' – they expressed their hatred for the patriots in words rather than deeds; and, if one is to believe the accusations against them, they were especially hard towards patriots who had been captured and were being taken to prison or to the guillotine. The case of Catherine Blanc *veuve* Garrely shows this clearly,[2] for she stood at the door of her house and constantly attracted the attention – 'les caresses' – of the ardent sectionaries, above all by railing against victims who were being taken, under the bayonets of the Sections, to the scaffold. She accused the Savons of doing a lot of harm, said that the guillotine was too kind a fate for Abeille, Grimaud and Bazin, called the *abbé* Bausset 'anti-Christ', described the wives of three patriots as 'les trois putains des prisonniers', accused Isoard of stealing 300,000 *livres* worth of confiscated property, and said that red-hot pincers should replace the guillotine. She herself was merely given three years in prison. That this is not an isolated incident is shown by the cases of several other women – Marie Borie of Salon, accused of clapping her hands when she heard of the arrest of patriots,[3] Marguerite Aubert demanding the immediate murder of the patriots as a public spectacle and guilty of acts of petty vindictiveness towards the children and wives of imprisoned patriots.[4]

This sort of crime came to be considered by the Tribunal as a typically feminine expression of anti-revolutionary feeling;

---

[1] ABR, L3118, 26 *germinal* II (15 Apr. 1794), Pierre Brest.
[2] ABR, L3114; 19, 21 *frimaire* II (9, 11 Nov. 1793), Catherine Blanc, *veuve* Garrely.
[3] ABR, L3118, 29 *germinal* II (18 Apr. 1794), Marie Borie, *femme* Gonelle.
[4] ABR, L3119, 3 *floréal* II (22 Apr. 1794), Marguerite Aubert, *femme* Lambert. Condemned to death.

but several of these women had no difficulty in refuting such accusations and securing their release.[1] The Tribunal seemed resigned to the fact that many women had been glad of the opportunity to express their hatred of the patriots who had stirred up trouble and strife in Marseilles and the surrounding villages, and apart from severely punishing a few notorious baiters of the patriots – and quite a few women who testified against the patriots before the sectionary tribunals – generally showed a reluctant indulgence towards women accused of this offence. Often therefore, those who were accused of the most bloodthirsty threats towards patriots – to make two out of one by chopping off their heads, to extract their sinews to make whips to beat them with, to cut them open with their table-knives, to hang them from all the trees for miles about Marseilles – these men and women were frequently released when it became clear that they had played no real part in the counter-revolution.

Many men, however, claimed that they had protected the patriots against persecution, even explaining that they had accepted posts on counter-revolutionary bodies at the request of leading Jacobins in order to advance the revolutionary cause. Except in four or five cases involving men too poor or too ignorant to be politically dangerous, the Tribunal refused to accept such excuses, saying that one could not help the patriots by oneself becoming counter-revolutionary. Other citizens claimed that they had given refuge to patriots in their houses, or had visited patriots in prison to bring them comfort. Louis Seytres said that he had defended a Jacobin before the Popular Tribunal[2] but most others afforded more clandestine help. On the whole, these stories, even when backed by the testimony of leading Montagnards, were of little benefit to the accused.

(d) THE JUDICIAL REPRESSION OF THE PATRIOTS

Those implicated in the judicial repression of the patriots were the most hated of all sectionaries. This was not just because they replaced the Criminal Tribunal and narrowly failed to send

---

[1] For example, ABR, L3113, 5 Nov. 1793, Anne Raspaud.
[2] ABR, L3119, 2 *floréal* II (21 Apr. 1794), Louis Seytres.

its members, Maillet, Giraud and Chompré, to the guillotine. The Popular Tribunal was more than just the organ which had supplanted the legally-established Criminal Tribunal. It formed the corner-stone of the edifice which the Sections had erected to repulse Jacobinism and, as such, had been singled out by the Convention for special condemnation. A decree of 15 May 1793 declared liable to the death penalty judges of any tribunal which had been created without the consent of the Convention. When the judges of the Popular Tribunal of Marseilles received this decree they laid down their powers (27 May). But the Tribunal was re-established in June. On 19 June, the Convention outlawed its judges and also those who gave evidence before it; and so those who sat on the Tribunal after 27 May and those who testified after the publication of the law of 19 June were liable to the death penalty.[1]

Fifteen members of the Popular and Military Tribunals (and one member of the provisional Criminal Tribunal) were judged by the Revolutionary Tribunal – all were condemned to death.[2] Pierre Laugier, a *bourgeois* of Marseilles, was tried on 28 August, the first session of the Revolutionary Tribunal,[3] denounced as president of the Popular Tribunal of Accusation. The first article of the decree of 19 June was read out, describing the judgements of the Popular Tribunal as so many murders and its judges as murderers. The fact that Laugier had been the president of the Tribunal of Accusation was so well known that his condemnation was certain. He had had a long (in revolutionary terms) and conspicuous career in the magistrature of Marseilles. Elected, on 24 November 1792, to the presidency of the Criminal Tribunal, he had stood down in favour of Maillet *cadet*,[4] since he preferred to give his full attention to the Popular Tribunal, of which he had been elected joint president on 26 September 1792 by the other judges of the Tribunal.[5]

Laugier had taken part regularly in the meetings of the

---

[1] ABR, L3100, papers of Popular Tribunal.

[2] They were 3 *négociants*; 3 *propriétaires*; 2 *hommes de loi*; 2 *bourgeois*; a *capitaine de navire*; an *imprimeur*; a *maître d'école*; a *constructeur de navires*; an *officier de la marine* and a *chirurgien-dentiste*.

[3] ABR, L3023, 28 Aug. 1793, Pierre Laugier.

[4] ABR, L278, Electoral Assembly, session of 24 Nov. 1792.

[5] ABR, L3100, Popular Tribunal, *procès-verbal* of election by members of the Tribunal, 26 Sept. 1792.

Tribunal throughout the autumn of 1792 when the vast majority of prisoners who appeared were released. Also, he had signed most of the proclamations of the Popular Tribunal, proclamations which emphasised the need to protect individual liberty and to preserve the rule of law, pledging impartial justice, from judges chosen by the people themselves.[1] He signed the address of 12 October 1792 drawing attention to lists of proscription which were circulated by 'aristocrats' with the intention of dividing the patriots,[2] and also that of 17 January 1793 pledging respect to persons and properties.[3] Thus far, Pierre Laugier had acted in concert, not only with his colleagues in the Popular Tribunal, but with the Club of Marseilles – indeed, he was president of the Club in December 1792 and showed that he was in full agreement with its principles by an outspoken speech denouncing the *appelants* and demanding the immediate execution of the king.[4] In this period, Club and Popular Tribunal and Criminal Tribunal worked in the same harness; Maillet *cadet*, president of the Criminal Tribunal, was a judge of the Popular Tribunal, and so was Étienne Bompard, soon to be a colleague of Maillet on the Revolutionary Tribunal.

It was in May 1793 that the careers of Maillet and Laugier diverged and former colleagues became bitter enemies. Laugier played a prominent part in evaluating evidence given before the Popular Tribunal by Seytres, Georges Manent and others, who attacked the clubists for attempting to massacre the peaceable citizens and magistrates of Marseilles.[5] This evidence was instrumental in effecting the arrest of the members of the Central Committee of the Club, including that of Maillet *cadet* and Joseph Giraud. It also led to the arrest and subsequent execution of Abeille, Grimaud and Bazin following the judgement of the Popular Tribunal.[6] Thus, the Popular Tribunal had openly joined the Sections in their battle with the Club, and had become their main instrument against the clubists. Even earlier, at the end of April 1793, Pierre Laugier had taken part

[1] ABR, L3100, Popular Tribunal, address of 1 Oct. 1792.
[2] loc. cit., address of 12 Oct. 1792.
[3] loc. cit., address of 17 Jan. 1793.
[4] ABR, *Jnal. Dépts. Mérid.*, cxxiii, 13 Dec. 1792.
[5] See above, pp. 46–8.
[6] See above, p. 113; and ABR, L3104, Popular Tribunal, interrogations of Abeille, etc., from the second half of May 1793.

in the trial of the Savons and their accomplices.[1] And as early
as 10 May 1793, he, and the Popular Tribunal, had been
obliged to issue an Address to the People of Marseilles, appeal-
ing to them for a renewal of their confidence to enable the
judges to pursue their struggle against the violators of individual
liberty; also, the Tribunal found it necessary to proclaim that

> ce n'est pas le procès à la Révolution que nous voulons
> instruire.[2]

Obviously, the clubists had attacked the Popular Tribunal as
an instrument of the Sections. Thus Laugier's attacks on the
appelants in December 1792, his attack on Barbaroux in January
1793,[3] and his term as president of the Club in February 1793,[4]
had not implied that he had permanently embraced Jacobin
principles – it was his position as one of the most eminent
judges of the Popular Tribunal which provided the element
of continuity in this stage of his career. For whereas Maillet
cadet had resigned from the Popular Tribunal at the end of
April when he had been summoned by Section 6 to choose
between his place on the Popular Tribunal and his presidency
of the Criminal Tribunal, Laugier (who had no second post)
continued to occupy his position in the Popular Tribunal,
embracing more and more closely the principles of the Sections.
This was not necessarily solely because he wished to keep his
post, but perhaps also because his participation in a Tribunal
noted for its opposition to arbitrary acts in the autumn of 1792
predisposed him to a moderate policy of opposition to the
Montagnard offensive of the spring of 1793. This offensive,
including the creation of a Revolutionary Tribunal to replace
the Popular Tribunal, obviously struck at the position of the
Popular Tribunal, while the action of Bayle and Boisset in
suspending that body had a similar result.

Laugier's career in Section 23 shows how he moved from
Jacobinism to a more moderate philosophy. In fact his career

---

[1] ABR, L3100, Popular Tribunal, minutes of session of the Tribunal of
Accusation, 27 Apr. 1793.

[2] ABR, L3100, Popular Tribunal, address of 10 May 1793.

[3] *Jnal. Dépts. Mérid.*, cxxxviii, 17 Jan. 1793.

[4] ABR, L2076, Club – Laugier signed as president the address to Barbaroux of 7/8 (?) Feb. 1793, bitterly condemning his vote for the *appel*.

is typical of the evolution of the Sections themselves. He was among the first to demand the creation of a central committee for the Sections,[1] he replaced Joseph Giraud, the public prosecutor of the Criminal Tribunal, as president of Section 23 on 30 April 1793,[2] and in this capacity he voted the sending of an address to the Convention attacking arbitrary disarmaments and so on. He led the opposition to Bayle and Boisset's *arrêtés*, demanded the recall of the 6000 men levied by the *Représentants* and adhered to all the addresses which attacked Marat and the Montagnards and which praised Barbaroux. Thereafter, his approval was given to all the important measures of the Sections.

However, when the decrees of 12 and 15 May were received, Laugier and his colleagues of the Popular Tribunal agreed to lay down their functions, though they expressed the wish that the Convention would, when it had heard the case of the Marseillais, authorise the restoration of the Popular Tribunal.[3] But, when the news of events in Paris on 2 June reached Marseilles and the Sections decided to restore the Popular Tribunal, Laugier resumed his post, though in doing so he was for the first time in his capacity as judge contravening the law. During the re-installation ceremonies, Laugier pledged their obedience to the will of the sovereign Sections and affirmed that threat of the death penalty did not intimidate them. Thus it is hardly surprising that the decree of 19 June should leave Laugier and his colleagues unmoved and that he is seen co-operating in the trial of Abeille, Grimaud and Bazin and in the interrogations of the clubists.[4] Clearly, he had placed himself in the category of those outlawed by the decree of 19 June.

Indeed during the later part of the rule of the Sections Laugier became indispensable – *chef de légion* in the National Guard and *commissaire* sent to restore the failing morale of the Departmental Army.[5] Finally, he was appointed on 14 August one of the five members of the Committee of General Security,

[1] ABR, L1950, Section 23, 29 Apr. 1793.

[2] ABR, L1947, Section 23, 30 Apr. 1793. This register contains most of the evidence as to Laugier's career in the Sections.

[3] ABR, L3100, Popular Tribunal, session of 27 May 1793.

[4] ABR, L3105, Popular Tribunal, Tribunal of Accusation, sessions of 13, 15 July 1793; L3106, sessions of 25 May, 11 June 1793, etc.

[5] ABR, L48, Three Administrations, 27 July 1793.

designed to tighten still further the direction of the sectionary revolt.[1]

Thus Laugier's career mirrored the evolution of the Sections, as he and many of his friends, once ardent colleagues of the Jacobins, became their most determined opponents. The careers of Maillet *cadet* and Pierre Laugier, which were so closely bound together in the autumn of 1792, diverged, so that, in successive phases of the Revolution in Marseilles, they became each other's judges.

The Montagnard judges had no high opinion of the justice dispensed by their predecessors. In condemning Louis Meyfrédy, a merchant, to death, they commented on its arbitrary nature.[2] The Revolutionary Tribunal, which was always most careful to give each judge the opportunity to explain the reasons for his verdict, and to quote in full the texts of the laws, found its predecessor's justice lacking in this respect and therefore considered the Popular Tribunal a vicious instrument by which the Sections, hypocritical upholders of law and order and worshippers of the sanctity of legal forms, had waged a bitter and bloody war against the most patriotic inhabitants of Marseilles.

No mercy was therefore to be expected from the Revolutionary Tribunal by those other 'juges populaires' who appeared before it. Once it had been established that they had taken part in its activities after 19 June, they were outlawed, despite their pleas that they had been obeying the sovereign people or had been forced by poverty to accept posts.[3] Moreover, two men who had served as *huissiers* to the Tribunal were likewise condemned to death.[4]

The Popular Tribunal had not been the only judicial organ used by the Sections. Indeed the Military Tribunal, even more

[1] ABR, L48, Three Administrations, 14 Aug. 1793.

[2] ABR, L3112, 21 Sept. 1793, Louis Meyfrédy; and L3023, 21 Sept. 1793.

[3] ABR, L3112, Jean Francoul, 16 Sept. 1793; Nicolas Clastrier, 26 Sept.; Jean-Baptiste-François Nicolas, 28 Sept.; L3115, Paul-Augustin Espitalier, 27 *nivôse* II (16 Jan. 1794); L3116, Antoine Étienne *dit* Blégier, 25 *ventôse* II (15 Mar. 1794); L3118, 15 *germinal* II (4 Apr. 1794), Claude Bontoux, Lazare Périer Meynard, and Henri Yvan.

[4] ABR, L3112, Pierre Mignonnat, 30 Aug. 1793; L3113, Jean-François Chauvet, 4 Nov. 1793.

abhorrent to the patriots, had been a sectionary creation, established after the riot of 21 July. Five of its members were outlawed by the Revolutionary Tribunal. Maillet said that the Military Tribunal was even more sanguinary than the so-called popular body, judging in twenty-four hours with no hope of appeal. This was true: moreover, its sentences, though never it seems fatal, were extremely severe in relation to the crime involved, the penalties including imprisonment in chains, even for expressing views which went against the policies of the Sections. *Femme* Fassy, who was to become a frequent witness against sectionaries before the Montagnard judges, had been condemned to twelve years in prison: a relative secured the identification and conviction of at least one judge of the Military Tribunal.[1]

It is obvious from the cases heard by the Montagnards that some of the 'judges' of the Military Tribunal were press-ganged into accepting posts to which they were elected. They had no knowledge of the law in general and no experience of judicial work. The Tribunal's powers had been the object of much dispute and the quick turn-over of judges had not been conducive to good justice. Perhaps these circumstances help to explain the confusion in the minds of those accused of having sat on the Tribunal; but to the Revolutionary Tribunal at least, they did not excuse their participation in an ill-conceived and outlawed travesty of justice. De la Ferté at least was appointed judge

> A l'effet de juger militairement le prévenu de révolte qui a été arrêté la nuit dernière –

powers which were later extended to cover all crimes against the policies of the Sections. Proclaimed by the General Committee, these facts were well known to the whole of Marseilles. All five members of the Military Tribunal judged were condemned to death – one of them, François Carnelli, a dentist, for attending a single judgement which was not among the most severe.[2]

Men who had co-operated with the sectionary Tribunals –

[1] ABR, L3118, 16 *germinal* II (5 Apr. 1794), identification of Pierre Bagarry.

[2] ABR, L3112, 6 Sept., Jean-Baptiste Chaulan and François Carnelli; 9 Sept., Mathieu-François de la Ferté; L3113, 23 Nov., Jean-Pierre Gérard-Reissolet; L3118, 16 *germinal* II (15 Apr. 1794), Pierre Bagarry.

national guardsmen who had arrested men and escorted them before their judges,[1] and prison officers who guarded patriots before trial[2] – were condemned to death, even if ignorant and of lowly social status. A drum-major was executed for drumming at the execution of the victims of the Sections' justice, in an attempt to drown the patriots' appeals to the people.[3]

Recognition of the Tribunals' jurisdiction was also a most serious crime. Thus Honoré Audiffren, a sailor of La Ciotat, a member of that town's general committee, wrote to the Popular Tribunal in August 1793 that his town was glad to have been adopted among the Tribunal's justiciables. He sent two patriots before the court. Such whole-hearted co-operation was fatal to Audiffren.[4]

Those who threatened to arrest the wives of patriots who had fled to escape persecution by the Sections, those who had seized the clubists of Marseilles who had fled to Toulon and those who had demanded the transference of the prisoners of Marseilles to Toulon, were all sentenced by the Tribunal. Men who brought evidence against patriots before the Popular or Military Tribunals or before the committees of the Sections were also dealt with. The denunciation of patriots before these sectionary bodies was perhaps the most common crime brought before the Tribunal for, by the law of 19 June, even those who merely testified were outlawed. But whereas the Revolutionary Tribunal assumed that the judges of its infamous predecessor knew the provisions of this decree, there was some doubt as to whether those who had come forward as witnesses had had this opportunity. Giraud wrote to the Minister of Justice to ask if a law which had not been published in Marseilles could be used to punish those who had offended against it unwittingly. Gohier replied that, though in normal circumstances a law would have to be published to be valid, if those who were liable to punishment under the law themselves suppressed it, they were to be punished as if the law had been published.[5] Thus

---

[1] ABR, L3115, 6 *nivôse* II (26 Dec. 1793), Pierre Gueyrard and Honoré Peyre.

[2] ABR, L3118, 23 *germinal* II (12 Apr. 1794), Antoine Monier.

[3] ABR, L3118, 24 *germinal* II (13 Apr. 1794), Antoine Chevalier.

[4] ABR, L3114, 28 *frimaire* II (18 Dec. 1793), Honoré Audiffren.

[5] ABR, L3127, Gohier to Giraud, 18 Sept. 1793.

a policy of severity had been sanctioned by the Minister of Justice.

As far as can be seen, the Revolutionary Tribunal took considerable trouble to establish if denunciations had been made after 19 June. One cause of this thoroughness was obviously the desire of the judges to obtain convictions; but their scanning of the minutes of the Popular Tribunal also forced them to postpone judgement when they found no evidence for allegations.[1] Generally, when the Tribunal condemned a person for having testified before the Popular Tribunal, it gave the date of the deposition: these dates are accurate, despite the accused's protestations to the contrary. As regards the Military Tribunal, evidence was often even more difficult to come by. Two citizens had to be freed provisionally because Chompré confessed that he had been unable to find the papers of that counter-revolutionary body.[2]

Many more suspects were convicted of having denounced patriots before the committees of their Sections. This was an offence only slightly less serious than denunciation before the 'tribunaux de sang', for the sectionary committees sent the depositions to the tribunals of Marseilles. In so far as people who went to Marseilles to testify before the Popular Tribunal showed a determination which guaranteed the virulence of their hatred for the patriots, their's was the more serious offence. Those who deposed before their local committees were more likely to have been misled into doing so. Certainly the committee of surveillance of Salon thought so. It appealed to the Tribunal to postpone the trials of those who merely testified before the Sections and did not confirm their deposition before the Popular Tribunal. It pointed out that about two hundred and fifty people of Salon, mostly peasants, had made depositions before the central committee of the Sections; but that few of them went to the Popular Tribunal.[3]

Many of those who had testified before the Popular Tribunal

[1] For example, ABR, L3118, 24 *germinal* II (13 Apr. 1794), Dominique Ravel and the Rougier *frères*; L3119, 1 *floréal* II (20 Apr. 1794), François-Victor Casserin.

[2] ABR, L3113, 4 Oct. 1793, *femmes* Blacas and Astrevigne. Some judgements survive dispersedly.

[3] ABR, L3109, *Comité de surveillance* of Salon to the Revolutionary Tribunal, 4 *frimaire* II (24 Nov. 1793).

had been members of 'la bourgeoisie villageoise' of Salon –
lawyers, *bourgeois*, *propriétaires*, doctors and so on. Their denunciations had been mostly against those who had levied forced
loans. It was these men who were most severely punished by the
Tribunal,[1] though others also received the death penalty.

Some citizens were accused of having received or collected
denunciations, sometimes in considerable quantity, 120 being
the highest recorded number.

Thus the Sections hardly differed from the clubs as far as
violence of deed and language was concerned: many sectionaries had learnt their tactics in the clubs and, when pressed
hard by opposition, resorted to the methods of their enemies.
Little wonder therefore that as soon as events in Paris in early
June had become known, the Marseillais thought in terms of a
punitive expedition to the capital. Unfortunately for the
Sections however, their warrior ardour, not backed by any
deep conviction or philosophy, proved unequal to the tasks
which faced it.

[1] ABR, L3118, 16 *germinal* II (5 Apr. 1794), Pierre Lagier; L3119, 5
floréal II (24 Apr. 1794), Jean-Jacques Rastèque; L3113, 11 Nov. 1793,
Jean-Baptiste Blanc; L3114, 8 *frimaire* II (28 Nov. 1793), Jean-Joseph
Barlatier.

CHAPTER TEN

The Convention in Danger

(a) ATTITUDES TO THE CONVENTION

The Revolutionary Tribunal naturally concerned itself with the opinions which the accused men had expressed as regards the Convention and the Jacobin Constitution. Those who followed the Sections in rejecting the authority of the Convention were treated with special severity by the Tribunal – and often the mere expression of distrust of the Convention was enough to secure conviction. The views attributed to those who appeared before the Tribunal sometimes reveal the extent to which the anti-Montagnard, anti-Parisian propaganda of the General Committee and other leading bodies had permeated the rank and file of the sectionary movement, to those who were often considered as more or less passive instruments in the hands of their more sophisticated and better-educated superiors.

Obviously those who had held offices in the Sections had often initiated policies directed against the Convention, while those who marched in the Departmental Army were often similarly conscious that the Convention was their principal enemy. Those who took part in the meeting which elected deputies to go to the proposed assembly at Bourges were likewise engaged in actions which aimed at the downfall of the Convention. All those in the Sections who refused to accept decrees voted after 31 May were in the vanguard of the attack.

In most cases, however, the opinions of the general run of people as regards the Convention seem pale reflections of the more coherent views expounded by office-holders when they appeared before the Tribunal. The accused had been more inclined to insult the Convention and to vilify its members than to argue with them. On the other hand, when Mathieu-

François Romieu, an employee of the customs at Sète, was asked by the president,

> N'avez-vous pas dit à un citoyen, que la Convention nationale était remplie de scélérats, que la République française était une monstruosité, et que vous étiez assuré de la Coalition de 66 départements, qui ne la voulaient pas?

he replied,

> Jamais ce blasphème n'est sorti de ma bouche. J'ai pu dire que dans la Convention il yavait des scélérats parce que je jugeais tels Barbaroux, Brissot et les autres, que la République fédérative ferait le plus grand mal à la France. . . .

This was, as Romieu no doubt knew, Jacobin-Montagnard dogma, the answer the judges would expect to hear from the tribune of the Club, not from a man 'targué d'être Girondin'.[1]

Thus attacks on the Convention generally took the form of denunciations of the factions which dominated that assembly, preventing it from debating freely.

> Ce sont des coquins qui sous peu recevront le prix de leurs forfaits

– this phrase was attributed to Bonaventure Estuby,[2] a former advocate (*avoué*); but it had been on the lips of many of the sectionaries. Others, according to the Tribunal, rejoiced that the British and Spanish were coming to march to Paris to destroy the Convention. Generally, attacks on the Convention can be summed up as centred round references to the 'anarchists' in that assembly. The belief that the Convention was dominated by 'anarchists' sank deep into the lower reaches of the population of Marseilles and the surrounding area; and this helps explain why the bulk of the population was held in acquiescence at the measures of the Sections. Apart from this, the only detailed criticism of the Convention's policy concerned

---

[1] ABR, L3115, 22 *nivôse* II (11 Jan. 1794), and A. Nat., BB 3 7, condemned to death by Military Commission of Marseilles, 26 *pluviôse* II (14 Feb. 1794), Mathieu-François Romieu.

[2] ABR, L3117, 8 *germinal* II (28 Mar. 1794), Bonaventure Estuby.

the issue of *assignats* – considered excessive by many Marseillais. It was generally thought that the deputies were growing rich on the proceeds of forced loans, taxes and speculation in *assignats*. 'La Convention a volé la République un milliard' was a popular belief: the deputies, it was thought, foisted *assignats* on the people and kept the gold for themselves.[1] Otherwise neither the great revolutionary measures of the spring and summer of 1793, nor the conduct of the war, were subjected to any real criticism or denunciation from the rank and file of the sectionaries.

Outrages against individual deputies were also punished – that of Rousselet, who had been to the lodgings of Bayle and Boisset to seize their correspondence,[2] of Antoine Maurin, who as general procurator syndic of the Department ordered the transference of Bô and Antiboul from Aix to the prisons of Marseilles and had kept them there.[3] One body of men who had seen the Convention at close quarters were the *fédérés* of the Second Battalion: one of their number, François Allemand, told his judges how Marat had come to the barracks where the Battalion lodged at Paris and told them that France would never be happy until ruled by one man.[4] Such reports, reaching Marseilles in March 1793, help explain the hatred of Marat and the Montagnards felt by sectionaries who detested any form of tyranny.

Many sectionaries were alleged to have insulted the Convention by tearing down its decrees which were placarded throughout the town; many were said to have 'forgotten' the Convention, to have disregarded its laws or to have protested against them. But these charges were generally vague and trivial. Only with regard to the Constitution was the impression of apathy at all shattered.

In the autumn of 1793, it was as advisable to praise the Jacobin Constitution of June 1793 as it had been to disparage it in the summer of that year. 'J'ai demandé la constitution'

---

[1] ABR, L3116, 29 *ventôse* II (19 Mar. 1794), Sauveur Ventron.

[2] ABR, L3112; 11, 12, 16 Sept. 1793, Jean-Marie Rousselet.

[3] ABR, L3114; 19, 21, 22 *frimaire* II (9, 11, 12 Dec. 1793), Antoine Maurin, and see above, pp. 165–71.

[4] ABR, L3112, 27 Sept. 1793, and L3113, 10 Oct. 1793, François Allemand, condemned to death.

was an affirmation repeated by many of those appearing before the Tribunal. Pierre Borrely, the priest of Saint-Antonin,
claimed that he had persuaded his village to accept the
Constitution, when the Marseillais used every effort to prevent
this happening –

> ce seul fait, puisqu'enfin je dois le dire, ne me méritait-il
> pas une couronne civique?[1]

Hyacinthe Bertrand, a lawyer of Apt, affirmed that he had
refused to come to do business in Marseilles until the city
accepted the Constitution,[2] while another man, a very suspect
dancing-master, was released after a witness had described
how he had demanded the acceptance of the Constitution in
his Section, saying that all France would oppose Marseilles
if the city did not agree to live under the Constitution: he had
been booed for his pains.[3]

Perhaps the most succinct expression of the case against the
Constitution was argued by one Blanc, a former procurator
and notary of Les Baux who was arrested as a suspect but who
was not judged by the Tribunal. He was alleged to have said
that

> La Convention a perdu la France, la plaine est la partie
> saine de la Convention, la Convention n'était plus libre
> depuis l'arrestation des trente-deux, que la Constitution
> n'était que l'ouvrage de quelques intrigants, un ouvrage de
> 24 heures, que la politique avait inventé parce que la
> Montagne prévoyait que le peuple allait lui tomber dessus;
> que cette politique était d'autant plus raffinée que la
> Montagne voulait Orléans pour Roi.[4]

With this assessment of the motives of the Montagnards many
sectionaries agreed; for, if we are to believe the testimony

[1] ABR, L3115, 29 *nivôse* II (18 Jan. 1794), in this dossier by mistake.
Pierre Borrely was condemned to death on 26 *ventôse* II (16 Mar. 1794),
L3116.

[2] ABR, L3117; 2, 8 *germinal* II (22, 28 Mar. 1794), François-Hyacinthe
Bertrand: and see above, pp. 183–7.

[3] ABR, L3118, 26 *germinal* II (15 Apr. 1794), Marcellin Arnaud.

[4] ABR, L3127, letter of the *Représentant du peuple* Leblanc to Giraud, from
Paris, dated 26 *messidor* II (14 July 1794), asking Giraud to send one Blanc
to the Popular Commission of Orange.

of a hostile witness, Catherine Blanc, speaking of the approach of Carteaux's troops, asked

> Que viennent-ils faire ici, nous apporter une constitution faite dans vingt-quatre heures; nous n'en voulons pas.[1]

The Constitution had reached Marseilles when the city had committed itself against the Convention and all its works and so, to the sectionaries, it was merely one product of a body whose decrees they refused to recognise. There could therefore be no question of considering it on its merits. It was not subjected to a clause-by-clause discussion and criticism – though some members of the Department had desired this. It was rejected *en bloc*, not so much because its principles were considered harmful to the State, but because it came from a body which, being bad itself, could only produce bad fruit. Recognising it as the main weapon in the campaign of the Montagne to win back the allegiance of the disaffected departments, the Sections tried to suppress discussion of it, and attempted to prevent individual provisions – which might not have substantiated their claim that the Convention was devoted only to the fostering of civil war and social discontent – from being known to the people of Marseilles. That they were largely successful in this, is suggested by the fact that few of the suspects of the autumn of 1793 were accused of making detailed refutations of the Constitution.

In some other departments, the Constitution afforded an excuse for those who had entered timidly into rebellion to scramble out again, saving a modicum of self-respect, and gaining a great measure of clemency from the Convention. Marseilles however had plunged too impetuously into the flood-current of rebellion for such an easy escape to be possible, even had its people desired it; and so, instead of serving the Montagnard purpose of reconciliation, the Constitution had the effect of dividing yet further the sectionaries from the republicans. The Constitution rejected, there could be no recourse but to arms.

Also, what helped to keep standing the whole edifice of Marseillais resistance to the Convention was the oath which

[1] ABR, L3114; 19, 21 *frimaire* II (9, 11 Dec. 1793), Catherine Blanc, *veuve* Garelly.

public officials had to take, renouncing the authority of that body and denying the validity of its acts.[1] Naturally, therefore, those who had sworn this oath were clearly designated as suspects. The Convention offered indulgence to those who had been coerced into taking such oaths, by giving several days in which to retract, but few did so in Marseilles before the arrival of Carteaux. Only some of the administrators of the District had the courage to do so. Thus many men were charged by the Tribunal with having taken the oath, or having forced others to do so. Any office-holder who came before the Tribunal was considered to have offended in this way. Only for outlying areas was the claim allowed that the decree of 26 June, allowing retraction, had not been published.

Priests were sometimes accused of encouraging their flocks to swear the oath. But many of those accused of taking the oath must have been like Jérôme Mathieu, who, as a member of the National Guard, found himself

> comme les autres sur le Cours – le capitaine lut le serment à haute et intelligible voix, mais je ne savais ce que c'était ce serment.[2]

Another of the accused claimed 'Je ne mettais pas de mal à ce serment'. Thus it seems that while in theory the oath served to bind the sectionaries together in their struggle against the Convention, its imposition as a test to be taken by those who wanted even the humblest job weakened its effect. On the whole, this was recognised by the Tribunal, which tried to distinguish between those who believed in what they had sworn to uphold, and those who took the oath without committing themselves to the policies therein contained. This of course was a delicate – an impossible – task but, frequently, those who had no record of active service on behalf of the Sections were freed even if they had taken the oath. Obviously many office-holders who had taken the oath to get their jobs were freed in this manner.

The Section's boldness in word has already been noted: but their offensive against the Convention went beyond the stage of words. By entering the realm of deeds, the Sections overreached themselves.

[1] See above, pp. 114–15.
[2] ABR, L3115, 17 *nivôse* II (6 Jan. 1794), Jérôme Mathieu *dit* Bertrand.

(b) THE DEPARTMENTAL ARMY

Naturally, any action which contributed to the formation and dispatch of the Departmental Army was regarded as counter-revolutionary. Here too the Tribunal distinguished between leaders and led, in this case between officers and men who had served in the ranks, the latter usually being acquitted. Officers were regarded as having acted in full knowledge of the expedition to Paris: moreover they were further accused of having led others astray. This discrimination was all the easier in that the Tribunal was under no illusions about the willingness of many 'volunteers' to join the army: it suited the Tribunal's purpose to emphasise the intimidation or deception employed by recruiters for the army.

At least seventy-two of the accused were agreed to have served in the Departmental Army: of these, twenty-seven were condemned to death; thirty-five were freed; two condemned to *réclusion* and one to prison. The cases of seven men were not terminated. The number condemned to death includes three *propriétaires*, three *négociants*, and a *notaire* whereas men of such standing are absent from those released: but the bulk of both categories is provided by artisans. It has not always been possible to establish whether an accused man had served as officer or volunteer.

By far the biggest fish caught in this particular trawl was Jean-Marie Rousselet, who commanded, for a time, the Departmental Army.[1] A tailor in civilian life, resident at Marseilles, he was a retired *militaire* and so was chosen for the job. But the defeats which shattered the army under his command, and the unanimous condemnation of his generalship, suggest that he had little professional expertise.

He appeared before the Tribunal on 11 September. 'Je n'ai point vu de contre-révolution' were his first words. Like those who held civil office, his main task was to maintain that he was an innocent victim of events; that he had obeyed the orders of the legal administrative bodies; that he was ignorant of the purpose of the levy of the Departmental Army. Such ignorance

[1] ABR, L3112; 11, 12, 13, 16 Sept. 1793. And L3121, Jean-Marie Rousselet.

was straightway ruled out as a means of defence:

> toute la ville savait que le bataillon allait combattre Paris et la Convention,

said the president. It was also the Tribunal's task to establish the responsibility of Rousselet for anti-Jacobin incidents which took place during the march of the army up the Rhône valley. Thus Rousselet was driven to confess that at Arles he had obeyed the orders of an envoy of the Sections of Marseilles to disarm the patriots of that city. The next stage in the army's advance was the crossing of the Durance. Rousselet claimed that the troops sent from Avignon to resist the attacks of the Marseillais had fired upon him first. The president replied that,

> Si vous aviez été républicain, dès cet instant vous auriez donné votre démission, puisque vous voyiez que c'était une guerre de frères contre frères. [Rousselet replied] Je ne croyais pas que ce fussent des frères. Ils firent feu. S'ils m'avaient parlé, nous nous serions entendus.

The next incident concerned the arrival of the Departmental Army before the walls of Avignon. To what extent had Rousselet used the threat of force to make the Avignonnais open their gates to him? Did he threaten to beat down the gates and enter the city as conqueror? 'Je demandai seulement le logement', said Rousselet. In Avignon, his soldiers got out of control and massacred some of the citizens – was Rousselet responsible for this? The massacres, he said, were the work of troops outside his command. Avignon in his hands, did he not wish to press on to Lyons, to attack the army of Dubois-Crancé?

Witnesses were called to undermine the commander's position. A *canonnier* of the Château d'If testified that Rousselet had told him that the Marseillais had killed a French king and that they would therefore have a British, Spanish, Imperial or Prussian monarch. Another witness said that Rousselet had appeared discontented with the Constitution while another *canonnier* alleged that, given a mission to repair the coastal batteries of Marseilles, Rousselet had refused to do this, and, on the contrary, said he would not oppose a British landing.

The most interesting evidence against Rousselet, however, came from an envoy of Carteaux, who held a parley with the 'general' at Avignon. Rousselet refused to recognise the legality of the republican army marching against him, since it had been levied by the outlawed Convention: instead he demanded that Carteaux's troops should march straight to the frontiers. At this appeal to patriotism, the envoy of Carteaux challenged him to lead *his* troops to the frontiers, to join *his* arms to those of the patriots. The Marseillais displayed their banners, embroidered with the device,

> Liberté, Égalité, République Française une et indivisible, Respect aux Lois et aux Propriétés.

Indignant, the republican denounced the hypocrisy of this device. When the president further underlined the contrast between these principles and the actions of the army – an army which killed more than sixty patriots in Avignon – the weakness of Rousselet's reply suggests the weakness of the man, and, above all, the weakness of the commanding officer –

> J'ai fait défense à mon bataillon de commettre aucun acte arbitraire. . . . Je ne sais quels sont les gens qui ont commis ces horreurs.

Another point which emerged from the interrogation was that Rousselet had forbidden his troops to read propaganda sent by General Carteaux to persuade them to join the republican cause. He could not therefore have wished to join Carteaux. Moreover Rousselet, at the very start of the revolt of the Sections, had been sent to seize letters addressed to Bayle and Boisset, and this arbitrary act had, in the opinion of Maillet, set in motion the events which led Marseilles to oppose by force the laws of the Convention.

To confirm the justice of its sentence of death against Rousselet, and to provide the basis of the accusations against him, Giraud and Chompré had gathered several documents which firmly established his individual responsibility for the acts of his army – a letter written from Arles on 29 June, referring to provisions to be gathered in towns all the way to Paris and which shows him actively recruiting soldiers; and a letter announcing his decision on 13–14 July to abandon Avignon because the municipality and citizens of that town were not prepared to resist an attack from Carteaux and reporting that the morale of the troops was high, especially when it was announced that the Toulonnais were sending reinforcements.

Thus Rousselet was an out-and-out defender of the departmental coalition against Paris. He withdrew from Avignon only to return and occupy the town a second time; and before the final retreat his soldiers had massacred many of the townspeople. Not till 21 July did he resign. Four days later, Avignon finally fell to Carteaux, and Rousselet returned to Marseilles and was replaced by Villeneuve, who was, it seems, more of a royalist than Rousselet, but no better general (Villeneuve escaped the clutches of the Tribunal). From the interrogation, it appears that Rousselet was a man without great character or ability who was nevertheless a firm defender of the principles of the Sections.

Jacques-Joseph Sauvage, a 46-year-old hairdresser was accused of having served as a lieutenant. In August, he related, he had marched under duress – 'J'ai ignoré qu'il y eut une armée républicaine'. Told they were going to Arles to protect the harvest against marauding bands (an excuse which recurs), when he realised what was happening, he left. He certainly did not encourage young men to volunteer: 'Je trouvais abominable d'enlever des citoyens pour marcher contre des frères'. Despite his assurances of patriotic behaviour, he too was condemned to death, for an excuse which the Tribunal accepted from lowly-placed men was thought of as effrontery coming from a man who had been a lieutenant in the Departmental Army.[1]

Alexis Favier was unfortunate in being a lieutenant in the customs and, as such, in the habit of receiving strict discipline from the top of his organisation. But the public prosecutor showed little appreciation of the delicacy of his position, pointing out however that the General Committee had had the astuteness to make use of the hierarchy of the customs officers in the levying of the army. Since the requisition by which he was called up had been read in court, Favier could only admit to having served. Ignorance was again an unsuccessful plea. Forced to confess that he had gone to Martigues to recruit

[1] ABR, L3117, 2 *germinal* II (22 Mar. 1794), Jacques-Joseph Sauvage.

members of the customs posts to go to Avignon, he pleaded that

> dans les douanes l'obéissance est forcée et la subordination très soutenue.

He confessed his guilt:

> J'ai été trompé et ayant servi le 10 août, j'aurais cru manquer de ne pas servir.

For Favier – and for how many others? – this expedition by the Departmental Army was merely one of a number of such sorties by the armed force of Marseilles – sorties to Aix, to Arles, to Avignon and to Paris, designed to advance the cause of the Revolution.[1] Indeed for an unsophisticated citizen, exposed to propaganda from above, subservient to orders from above, such an interpretation of events may well have seemed natural.

Moreover, when Favier had seen the tricolour floating above the troops of Carteaux on the far bank of the Durance, he had deserted and had prevented his company from firing a shot at Carteaux's army. Forced to rejoin the army, he went determined to sabotage its effort. When Carteaux entered Marseilles, Favier was quick to offer his services to the republican general. He and his company were incorporated – no questions asked – into the republican army marching against Toulon. Unfortunately for Favier, the Committee of Surveillance of Marseilles was active ferreting out ex-federalists in Carteaux's army, so he was arrested, brought to trial and executed.[2]

This interference with his army annoyed Carteaux who wrote on one of Favier's petitions,

> Je certifie que s'il faut purger de l'armée que j'ai l'honneur de commander tous les sujets qui ont marché contre moi,

---

[1] See ABR, L3117, 12 *germinal* II (1 Apr. 1794), the case of Jean-Baptiste Gayde, a 22-year-old *tonnelier* from Marseilles, who was released, despite the fact that he marched as far as Orange. 'Je croyais marcher pour l'indivisibilité et j'ai fait comme autrefois', he explained. No doubt he, like many others, marched once too often, without too clearly distinguishing the causes for which he volunteered. A certificate showed that he had gone on the expedition to rescue the patriots of Arles, and had also been in the levy of 6000 men raised by Bayle and Boisset.

[2] ABR, L3113, 29 Oct., 8, 13 Nov. 1793, Alexis Favier: also L3120.

l'on peut donner des ordres à la boulangerie pour faire 6000 rations de pain de moins chaque jour.

Carteaux was a staid realist, unexcited by the frenetic man-hunts of the civilian authorities of Marseilles, unconcerned with the niceties of political allegiance. Favier – and the hundreds like him with a past to live down – might have given devoted service to the army of Toulon: most no doubt did.

But the death penalty was not enforced against André Bens *fils*, tiler from Aubagne, though he was denounced as a lieuten-ant in the Departmental Army – probably not so much because he deserted the army and then joined Carteaux on his march against Toulon, as because he was only 20 years old and could therefore be thought to speak the truth in describing himself as a 'simple soldat'. He and his friends were forced to go to the army 'la bouche du fusil sur l'estomac'.[1] Also from Aubagne was Honoré Bens, a 47-year-old *cultivateur* who appeared before the Tribunal charged with having gone to Roquevaire as sub-lieutenant. He also deserted the army. According to an attesta-tion from the club of Aubagne, he had been forced to join the army:

> En cas de refus on lui saisirait tout ce qu'il avait dans sa maison et qu'on mettrait garnison chez lui. Ces menaces l'effrayèrent au point que pour conserver un pain à sa famille, il obéit avec la plus grande répugnance. . . . L'exposant ignorant, timide et craintif, il adhéra à marcher contre sa volonté.

The club of Aubagne gave identical certificates of civism to other villagers and, like Honoré Bens, many of them were released by the Tribunal.[2]

Obviously, with the army of the Sections being driven back to Marseilles, it disintegrated rather than fell in battle; obviously also, many of those who fled in panic were captured by the advancing Allobroges and taken to the prisons of Marseilles. These men were only too anxious to portray their terror-struck flight from the field of battle as a patriotic refusal to fight against their brothers. This excuse, often accepted from

---

[1] ABR, L3118, 18 *germinal* II (7 Apr. 1794), and L3119, 5 *floréal* II (24 Apr. 1794), André Bens.

[2] ABR, L3118, 25 *germinal* II (14 Apr. 1794), Honoré Bens.

volunteers and 'simples soldats', rarely sufficed to obtain ex-officers their freedom.

Not at least for men such as Dominique Girard, shoemaker and *sergent du port*, who, according to Giraud, had been *aide-de-camp* in the Departmental Army, and also captain of cavalry.[1] A close friend of Barbaroux, and commander of the Second Battalion of Marseilles, on his return from Paris, he had acted as instigator of the sectionary 'system' about which he had learned at Paris. Giraud suggested that Girard had thrown in his lot with Barbaroux and had tried to get the *fédérés* to follow suit; had planned, in Paris, the revolt of the Sections which took place after the Battalion had returned home. As to service in the Departmental Army, Girard confessed to this – but he had joined solely to spread disorder among its ranks. However, a document shows Girard receiving at Lambesc in mid-August pay as *chasseur à cheval* and *capitaine de cavalerie*.

But it was the relations between Girard and Barbaroux which interested the court – a letter was read showing that Girard was an intimate friend of Buzot and Barbaroux, a letter dated 27 May 1793, which referred to the progress which the 'good cause' had made at Marseilles since the Battalion's arrival and to the happy imprisonment of the anarchists. As commander of the *fédérés*, he was accused of trying to use them against the Convention in order to force through the appeal to the people. When he arrived back at Marseilles – contaminating Lyons *en route* – he reported to the Club but was violently attacked for his intrigues with Barbaroux, some of his own men denouncing him and shouting him down.[2] One of their accusations was that, in Lyons, he had urged that the head of Chalier should have been struck off.

Girard stood condemned. Above all, his letter referring joyfully to the imprisonment of the anarchists of Marseilles – who included his examiner and prosecutor on the Tribunal – served to condemn him. A member of an earlier levy, an ardent admirer of Barbaroux, he was obviously good material

---

[1] ABR, L3113, 30 Oct. 1793; also L3023. See also A. Nat., AF II 45³⁵⁰, (Correspondence of Barbaroux), and see above, pp. 61–3; Dominique Girard.

[2] ABR, L2071, Club, 27, 28 Mar. 1793.

for the Departmental Army. He was evidently devoted to the cause for which it fought.

Many citizens had been dragooned into service. On 17 September several of these men appeared before the Tribunal – a *cultivateur* from the outskirts of Marseilles, an 18-year-old *tisserand*, two 15-year-old butchers from La Fare, a 17-year-old *cultivateur* and a 16-year-old *ménager* with his younger brother, also from La Fare. One of them, asked why he joined up, replied

> Je croyais que nous allions à Paris, et comme j'avais des papiers importants à y retirer, je profitai de l'occasion de m'y transporter sans frais.

A question put by Maillet showed that he understood the situation –

> Ne vous dit-on pas que vous alliez contre les brigands?
> On nous disait que nous allions détruire les tyrans, les intrigants –

replied one of the accused. Another man – or boy – said that he had been forced to go because 'they' had threatened to take away his coat if he did not – and that was the only coat he had. Obviously they were village youths who had been cajoled into leaving their homes. Accordingly, the final account of their trial says that

> ils ont été forcés de marcher comme volontaires dans l'armée rebelle, élus par le sort, sous les ordres et la contrainte de la municipalité d'Aix . . . ils n'ont pas été plus loin que le hameau de la Gavotte et ont été induits en erreur, au point de croire qu'ils allaient combattre des brigands.

The Tribunal wrote of one of them,

> Louis Doucelet . . . n'a été engagé dans le bataillon rebelle, allant sur Paris, que par manque de pain, et sur le fol espoir de retourner dans cette ville sans frais, pour y relever des papiers de famille.

Summing up, the Tribunal explained that they were freed because they had been contraints, forcés par menaces et sous la certitude d'une extrême misère à marcher comme volontaires dans l'armée rebelle.[1]

Rémi Magnier, a cutler of Marseilles, was acquitted by the Tribunal, which reproduced his exact words on the printed judgement sheet and added, as if to excuse him, that

> père d'une nombreuse famille, il était facile de l'induire en erreur, parce que son genre de travail l'empêchait d'aller le soir s'instruire ou au club ou dans les sociétés qui auraient pu l'éclairer; qu'au surplus, devant tout à sa famille, il se croit bien puni de son erreur, et en a tous les regrets, quoique cette erreur soit involontaire de sa part.[2]

Those soldiers who had given no evidence of 'incivism' in civilian life – had been too busy to attend the Sections, had not denounced patriots – were generally freed: thus Antoine Mégy, a baker from Aix, who pleaded that 'on nous disait que nous allions en fête' and who, on seventeen days' service, had never seen the republican army.[3] François Michel, a cobbler, said he marched because he was unemployed.

> On nous faisait accroire que d'aller à Paris était une partie de plaisir. J'ai eu le malheur, faute d'une certaine intelligence, d'avoir été trompé par ces méchants.

This excuse was repeated verbatim in the final account of the judgement which acquitted Michel.[4] Eighteen-year-old Pierre Jurami, *tonnelier* from Marseilles was likewise granted the indulgence of the Tribunal for his tale of forced service and attempted desertion. He tried to desert but was, in the words of the judgement,

> poursuivi, atteint, maltraité et contraint de retourner . . . avouant n'avoir nullement voulu se battre et le sang lui bouillit de voir ses pareils, en même uniforme que ceux de la

---

[1] ABR, L3112, 17 Sept. 1793, Jacques Chauvet, Joseph Davin, Louis Doucelet, etc. (La Fare-les-Oliviers, *arrond.* of Aix; *canton* of Berre-L'Étang). Also L3023, 17 Sept. 1793.

[2] ABR, L3112, 21 Sept. 1793; also L3023, 21 Sept. 1793, Rémi Magnier *dit* Barrois.

[3] ABR, L3112, 21 Sept. 1793, Antoine Mégy.

[4] ABR, L3112, 19 Sept. 1793, François Michel. Also L3023.

République, chercher à se battre; qu'on l'a trompé méchamment.[1]

Some of the tensions which arose in the smaller villages when Marseilles demanded a contingent for its army are illustrated in the testimony of four members of the municipality of the small town of Gémenos, who related that,

> Nous eûmes ordre de faire seize hommes, il y eut quelques difficultés entre les hommes mariés et les garçons. Dans cette intervalle, un bon patriote nous avertit que nous ne devions pas consentir à faire marcher contre nos frères. Le maire le voulut, nous menaça même de faire venir du monde de Marseille. Nous nous y opposâmes et personne ne marcha. On voulait faire marcher les patriotes pour les sacrifier, mais nous tînmes bon et nous forçâmes le commandant de la garde nationale à se démettre et il a disparu.

The Tribunal took this tale at its face-value and freed the four accused.[2] Leydet, mayor of the hamlet of Cornillon (near Salon), refused the demand of Urtin, notorious *commissaire* of the Sections of Marseilles, to levy men for the Departmental Army, on the grounds that the village's young men were at the frontiers and would not turn their arms against the nation.[3]

A final excuse for marching comes from Jean-Baptiste Sardou – arrested but not judged – who said

> on me faisait accroire qu'on voulait mettre d'Orléans sur le trône, je croyais faire pour le bien.[4]

It seems therefore that the Revolutionary Tribunal was extremely lenient to many who admitted marching in the Departmental Army. The freedom with which many of the accused admitted their offence, the extreme youth of some of them, their lowly social station, the naivety of many of their excuses, the absence of any other counter-revolutionary activities – all these factors helped to secure their release. Others

---

[1] ABR, L3023, 19 Sept. 1793; also L3112, Pierre Jurami.

[2] ABR, L3113, 22 Oct. 1793, Joseph Thobert, etc., from Gémenos (*arrond.*, Marseilles; *canton*, Aubagne).

[3] ABR, L3113, 23 Oct. 1793, Jean-Joseph Leydet, from Cornillon (*arrond.*, Aix; *canton*, Salon).

[4] ABR, L3130, Military Commission, petition from Jean-Baptiste Sardou.

who had served in the army of Marseilles without rank were not so lucky, mainly because they had taken part in other anti-patriotic outbursts.

If service in the Departmental Army was one of the main manifestations of a federalist disposition, refusal to serve was taken as a proof of patriotism. Thus anyone who, too lazy or fearful to serve federalism in an active way, had managed to escape the press-gang or the lottery (*le sort*), could advance this as evidence that he had actively opposed the designs of the Sections. Louis-François Hérault was freed after being able to affirm that he had not served in the army;

> Dieu m'en préserve! je n'ai jamais voulu marcher; je me fis garçon cafetier à la comédie neuve pour éviter d'être contraint à marcher.

Certainly a heroic way to resist the pressures of the Sections.[1] André Ambard, an Aubagne stone-quarrier, affirmed, 'J'ai profité de mon âge pour mieux assurer mon refus d'aller'. He was 48, an age at which many men marched with the Marseillais.[2] Several men were executed for urging men to march, for the Tribunal regarded recruitment for the Departmental Army as one of the most serious crimes with which it had to deal and almost all men who had served in sectionary committees had been implicated. According to the law of 5 July anyone who helped in any way the mission of the Departmental Army might be condemned to death, and at Marseilles even those who merely urged men to march were treated severely, especially if they threatened the recalcitrant with summary justice from the Popular Tribunal. One man was accused of having demanded that deserters should be severely punished, or the whole army would desert.[3] Certainly some cases provide corroborative evidence regarding resistance to the Sections' recruiting drive. In the lowerclass Section 9, the first requisition for the army met with no success and had to be repeated in a more coercive

[1] ABR, L3113, 26 Oct. 1793, Louis-François Hérault.

[2] ABR, L3113, 24 *brumaire* II (14 Nov. 1793), André Ambard.

[3] ABR, L3118, 21 *germinal* II (10 Apr. 1794), Cabrol *dit* Montcoussou. The register of Section 5, (L1938, 1 Aug. 1793), shows him trying to find ways and means to purchase arms for the sectionaries, listing property-owners who had horses and carts which might be used by the army. He was condemned to death.

manner.[1] And one man, Honoré Lieutaud, a clock dealer, complained:

les ouvriers ne veulent pas marcher [contre Carteaux]. Ils avaient marché pour les intrigants. Il faut qu'on les emprisonne ou qu'on leur ôte le pain.[2]

One form of help for the Departmental Army which was evoked before the Tribunal concerns money. Only on a few occasions were men accused of giving money in any quantity for the army. Only under the *Commission militaire* were men convicted of subsidising the army with sums of more than a few pounds. This fact, together with the almost complete absence of information regarding the subscribers to the Departmental Army and the fact that the Sections had to pillage public funds, suggests that its financing was an affair of spasmodic expedients – a gift of money here and there, collections from rich men in the Sections, gifts of coats, of rifles and so on, requisitions of horses and carts. This fits in quite well with the general picture of hasty improvisation and make-shift bustle afforded by much else of the Sections' activity.[3]

Finally, since every accusation had as its obverse a means of defence, many of the accused described to the Tribunal how they did all in their power to refuse to recruit men for the army, or to dissuade men from marching.

Also thought of as contributing to the war-effort of Marseilles were those who served to keep up fighting spirits by describing in vivid terms the moral shortcomings of the soldiers of Carteaux. Those who slandered the army of Carteaux were treated with almost as much severity as those who fought it. But in fact the Marseillais seemed bolder in word than in deed and it may well have been the case that the slanders were more

[1] ABR, L3113, 11 Nov. 1793, case of Joseph Allen, *fripier*.

[2] ABR, L3117, 8 *germinal* II (28 Mar. 1794), Honoré Lieutaud, *horloger*, condemned to *réclusion*.

[3] No doubt the supplying of money for the army was heavily disguised; and anyway, money paid as taxes went straight into the coffers of the Sections. On 6 Aug. 1793, the Municipality referred to the payment of 3.27 million *livres* by the *Compagnie de l'Arsenal*, a consortium of some of the richest citizens in Marseilles engaged in redeveloping the site of the former Royal Arsenal at the head of the Vieux-Port. This money might well have helped to finance the rebellion of the sections. A. Comm., 4D7.

dangerous to the republican cause than the armed resistance of the sectionaries. Typical was the case of Honoré Lieutaud, a clock dealer, who allegedly described Carteaux's army as a gang of deserters and thieves who pillaged and raped wherever they went – at Aix, for example, they had sold in the town square drapery and silverware which they had stolen.[1] Many Marseillais thought Carteaux was coming to put their city to fire and to the sword. Such cases suggest that many who marched in the army were indeed misled by the propaganda effort of the Sections. And to convict some men for spreading false allegations about Carteaux's army was to acquit other men for being misled by them.

The conflict in Section 11 formed the postscript of the fighting.

(c) SECTION 11

This skirmish gave rise to many arrests and accusations, and it was standard tactics for the Tribunal to ask an accused man what he had been doing on 23 and 24 August. Those who had stayed indoors were fortunate. Only a few men claimed that they had joined forces with the inhabitants of Section 11 to resist the attacks upon the patriots.

Serious accusations were however levied against those who were said to have led the attack. Joseph Lenthéric, who commanded Section 1's company of the National Guard, was accused of leading his men against Section 11.[2] A witness described how Lenthéric had manœuvred a piece of artillery which had fired on the patriots of Section 11. He was also accused of going aboard ships in the harbour to take gunpowder from them to use against the patriots. Lenthéric had a long counter-revolutionary record; for, as captain in the National Guard, he had led expeditions to disarm patriots and he had also been a frequent participant in the meetings of Section 1 and a member of its committee of surveillance. For all these reasons, he was condemned to death.

Some sailors took part in this engagement; of these François Boulle, a naval captain, appeared before the Tribunal to be

---

[1] ABR, L3117, 8 *germinal* II (28 Mar. 1794), Honoré Lieutaud.
[2] ABR, L3113; 17, 21 Oct. 1793, Joseph Lenthéric. Also L3121.

denounced for having

> renoncé ouvertement à tous les avantages que la Révolution a procurés à la classe des marins. Il a voulu faire revenir l'ancienne servitude et l'ancien avilissement. . . .

He was convicted of having guarded the Maison Commune throughout this period, of having provided a guard for the General Committee, of having ordered his sailors to obey the Sections' orders and of having removed two cannon from the ship which he commanded. Finally, after the patriots who had led the resistance in Section 11 had broken out, he had led his soldiers into the Section and had disarmed and taken to prison those who remained. For these crimes, he was sentenced to death.[1]

Two artillery officers left their posts on the coast – leaving it unprotected against a possible incursion by the British – to take part in the attack against Section 11. They too were condemned to death.[2]

Those who supported the attack by providing arms and munitions were likewise convicted. (And, according to Lautard, the great merchant Jacques Rabaud was condemned to death by the Revolutionary Tribunal of Paris for supplying cannon to be used against the patriots.)[3]

In this affair, too, the Tribunal distinguished between those who led and those who followed and recognised that a considerable degree of force had been used by those who mounted the attacks to compel the apathetic or hostile populace to fight against their fellow-citizens. Often citizens who had been mere bystanders had been dragooned into squadrons and forced to march against 'their brothers'. Generally these men were released by the Tribunal.

Thus the military ventures of the sectionaries were not very happy. They were troublesome to the Republic: but the failure to link Marseilles with Lyons brought the downfall of federalism in both cities and saved the Convention.

[1] ABR, L484, 8 *nivôse* II (28 Dec. 1793), François-Bernard Boulle.
[2] ABR, L3112, 20 Sept. 1793, Valentin Pioche and Imbert Calas.
[3] Lautard, 1, p. 324.

CHAPTER ELEVEN

A Counter-Revolutionary
Fournée

(*a*) SUSPECT TRAVEL

During the Revolution it was often impossible to make a journey from one's home town without incurring suspicion. Travellers seen approaching a town were awaited with apprehension; on arrival their papers, and often their baggage, were searched. An elaborate system of passports was introduced to enable checks to be made on those who went on journeys, whether these journeys were made for business, or, more rarely, for pleasure. Travellers were regarded as fugitives from justice, as bandits, or *gens sans aveu*, as troublemakers, until, at the municipal offices of the towns through which they passed, they produced their papers for local inspection. To remain at one's post was the most important duty of an administrator; to stay at home, and at work, was an important duty of the ordinary citizen. The rural disturbances of the early years of the Revolution, and the conviction that plotters, both foreign and domestic, were travelling through France preparing the ground-plan for a general counter-revolutionary rising, were powerful factors tending to turn each traveller into a suspect. It is not surprising therefore that the Revolutionary Tribunal had to deal with numerous cases where suspicion had been aroused initially because Marseillais or Provençaux had strayed from their home town.

Jérôme Rouquet, a carter of Éguilles, had been arrested because his profession was one which gave rise to suspicion, even though Rouquet himself had done nothing to warrant that suspicion.[1] For François Arnaud, a *courrier* who lived at Lyons, such suspicion was likewise an occupational hazard. He was

[1] ABR, L3115, 3 *nivôse* II (23 Dec. 1793), Jérôme Rouquet of Éguilles (*arrond.*, Aix, *canton*, Aix-Sud).

accused of having carried 'les communications liberticides' between Lyons and Marseilles and of thereby helping to co-ordinate the revolts of the two cities; but since no proof was advanced, he was set at liberty.[1]

Other travellers did not have their work as an excuse but were not generally backward in suggesting justifications for their journeys – business trips, visits to *bastides*, hunting expeditions, visits to relatives or journeys to return to their place of birth.

All those who had journeyed during the régime of the Sections were suspected of having been their emissaries; but most affirmed that they had been on private business and were released. Those who travelled after the fall of the Sections were suspected not only of being sectionaries who were fleeing from arrest, but also of being deserters from the Army of Italy, or *gens sans aveu* who terrorised the countryside, who preyed on farmers and hi-jacked vehicles on the roads. Bands of these homeless men roamed the hills around Marseilles and Aix, and it was thought that they might attempt to descend *en masse* upon the towns, plunder them and massacre their inhabitants or, by holding up the traffic on the roads, try to provoke a famine in the towns. The case of the soldiers, over sixty of them, who broke away from the Army of Italy and who went through the countryside requisitioning food and clothing and horses shows that such fears, if grossly exaggerated, were not entirely unfounded.[2]

Many of those arrested on the highways or in the fields were fugitives from justice for, as the army of Carteaux entered Marseilles, troops of those implicated in the revolt of the Sections streamed towards Toulon. As the instruments of the Terror began functioning in Marseilles, others fled from the city and tried to escape into Italy or Switzerland.

Among prominent sectionaries who confessed their guilt by fleeing were Antoine Maurin, the former general procurator syndic of the Bouches-du-Rhône, Jean-Baptiste Vence, one of the deputies elected to the proposed assembly at Bourges, and Louis Meyfrédy, one of the presidents of the Popular Tribunal. Often the fugitives affirmed that they had not intended to

---

[1] ABR, L3115, 29 *nivôse* II (18 Jan. 1794), François Arnaud.
[2] See below, pp. 300–1.

flee beyond the frontiers of France; but this was – and is – something impossible to establish. Some of them, well-off sectionary office-holders, had to undergo considerable hardship as they fled often by night through the mountains, living in a hand-to-mouth fashion, begging alms or eating what they could pick up in an inhospitable countryside. Certainly some men and women came before the Tribunal accused of sheltering such fugitives – generally pleading ignorance of their identity and saying that they had acted from pure hospitality – but such cases were not frequent.

Because flight was seen as an admission of guilt, some of the accused stressed the fact that, because they might have fled, but had remained at home instead, they were therefore out of the reach of suspicion.

Despite the cases where fugitives were arrested before they escaped from the clutches of revolutionary justice, it was obvious that many of the sectionaries had escaped by flight. Unfortunately, until a complete survey of the emigration from the Bouches-du-Rhône has been undertaken, it will be impossible to ascertain the number of sectionaries who successfully escaped from Marseilles. After the collapse of the Sections therefore, their leaders, it must be assumed, were dispersed far and wide – in Spain, in Italy, in Switzerland, and no doubt in Marseilles.

(*b*) RESIDENCE AT LYONS

If travel in general was liable to expose a man to suspicion, residence at, or visits to, certain areas of France were even more dangerous in this respect. Of the areas where residence had been inadvisable for a stranger, Lyons and Toulon were the most important from the point of view of the Marseillais. During the time in which these two towns had been in open revolt against the Convention, the inhabitants of other towns had been required to leave them and if possible return to their homes. Those who had not done so, and who were caught in Lyons or in Toulon when the republicans entered those towns, were often arrested and sent back to the department in which they habitually resided. Thus, several citizens of Marseilles and the Bouches-du-Rhône were 'returned' under arrest from

Lyons and Toulon; also, some citizens of the Var, who had co-operated with the enemy in Toulon, were sent to the Revolutionary Tribunal of Marseilles because of the temporary lack of such a tribunal in their own department. Moreover those who had remained in the rebel cities had been declared *émigrés*.

Some of the dozen or so people accused of having resided at Lyons were nobles whose cases have already been examined. Obviously all stressed that they had not taken part in the rebellion, Bournissac stressing that he had left the city for a nearby village whose principles were diametrically opposed to those of the Lyonnais. To the president, however, residence in the vicinity of Lyons was just as bad. Maillet had himself been to Lyons and returned convinced that the city was full of aristocrats: he described it as a city 'habituellement en contre-révolution'. To those who had stayed there, however, that city seems to have enjoyed the reputation of a health-resort, for reasons of health were given most often as the motive for residence there. Since one of the greatest fears of the Monta-gnards, however, had been the counter-revolutionary union of Lyons and Marseilles, it was not surprising that those who had gone to stay at Lyons were severely treated by the Tribunal. Of course in some ways the loss of Toulon, providing France's most powerful enemy with an *enclave* on French soil, had been even more dangerous. But the thirty or so suspects accused of having remained in Toulon were accused of treason and royal-ism – for having co-operated with the British and Spanish authorities and troops and for having thereby aided the avowed purpose of the coalition powers – the restoration of the French monarchy.[1]

Of course, travel and absence from Marseilles or Aix led to the accusation of emigration or attempted emigration.

(c) EMIGRATION[2]

Some of those who stood before the Tribunal were facing charges of emigration, or were accused of having given help

---

[1] See above, pp. 221–3.

[2] D. Greer, *The Incidence of the Emigration during the French Revolution* (Princeton, 1951), places the Bouches-du-Rhône third among French de-partments for the number of *émigrés* (5125); these represented 1·8 per cent

to *émigrés* or would-be *émigrés*. Those who had been at Lyons were also involved in such charges of emigration. Marseilles and the Bouches-du-Rhône were well placed for those of their inhabitants who wished to leave France – by land or sea, the Italian States offered a convenient destination. Some of those implicated in the sectionary movements took to flight and were captured before they reached the frontiers. Some of these may have had no intention of emigrating; instead, they wished to hide in the small towns and villages of upper Provence or along the coast. But many of them were undoubtedly heading for Piedmont (Turin) and Genoa. Those caught at sea must almost certainly have had the intention of emigrating. Joseph-Bonaventure Bonardel, a famous sectionary, was found on a Genoese boat off the coast of Provence, obviously destined for Genoa; Joseph-Marie Rostan, a merchant of Marseilles, was likewise apprehended at sea. In these cases, the fact that those arrested had had prominent careers under the Sections, suggests strongly that they were going to join their friends and colleagues who had already found refuge in Turin and Genoa.[1]

---

of the total population, a percentage exceeded by three departments (the Var had 5331 *émigrés* or 1·96 per cent of the total population). According to M. Vovelle, *Histoire de la Provence*, p. 429, 2000 people emigrated from the district of Marseilles, out of a population of 130,000 (1·5 per cent): of these, 40 per cent left in a wave following the downfall of federalism. Of these, 90 per cent were members of the Third Estate – 'le négoce et la bonne bourgeoisie marseillaise, compromis dans le fédéralisme, constituent un apport massif': a quarter of all emigrants from the district of Marseilles were *négociants, marchands, courtiers*, and *fabricants*. Of the 5125 *émigrés* of the Bouches-du-Rhône (a figure established by the Prefect Villeneuve in the 1820's and used by Greer), 360 were nobles, 480 clerics, 447 *fonctionnaires et employés*, 135 *gens de loi et médecins*, 1940 *négociants et marchands*, 1416 *propriétaires et cultivateurs*, 220 *artisans et ouvriers*, 127 *domestiques* (quoted in Moulin, 1, p. xii). Greer classifies these into broader categories: 40 per cent of *émigrés* from the Bouches-du-Rhône belonged to the 'upper middle class' – the highest percentage for any French department (national average 11 per cent). Though Greer's calculations (and sources) call for many reserves, the fundamental picture has been confirmed.

[1] ABR, L3117, 3 *germinal* II (23 Mar. 1794), Joseph-Bonaventure Bonardel; L3118, 27 *germinal* II (16 Apr. 1794), Joseph-Marie-Honoré Rostan. Note, however, that D. Greer, p. 10, remarks that the law of 8 Apr. 1792 designated as *émigrés* not only those who left France but those who were absent from their home departments and could not prove that they had not left France.

The committees of surveillance denounced to the Tribunal those who had been included on the lists of the *émigrés* of the Bouches-du-Rhône. It was generally believed that during the régime of the Sections many *émigrés* had returned to Marseilles, hoping to find the political climate there more congenial than it had been in the previous months. To some extent, the truth of this belief is confirmed by several cases involving returned *émigrés* who were judged by the Revolutionary Tribunal. Presumably those who were convicted of emigration by the Tribunal had returned to see their friends and parents or to help the work of the Sections, hoping that their presence would either go unnoticed or be disregarded. The Sections themselves had not shown much concern with the *émigrés*, as far as can be seen from their registers, though attempts to enforce the legislation as regards the *émigrés* were made by the authorities of Marseilles.[1] Since however the commander of the Departmental Army, Villeneuve, had at least the reputation of having emigrated, doubts may be expressed – and certainly were expressed at the time – as to the conviction and sincerity of those responsible for enforcing the laws against the *émigrés* – laws which punished the returned *émigrés* with death.

Those who could not prove continuous residence on French soil were held by law to have emigrated. Several of the accused who fell into this category were executed. The basis of such prosecutions seems to have been the lists of *émigrés* published by the Department, but these are of dubious accuracy. Few other categories of crimes covered by revolutionary justice gave a man's personal enemies so easy an opportunity to denounce him and bring about his downfall, especially as the whole process of keeping oneself supplied with valid residence certificates was extremely involved, above all for men who had to travel on business or for other *bona fide* reasons. Moreover, in areas where many of the administrative organs were in open revolt against the Convention, it was often difficult to get a certificate or a passport which would later be recognised as valid by the revolutionary authorities of the autumn of 1793. Not only were men who had been on quite justifiable journeys often denounced, but men who to avoid the strife and strain of urban political battles had retired to their country houses,

[1] ABR, L346.

were likewise accused of emigration – even those whose retired way of life had caused their neighbours not to see them, sometimes found themselves before the Tribunal.

Another aspect of this matter was illustrated by the struggles at Salon in the early months of 1793, when many of the people who were forced to leave their houses and their villages by the depredations (real or alleged) of the Jacobins were declared *émigrés* by the Jacobin municipality, even though the fugitives had fled no farther than Martigues or Manosque. Furthermore, those who fled had left behind them their lands and their houses, and these, confiscated for the benefit of the nation, were 'managed' by those who had driven out the fugitives in the first place. Those who fled were not the only people who alleged that the prime motive, in some communes at least, for declaring a man an *émigré* was to seize and enjoy his possessions.

Other men accused of emigration maintained that they had fled because they feared arrest by the revolutionaries who returned after the fall of the Sections. The fact that so many who fled in such circumstances went eastwards through the Var casts much doubt on the truth of such pleas. Many others, however, probably escaped without trace into the interior of the Republic, where surveillance was perhaps rather less strict and so they were not intercepted and accused of flight. The Army of Italy provided a barrier which entrapped many of those who wished to escape to the frontiers by the shortest route.

The case of Jean-Joseph Franchicour, a priest living in Marseilles, was rather different from the others, since he had returned after a stay in Turin. According to the public prosecutor, he was subject to deportation for having preached in a church without having sworn the oaths demanded from practising priests. At the end of July 1792, he had left Marseilles – at a time when many such priests were expelled – and had tried to return in August 1793 but was intercepted at Nice. He admitted that he had been expelled on the orders of the Municipality of Marseilles, and, disguised as a grain-merchant, he reached Turin, but then returned to France impelled 'par le désir naturel à toute personne de revoir sa patrie'. He claimed that he had not thought it necessary to take oaths, since he had resigned his priestly functions in 1789, and he denied that he had tried to come back to Marseilles in August 1793 because the counter-revolution was supreme there. And though he further denied having attended the meetings of *émigrés* at Turin, he was nevertheless condemned to death.[1]

In general however, the crime of emigration, though very serious, did not feature to any great extent in the records of the Revolutionary Tribunal – neither the importance of the individual cases, nor the number of such cases was sufficiently great to confirm the frequently held belief that the *émigrés* of the Bouches-du-Rhône had returned in large numbers to take part in the counter-revolution. Nor can much light be shed on the extent of emigration from the department, since those *émigrés* who appeared before the Tribunal had either failed to leave the territory of France, or had returned from foreign parts.

Those who had escaped however were fairly numerous, and, in a negative way, this is reflected in the minutes of the Revolutionary Tribunal. For a large number of people – almost treble those who were accused of emigration – were accused of having relatives who had emigrated, of helping men to emigrate, or of corresponding with *émigrés*. For instance, it was a stock question of the president, when confronted with a woman suspect who was accused of no very definite crime, to ask whether she had a husband or a son who had emigrated. Generally such a question was a pure formality and was brushed aside by the accused. Even those who did have relatives who had emigrated were not punished, for this in itself was not a crime. If however they had engaged in active work themselves on behalf of the Sections, the fact that they were related to *émigrés* told against them. Those accused of having aided *émigrés* faced a definite charge, though relatives of *émigrés* were generally suspected of having helped them escape and of having corresponded with them.

A priest, Jean-Pierre Pidoux of Aix, was accused of having bought up their lands in order to preserve them against their return, but he denied this, saying he had resold all his purchases.[2] Another man was accused of having sheltered *émigrés* at Toulon but was freed when he proved the falsity of this

---

[1] ABR, L3113, 8 Nov. 1793, Jean-Joseph Franchicour; and L3120.

[2] ABR, L3113, 8 Nov. 1793, Jean-Pierre Pidoux.

accusation.[1] A woman who hired out furnished rooms was charged with lodging *émigrés* but she too was freed.[2] Two sailors who took prominent sectionaries in their boats were released because they acted in ignorance.[3] Aimé-Victor Lieutaud, a soldier of Marseilles, was accused of having helped an *émigré* return, for as secretary of the general committee of Aubagne he had signed the *émigré's* recall. Lieutaud denied knowledge of the emigration of the citizen in question. But his position on the general committee of the Sections of Aubagne ensured that he was condemned to death.[4] His case is unique for no other mention is made of a specific case in which the sectionaries recalled *émigrés*. Finally, a much less serious case; that of Antoinette Ferrary who received from Genoa letters from a person who, in her own words, 'avait de l'inclination pour moi'. The girl was released because there was no proof of a sinister relationship.[5]

(d) SERVICE TO THE REPUBLIC

In order to counteract the bad effect produced on the judges of the Tribunal by the recital of their misdeeds, some of the accused tried to establish their devotion to the Revolution by describing their gifts to the Republic or their service in the armies of France. The most common gifts were those of money for the volunteers, rifles, coats, and shoes, though some merchants claimed that they had given corn and meat. The true republican was one who, in difficult circumstances, 'consulted his heart rather than his purse'. Other citizens had done what they could to help the war-effort –

J'ai eu des volontaires chez moi qui m'ont quitté la larme à l'œil.

Some had aided the poor families whose bread-winners had gone to the front, others pleaded that they had sent their children to the frontiers, even though they were aged 16, 14 and 12.

[1] ABR, L3112, 19 Sept. 1793, Jean-François Galopin.
[2] ABR, L3119, 4 *floréal* II (23 Apr. 1794), Marie Serre.
[3] ABR, L3113, 8 Oct. 1793, Sauveur Marin and Louis Icard.
[4] ABR, L3115, 6 *nivôse* II (26 Dec. 1793), Aimé-Victor Lieutaud.
[5] ABR, L3112, 13 Sept. 1793, Antoinette Ferrary.

It seems that the poorer the men were who made these sacrifices, the more sincere were their republican sympathies and the more indulgent was the Tribunal towards them, while many of the more well-to-do stressed their sacrifices a bit too raucously for the tastes of the Tribunal. Thus Jean-François Mestre – a 'bourgeois riche ci-devant noble' – asked the Tribunal to take into consideration his gift of 4000 *livres* for Carteaux's army. But the judges knew very well that this was a forced loan levied on the trading community of Marseilles and that many paid up less from a desire to serve the Republic than from fear of the Revolutionary Tribunal. Mestre was freed – but not before he had paid a large fine.[1]

Those who had themselves served in the armies of the Republic were better placed to win sympathy; hence the accused were rarely slow in describing their military service – in the National Guard, in the expeditions to Aix and Arles, in the two Battalions which marched to Paris, even, in one instance, in the French forces fighting for American independence. In the service of the Republic, some had been on the ill-fated expedition against Sardinia in the early months of 1793, while others had been at the capture of Nice. Joseph Tassy, not judged by the Tribunal, had served on the *corsaires* of the Republic. Some had served in the batteries along the sea-coast: others had joined Carteaux and went to fight against the rebels of Toulon. But this last service was no sure guarantee of the goodwill of the Tribunal since it realised that many who fought against Toulon had done so to hide a counter-revolutionary past. Like Ambroise Le Roi, who took the oath against the Convention, they felt they had 'fait une faute' and so explained that they wished to expiate it by serving at Toulon.[2] Some, like Pierre Oderieu, had been forced to go in the Departmental Army but had thrown down their arms and joined Carteaux.[3] Sometimes the most valorous service in the army before Toulon did not secure acquittal, as is shown in the case of a surgeon-major who fought well – as patriots attested – but

[1] ABR, L3116, 29 *ventôse* II (19 Mar. 1794), Jean-François-Melchior Mestre.

[2] ABR, L3115, 17 *nivôse* II (6 Jan. 1794), and L3119, 2 *floréal* II (21 Apr. 1794), Ambroise Le Roi.

[3] ABR, L3115, 29 *nivôse* II (18 Jan. 1794), Pierre-Vincent Oderieu.

who had a counter-revolutionary past.[1] Other men were accused of misconduct or negligence under arms, though two soldiers accused of insubordination were freed after they had denounced the aristocratic ways of their commanding officer.[2] The case of Jacques Marchand was more serious: he was condemned to death for having transferred his allegiance from the Army of Italy to the forces of Britain and Spain.[3] However, a man who joined Carteaux because he did not want to fight against the Piedmontese was released.[4]

The case of Joseph Martel, a captain in the Army of Italy, was more complicated. He was condemned to death for having, in the autumn of 1793, swindled a commission from his superiors, giving him powers to requisition cattle and sheep. Posing as an agent of government, he requisitioned livestock from the poor farmers of the Crau and disposed of them for his own profit. The Tribunal, in condemning him to death, underlined that Martel had been an agent in a vast plot, designed to starve Marseilles and Toulon and to call upon these two 'regenerated' cities 'l'animadversion de la Convention nationale'. No evidence was produced to prove this highly unlikely story.[5]

Finally, the Tribunal was occupied for several days in judging sixty-one individuals who had formed an armed band, having forged their marching orders, broken away from the Army of Italy, and, marching towards the centre of France, had requisitioned food from the towns through which they had passed, recruiting new men as they went along. Men were persuaded to join by being made officers or given horses or shoes – many soldiers who were heading for the army at Toulon turned round and marched the other way. Seven of these soldiers were condemned to death, thirty-nine to five years in irons, and the rest were freed. This was done by virtue of a clause in the *Code pénal militaire* stating that anyone who recruited for the foreign enemies of the Republic or for the

---

[1] ABR, L3119, 5 *floréal* II (24 Apr. 1794), Pierre-François Demaine.

[2] ABR, L3115, 18 *nivôse* II (7 Jan. 1794), Aimé Dessex and Georges Souviran.

[3] ABR, L3115, 18 *nivôse* II (7 Jan. 1794), Jacques Marchand.

[4] ABR, L3113, 23 Oct. 1793 and 19 *brumaire* II (9 Nov. 1793), Didier Laureil.

[5] ABR, L3118, 23 *germinal* II (12 Apr. 1794), Joseph Martel.

rebels should be condemned to death and which also punished deserters.[1]

(e) ECONOMIC OFFENCES

As regards economic offences, the Revolutionary Tribunal was hardly over-worked. The economic legislation of the spring and summer of 1793 had often been criticised by the Sections of Marseilles – especially the *maximum*, the forced loans, and the continued issue of *assignats*.[2] This legislation was not of course put into effect at Marseilles until the city had been retaken by the republicans. Maillet and his colleagues seem to have tacitly assumed that no prosecutions could be made for neglecting to implement this legislation.

Most of the economic offences concerned the use and abuse of the *assignats*, generally involving the charge that the offender had tried to discredit the *assignats* – and hence the Convention and the Republic – by insisting upon the discrepancies between them and metallic money 'à face royale'. Such crimes were more political than economic, however, casting doubt on the longevity of the Republic. Pierre Timon-David, one of the most notable merchants of Marseilles, was condemned to death for, among many other illegal acts, having accepted a post on a bureau designed – according to the Tribunal – to continue the circulation of *assignats à face royale* and thereby discredit those of the Republic.[3] The possession of large sums of gold and silver aroused suspicion, partly because this too might indicate distrust of the *assignats*. Only one person was accused of circulating false *assignats*; and she, Marie Martin of Jouques, was acquitted.[4]

More general criticism of the Convention's policy as regards the issue of *assignats* was likewise evoked during the sessions of the Tribunal. Thus Antoine-Blaise Colombon, a former lawyer of Marseilles, was blamed for having voted the formation of a committee,

---

[1] ABR, L3114, 11–15 *frimaire* II (1–5 Dec. 1793).
[2] See above, pp. 120 ff.
[3] ABR, L3118, 27 *germinal* II (16 Apr. 1794), Pierre Timon-David.
[4] ABR, L3113, 3 Nov. 1793; Marie Martin of Jouques (*arrond.*, Aix; *canton*, Peyrolles).

pour prendre des mesures afin d'empêcher la dilapidation
que l'abus de notre papier-monnaie ne rend que trop facile.[1]

Ange Ferroul, a notary's clerk, was accused of blaming high
prices on the excessive issuing of *assignats* and of alleging that
the deputies of the Convention made fortunes by speculating
with *louis* and *assignats*.[2] Speculation was considered blameworthy by the Tribunal, though few cases were brought to its
notice and these were of a very trivial nature.

The most important – the only important – case from two or
three involving hoarding was that of Basile Samatan, one of the
most wealthy and notable of all the merchants of Marseilles.[3]
He had failed to declare within the required delay of a week,
imposed by the law of 26 July 1793, some wool stored at
Tarascon. The public prosecutor commented:

Cette infraction coupable confirme la réputation plus
qu'équivoque qu'il s'est faite dans la Révolution.

The case shows the difficulties which merchants with national
and international trading commitments had in obeying the
letter of the Revolution's economic legislation. Samatan said
that he thought his agents at Tarascon had declared the wool.
It had remained unsold at the fair of Beaucaire: local woollen
manufacturers had demanded that it should be sold to them
at the price fixed by the *maximum*, thus enabling them to keep
their manufactures going and their workers in jobs. Samatan
pointed out that he had declared his merchandise stocked at
Marseilles. Baffled, the Tribunal wrote to the Minister of
Justice, who replied that the Convention was studying the
matter, but had meanwhile suspended the execution of the
death penalty prescribed by the law. Samatan was not judged
before the Tribunal was suppressed, but later, to the delight
of Barras and Fréron, was condemned to death by the Military
Commission, (on 4 *pluviôse* II – 23 Jan. 1794), for having given
financial support to the Sections.

The case shows that the Revolutionary Tribunal, at least, was

[1] ABR, L3115, 18 *nivôse* II (7 Jan. 1794), Antoine-Joseph-Blaise
Colombon.

[2] ABR, L3118, 25 *germinal* II (14 Apr. 1794), Ange-Henri Ferroul.

[3] ABR, L3114, 21 *frimaire* II (11 Dec. 1793), and see above, p. 24.

willing to consider scrupulously the points raised by Samatan
about the practicability of the law of 26 July 1793 and that a
closely-argued and articulate defence might make the judges
draw back from an over-hasty judgement. But it also gives the
impression of having been a mere pretext to entrap a man who,
for reasons which are by no means clear, had, in the parting
jibe of the public prosecutor, a 'réputation plus qu'équivoque'.
Obviously Samatan was really suspected of having used his
great wealth to aid the sectionaries; his loan of money to the
Municipality for the purpose of buying food for Marseilles was
regarded, not so much as an act of charity, as an act which had
buttressed the crumbling edifice of sectionary power. That this
is so, is suggested by the verdict of the Military Commission,
though about this we have no information.

But equivocation was rife in Samatan's case: he had been
arrested on 6 October 1793, released by order of Maillet early
in November – to help to provide food for his city – but had
been arrested once more on 6 December, after which his trial
came quickly.[1] Perhaps this was a case of the Tribunal bowing
to the pressure of Barras and Fréron.

We have few indications as to Samatan's political views,
though a letter to Jean-Baptiste Vence – executed as a leading
agent of the Sections[2] – survives, in which Samatan stressed the
need to find out if the government (in May or June 1793,
probably) was strong enough to stand up against foreign
powers and spoke of how 'les fortunes s'éclipsent'.[3] More
incriminating was his election as *suppléant* to the Tribunal of
Commerce – for service on which, three of his colleagues were
executed.[4] He was also one of the merchants denounced by
Nicolas Clastrier,[5] a ship's captain, who said that his patriotic
principles had indisposed the merchants against giving him
employment –

tout le monde sait qu'à Marseille les amis les plus chauds de
la Révolution n'ont pas été les négociants.

Certainly, members of the upper ranks of the trading

[1] For this episode, see Odon de Samatan, *Basile Samatan* (Marseilles,
1894).   [2] See above, pp. 176–9.   [3] ABR, L3114.
[4] ABR, L3118, elections took place on 3 July 1793.
[5] ABR, L3112, 26 Sept. 1793, Nicolas Clastrier.

community were accused of having aided the counter-revolution by co-operating in the provision of foodstuffs for the city. Thus Laurent-François Tarteiron, like Samatan a prominent merchant, appeared before the Tribunal on this charge.[1] Unlike Samatan, however, he had played a conspicuous part in his Section. In the words of the accusation,

> il a coopéré aux subsistances d'une ville rebelle, à la délibération qui établissait un impôt qui intimait des achats de comestibles avec la coupable différence que les contre-révolutionnaires mettaient entre l'assignat et l'argent . . . il a souscrit aux différentes contributions qui se sont faites par les rebelles pour alimenter la contre-révolution, la force départementale et la dégradation de l'esprit public. Il était président de la corporation des négociants pour l'élection des juges illégaux de commerce.

Thus, in the eyes of the public prosecutor, Tarteiron was one of the few merchants of the first rank who had devoted much of his time to attending the Sections. Certainly, his actions in the rebellion are very much in evidence in the pages of the registers of Section 2.[2] He had early been appointed to the *Comité de bienfaisance*; he had communicated to the Section a letter from Barbaroux in his possession; throughout August, he had been vice-president of his Section, often presiding in the absence of the president; and in this capacity he had co-operated in the functioning of the Military Tribunal, in the election of new municipal officers, in the working of the Popular Tribunal. He was present at the meeting of the Three Administrations on 10 August, which debated means of providing food for the city, a meeting which decided upon a tax to be imposed on the *gens aisés*, to import foodstuffs, and also envisaged the possibility of using public money for this purpose.[3] Both these measures lay within the competence of the Convention alone, and so Tarteiron was undoubtedly one of the main supporters of the Sections' revolt and, as such, could hardly have expected to escape from the death penalty imposed upon him.

[1] ABR, L484, 13 *nivôse* II (2 Jan. 1794), Laurent-François Tarteiron.
[2] ABR, L1934, L1935.
[3] ABR, L48, Three Administrations, 10 Aug. 1793.

Other members of the trading community of Marseilles had been accused of similar offences, though none of the accused was as important as Tarteiron, nor were the charges particularly specific or convincing. Étienne Mouret, described as a 'voiturier sur le Rhône', and living at Tarascon, was confronted with the accusation that he had been given a commission by the Municipality of Marseilles to get corn for the city.[1] Siffren Boulouvard, a merchant captain of Arles, was closely questioned to find out whether he too had supplied Marseilles with corn.[2]

In fact, in cases involving *subsistances*, as in other offences concerning economic matters, action was usually taken only if the accused had played an overtly political rôle in the rebellion. Such offences were regarded as subsidiary to those which primarily occupied the attention of the Tribunal. Only a minute proportion of those guilty of contravening the economic legislation of the Convention were brought to trial. The great merchants had acted discreetly in the counter-revolution, having rarely occupied conspicuous places and, more often than not, their gifts to the Departmental Army were camouflaged. Certainly the Tribunal had little success in providing evidence of such gifts. Inevitably it was to the merchants and shipowners of Marseilles that the local authorities – royal or popular, revolutionary or counter-revolutionary – looked for subsidies and contributions to sustain their activities. Concerned primarily with managing their commercial empires – or, as seemed often the case, with winding them up – the merchants complied, albeit reluctantly, without bothering too much about the legitimacy of the organs which made the demands. It must therefore be assumed that the merchants had paid the money, which in normal times went as taxes to the national treasury, to the Sections when Marseilles was in rebellion against the government. Certainly, whenever there was a subscription to finance the Departmental Army or to pay the running expenses of the Sections, it was the merchants – 'gens aisés' to a degree – who were most strongly pressed to contribute.

[1] ABR, L484, 11 *nivôse* II (31 Dec. 1793), Étienne Mouret.
[2] ABR, L3113, 18–19 Oct. 1793, Siffren Boulouvard – he had indeed been very active in providing corn for sectionary Marseilles.

But there is also little doubt that the sectionaries expected the merchants to be sympathetic to their cause. Jacques Seimandy, for example, was elected a member of the General Committee of the Sections on 30 July, though he refused to accept his appointment:[1] he had however accepted commissions which had political implications – to debate means to restore the nation's finances, to prevent abuses in the supply of goods to the armies, and so on. Joseph-Marie-Honoré Rostan was condemned to death as a member of the General Committee.[2] Pierre Bernard, an important soap-manufacturer, had been a provisional municipal officer[3] – while one of his fellow *fabricants*, Honoré Maysse, had announced that the 'honnêtes gens' should now get on top and had urged the merchants to attend the installation of this provisional Municipality.[4] He had been a member of the *Comité secret* of Section 4. Lazare Périer Meynard, reputed to enjoy 50,000 *livres* of revenue, purchaser of *biens nationaux*, owner of three ships and 3 *bastides* (at the very least) had been a 'juge populaire'.[5] Though Jean-Joachim Dragon was liquidating his own commercial company, this had not prevented him from accepting jurisdiction over the mercantile community as a whole by becoming an illegal judge of commerce.[6] Nor were all the merchants employed in sedentary occupations. Besides Vence, others had gone to the Departmental Army. Jean-Pierre Reynier, *capitaine de grenadiers* of Section 23, went twice; the second time to reinforce the last-ditch stand at Septèmes. He was one of the more wealthy men to suffer the death penalty. Assessed at nearly 48,000 *livres* for the tax of 3 September 1793, he had purchased extensive *biens nationaux* on the outskirts of town: his stocks

---

[1] ABR, L1935, Section 2, 30 and 31 July 1793.

[2] See above, p. 211.

[3] ABR, L3113, 24 Oct. 1793, Pierre Bernard.

[4] ABR, L3118, 24 *germinal* II (13 Apr. 1794), Honoré Maysse.

[5] ABR, L3118, 15 *germinal* II (4 Apr. 1794), Lazare Périer Meynard, condemned to death.

[6] ABR, L3115, 22 *nivôse* II (11 Jan. 1794), Jean-Joachim Dragon, now described as a *bourgeois*, though still owning massive stocks of cotton, lead, iron, sugar, coffee, wine; owner of large rural properties, numerous town houses, the *mobilier* of one of which came to over 18,000 *livres*. See ABR, 4Q193; Moulin, 3, pp. 226, 238, 308; 4, p. 251. He was summoned to pay over 28,000 *livres* for the tax of 3 Sept. 1793 (A. Comm., 2G33).

included cotton, various exotic woods – some of which were used to warm the administrations of Marseilles – indigo, tobacco, soap, alum and various roots whose identity baffled the inspectors of the Republic. It is noteworthy that he pur-chased his *campagnes* (former ecclesiastical estates) in June 1793.[1] Several other of the richest merchants made big purchases of clerical land in June and July 1793.[2]

Economic activity in this period had profound political implications, but what these implications are – or were – is difficult to define. Lefebvre backs up Lautard in picturing many of the merchants of Marseilles speculating furiously in *assignats* as Carteaux marched towards their city[3] at a time when several served on a committee designed to bolster the value of the revolutionary money. To the sectionaries, as well as to the Jacobins, merchants were often rich egoists who benefited from public misfortune by hoarding corn, who preferred private profit-making to service in the National Guard or in political and administrative bodies.[4] But to put money in *biens nationaux* was to defend the Revolution and several of the accused mentioned their purchases in their defence. To pursue profit too ardently was dangerous, however – Pierre Decroi, a rich banker, said in his defence that he had lost three-quarters of his fortune by not speculating. He had also used his financial experience to the benefit of his fellow-citizens by his activities in organising subscriptions for food supplies.[5]

[1] ABR, L3115, 27 *nivôse* II (16 Jan. 1794), Jean-Pierre Reynier; see also 4Q231 and Moulin, 3, pp. 121–2, 168–9. He had merchandise valued at over 600,000 *livres* but he complained that the *maximum* had not only anihilated his profits for 1793 but had also eaten into his capital.

[2] Pierre Rolland, executed after judgement of the Military Commission, 13 *pluviôse* II (1 Feb. 1794); Jean-Baptiste-Scipion Fabre, condemned to death 26 *pluviôse* II (14 Feb. 1794). See Moulin, 3, pp. 171–2.

[3] Lautard, 1, p. 323, says that Jean Payan, executed after judgement of the Military Commission, established a vast fortune by this speculation. See also G. Lefebvre, 'Le commerce extérieur en l'an II', in *Études sur la Révolution française* (Paris, 1963), p. 240.

[4] Pierre Timon-David (see above, p. 301) told the Tribunal that he was fined for not going to the Sections.

[5] ABR, L3119, 5 *floréal* II (24 Apr. 1794): Pierre Decroi was subjected to the demand for 88,334 *livres* for the tax of 3 Sept. 1793. His case was not decided before the Tribunal ended its sessions. For his tax assessment, A. Comm., 2G33.

And, in fact, he served the *Bureau des comestibles* well into the winter of 1793. Wealth, or forceful economic activity, might always be turned by skilful *prévenus* into a means of defence. For instance, some boasted of giving employment to thousands of workers: almost all detailed the money they had given in 'forced' loans or 'voluntary' subscriptions. Just as some landowners were blamed by the judges for letting their land lie fallow, thus sabotaging the well-being of the republicans, those who let their wealth lie inactive were guilty of egoism or indifference[1] and might be fined by the Tribunal, as was, for example, Joseph Audibert, one of the group of closely-related merchant 'aristocrats'.[2] One wealthy *fabricant tanneur* was so ill-advised as to use his money to try to bribe a public official – in fact the acting public prosecutor. He was freed but fined 60,000 *livres*.[3] But Jacques Grenier, though 'inutile' to the patriots, was not even fined. It is true that his commercial empire was in bad shape by 1794; it had declined steeply since the end of 1792, hit by the war – with the end of expeditions to the West Indies – by the *maximum*, by an accumulation of hopeless debts, by requisitions and by the lack of raw materials for sulphur-refining (he had thus been forced to dismiss all his workers 'jusqu'à la paix'). Perhaps a demand for 69,083 *livres* for the *impôt forcé* had dealt a further crippling blow to his fortune.[4] But such circumstances were rarely taken into account by the Tribunal.

Such circumstances however seem to have been general among the mercantile community. Forced loans, imposed on fortunes reputed to be much higher than they actually were – or had become – had eaten into capital. Troubles in the West Indies had disrupted trade, made many merchants write off massive debts as hopeless, caused the loss of stocks and plantations. The war had brought the loss and seizure of ships;

---

[1] See below, pp. 312ff., for concept of 'indifference'.

[2] ABR, L3116, 29 *ventôse* II (19 Mar. 1794), Joseph Audibert, freed but fined 20,000 *livres*. He said he was 'riche de 300,000 *livres*'.

[3] ABR, L3116, 19 *germinal* II (8 Apr. 1794), Marc Aillaud.

[4] ABR, L3118, 28 *germinal* II (17 Apr. 1794), Jacques Grenier, *oncle*. See also A. Comm., 2G33, for information regarding his financial situation. This information is accepted as veracious by C. Carrière; see 'Un hôtel de grands négociants, 42 rue Sainte, 1785–1820', *Marseille*, No. 46, 1962, pp. 3–20; No. 47, 1962, pp. 25–32. It was of course a family fortune.

insurance rates increased greatly; stocks, confined in far-off ports, deteriorated; markets for exports were cut off and so French-produced goods rotted in warehouses; anti-French acts in foreign lands hit some merchants hard. Many merchants had been owed money by their colleagues who had emigrated, who had gone bankrupt or been executed. Others had lent large sums to the Commune, which proved a bad debtor. Those who had invested large sums of money in urban property found it difficult to find tenants. And, in complaining of the exorbitance of their tax assessments, some merchants did not hesitate to blame their lack of profits on requisitions, forced taxes, subscriptions for foodstuffs, and the *maximum*.[1]

But so varied were the activities of the really great merchants that they might turn circumstances to advantage and balance profit and loss, invest in land in preparation for a more stable future. Certainly, each of these merchants had huge commercial empires, with multifarious aspects – activities which had varied and sometimes contradictory implications in the social and political spheres. Sometimes such merchants were able to put a public 'front' on their activities – notably by participation in organisations designed to facilitate the supply of foodstuffs to the city. The records of the *Bureau des subsistances* show Samatan, Solier, Rabaud, Payan, Hugues *l'aîné*, Dragon etc. playing a part in this official body throughout the autumn and into the winter of 1793.[2] Another public glimpse of the merchants' activities – or some of them – is afforded by tax declarations and assessments, while inventories of those merchants who had emigrated or who had been executed show more aspects of the empires of the *négociants*. Combined, these sources often reveal massive investment in land, the virtual suspension of many trading and industrial ventures and the collapse of profits from commerce in 1793. They reveal that a merchant might plead poverty, just after having invested

[1] See especially the tax declarations and assessments of many of the more wealthy merchants in the A. Comm., *Série* 2G, especially 2G28–33.

[2] A. Comm., 46F12, *Bureau des subsistances*. Also, on 24 *nivôse* II (13 Jan. 1794), the *Commission des subsistances* of Paris appointed Rabaud, Samatan, Payan, etc., members of the *Comité d'approvisionnements maritimes*: P. Caron, *La Commission des subsistances de l'An II*, 2 vols. (Paris, 1924–5) p. 241.

hundreds of thousands of *livres* in the 'lands of the Nation'.[1]

To navigate a great commerce through the rocks of the Revolution was a very delicate business. Such was the position of the merchants and the nature of their activities that they were easy prey to terrorists who wished to give themselves a reputation for ruthlessness. It seems that the Revolutionary Tribunal – in its treatment of the merchants – deserved the attacks of Barras and Fréron: it did not go out of its way to seek out those who financed the sectionary revolt. Not till the advent of the Military Commission did scenes occur at Marseilles at all similar to those at other great ports, where merchants were arrested – sometimes in their hundreds – and subjected to ruthless judicial terror culminating in massive fines and executions.[2]

(f) INCRIMINATING RELATIVES

Sometimes, usually incidentally to more vital questions, the president asked a *prévenu* about the activities of his or her relatives. In a few cases the relatives of eminent sectionaries appeared and had to dissociate themselves from their unpatriotic doings. Thus Louis Seytres, brother of Étienne Seytres, the former procurator general of Marseilles, had great difficulty in defending himself against the charge that he had paid for the printing of one of his brother's pamphlets.[3] Marie Simai, wife of Castelanet, and Pierre Simai and Charles Seren were introduced as 'simples parents du traître Castelanet'. Marie Simai was questioned as to whether she had known the 'projets liberticides' of her husband, but such knowledge was denied. Pierre Simai, Castelanet's brother-in-law, likewise denied knowledge of the projects of the leader of the General

---

[1] Samatan, however, after relating his commercial losses, adds 'Il résulte de ce que dessus que non seulement ma société de commerce a perdu tous ces bénéfices, et mon fond capital, mais que mon état peut encore empirer au point que partie de mes immeubles suffira à peine pour recombler le déficit que j'éprouverai sur la liquidation de mes dettes qui se montent à £2,500,000 environ' (Tax declaration, A. Comm., 2G28).

[2] At Bordeaux, for example, a batch of two hundred merchants was arrested: fifteen were executed, fines of seven million *livres* exacted. See *Bordeaux au XVIIIe siècle*, ed. G. Pariset (Bordeaux, 1968) pp. 430 ff.

[3] ABR, L3119, 2 *floréal* II (21 Apr. 1794), Louis Seytres.

Committee of Marseilles. These three citizens were sentenced to *réclusion* until the Convention had given a ruling on their case. In the official account of their judgement, they are described as having been sentenced to *réclusion*,

n'étant convaincus d'aucunes plaintes ou inculpations . . . sinon d'être alliés à des traîtres à la patrie.[1]

This rigorous judgement was unique in the records of the Tribunal – generally some other proof of counter-revolutionary principles was needed to secure conviction. Fathers were often reprimanded for not keeping their sons on the straight and narrow path of republican virtue but generally it was the women who were most vulnerable to this accusation for they were often held responsible for the misdeeds of their husbands. The wife of Ferréol Beaugeard, (the journalist of the Sections, who had emigrated from Marseilles), was freed after she affirmed that she had never read his newspaper.[2] *Femme* Bouffier, wife of an office-holder, showed that she did not share his opinions by saying that she wished to divorce him.[3] Most frequently, however, women were considered suspects because their husbands were thought to be *émigrés*. Sometimes the husbands in question had been dead for a couple of months – or for twenty years – or the women had never been married; but sometimes they had indeed disappeared. *Femme* Aubert, asked why she had not prevented her husband, a member of a sectionary committee, from emigrating, replied that:

j'ai fait tout ce que j'ai pu, mais mon mari ne m'a jamais écoutée; comme bien des hommes font, il m'a méprisée. Je ne le regrette pas, il m'a donné trop de chagrin.[4]

The arrest of many of these women seems to have been haphazard and unfortunate. Though most were released, they had often spent several months in prison in horrible conditions.

Another negative crime occupied the attention of the Tribunal – the crime of indifference.

[1] ABR, L3113, 6 Oct. 1793, Marie Simai, *femme* Castelanet; Pierre-Philippe Simai; Charles Seren.
[2] ABR, L3118, 28 *germinal* II (17 Apr. 1794), Maurel *femme* Beaugeard.
[3] ABR, L3113, 12 Nov. 1793, Marie-Jeanne Monier, *femme* Bouffier.
[4] ABR, L3118, 28 *germinal* II (17 Apr. 1794), Thérèse Pottier.

(g) INDIFFERENCE

Some of the accused were convicted of having been indifferent to the Revolution. This category of suspects was included under the provisions of Article 10 of the law of 17 September 1793, which empowered tribunals to imprison as suspects men who had been acquitted of definite charges, but whose release might jeopardise the safety of the Republic. This decree was supplemented by *arrêtés* of the *Représentants*. Thus an *arrêté* of Saliceti, Gasparin, Escudier and Albitte of 27 August authorised the Department to arrest all those people 'dont les principes lui paraîtront dangereux pour l'affermissement du système républicain'.[1] But it was Maignet who was chiefly responsible for introducing the concept of 'nullity' into the judicial nomenclature of Marseilles; for he was a confirmed enemy of all those who had refused to commit themselves in the Revolution and he believed that the troubles in Marseilles had been largely the work of such people. In his proclamation of 19 *pluviôse* II (7 Feb. 1794), he defined his ideas regarding this type of suspect –

> S'il est quelque époque où ils aient vu la liberté en péril, et qu'ils aient demeurés tranquilles et froids spectateurs au milieu du déchirement de leur patrie, dites que ces hommes sont des fourbes, que les actes de civisme qu'ils ont faits quelquefois, ne sont que des moyens qu'ils ont voulu se ménager pour tromper l'opinion publique et pour se donner un brevet, afin de conspirer plus tranquillement; assurez-vous de leurs personnes; que leur détention donne à la République la garantie pleine et entière que leur conduite ne peut lui offrir.[2]

Elsewhere, Maignet defined such a man as

> un homme pour qui la Révolution a été jusqu'aujourd'hui un supplice.[3]

It was however in an *arrêté* of 10 February 1794 that Maignet came to the heart of the question of nullity.[4] This decree,

---

[1] ABR, L363.'   [2] ABR, 100E32.
[3] ABR, L1039 (papers of District Admin.).   [4] ABR, L3127.

allowing the Military Commission to levy fines on suspects, was later extended for the benefit of the Revolutionary Tribunal. By its provisions, men who had been recognised as innocent or guilty of only minor offences, whose release would not endanger the security of the Republic, were to be set free. But if it was thought that well-off people had not paid a proportionate sacrifice to the Republic, they should be fined according to their wealth, to the number of children they had, and to the gravity of the offences or negligences which they had committed. Until this fine was paid, they had to remain in prison.

On the day that this decree was applied to the Revolutionary Tribunal, the judges took advantage of its provisions to punish several citizens convicted of nullity. Four were described as having done nothing to advance the cause of the Revolution; another was stigmatised as 'au moins un être nul'. Joseph Audibert, a retired merchant of Marseilles, described as 'riche de 200,000', was fined 20,000 *livres* for his indifference – an indifference which he explained by pleading a long illness. Jean-Joseph Gaillard was a *bourgeois* of Marseilles, 'riche de 130,000', who was acquitted of the charge that he had denounced the clubists, but who was nevertheless fined 4000 *livres*. Janvier d'Amice *père*, who made violin strings, was not convicted of speculation but was fined 3000 *livres*. The Mestre brothers were fined 20,000 each. One was 48-years old and described himself as a 'célibataire bourgeois riche de 600,000 livres, mais dépendant encore de mon père'. They were accused of being nobles[1] but were freed after being heavily fined. Though these were not the only citizens fined by the Tribunal, Maignet's decree was not used very frequently as a weapon against the indifferent and 'useless'; nor was it used as an indiscriminate weapon against the rich, who were either subjected to forced loans or executed (principally by the Military Commission). There was no equivalent of the seven million *livres* in fines imposed by the Military Commission of Bordeaux.[2] Instead, the Tribunal continued its previous policy towards men who had done nothing to advance the revolutionary cause. Long before Maignet's decree, the Tribunal had denounced such men.

[1] See above, pp. 211–12.
[2] *Bordeaux au XVIIIe siècle*, ed. G. Pariset (Bordeaux, 1968) pp. 432–3.

On a rather arbitrary calculation, it would seem that about forty men and women were accused of indifference and very little else: in fact, of thirty-nine people we have assigned to this category, the cases of thirty-three were terminated. All but one of these were freed and one person was sentenced to *réclusion*. The majority (twenty-five) were sentenced on or after 29 *ventôse*. Socially, they represent a fair cross-section of all who came before the Tribunal. A further seventeen suspects were accused of 'nullity' – hardly distinguishable from indifference – fifteen were freed, two condemned to *réclusion*. Thirteen were said to be 'egoists' but all were freed. Though the phrase 'riche égoïste' was common during the Revolution, it does not seem that this particular category – nor the indifferent in general – contained a specially high percentage of men drawn from the upper classes. Also, one hundred men and women were confronted with vague accusations which cannot be categorised as other than 'indefinite': their denunciation by the public prosecutor was perfunctory, their interrogation short and shapeless, with the president obviously at a loss, drifting through a few ritual questions before the Tribunal ordered the release of the accused. Of these one hundred, the ninety-four whose trial was terminated were released.

A classic statement of nullity was levied against Jean Sellon, a lawyer:

> Il a un patriotisme fort modéré. S'il peut donner des preuves de civisme, ce n'est que par des actes néanmoins fort communs. Il n'a jamais voulu prendre un parti fort décidé. S'il n'a pas été fréquemment à la section, c'est plutôt par crainte de se compromettre que de servir la chose publique. Il a laissé dans le plus grand danger de la liberté inutiles ses lumières et ses connaissances. Il ne peut pas dire qu'il ait ouvertement blâmé la contre-révolution.[1]

Of some women, the public prosecutor remarked,

> Elles n'ont jamais fait pour la liberté ce que tant de femmes patriotes de la société populaire ont fait avec tant de zèle,[2]

---

[1] ABR, L3118, 27 *germinal* II (16 Apr. 1794), Jean-Joseph-Claude Sellon. He was freed.

[2] ABR, L3118, 27 *germinal* II (16 Apr. 1794).

thus incidentally suggesting that the Jacobin Club of Marseilles contained women.

Often accusations of indifference were coupled with taunts of egoism. Thus Joseph Méritant, a shoemaker of Marseilles, was denounced because

> l'amour de son intérêt propre l'a rendu indifférent pour la Révolution : il a toujours dit qu'il s'occupait de lui et non des autres.[1]

Likewise Antoine-Félix Reboul, a young merchant of Marseilles, who

> n'a jamais eu de zèle pour la Révolution. Il n'a jamais fréquenté que des gens suspects. Il a entretenu une correspondance très équivoque. . . . il est un de ces jeunes gens que les plaisirs guident, que l'intérêt personnel occupe, réfléchissant rarement sur l'intérêt général. . . .[2]

Both Méritant and Reboul were released.

The president told Dominique Tacussel, a paper manufacturer of Jouques, who had pleaded that the supervision of his manufacture had left him no time to play an active part in the Revolution, – 'vous devez savoir qu'un homme nul dans la République est un ennemi'.[3] But despite this stern warning, Tacussel was released. Most often, indeed, those accused of nullity were, as one would perhaps expect, timid and colourless individuals – it was no danger to the Republic to release such men.

In all, besides the sixty-seven men and women sent to prison, forty-four were sentenced to be detained as suspects until the peace – there was nothing definite held against them, though they had usually been faced with a definite charge.[4] But how, asked some of the accused, could they be indifferent to so glorious a Revolution?

[1] ABR, L3118, 23 *germinal* II (12 Apr. 1794), Joseph Méritant, released.
[2] ABR, L3115, 29 *nivôse* II (18 Jan. 1794), Antoine-Félix-Timothée Reboul.
[3] ABR, L3113, 9 Nov. 1793, Dominique Tacussel.
[4] See ABR, L586, motives of suspicion of various citizens (who did not appear before the Tribunal), described as 'peu entreprenant; souple, pusillanime; insouciant, peu prononcé; hautain et orgueilleux; peu décidé et docile; timide et dissimulé; taciturne et sournois, triste et taciturne. . . .' etc.

(*h*) ATTESTATIONS FOR THE REVOLUTION

> Belle foutre Révolution! J'ai commencé savetier et je finirai savetier![1]

Sometimes the men and women who appeared before the Tribunal took the opportunity to praise the Revolution, hoping by this to win the indulgence of the Tribunal. Often, the instances which they chose are very revealing – both as regards the character of the accused and their conception of the Revolution. Taken at random they present a somewhat curious picture.

When Jacques Grenier and his nephew, both merchants of Marseilles, wished to prove their devotion to revolutionary principles, they asked

> peuvent-ils mieux manifester leurs sentiments républicains que par l'éducation qu'ils font donner à Paris depuis deux ans à leur fils Achille, enfant âgé de neuf ans, qu'ils ont confié à l'ex-abbé Chautevot qui a troqué ses titres de prêtrise contre une femme pour donner des défenseurs à la patrie?[2]

Another question with the same purpose was asked of the Tribunal by Antoine Bœuf, an officer in the customs;

> peut-on présumer qu'un homme qui n'avait avant la Révolution qu'un très modique emploi et après la République vient de lui en procurer un qui le met dans la plus parfaite aisance puisse être contre-révolutionnaire?[3]

---

[1] British Museum, F1028(2), *Mémoire sur le Midi présenté au Directoire exécutif par Ls. Jullian et Alexandre Mechin*. This ridicules the ambitions of the lower classes in Marseilles: artisans will not go back to their workshops but are layabouts, expecting administrative jobs. The *savetier* (cobbler) in question expected to be put in charge of a hospital. Elsewhere a gardener wanted the job of maintaining the trees in the streets (the present incumbent being rich and unpatriotic) – he affirmed, 'le patriote doit être l'enfant gâté de la patrie'. (A. Comm., 2I4). When Maillet *cadet* became J.P., he reported that many artisans, many of whom could not read or write, flocked to apply for the post of secretary – A. Comm., 2I18).

[2] ABR, L3118, 28 *germinal* II (17 Apr. 1794), Jacques Grenier, *oncle*, and Jean-Rémond Grenier, *neveu*.

[3] ABR, L3114, 18 *frimaire* II (8 Dec. 1793), Antoine-Daniel Bœuf.

Another petitioner, Pierre Vérone, a young advocate's clerk, explained that, but for his arrest, he would have married.

> L'intérêt que j'avais à épouser cette femme qui a pour quatre-vingt mille livres de bien en immeubles doit être un sûr garant de mon zèle, de mon attachement pour la République. . . .

When the judges read this, he continues,

> ils diront, 'Voilà un homme qui allait épouser une femme qui faisait sa fortune. Aurait-il pu parvenir à cela sans la Révolution, pouvait-il sans les lois émanées de la Convention s'attendre à jouir d'un bien-être qu'il désire depuis tant de temps?'[1]

Antoine Vigne, a mason of Salon, affirmed that the Revolution favoured him by giving him more work than before,[2] while Jacques-Joseph Liautard likewise had a professional reason to appreciate the Revolution which had, he said, enabled him, as a maker of lead shot, to furnish that commodity to the interior of the Republic, because of the reduction of duties.[3] Another man, as a guarantee of his goodwill towards the Revolution, advanced the fact that he had bought a *bien national* – a purchase he would surely not have made had he not expected and desired the complete success of the Revolution. Joseph-Gabriel Isoard, a *huissier* of Marseilles, wrote that under the *Ancien régime* he had been oppressed by the lawyers and he had therefore been among the first to welcome the Revolution and to support it. Furthermore, he continued,

> un autre acte d'un vrai révolutionnaire est le divorce qu'il a provoqué depuis plus d'un an et fait prononcer, parce qu'il avait eu le malheur d'être du nombre des mal mariés. Sans la Révolution, qui a brisé diverses chaînes, il porterait encore celle d'un mariage malheureux, nœud qui dans les temps de la tyrannie était indissoluble et si, comme il a lieu de l'espérer de la justice de la Commission, la liberté lui est rendue, il se propose de se marier avec une vraie Républicaine

---

[1] ABR, L3130, Military Commission, Pierre Vérone.
[2] ABR, L3115, 17 *nivôse* II (6 Jan. 1794), Antoine Vigne.
[3] ABR, L3117, 2 *germinal* II (22 Mar. 1794), Jacques-Joseph Liautard.

pour donner d'autant plus de preuves de sa foi et de son observation aux lois qui gouvernent la République.[1]

Antoine-Lazare Isoard *fils*, a 21-year-old student, pledged his devotion to the Revolution by marrying a relative, something he could not have contemplated under the *Ancien régime*.[2] Another suspect wrote of himself that

> on peut le calomnier, mais on ne parviendra jamais à le détacher d'une Révolution à laquelle il doit la partie la plus grande de sa fortune.[3]

Jean-Baptiste Blanc, a *ménager*, affirmed that he would have been an imbecile to declaim against a Revolution which had abolished tithes and feudal dues,[4] while a shopkeeper (probably from the Doubs) who had been born a serf said that he had consequently been a good republican.[5] An exchange broker likewise stressed his interest in the Revolution, for, could he have risen to be a *courtier* under the former régime?[6]

Other suspects however spoke of the benefits of the Revolution in more general terms. Thus Louis-Marie Berger, an organist of Marseilles, explained that

> l'intérêt public et la Révolution lui ont toujours été très agréables, parce qu'elle élevait à sa hauteur le peuple en lui restituant ses droits anciens, que les despotes et les grands lui avaient ravis,[7]

while Honoré Liane, a miller (*meunier*) in a bonnet manufacture, pictured himself as a

> citoyen paisible et soumis aux lois, bénissant toujours l'heureuse révolution qui a réintégré l'homme dans tous ses droits.[8]

---

[1] ABR, L3118, 26 *germinal* II (15 Apr. 1794), Joseph-Gabriel Isoard.
[2] ABR, L3118, 26 *germinal* II (15 Apr. 1794), Antoine-Lazare-Joseph Isoard.
[3] ABR, L3127, Jean-Louis Coppeau.
[4] ABR, L3113, 11 Nov. 1793, Jean-Baptiste Blanc.
[5] ABR, L3112, 7 Sept. 1793, Claude Fey.
[6] ABR, L3109, petition of Augustin Pelard.
[7] ABR, L3118, 24 *germinal* II (13 Apr. 1794), Louis-Marie Berger.
[8] ABR, L3118, 21 *germinal* II (10 Apr. 1794), Honoré Liane.

Finally, François Magny, a landowner of Aubagne, had his own vision of the Revolution. From the start of the Revolution, he wrote,

> je n'ai cessé de la regarder comme un bienfait de l'Être Suprême. . . . que je croyais sincèrement devoir être l'époque du bonheur de la France par le renouvellement des mœurs, la suppression du luxe, l'encouragement de l'agriculteur et l'admission du seul mérite aux emplois.[1]

Perhaps Magny wrote in the past tense because he felt that his noble expectations had been disappointed. But, to judge from some of the other tributes to the Revolution pronounced before the Tribunal, the Revolution had more than satisfied some men's triple quest for profit, prosperity and pleasure.

But of course it was rather dangerous to admit that one had benefited from the Revolution in too blatant a way; for then one incurred the charge of egoism. Thus Jérôme Mathieu, a public scribe, was accused by the president of having shown 'beaucoup plus d'aisance' during the period of the Sections than before.[2] A man who had made a career in the revolutionary bureaucracy – Jacques Marchand, 'commis dans la distribution des vivres' – was designated as

> de la classe de ces jeunes gens qui cherchent des places dans la République sans aimer les principes républicains, qui portent partout l'esprit de fatuité, les maximes erronnées, les préjugés de distinction.[3]

He served in the armies against France and was therefore executed. Other suspects were said to have 'forgotten' or been ungrateful for the benefits which the Revolution bestowed on various professions. In fact, Jean-Baptiste Capefigue complained of all the laws which dealt with his profession – he was a *marchand drapier*: if, said the public prosecutor, he had had the least zeal for the Revolution, the *maximum* would have killed it.[4]

[1] ABR, L3114; 23, 24 *frimaire* II (13, 14 Dec. 1793), François Magny.

[2] ABR, L3115, condemned to death 17 *nivôse* II (6 Jan. 1794), Jérôme Mathieu *dit* Bertrand, *écrivain public*.

[3] ABR, L3115, 18 *nivôse* II (7 Jan. 1794), Jacques Marchand.

[4] ABR, L3118, 27 *germinal* II (16 Apr. 1794), Jean-Baptiste Capefigue: released.

A former wig-maker was one of a class of people who regretted their former profession and showed himself a supporter of those who had given him their custom: the fear of losing that custom made him sacrifice the interests of the Revolution.[1]

Some of these cases are revealing for the light they shed on the judges' conception of the Revolution. A warehouse-porter renounced the benefits of 'la révolution populaire';[2] a *cultivateur* forgot that he owed everything to the Revolution.[3] But perhaps the most surprising of these is the case of Jean Gourel, a former merchant captain of Berre, who forgot

> tout ce que la marine commerçante gagne à la Révolution. . . . il était uni avec tous les propriétaires de sa commune, qui formaient une masse de contre-révolutionnaires.[4]

With the collapse of France's overseas trade, such a verdict is rather astonishing.

Others, of course, had suffered during the Revolution. Most of these did not care to discuss this aspect of their experience under the Revolution. *Robins* who had witnessed the demise of the *Parlement* of Aix; merchants whose trade had shrunk as a result of the Mediterranean blockade; workers in the manufactures of sulphur and soap and the refiners of sugar who had seen their employment vanish because of the dearth of raw materials; domestics, valets, cooks, hairdressers, dancing-masters who had had to make do as best they could while their masters and mistresses were absent in Italy or Switzerland; the poor people who had suffered from the decay of charitable institutions; priests who had been forced to exchange their priesthood for matrimony; peasants who had had their sons killed at the front – all these people, and many others, did not regard the Revolution with the same blithe eyes as did those who had gained new jobs and won new fortunes. But to have expressed their discontent in front of the Tribunal would have been to incriminate themselves; for it was necessary in these

[1] ABR, L3114, 27 *frimaire* II (17 Dec. 1793), Pierre Lamoureux of Berre.
[2] ABR, L3115, 27 *nivôse* II (16 Jan. 1794), Joseph Julien.
[3] ABR, L3115, 27 *nivôse* II (16 Jan. 1794), François Autran.
[4] ABR, L3114, 27 *frimaire* II (17 Dec. 1793), Jean Gourel, condemned to *réclusion*.

circumstances to stress the benefits of the Revolution rather than its drawbacks.

In fact, success in artisanal and shopkeeping trades might lead to denunciation by discontented competitors; at least this was given as the reason for their imprisonment by several men who appeared before the Tribunal. It is petitions regarding taxation which reveal the extent of the distress of large sections of the working population under the Revolution: a pork-butcher who lamented that for more than a year he had been selling off the remnants of the sausages which remained; a *brodeuse* saying that her profession had left her, rather than the other way round; war-widows; *hôteliers* catering for foreigners who became rare; *bourgeois* whose incomes, often inconsiderable in the first place, were rendered almost worthless by high prices; private tutors with no pupils; creditors of the Commune who had received virtually no payment for years; small investors in trade and shipping – numerous, of course, in Marseilles – who had lost much of their capital.[1] All these men and women had precious little to thank the Revolution for, especially during the hard winter of the Year II (there was snow in *pluviôse*), with bread rigorously rationed and fuel scarce and costly.

Some men, however, made a virtue of necessity by stressing the sacrifices which they had made to the Revolution and all its works. Jean-Baptiste Vence, driven out of both Sicily and Britain because of his outspoken defence of French revolutionary principles;[2] Nicolas Clastrier, merchant captain, deprived of employment because of the aristocracy of the great merchants of Marseilles;[3] Jacques Cayras, forced by the aristocrats to leave Santo Domingo abandoning his possessions[4] – these, and other citizens, were able to claim that they had suffered under the Revolution because they had suffered for the Revolution, at the hands of the enemies of the Revolution.

Some men had other instances of patriotism and self-sacrifice to relate; Ange Ferroul who abandoned his dying

[1] These cases are taken from the *Série* G (taxation), of the Archives communales.
[2] ABR, L3112, 11–12 Sept. 1793, Jean-Baptiste Vence. And see above, pp. 176–9.
[3] ABR, L3112, 26 Sept. 1793, Nicolas Clastrier.
[4] ABR, L3118, 25 *germinal* II (14 Apr. 1794), Jacques Cayras.

father to do his duty in the National Guard, those who had been oppressed by Bournissac or by the General Committee and Popular Tribunal when they came to the aid of the patriots, even those who paid their taxes, contributed to collections for the volunteers sent from Marseilles to the frontiers, or who, most difficult of all, led irreproachably moral lives. These men advanced such facts in order to win the indulgence of their judges. 'Il n'a fait que son devoir, mais il l'a fait' was a tag which could be applied to many of those who thought that they had special claims to the clemency of the Tribunal.

In most cases however, such claims failed to impress the judges, some of whom had suffered worse deprivations at the hands of the sectionaries. Those claims which had most effect were, it seems, the most modest – the pleas of men who, when asked the usual question, 'what have you done for the Revolution?', replied

> tout ce que j'ai pu selon mes petits moyens . . . Par mes petits moyens, par ma garde, mes payements aux contributions; avec peu de fortune, une femme malade, je pouvais peu. . . . j'ai peu de moyens et j'ai fait tout ce que j'ai pu selon mon physique et mes lumières. . . . j'ai donné selon mes moyens, je me suis conduit en honnête citoyen.

People such as these, who, in truth, exhibited a nullity in the Revolution which would have been severely punished if shown by a landowner or a merchant, were invariably released by the Tribunal because, if they had little positive to advance in their favour, they had similarly little with which to reproach themselves. It was an unusually honest retired sea-captain who apologised because, though a good patriot, his age had not allowed him to develop 'comme les autres'[1] 'Sicard, dit fa-tout, n'est qu'un simple cultivateur, qui n'a jamais été rien . . . il ne s'est occupé que de son bien et de rien de plus.'[2] These were the minnows who had been drawn into a net which was intended to catch only the big fish. Their arrest and continued incarceration was not without danger to the Tribunal and the Revolu-

---

[1] ABR, L3117, 12 *germinal* II (1 Apr. 1794), Jean-Baptiste Lambert.
[2] ABR, L3113, 29 *brumaire* II (19 Nov. 1793), Jean Sicard.

tion in general. As one shopkeeper warned,

> Observez que je suis patriote et que ceux de ma classe qui
> professent mes sentiments et qui sont détenus font rire les
> ennemis des sans-culottes.[1]

When the Tribunal was subjected to criticism and denunciation
from all sides, such a warning was significant.

[1] ABR, L3119, 1 *floréal* II (20 Apr. 1794), Silvestre Paris, acquitted.

CHAPTER TWELVE

Judicial Misconduct?

The impression which emerges from reading the papers of the Revolutionary Tribunal is of judges determined to enforce with vigour the revolutionary laws relating to suspects, yet seldom blinded by too strong a desire to avenge themselves for the imprisonment which they had suffered under those they later judged. During the exercise of their functions, however, they were exposed to various accusations. Barras, Fréron, Saliceti and Ricord, in an *arrêté* of 17 *nivôse* II (6 Jan. 1794), sending Maillet and Giraud to the Revolutionary Tribunal of Paris, accused their Tribunal of passing

> chaque jour des jugements arbitraires en appliquant pour des délits contre-révolutionnaires d'autres peines que celles portées au Code pénal.[1]

But, as Maillet and Giraud pointed out in their defence,

> il existe des lois de circonstance, et c'est d'après ces décrets qu'on doit juger la contre-révolution et le fédéralisme.[2]

This argument seems impregnable, for laws such as those of 19 June 1793 and 5 July 1793 were clearly forged for the punishment of the federalists, and particularised the more general condemnations pronounced in the *Code pénal*.

The *Représentants* alleged

> que les provocateurs de la guerre civile lèvent insolemment la tête; que les plus acharnés sectionnaires échappent au supplice; que des négociants, sangsues du peuple, continuent

---

[1] A. Nat., AF II 90663. *Arrêté* of Barras, Fréron, Saliceti and Ricord, at Toulon, 17 *nivôse* II (6 Jan. 1794). Enforced 1 *pluviôse* II (20 Jan. 1794).

[2] *Mémoire justificatif des citoyens Augustin Maillet et Joseph Giraud*, n.d. (British Museum, F 1012(10)).

à affamer leurs concitoyens, en se jouant, à l'ombre de ce tribunal, des lois les plus précises.

It is true that the Tribunal was not very active in enforcing laws against hoarding and speculation,[1] though even by 17 *nivôse* II several eminent *négociants* had been condemned to death.

Finally, the *Représentants* accused the Tribunal of letting the friends of Barbaroux escape justice (i.e. the death penalty), and of being the instrument, not of 'la vengeance nationale' but of 'les haines particulières'. However, Maillet and Giraud were able to give the names of four friends of Barbaroux who had been executed – including Girard the commander of the Second Battalion of Marseilles and François Allemand, thought to have acted as secretary to Barbaroux. The two arrested men asked why Barras and Fréron had not arrested those who were plotting in the shadow of the Tribunal, why they had not sent proof of the plotters' offences so they might be judged. They demanded proof of the allegation that the Tribunal 'appeared' ('paraît') to satisfy the passions and hatreds of the judges. Moreover, if the *Représentants* had read its judgement sheets and found them irregular, why had they waited till 17 *nivôse* to do something about it? (And, even then, they took another fortnight to enforce their decree!) The judgement sheets, wrote Maillet and Giraud, were published and placarded, copies were sent to the Minister of Justice, the literal text of the law was quoted on each judgement. The two judges considered that the accusations levied against them by the *Représentants* (responsible for the massacre of hundreds of citizens at Toulon) sprang from their opposition to Barras and Fréron in December.

Elsewhere, Barras and Fréron accused the clubists of Marseilles of wishing to massacre the prisoners, of extorting 100,000 *livres* from them, of planning to kill the *Représentants* if they intervened to protect the prisoners.[2] These allegations were repeated by Ricord who, on 1 *pluviôse* II (20 Jan. 1794), wrote to the Committee of Public Safety that the *Comité de surveillance* freed guilty men and arrested men who were

[1] See above, pp. 301–3.
[2] A. Nat., AF II 90⁶⁶². Proclamation of Barras and Fréron, Marseilles, 3 *pluviôse* II (22 Jan. 1794).

creditors of its members. When he came to Marseilles,

> Je vis un tribunal révolutionnaire dans une apathie crimi-
> nelle, ne faisant justice d'aucun scélérat et accusé d'en avoir
> acquitté pour de l'argent.[1]

Barras and Fréron reported to the Committee that Maillet and
Giraud were accused by public opinion of having 'trafiqué de
leur ministère'. They instanced the case of Henri Larguier,
substitut du procureur de la commune during the Sections, who,
a friend of Barbaroux, had been condemned to six years of
gêne, on 24 *frimaire* II (14 Dec. 1793).[2] The clause of the *Code
pénal* quoted by the judges condemned men who made illegal
arrests to six years' *gêne*.[3] No doubt the Tribunal might have
condemned him to death for his friendship with Barbaroux;
but it seems that such offences of Larguier took place in May
1793, when it was no crime to support the policies of the
deputy of Marseilles. The Tribunal printed a letter from Larguier to Barbaroux rejoicing that 'l'hydre de l'anarchie' had
been defeated at Marseilles;[4] but he had refused to attend the
re-installation of the Popular Tribunal on 9 June,[5] while, on 19
August, Section 8 had protested that, in defending citizens
before the Popular Tribunal, Larguier had declaimed against
that Tribunal.[6] In fact, Larguier, displaced from the Municipality by the Sections, seems to have played no part in the
events of June, July and August and it was no doubt for this
reason that the Tribunal was lenient to him.

Barras and Fréron cited only one other case[7] – that of Ange
Rambaud, who as president of Section 23 in June 1793 had

[1] Aulard, x, p. 350, Ricord to Committee of Public Safety from Nice, 1
pluviôse II (20 Jan. 1794).

[2] For Barras and Fréron's accusations see Aulard, x, pp. 427 ff., letter
from 'Sans Nom', 5 *pluviôse* II (24 Jan. 1794); for the trial of Larguier,
ABR, L3114, Revolutionary Tribunal, 24 *frimaire* II (14 Dec. 1793).

[3] *Code pénal, Deuxième Partie, Premier Titre, Troisième Section, Article XIX.*

[4] ABR, L3024, Revolutionary Tribunal, 24 *frimaire* II (14 Dec. 1793),
written 28 May 1793.

[5] ABR, L2006, Popular Tribunal, letter of Municipality of Marseilles
to the General Committee, 9 June 1793.

[6] ABR, L2006, Section 8, 19 Aug. 1793.

[7] A. Nat., W329, Revolutionary Tribunal of Paris, No. 545, *Affaire
Maillet et Giraud*. Barras and Fréron to the public prosecutor, 6 *pluviôse* II
(25 Jan. 1794).

been sentenced to *réclusion* as a suspect on 6 October 1793.[1] It seems that Rambaud – or at least his Section – had played a large part in the counter-revolution. A list of those condemned by the Tribunal reports, enigmatically, that he was sent to detention 'jusqu'à la Convention se soit expliquée'.[2] He was later interrogated by the Military Commission but this court, a creation of Barras and Fréron, did not see fit to condemn him.[3] Moreover, if the Revolutionary Tribunal had been excessively lenient towards Larguier and Rambaud, both men might have been sent by Barras and Fréron for a new trial.

Unfortunately the account of the trial of the two Marseillais before the Revolutionary Tribunal of Paris is not very communicative, concentrating mainly on the two men's resistance to the *Représentants*. Nevertheless their judicial 'crimes' were the subject of a brief cross-examination and enquiry. Several *Représentants* testified to their good reputation and agents of *le pouvoir exécutif* spoke of

> la sagacité et la justice que ces deux fonctionnaires publics mettaient dans tous leurs jugements.

The jury found that the two men were not liable to be deprived of their posts for imposing sentences at variance with the *Code pénal* and later laws.[4]

Maillet and Giraud were triumphantly received at the Convention, the Jacobin Club, and the Cordeliers and returned to resume their offices.[5] They won the esteem and consideration of Maignet, who, often accused of cruelty but never of corruption, was very demanding in his relations with public officials.[6]

[1] ABR, L3113, Revolutionary Tribunal of the Bouches-du-Rhône, 6 Oct. 1793.

[2] ABR, L3122, Revolutionary Tribunal, *Liste des personnes condamnées à la détention jusqu'à la paix.*

[3] ABR, L3113, Revolutionary Tribunal, Ange Rambaud, 6 Oct. 1793.

[4] A. Nat., W329, loc. cit., judgement 5 *ventôse* II (23 Feb. 1794).

[5] For the Convention see L3012, extract from deliberation of the Convention, 8 *ventôse* II (26 Feb. 1794), congratulating the two Marseillais and restoring them to their functions; for the Jacobin Club see *Moniteur*, XIX 590, No. 162 of 12 *ventôse* II (2 Mar. 1794), and for the Cordeliers, *Moniteur*, XIX 664, No. 171 of 21 *ventôse* II (11 Mar. 1794).

[6] Re-installation of the Tribunal, ABR, L3127, *arrêté* of Maignet, at Marseilles, 23 *ventôse* II (13 Mar. 1794). Also correspondence between Maignet and the Tribunal in ABR, L3012.

But the truth about such allegations of bribery, by their very nature, can rarely be established beyond doubt – perhaps the confidence which Maignet showed in the Tribunal is the most weighty argument against them.

Other criticisms of the conduct of the repression in the Year II largely concerned the activities of other clubists – though Antoine Riquier, who was for a time assistant to Giraud, was accused of bringing his creditors before the Revolutionary Tribunal. Men were accused of threatening people with punishment by the Tribunal if they did not pay them money. Isoard, Carles, Giraud, and the Maillet brothers were said to have lived miserably before the Revolution, but to have acquired great wealth[1] by demanding protection-money from the aristocrats, and so made progresses through the countryside in gilded carriages in company with their 'maîtresses dorées'.[2] But during his trial in the Year III, Isoard denied close collaboration with Maillet and Giraud and no evidence was produced which incriminated Maillet and his colleagues in the exactions which Isoard was accused of having effected.[3]

Finally, one person – Jean Escavi – when interrogated by the Military Commission and having been asked to obtain certificates from patriots defending his actions during the Revolution, had regretted not being able to do this; for, he said, it was common knowledge in Marseilles that anyone who signed such certificates would be sought out and molested. This did not, in fact, concern the Revolutionary Tribunal. But, for men being judged by both tribunals, large numbers of Marseillais and Provençaux signed *attestations*. Some of these came from the prisoner's employer, from his neighbours – the 'vrais sans-culottes du quartier' – from members of the committees of surveillance, from municipal authorities and so on. In fact, the signing of *attestations* may have been as widespread as the signing of denunciations. Both the Revolutionary Tribunal and the Military Commission sent back men to prison to allow

---

[1] Maillet earned 6000 *livres* a year as president of the Tribunal, Giraud 4500 as public prosecutor, and each judge 3000. ABR, L47, Dept. Admin., 24 *frimaire* II (14 Dec. 1793) (*Comité de comptabilité: dépenses du Tribunal criminel*). There is no evidence that Maillet enjoyed affluence.

[2] A. Nat., W86, accusations against the clubists of Marseilles.

[3] ABR, L3037, Criminal Tribunal of the Bouches-du-Rhône, depositions against Isoard, Year III.

them time to provide favourable *certificats* – the case of Escavi shows this.

Nearly one hundred of the accused were, after cross-examination, sent back to the prisons so that the Tribunal could get more information about them, and those who appeared again were not invariably condemned. Generally, the Tribunal was extremely conscientious in obtaining factual information – not just denunciations – on which to arrive at judgement. It would be absurd to suggest that Maillet and his colleagues never made a mistake, never, in other words, condemned an innocent man to death, yet it would be unjust to them to underestimate the scrupulous seriousness with which they undertook their task. Revolutionary laws gave ample scope to violent and vindictive men and revolutionary storms were of a violence which might easily overwhelm the most impartial mind. Revolutionary tribunals, judging without jury and denying the accused any right of appeal, confronting the prisoner with charges which might, until his appearance, have been unknown to him, and providing him with no legal aid, no *défenseur officieux*, were, by their very nature, tribunals of quick, not to say summary, justice. In these circumstances, Maillet, Giraud and their colleagues seem to have acquitted their task with dignity and, on occasions, a measure of understanding of the plight of those who were caught up in the troubles which had afflicted the Bouches-du-Rhône.

CHAPTER THIRTEEN

Epilogue

After the end of the Revolutionary Tribunal – on 5 *floréal* II, (24 Apr. 1794) – some Marseillais awaited trial by the *Commission populaire* established by Maignet at Orange.[1] But *thermidor* brought their release. Though *thermidor* was welcomed by Maignet – and the Club of Marseilles[2] – the *Représentant* had worked in too close collaboration with Robespierre not to be involved in accusations of bloodthirsty terrorism – his record in the Vaucluse, where he had burned down a whole village when its inhabitants refused to disclose who destroyed a tree of liberty and had sent numerous suspects to the *Commission populaire* and the Revolutionary Tribunal of the Vaucluse, had been attacked to the exclusion of his activities in the Bouches-du-Rhône.[3]

Recalled as early as 24 *thermidor* (11 Aug. 1794), Maignet was replaced by Auguis and Serres, two of the most moderate and colourless of the deputies of the Convention, who saw as their main duty at Marseilles the ending of the Terror and the dismantling of its machinery.[4] To this effect, they released most of

---

[1] See Lautard, 1, pp. 381 ff. In ABR, L3122, is a list of 83 prisoners from Marseilles sent to Orange, *Liste des individus traduits à Orange*. For the co-operation between Maignet and the Popular Commission of Orange and the Revolutionary Tribunal of Marseilles see the documents in ABR, L3127 and L3103, Maignet to Criminal (ex-Revolutionary) Tribunal, 25 *messidor* II (13 July 1794).

[2] ABR, L2076, Club's address of 1 *fructidor* II (18 Aug. 1794); *Procès-verbal* of Club, 17 *thermidor* II (4 Aug. 1794), including address by Maignet. But Maignet arrested many suspects in the period from the end of the Tribunal to his recall at the end of *thermidor*: he ordered the arrest of all former nobles and priests at Aix, ABR, L584.

[3] See A. Nat., D III 354 and 355; AF II 82[604] and AF II 42[336] for these accusations against Maignet.

[4] Pierre-Jean-Baptiste Auguis, deputy of the Deux-Sèvres; voted for imprisonment of king; sent to the Bouches-du-Rhône by decrees of 4 and 9 *fructidor* II, recalled 29 *brumaire* III; became member of the 500; Jean-

the prisoners who had either escaped trial by the Revolutionary Tribunal, or who had been condemned to terms of imprisonment.[1] This activity brought them into conflict with the local patriots who, as always, were determined to impose their views on the *Représentants en mission* and who, terrorists by profession, habit and conviction, came to regret Robespierre and openly defend Maignet, calling once more on Moïse Bayle and Granet to defend their principles, protesting to the Convention against measures of clemency which weakened the coercive power of the revolutionary government – a government embodied, to them, most satisfactorily in the Law of Suspects of 17 September 1793 and in the revolutionary tribunals.[2]

Demands for a restoration of the Terror, for an end to the release of suspects, reached the Convention and the Jacobin Club and caused great fermentation. At Marseilles, things came to a head when Auguis and Serres arrested the clubist Reynier who, as early as 26 August 1794, had written a letter demanding – in retaliation for the continued release of the federalists – a new September Massacre.[3] However, Reynier, when being taken to Paris for trial by the Revolutionary Tribunal, was seized by a band of patriots not far from Marseilles.[4] Auguis and Serres suspected that the leading clubists – Maillet *cadet*, Maillet *aîné*, Giraud, Chompré, Isoard, Carles and associates – had organised this 'enlèvement'. They therefore decided to arrest them. The Committee of Surveillance was quashed and the Municipality replaced. After being regaled on 5 *sans-culottide* (21 Sept. 1794) at a feast at the Temple de la Raison, to cries of 'Marat n'est pas mort' and 'Merde aux appelants' from Maillet *cadet*, Auguis and Serres arrested some of the leading clubists on the night of 4–5 *vendémiaire* III

Jacques-Joseph Serres, deputy of Île-de-France, wrote in favour of imprisonment of king; entered Convention, Oct. 1793; after mission in Midi, led attacks on clubs, etc.

[1] ABR, L1041, L1059, documents of the Committee of Surveillance of Marseilles, orders of the *Représentants* for the release of prisoners, etc.

[2] Most of the documents concerning the Club, at this time, are at A. Nat., W86 and W87 (papers of the Revolutionary Tribunal of Paris).

[3] A. Nat., AF II 58⁴²⁶, Reynier to *Agent national* of Chabeuil, 9 *fructidor* II (26 Aug. 1794).

[4] ABR, L3041, Criminal Tribunal, *procès-verbal* of 'enlèvement'.

(25–26 Sept. 1794). This sparked off more disturbances next day, culminating in a riot, grossly exaggerated by the *Représentants*, where the rioters demanded the release of the clubists.[1]

Some of those who had been marked down for arrest on 4–5 *vendémiaire* had for a time escaped, but soon Maillet, Giraud and Chompré were arrested and were sent with twenty-five of their colleagues to the Revolutionary Tribunal of Paris.[2]

With the purges of this period, all the authorities of Marseilles were staffed by the men of Auguis and Serres, the leading clubists had been arrested and five of the *émeutiers* of 5 *vendémiaire* condemned to death.[3] The Club was purged of Jacobins. The Convention approved the measures of its deputies,[4] which were championed at Paris by Fréron, who did not forgive the Montagnards of the deputation of the Bouches-du-Rhône – especially Moïse Bayle and Granet – for defending in December 1793 the patriots of Marseilles and for persuading the Convention to recall him. Fréron's journal, *L'Orateur du peuple*, referred to

> une faction méridionale, attachée sans relâche, depuis cinq années, à faire de Marseille un état à part, indépendant de la République française.

This had been the policy of Barbaroux, Rebecquy and De Perret; now it was the policy of Moïse Bayle and Granet. Fréron denounced Granet for opposing the releases of suspects which had followed 9 *thermidor* – once more, he said, Bayle and Granet had conspired to make Marseilles rebel against the Convention.[5] Moïse Bayle and Granet took their complaints

[1] See Aulard, xvii 94 ff., Auguis and Serres to Committee of Public Safety from Marseilles, 5 *vendémiaire* III (26 Sept. 1794), and, for the riot, ABR, L3041, the *procès-verbal* drawn up by Auguis and Serres on 5 *vendémiaire* III, and Aulard, xvii, 108 ff., Auguis and Serres to Committee of Public Safety, 6 *vendémiaire* III (27 Sept. 1794).

[2] A. Nat., W86 and W87, etc. ABR, L1248, *arrêté* of Auguis and Serres, 21 *vendémiaire* III (12 Oct. 1794).

[3] ABR, L3131, papers of the Military Commission set up by Auguis and Serres.

[4] Aulard, xvii, p. 201, note 1, decree of Convention, 12 *vendémiaire* III (3 Oct. 1794).

[5] A. Nat., AF II 90⁶⁶⁴, *L'Orateur du peuple, par Fréron*, No. vi, 1 *vendémiaire* III (22 Sept. 1794).

against Fréron before the Convention[1] – reiterating the defence of Marseilles which they had pleaded successfully in the winter of 1793–4. In reply, Fréron wrote that if Marseilles was in open revolt, this was the work of Bayle and Granet who defended the so-called patriots, the troublemakers who had been sent by Auguis and Serres – as by Barras and Fréron – to the Revolutionary Tribunal of Paris, who had wished to get rid of the suspects by a new September Massacre, or by drowning them in the Durance, or sending them to the Lazaret of Marseilles to die of the plague.[2]

Throughout the Year III, the principles of Auguis and Serres seem to have prevailed at Marseilles. The leading clubists were imprisoned in Paris, at Amiens and the château of Ham, thus escaping the massacres and murders which marked the hatred of those who had suffered under the Terror for their oppressors, though some of their colleagues, and the wife of Maillet *cadet*, were struck down by the *compagnies du Soleil* and *de Jésus* which roamed the department, openly tolerated by the *Représentants*.[3] Finally, events in Paris saved the 'patriots of '89'. Released to defend the Convention against the Sections of Paris during the insurrection of 12–13 *vendémiaire* IV (4–5 Oct. 1795), they were in the army commanded by Barras which was hastily formed to drive back the sectionary rebels. After this service, they received the thanks of the Convention and were given enough money to get them back to their native city.[4]

It is doubtful whether all the 28 terrorists of Marseilles

[1] A. Nat., AF II 90⁶⁶⁴, *Moïse Bayle à ses collègues du comité de salut public.* N.d. And *Moïse Bayle et Granet au Peuple Français.* Undated, but with the stamp of the Committee of Public Safety dated *vendémiaire* III.

[2] On 5 Apr. 1795, the Convention decreed the arrest of Granet, Bayle and Maignet: they benefited however from the amnesty ordered by the Convention in its last hours of existence. Granet returned to Marseilles and caused a certain amount of trouble to the successors of Auguis and Serres; Maignet pursued his career of *avocat* at his native town of Ambert in the Puy-de-Dôme, though he was forced to flee for a time in 1815. Moïse Bayle, after having a post in the bureau of *émigrés* of the *Ministère de police générale*, was exiled to his native Switzerland till 1803, at which date he returned to France.

[3] For the bulk of these events, see Lourde, vol. 3, pp. 380 ff.

[4] A. Nat., AF II 52³⁸⁷⁻³⁹¹, for decrees freeing 'patriots', 12–13 *vendémiaire* IV (4–5 Oct. 1795); also a petition of the Marseillais for enough money to

returned home, there to flock round Fréron in an attempt to persuade him to restore the revolutionary government of 1793, or whether some of them remained in Paris and took part in the conspiracies of the patriots of 1793 against the Directory. At Marseilles virtually all those who had been held as suspects under the Terror had been released by the end of 1794[1] – only terrorists remained in the prisons – and so the Midi, racked by the activities of royalist murder-gangs, offered no refuge for the patriots of Marseilles.

Only a few documents in the dossiers of the Babouvists implicate specifically the terrorists of Marseilles. Maillet *cadet* was said to be an agent for a fantastic plot, in *prairial* IV (25 May 1796), designed to massacre all landowners with property exceeding six or ten thousand *livres*, all *émigrés*, all educated men (and to burn all papers) and to distribute land to every citizen of France (after the destruction of all towns and trade).[2] Subsequently, terrorists appeared from time to time in police reports – Maillet *cadet* in June 1796 threatening people with a resurrection of 'his' Revolutionary Tribunal,[3] François Brogy, Étienne Bompard and Antoine Riquier, ex-judges of the Tribunal, protesting at the quashing of elections in the Year IV, the ex-*abbé* Bausset, Maillet *cadet* and the ex-*Conventionnel* Granet conspiring against the Directory and building up an armed force to separate Marseilles from the rest of the Republic and, in the Year VI, forming a *cercle constitutionnel* to preserve the traditions and the traditional leaders of the Club of Marseilles.[4]

After this epoch however, it is extremely difficult – indeed impossible – to trace the careers of the ex-terrorists in Marseilles in the confusing waves of struggles which overwhelmed the Bouches-du-Rhône. It seems that Maillet *cadet* and Giraud

---

return to Marseilles and an *arrêté* of the *Directoire exécutif*, of 29 *brumaire* IV (20 Nov. 1795), granting to Maillet *aîné*, Maillet *cadet*, Giraud, etc., 500 *livres* each.

[1] ABR, L1059, reports from prisons of Marseilles by the Committee of Surveillance.

[2] A. Nat., F⁷3054; F⁷4277, *Extrait des lettres écrites d'Aix*, 6 *prairial* IV (25 May 1796); also, A. Nat., F⁷4278.

[3] A. Nat., F⁷4268, letter from Marseilles, 25 *prairial* IV (13 June 1796), to Minister of *Police générale*.

[4] A. Nat., F⁷4268. See also F⁷3659⁴; FI°III B.-du-Rh. 1 and FI°III B.-du-Rh. 8.

escaped from the eternal round of oppression and counter-oppression, stronger in the Midi than elsewhere, by leaving the area and finding positions elsewhere. According to Poupé, Maillet *cadet* was employed in the offices of the Ministry of the Marine and Giraud was a *conseiller* at the appeal court at Caen under the Restoration,[1] while Chompré retired to Versailles and died at Paris in 1811.[2]

[1] Poupé, p. 126, note; and Lautard, 1, 406.

[2] J. Viguier, 'Marseille et ses représentants à la Constituante', p. 201, note 2. (*La Révolution française, tome* 40, 1901, pp. 193–209.)

CHAPTER FOURTEEN

Conclusion

We must try to place the Revolutionary Tribunal at Marseilles in the wide spectrum of the Terror. According to an obvious criterion – that of numbers – the Tribunal at Marseilles was eclipsed, in the total of death sentences passed, by nine revolutionary courts in the French provinces, according to statistics compiled by Donald Greer.[1] Besides five tribunals dealing mainly with the rebels of the Vendée, courts at Lyons (1665 death sentences), Arras (392), Orange (332) and Bordeaux (299) exceeded the total passed by the Revolutionary Tribunal at Marseilles (289). Including the department of the Seine (i.e. Paris), the Bouches-du-Rhône was 9th out of eighty-seven departments for the number of death sentences. The Revolutionary Tribunal of Paris judged 5283 persons, of whom 2747 were condemned to death and 1273 freed, 973 cases being dismissed for lack of information.[2] At Bordeaux, the Military Commission condemned 302 to death to 376 acquitted (out of 898 judged in all).[3] Thus the 289 death sentences to 476 acquittals by the Revolutionary Tribunal at Marseilles seem moderate.

Though the pace of the repression quickened towards the end of the Tribunal's existence – but more were freed than executed – Marseilles did not experience the phenomenon of the 'Great Terror', which saw 1376 executions at Paris from 10 June to 27 July 1794. In establishing comparisons, we must include the *fusillades*, *mitraillades* and *noyades* which disposed of at least 350 of the enemies of the Revolution (and others) at Lyons, over 800 at Toulon and up to 2000 at Nantes.

At Marseilles, the Terror was thoroughly regular, judicial, institutionalised: no one was condemned to death without an interrogation in which he could defend himself, provide

---

[1] D. Greer, *The Incidence of the Terror during the French Revolution* (Cambridge, Mass., 1935) Tables, pp. 135 ff.

[2] J. L. Godfrey, *Revolutionary Justice* (Chapel Hill, 1951) pp. 136 ff.

[3] P. Bécamps, in *Bordeaux au XVIIIe siècle*, pp. 432 ff. (an understandable discrepancy from the figure for deaths given by Greer).

attestations etc. In fact the first few sessions of the Revolutionary Tribunal, immediately after the collapse of the revolt and following the release of the judges from prison, were not rushed through with a haste which might indicate a thirst for vengeance. On the contrary, debates were often prolonged and documentary evidence was invariably produced. The records of the Sections were scrutinised.

The Tribunal was scrupulous in following judicial forms. The mere existence of verbatim minutes shows great devotion to bureaucratic practices. The demeanour of the judges indicates that they were very conscious of being magistrates, servants of the law, agents of the Convention – which they viewed with an almost religious awe.

If we accept a distinction between Jacobin and *sans-culotte* as being indicative of the range of political activity open to revolutionary militants in the Year II, it is quite clear that the Revolutionary Tribunal at Marseilles was firmly based at the Jacobin end of the spectrum. Cobb remarks that revolutionaries in the provinces were often more 'anarchical' than those of Paris:[1] this does not apply to the judges of the Tribunal of Marseilles. Maillet *cadet* seems to have been a Jacobin of impeccable orthodoxy, imbued with a Robespierrist view of the Revolution. His repudiation of direct democracy is couched in Robespierrist terms:

le peuple en masse est souverain, qu'aucune portion du peuple ne peut exercer cette souveraineté séparément, qu'il a délégué ses pouvoirs à ses représentants pour lui donner des lois.

He, and other clubists, maintained at the time of the appeal to the people (January 1793) that 'le gouvernement représentatif [est] le seul qui convienne à une République aussi étendue que la France' and repudiated 'la démocratie pure' as anarchical.[2] In the context of Marseilles' political life, where the Sections had been, for a time, every bit as 'popular' as the militant-run Sections of Paris, the concept of 'direct democracy', always fairly vague among the aspirations of the *sans-culottes*, was

[1] R. C. Cobb, *The Police and the People* (Oxford, 1970) p. 128.

[2] For the first affirmation, ABR, L3112, trial of J. B. F. Nicolas, 28 Sept. 1793; for the second, ABR, L2041, an address of the Club of Marseilles, signed by Maillet, to the Club of Aix, 18 Jan. 1793.

tarnished, fatally, by the royalist outcome of the sectionary revolt. And, despite the accusation of 'federalism' levied at Maillet and Giraud by Barras and Fréron in December 1793, despite the influence which events at Marseilles must have had in precipitating the centralising law of 14 *frimaire* II (4 Dec. 1793), there was little in the views of Maillet *cadet*, or in the activities of the Tribunal over which he presided, which might be termed 'ultra-revolutionary', though their pretensions to freedom of action in the local sphere were perhaps dangerous to the necessary unity of direction of the revolutionary government (but even more dangerous were the activities of Barras and Fréron).

The Tribunal was a regular court given revolutionary powers by the agents of government in the provinces. It was not created as a sop to popular pressure, as the result of an insurrection in which the *sans-culottes* demanded ruthless measures of terror not only against enemies designated by duly-passed decrees, but also against categories of suspects defined by the people themselves. Certainly many of the laws against suspects were passed as a result of popular pressure on the Convention – most directly, that of 17 September, but the decrees of *ventôse* to a large extent too – and so the actions of the Paris crowd had an important impact on the conduct of the Terror at Marseilles. But at Marseilles the Tribunal did not function amid scenes of crowd activity as did its counterpart at Paris, whose procedure was speeded up as a result of pressure from the streets, clubs, and Sections.[1] What indication of popular attitudes we can find, suggests a degree of repugnance at the extent of the repression, rather than popular zeal for the branding of ever-wider categories of people as suspects. Demands for a general amnesty may have been put about by 'aristocrats' but they obviously achieved an audience wide enough to worry the authorities, who moreover had to take measures to prevent the populace being repelled by the spectacle of frequent guillotinings.[2] So many men, as the judges admitted, had been misled by the sectionaries in a revolt in which issues

---

[1] J. L. Godfrey, *Revolutionary Justice*, pp. 18–19.

[2] A. Comm., 2143: on 18 *frimaire* II (8 Dec. 1793) an official ordered that the bodies of those executed after judgement by the Revolutionary Tribunal should be immediately taken away and buried, 'craignant que le spectacle n'occasionne quelque mouvement populaire'.

had been very blurred and distinctions of opinion finely balanced, that many citizens of Marseilles must have been frightened of being incriminated in the counter-revolution.

Much of the Tribunal's work was designed to distinguish between the leaders and the led. The judges were concerned with defining as precisely as possible those who had played a persistent rôle in the counter-revolution. They were not, on the whole, reckless in their interpretation of the term 'suspect' – their pursuit of nobles and priests was far from being unrestrained, even though those priests and nobles who were judged were severely dealt with. It was consistently admitted that nobles might serve the Revolution and in no sense was the Tribunal an instrument of dechristianisation. The judges did not push the revolutionary legislation to its limits in passing sentences, for the laws gave them virtually unlimited powers. In common with many other revolutionary tribunals, that of Marseilles did not enforce the largely crowd-imposed 'economic' legislation of the revolutionary government (laws on hoarding etc.)[1] – but, in contrast with Paris, there seems also to have been little outside pressure on the Tribunal to do so. As regards the merchants, the judges were extremely circumspect. Again, at Marseilles there is little evidence of the indiscriminate denunciation of 'négociantisme' which existed elsewhere: in fact the most vehement attacks on the merchants date from the early years of the Revolution. The Tribunal did not work in the midst of radical *sans-culotte* or *enragé* demands for the limitation of wealth, of the ownership of industrial and commercial property; nor were the Marseillais fertile in producing plans for wide-ranging social reform. There seems to be no Marseillais counterpart to the *Instruction* of the *Commission temporaire* of Lyons.

Compared with the aspirations voiced in that, and similar documents – the complete liberation of twenty-four million Frenchmen from all forms of domination, whether political, social or economic – the activities of Maillet and his colleagues seem rather restricted. Certainly these activities left large

---

[1] A. Soboul, *La 1re République*, p. 82, 'Il ne semble pas en effet qu'il y ait eu de condamnation capitale pour des motifs d'ordre purement économique.' R. C. Cobb, *The Police and the People*, pp. 290 ff., points out that no farmers were executed for contravening the economic legislation. D. Greer supports these conclusions (*The Incidence of the Terror*, p. 85).

areas of life untouched, because they largely concentrated on the political manifestations of resistance (on definite acts which left documentary evidence) rather than on the 'principles engraved in the heart', so frequently cited in the advanced rhetoric of the Year II. The Tribunal was a political body, which imposed political judgements on the people who stood before it. To the judges, the leaders of the revolt were primarily their fellow lawyers and professional men, their nearest rivals on the political stage. Certain social categories – the priests, nobles, men of wealth and education – were regarded with suspicion, but were generally punished only for overtly political acts to which, it was admitted, they were specially prone. But the criterion of guilt was usually the political test of participation in, or defence of, an institution of rebellion – the Sections, the administrative bodies under their control, the Departmental Army, etc. Thus many priests and merchants were punished as members of these bodies.

Certainly it is clear that the work of the Tribunal had a distinct social bias. There can be no doubt that poorer citizens sometimes got off more lightly, even if they had been as politically implicated as the rich and the educated. But clemency often came because many of the poor and ignorant people who came before the Tribunal could not – because of their social circumstances – have posed any serious political threat to the revolutionary régime. Greer makes the point that in the Terror, 'the open enemies of the Revolution were cut down regardless of their social caste', adding however that 'the social distribution of the victims varied from region to region, even from *département* to *département*, according to the social texture of the counter-revolution'.[1] It would appear that the Revolutionary Tribunal of Marseilles was socially discriminating, but on the primarily political criterion of participation in political move-

---

[1] op. cit. p. 105. By studying only death sentences, not considering acquittals, Greer may underestimate the degree to which the Terror was discriminating – socially, or otherwise. Also, while the social distribution of victims varied according to the social composition of rebellion, there was no absolute correlation: revolutionary judges did exercise a measure of discrimination. These observations are only minor compared with R. Louie's cogent criticisms of Greer's methods and conclusions in 'The Incidence of the Terror: A Critique of a Statistical Interpretation', *French Historical Studies*, Vol. III, No. 3, 1964, pp. 379–89.

ments. Because this participation was itself largely socially-determined, the Terror (at Marseilles or anywhere else) could hardly avoid having a socially-discriminating impact.

While the *greffier* of the Revolutionary Tribunal at Marseilles drew up numerous lists of those judged, there does not exist one in which these men and women are grouped according to social or professional categories. Yet the judges could hardly have been unaware of the social bias of their judgements. If, for a moment, one divides those judged into social categories similar to those devised by Greer, we find that the Tribunal's death sentences may be divided as falling upon 'upper middle', 'lower middle' and 'working class' victims in the respective proportions of 41·2, 42·6 and 16·2 per cent, while acquittals may be correspondingly calculated at 16·4, 39·0 and 44·6 per cent, revealing a strong tendency to free persons belonging to the lowest of Greer's categories.[1] It is not only the fact that such men occupied, on the whole, less prominent positions in the counter-revolution which accounts for this bias, though this is probably the most important factor. The judges revealed a tendency to idealise the poor people of the countryside, to regard them as unwilling victims of the rural bourgeoisie and their allies the priests, while they consistently maintained that the 'bon peuple' of Marseilles was virtually blameless in the revolt. They also tended to slip easily into an interpretation of the Revolution which saw it as a struggle between rich and poor. Does this mean that the judges really identified themselves with the poor?

In their attitude towards the peasants can be seen the very limited, vicarious nature of that identification. Rejection of the tutelage of nobles and priests, propaganda directed against the rural bourgeoisie cannot disguise the fact that the judges were townsmen with no real knowledge of the grievances of various sections of the peasantry. The clubists' attempts to stir up the peasants against the bourgeois of Salon were largely opportunist and political – to force the bourgeois to part with their money

[1] This is only a very rough-and-ready test to the impression which emerges from our treatment of the case histories. We have divided the suspects into only three categories, but, in general, have made use of Greer's divisions, though only to retain some degree of comparability with his study.

for the needs of national defence. The judges hardly seemed to be aiming at eliminating a deeply entrenched social group, as happened consciously in later revolutions, and with the elimination of the *Parlementaires* of Toulouse. For a peasant, an appearance before the Tribunal was an examination to find out if he was politically dangerous. If he was deemed to be harmless, he was sent back to his village to live a life of hard work (often as an employee of the bourgeois) and to obey the new authorities. Some of the comments written in the judgement sheets – no doubt designed to educate the poorer citizens in 'civisme' – amount to panegyrics of the poor toiling peasantry. They are fatalistic in the extreme: there is complete acceptance of the fact that the peasants were too busy earning their livelihood to take part in politics, and there is no indication that this state of affairs should or could be changed by a radical social revolution. Correspondingly, when rich merchants are released, they too return (privileged) to the unequal social relationships, which remain basically unchanged.

Thus the radicalism of the Tribunal's work, at least in its social impact, was limited. Detached from the lower classes – as judges are by definition – the Jacobins of the Revolutionary Tribunal shared an orthodox political conception of the Revolution. The Tribunal laid down political judgements which functioned within a specific social and economic context and which both influenced and were influenced by that context. It admitted the existence of a social sphere, and though legislators prescribed the limits of that sphere, within it, men were to be left alone to live their own lives. No doubt, under the Terror, the field of private life was restricted to a great extent, but it still remained: even Robespierre asserted in his speech of 25 December 1793 (5 *nivôse*, II) that the revolutionary government must 's'abstenir des mesures qui gênent inutilement la liberté et qui froissent les intérêts privés sans aucun avantage public'. Throughout the Revolution, legislators had been preoccupied with defining – or re-defining – the boundary between public and private life, the political and the social spheres; and the pages of the Revolutionary Tribunal are full of confrontations at the frontier of these spheres – men too busy to go to the Club, too engrossed in making money or pursuing a full family life to take part in politics.

This was accepted to a surprising extent by the Tribunal and those suspects who claimed that in their private and professional lives they had turned the Revolution to advantage were not miscalculating the temper of their judges, who continually pointed out the advantages which such and such a professional group had gained from the Revolution. Such appeals to material self-interest can be exaggerated but provide a useful corrective to the exclusive emphasis on the puritanism of the Terror, and the so-called 'Reign of Virtue'.

The judges of the Revolutionary Tribunal certainly regarded themselves as having a social mission – to redress the oppressive hold of the rich over the poor – and saw themselves and their Tribunal as agents for this transformation. Thus they declaimed against the bourgeois and against the aristocracy of wealth, derided those who had not progressed beyond the language of the 1791 Constitution, attacked those who used their monopoly of education to dupe the poor inhabitants of the countryside. Yet they operated in a situation where their activity could not – limited as it was to the political sphere, seeing social problems through political eyes – materially alter the social disharmonies and inequalities. In thinking otherwise, the judges were sharing the fallacy of the Jacobins, who, confronted with social problems of great acuity, overestimated the extent to which the political means at their disposal could solve these problems. Operating in a situation of the utmost fragmentation of national life – a fragmentation in many ways typified by the federalist revolts – they relied on political means to provide conditions for the unification of the country behind the revolutionary government; yet every attempt to strengthen that government aroused new opposition which, in turn, made imperative the further strengthening of the apparatus of political control and repression. This apparatus, in a disintegrating society at war with Europe, became more and more isolated, bureaucratised, frozen, divorced from the social forces which had given it life. As the ruling class's monopoly of politics became more and more intense, so its belief that social problems were amenable to political solutions became more extreme. The very recognition of the existence of grave social problems was a political matter: only when it was seen to be necessary to keep the poor alive if they were to fight for

the ruling group's continued hold on power, were 'lois populaires' passed, and then only with the greatest reluctance.
Throughout the Revolution, the 'people' were treated as
instruments in the battles of politicians and their intervention
in politics to solve their own social and economic grievances in
their own ways was discouraged, as they were trained into
designating as *their* enemies the political enemies of the revolutionary government. The only activity from the lower classes
which the revolutionary government tolerated was that which
contributed to the political aims of the Montagnards – the
elimination of the Girondins, the defeat of foreign enemies.

Consistently the Jacobins ignored the social demands of the
people, who had no right to be concerned with wretched
foodstuffs, but were to riot, not so that they might have bread
but to defeat the enemies of the Jacobins. Any emergence of the
people from social into political life was to be in a manner
approved by the government. Distress affecting the lower
classes was blamed by the Jacobins on the machinations of
their political enemies and so the need for radical social
reform was obviated. Not one of the groups which held power
had an interest in exposing the real causes of popular distress.
If the people took independent initiatives – strikes, for example –
they were threatened at Paris with the Revolutionary Tribunal
as agents of Pitt and at Marseilles treated as deserters – political
designations imposed from above. Even 'lois populaires' were
often designed as weapons against the government's political
enemies (such as the *ventôse* decrees against politically-defined
suspects) and, even if enforced, would only have been palliatives
for large sections of the population (again often defined politically as 'patriots'). At all times, the Jacobins considered that
the populace, though it 'wished the good', was incapable of
discerning it, far less attaining it, without their tutelage.

The Jacobins needed popular support to carry out their
revolutionary task, yet had to operate in a divided society using
means which divided it still further. In a situation of such
complexity and fluidity, where the aspirations of various
sections of a divided society were mutually contradictory, it
is futile to attempt to designate a social group as forming the
basis of Jacobin power, to make the ideology of Robespierre
express the aspirations of such and such a sector of the petty

bourgeoisie. In a situation of such disorientation, only those measures which worked with the profound social changes which had brought about the Revolution itself stood much chance of success. Political power was powerless to work against the conditions of its own existence, and in trying to do so became hopelessly – if heroically – utopian. The judges of the Revolutionary Tribunal of Marseilles were less visionary than some; but when they saw themselves as leading a battle against the 'aristocracy of wealth' they overestimated their powers and exaggerated the impact of their activities, and perhaps misunderstood their real significance. Their essential rôle was to force the 'rich egoists' to a more realistic assessment of their interests than they had shown in their involvement in the federalist revolt – interests which would hardly be served by the English at Toulon or the Prussians at Paris. The Terror at Marseilles was principally a means of national defence – the immense military effort of a city which was decidedly anti-militaristic – and the work of the Revolutionary Tribunal was part of this effort – to force the rich inhabitants of town and country to take this task seriously, to accept the sacrifices necessary for the successful prosecution of the war, and thus preserve the achievements of the Revolution. And these achievements were not enshrined in the Constitution of 1793 – immeasurably important though that was in every sphere but the practical – but in the Constitution of 1791, so scorned, verbally at least, by Maillet and his colleagues. Their activities ultimately can be seen as protecting the revolutionary achievements of 1789–92, not the laws of *ventôse* nor the *maximum*, but the abolition of the nobility, the reduction of the power of the Church, the creation of a unified nation, the final political consecration of talents and wealth as criteria for public office and status, the suppression of all forms of corporations, the abolition of feudalism and the defence of a society freed from ancestral restraints on all forms of competitive activity, especially in the economic sphere. The fact that the turbulent emergence of such a society was attended with unprecedented regulations and restraints should not blind us to the fact that, by its work, the Revolutionary Tribunal of Marseilles – in the context of the French Revolutionary Terror – played a significant rôle in the formation of modern bourgeois society.

Appendix

THE REVOLUTIONARY TRIBUNAL OF THE BOUCHES-DU-RHÔNE

List of Judgements

Occupation	Death	Freed	Réclusion	Prison	Renvoi	Total judged
MEN:						
agriculteur		1				1
agriculteur propriétaire	4					4
apothicaire	1					1
archiviste de l' Hôtel-Dieu		1				1
arithméticien	1					1
attaché au théâtre		1				1
aubergiste		3		1	1	5
avoué	2				1	3
balancier		1				1
banquier					1	1
barillat		1				1
berger		1				1
bonnetier		1				1
boucher		3				3
boulanger	3	7			2	12
bourgeois	4	1	2		2	9
bourrelier	2					2
boutiquier		1				1
boutonnier		1				1
cabaretier	1			1		2
caissier					2	2
calandreur		1				1
calfat		2		1		3
capitaine marin capitaine de navire capitaine navigant	7	7	4		1	19
chapelier	2	2				4
charcutier	3					3
chargeur					1	1
charpentier	1	1				2

Occupation	Death	Freed	Réclusion	Prison	Renvoi	Total judged
charretier		4				4
chaudronnier		1				1
chauffonnier					1	1
chimiste					1	1
chirurgien	4	3			2	9
chirurgien-dentiste	1					1
élève en chirurgie					1	1
citoyen	1	2				3
coiffeur de femme	1					1
colporteur	1					1
commerçant	1	1				2
commis	11	20	3	3	5	42
commissionnaire		5			1	6
concierge des prisons	2					2
conseiller au parlement	1					1
constructeur	1					1
consul		1				1
corbeau		1				1
cordier	1	1				2
cordonnier	5	12		1	5	23
courtier	3	5	1		1	10
coutelier		1				1
cuisinier		2	1			3
cultivateur	18	50	6	6	11	91
débiteur de tabac					1	1
défenseur officieux		1				1
directeur de verrerie	1					1
dirigeant les opérations de la monnaie		1				1
distributeur des billets au grand théâtre		1				1
domestique		2				2
doreur sur bois	1					1
droguiste					2	2
écrivain public	1					1
éducateur		1				1
emballeur		1				1
employé aux douanes		1			1	2
étudiant		2			1	3

Occupation	Death	Freed	Réclusion	Prison	Renvoi	Total judged
expert aux rapports	1					1
fabricant	4	8	1		1	14
fabricant faïencier	1	1				2
faiseur de chaises	1					1
faiseur de cordes de violon		1				1
ferblantier	1	1				2
fondeur					1	1
fontainier	1	1				2
fournier		4				4
garçon confiseur	1					1
garçon tisserand				1		1
garde de police		3				3
gendarme	3		1			4
geôlier				1		1
graveur sur métaux		1				1
greffier de Justice de la paix		1				1
guichetier des prisons	1					1
homme de loi	10	2	1	1 prison and 1 deportation		15
horloger		3	1			4
hydrographe	1					1
imprimeur	1	1				2
instituteur	2	1			1	4
jardinier		1				1
jaugeur		1				1
'je n'ai rien'			1			1
juge de paix	2					2
libraire				1		1
lieutenant, capitaine des douanes	3				1	4
limonadier	1				1	2
liquidateur du droit des huiles		1				1
liquoriste	1	2				3
luthier		1			1	2
maçon	1	5		3		9
magasinier	2	2				4
maître à danser		2				2
maître à langues	1					1
maître d'école	1					1
manœuvrier					1	1
marchand	11	18	1	1	5	36
maréchal de camp	1					1

Occupation	Death	Freed	Réclusion	Prison	Renvoi	Total judged
maréchal ferrant	1	3				4
marin	5	26	2		1	34
marinier	1					1
matelot		15				15
médecin	5		1			6
ménager	1	14			1	16
mendiant		1				1
ménétrier		1				1
meneur (?) dans une fabrique de bonnets			1			1
menuisier	3	2	1			6
meunier			1	1		2
mouleur en sable		1				1
musicien au théâtre		1				1
négociant	18	8	3		4	33
notaire	8	3			1	12
officier ministériel	2	1			1	4
orfèvre	1					1
organiste	1	1				2
ouvrier		5			1	6
patron de Madrague (a boat)		1				1
paysan		1				1
pêcheur		6				6
peintre		1				1
perclus ne faisant rien		1				1
perruquier	2	5				7
peseur public	1					1
pharmacien		1				1
plâtrier					1	1
poissonneur	1					1
portefaix	2	4		1		7
potier		1				1
poulieur	1	2				3
procureur de Cassis	1					1
procureur général syndic	2					2
propriétaire	42	38	2	4	7	93
receveur aux archives de commerce		1				1
receveur d'enregistrement et notaire	1	1				2

Occupation	Death	Freed	Réclusion	Prison	Renvoi	Total judged
receveur de loterie					1	1
régisseur des douanes	1	2				3
restaurateur-traiteur		1				1
saleur		1				1
secrétaire greffier	1					1
sellier		1				1
serrurier				1		1
tabletier		1				1
taillandier-forgeron		1				1
tailleur d'habits	3	3	1		1	8
tailleur de pierres		4				4
tailleur et gendarme		1				1
tanneur		2				2
tapissier		1				1
tisserand		2				2
tisseur en toile		1				1
tonnelier	2	5				7
tourneur	1					1
tripier	1					1
tuilier					1	1
vermicellier		1				1
vice-consul		1				1
vitrier	1	1				2
voilier	1	1				2
voiturier	1				1	2
volontaire		1	1			2
priests (including one ex-religieuse)	22	2	2		5	31
soldiers, *militaires* etc.	12	21	1	39	2	75
Prisoner of War				1		1
WOMEN:	7	62	3	1	13	86
Totals	289	476	44	69	97	975

Bibliography

I. PRIMARY SOURCES

A. MANUSCRIPT SOURCES

1. *Clermont-Ferrand.* In the Bibliothèque Municipale: the correspondence of Maignet.

2. *Marseilles*

   (a) *Archives de la Chambre de Commerce*
   B21 *Délibérations du bureau provisoire du Commerce de Marseille.*
   B74 *Cayer des délibérations du Comité de correspondance de Marseille avec MM. les députés extraordinaires du commerce de cette ville auprès de l'Assemblée nationale.*

   (b) *Archives communales*
   In many cases, only the main *Série* will be cited, with indications as to content.

Série BB	Deliberations and correspondence of the *Ancien régime* Municipality: consulted for the years 1788–90.
Série 1D	
1D1–1D6	*Conseil général de la commune.*
1D8–1D13	*Conseil municipal.*
Série 3D	
3D1	Municipal proclamations.
3D1*bis*	Municipal proclamations.
Série 4D	Correspondence of the revolutionary Municipality: consulted for the whole of the period to 1795. In particular:
4D2	*Registre des lettres écrites par la Municipalité de Marseille à Paris.*
4D3	*Registre des lettres écrites par la Municipalité de Marseille à Paris.*
4D44	*Registre des lettres reçues de Paris* (in winter of 1792–3, mostly from the Second Battalion and deputies at the Convention).
Série 13D	A very complete series of *Affiches* for the revolutionary period.
Série 20D	Letters from various municipalities to that of Marseilles.
Série F	Documents relating to food supplies. In particular:
44F11	*Souscription pour les subsistances.*

46F12–14	Documents of *bureaux* and *comités* occupied with supplying the city with food.
Série G	Relating to taxation: especially consulted for documents on the *Quart du revenu* of 1789 and the forced loans of 1793.
2G31	*Emprunt de 4 millions du 29 août 1793.*
2G32	*Emprunt de 4 millions du 11 septembre 1793.*
Série H	A largely military *Série*.
21H1	*Justice et tribunaux militaires.*
24H2	Funds for the Departmental Army.
Série I	An important *Série* devoted to matters of police.

(c) *Archives départementales des Bouches-du-Rhône*

Série L	An extremely thorough printed numerical inventory exists for this series. Because of this, and because of the large number of *liasses* consulted, only the most important are included below.
100 E 32	–*Lois, arrêtés, proclamations* . . .
L20, L21	–documents of Committee of Public Safety.
L45–L47	–deliberations of the *Conseil du département*.
L48	–deliberations of the *Trois corps administratifs* of Marseilles.
L79–L84	–deliberations of the *Directoire du département*.
L120, L121	–*arrêtés* of *Représentants du peuple*.
L126-L129	–correspondence of the Departmental Administration.
L276–L278	–electoral assemblies of the department.
L363	–documents on the Sections of Marseilles.
L364	–documents on the Sections of the department.
L365	–correspondence of the Club of Marseilles, 1791–Year VI.
L483–L501*bis*	–dossiers relating to judicial organs (Popular, Military and Revolutionary Tribunals) and to prisons.
L943–L945	–deliberations of the District Administration of Marseilles.
L1039–L1042	–dossiers relating to suspects (arrests, releases, etc.).
L1043–L1044	–troubles at Marseilles (1792–Year III).
L1059, L1059*bis*	–Committee of Surveillance of Marseilles (odd papers).
L1061	–Clubs of the department (various papers).
L1210*bis*	–*Journal Républicain de Marseille* (incomplete).
L1813, L1813*bis*	–papers of the Committee of Surveillance of Marseilles.

The papers of the Sections of Marseilles are to be found in the *liasses* L1932 to L2011*ter* beginning with the surviving registers (often incomplete) of thirteen of the thirty-two Sections. The remaining *liasses* are arranged according to subject matter (*Armée départementale, Tribunal populaire, Comité général* etc.), as indicated in the inventory.

L2071	–*Société des Amis de la Liberté et de l'Égalité de Marseille; délibérations*, (28 Feb. – 18 Apr. 1793). This is the

only *procès-verbal* of the Club's sessions in the period covered.

L2072–L2076   –dossiers of the papers of the Club of Marseilles.

Fonds du Tribunal Criminel du département

L3012–L3013   –*arrêtés* etc. concerning the Criminal and Revolutionary Tribunals.

L3023–L3025   –judgements of the Criminal and Revolutionary Tribunals (1792–Year IV).

L3032   –letters between Criminal Tribunal and Minister of Justice.

L3037   –trial of Louis-François-Dominique Isoard.

L3041   –*émeute* of 5 *vendémiaire* III.

L3044–L3047   –*Affaire de Salon,* 1793.

L3064   –*Contributions forcées,* 1793.

L3066   –*Actes arbitraires,* Year II.

L3069   –*Terrorisme,* Year III.

Fonds du Tribunal populaire de Marseille

L3100–L3108   –some of the surviving judgements (see also L3044–L3047 *Affaire de Salon*; L2006; L483), and diverse papers, especially accusations against clubists relating to their activities at Salon, Orgon, etc. in Feb.–Mar. 1793.

Fonds du Tribunal révolutionnaire séant à Marseille

L3109   –petitions addressed to the public prosecutor.

L3110   –denunciations before committees of surveillance.

L3111   –correspondence of public prosecutor.

L3112–L3119   –the series of verbatim accounts of the sessions, from 28 Aug. 1793 to 5 *floréal* II (24 Apr. 1794), with the exception (besides the period of 1 *pluviôse* II – 24 *ventôse* II when the Military Commission met) of some sessions in *nivôse* II, for which see L484 and L3024.

L3120–L3121   –petitions from the accused.

L3122–L3126   –lists of individuals judged, their penalties, etc.

L3127   –papers relating to the organisation of the Tribunal, its relations with the *Représentants,* with the Popular Commission of Orange, etc.

Commissions militaires

L3128–L3130   –papers of the Military Commission of the Year II, including rough drafts of preliminary (?) interrogations; petitions, etc.

L3131   –Military Commission of 5–7 *vendémiaire* III (set up by Auguis and Serres).

Serie Q   –the possessions of condemned Marseillais, in the dossiers from 4Q167 to 4Q243 (arranged alphabetically).

(d) *Bibliothèque Municipale de Marseille*

048728   – *Correspondance entre MM. Beleste et Roustan de Marseille et M. Mourgues de Martigues* (26 Oct. 1791–24 Nov. 1792).

049068   – letters from Roland, etc.

3. *Paris*

(a) *Archives de la Guerre* at Vincennes

B³⁶⎫
B³⁷⎬ various letters on Marseilles in the autumn of 1793.
B³⁸⎭

B³101 and B³102 – *arrêtés* etc. from *Représentants* at the Army of Italy.

(b) *Archives Nationales*

As in the case of the *Archives communales* and *départementales*, only the most important dossiers can be cited.

Série AF II: *Correspondance des Représentants en mission avec le Comité de salut public*

AF II 3¹⁸   – documents on Marseilles, Apr. 1793.
AF II 42³³⁶   – letters of Maignet.
AF II 42³³⁸   – police reports on *émeute* of 13 *vendémiaire* IV.
AF II 44³⁴⁵⁻³⁴⁶   – *affaire de Toulon*.
AF II 45³⁵⁰,³⁵⁵   – correspondence of Barbaroux.
AF II 58³⁸⁷⁻³⁹¹   – Marseillais and 13 *vendémiaire* IV.
AF II 58⁴²²   – Committee of Public Safety and Marseilles.
AF II 58⁴²⁶,⁴²⁷,⁴²⁸ – Auguis and Serres and Marseilles.

AF II 90⎫   – numerous documents relating to the missions to the
AF II 91⎬   Bouches-du-Rhône of *Représentants* from Bayle and
        ⎭   Boisset to Maignet.

AF II 185¹⁵²⁹,¹⁵³⁰ – letters of Pomme, Rovère and Poultier on the situation of the Bouches-du-Rhône in Oct. 1793.

Série BB 3: Justice: Affaires criminelles

BB 3 7   – Revolutionary Tribunals in the departments.
BB 3 9   – Revolutionary Tribunals . . . in the Bouches-du-Rhône.
BB 3 56   – arrests etc. by the Convention etc.

Série BB 30: Ministère de la Justice

BB 30 14   – containing much information on Bournissac's tribunal.
BB 30 15   – containing much information on Bournissac's tribunal.
BB 30 91   – containing much information on Bournissac's tribunal.

Série DS: Missions des Représentants dans les départements

DS 1 29   – mission of Maignet in the Bouches-du-Rhône.

Série D III: Comité de législation de la Convention

D III 29–31   –documents relating to the Bouches-du-Rhône.

D III 343–357   –denunciations against relevant *Représentants en mission*.

Série D XXIX: Comité des rapports

D XXIX 53   –these dossiers contain much information on Bournis-
D XXIX 54   sac's tribunal and on disturbances at Marseilles in
D XXIX 55   1789 and 1790.

Série D XLII: Comité de salut public

D XLII, 4   –various letters concerning federalism in the Midi.

Série F: Administration générale

FI^bII B.-du-Rh. 16 – on commune of Marseilles.

FI^cIII B.-du-Rh. 1, 2, 6, 7, 8, 10 – documents relating to Marseilles in
the series *Esprit public, élections*.

Série F^7: Police générale

F^73054   –*Club du Panthéon*, Year IV.

F^73281   –*Détenus par mesure de haute police, B.du–Rh.*

F^73301   –*Détenus par mesure de haute police, Seine* (prison de
Plessis).

F^73659   –dossiers 1, 2, 3, 4 – *Statistique personnelle et morale;
série départementale, B.–du–Rh.*

F^74268   –Marseilles and Aix, troubles, Years IV to V.

F^74276–8   –*Affaire Babeuf*.

Comité de sûreté générale

F^74435, *plaquette* 4 – correspondence of Maignet.

F^74554   –*Arrestations, détentions, mises en liberté, série départementale, B.-du-Rh.*

Série alphabétique: dossiers individuels

F^74585   –Barbaroux.

F^74589   –Moïse Bayle.

F^74628
F^74629   –Cadroy.

F^74701   –Escudier.

F^74716   –Gasparin.

F^74747   –Louis-François-Dominique Isoard.

F^74774^29   –Maignet.

F^74775^12   –Saliceti.

Série H: Administrative series for the *Ancien régime*: consulted for Provence.

H 1238
H 1240
H 1274   –principally correspondence between the *Intendant* and
Caraman and the government, dealing with dis-
turbances in Provence in 1789.

Série W: Tribunal révolutionnaire de Paris

W86, W87   –documents relating to the riot of 5 *vendémiaire* III at
Marseilles.

W329, No. 545   –*Affaire Maillet et Giraud*.

B. PRINTED SOURCES

(a) *Pamphlets.* The collections in the British Museum and the Bibliothèque Nationale of Paris are useful but contain little of essential interest not to be found in the dossiers cited above. That at the Bibliothèque Municipale of Marseilles, however, contains pamphlets of more immediate interest, especially valuable being the *Recueil de François Michel de Léon*, containing numerous documents (pamphlets, *cahiers* etc.) relating chiefly to the early years of the Revolution. See the catalogue of the *Fonds de Provence*.

(b) *Journals.* Of special interest to Marseilles are the following:

Journal des départements méridionaux et des débats des Amis de la Constitution de Marseille par une Société de Gens de Lettres (Ricord *fils*), Mar. 1792–May 1793.

Journal de Provence (1781–Jan. 1792), then

Journal de Marseille (till June 1793), then

Journal de Marseille et des Sections (till end of Aug. 1793, when its editor Ferréol Beaugeard emigrated). It re-appeared later.

Journal Républicain de Marseille et des départements méridionaux Oct. 1793–*pluviôse* II (with gaps).

Also, *Réimpression de l'Ancien Moniteur*, 31 vols. (Paris, 1854).

This was supplemented by the *Procès-verbal de la Convention nationale depuis et compris le 20 septembre 1792 An I au brumaire An IV*, 72 vols. (Paris 1792–1796).

(c) *Memoirs and Diaries*

Correspondance et mémoires de Barbaroux, ed. C. Perroud and A. Chabaud (Paris, 1923).

Mémoires de Charles Barbaroux, ed. MM. Berville and Barrière (Paris, 1822).

Mémoires de Barbaroux, ed. A. Chabaud (Paris, 1936).

Mémoires de Barras publiés avec une introduction générale . . . de Georges Dupuy . . ., 2 vols. (Paris, 1895–6).

F. A. Doppet, *Mémoires politiques et militaires du général Doppet* (Paris, 1824).

P. T. Durand-Maillane, *Histoire de la Convention nationale* (Paris, 1825).

Mémoires historiques de M. le chevalier de Fonvielle de Toulouse, 4 vols. (Paris, 1824) (B. F. A. Fonvielle).

Not strictly speaking memoirs are the volumes of Laurent-Marie Lautard, *Esquisses historiques: Marseille depuis 1789 jusqu'en 1815*, 2 vols. (Marseilles, 1844). Lautard was a witness of the events he describes and, imprisoned as a suspected federalist, he provides the most vivid descriptions of the conditions of the prisons of Marseilles in the Year II, as well as an extremely readable, if partisan, account of the Revolution at Marseilles.

Mémoires de S.A.S. L. A. Philippe d'Orléans, duc de Montpensier (Paris, 1824).

Mémoires de A. C. Thibaudeau, 1799–1815 (Paris, 1913).

(d) *Other contemporary works: travellers and topographers.*

C. F. Achard, *Description historique, géographique et topographique des villes . . . de la Provence* (Aix, 1787).

C. F. Achard, *Dictionnaire de la Provence et du Comté Venaissin*, 4 vols. (Marseilles, 1786–1787).

C. F. Achard, *Tableau historique de Marseille et de ses dépendances* (Lausanne, 1789).

F. Benoît (ed.), *Voyage en Provence d'un gentilhomme polonais, le comte Moszyński, 1784–1785* (Marseilles, 1930).

L. P. Berenger, *Soirées provençales*, 3 vols. (Marseilles, 1787).

J. Chardon, *Almanach historique, politique et commercial de Marseille, pour l'an XII de la République* (Marseilles, 1803–4).

J. Chardon, *Précis historique de tous les événements remarquables arrivés à Marseille depuis 1789 jusqu'au 25 juin 1815* (Marseilles, 1829).

J. Chardon, *Tableau des noms anciens . . . de la ville de Marseille* (Marseilles, 1806, etc.).

J. Chardon, *Tableau historique et politique de Marseille ancienne et moderne* (Marseilles, 1806 etc.).

l'abbé Expilly, *Dictionnaire des Gaules*, vol 4 (Paris, 1766).

Piganiol de la Force, *Notes et notices sur Marseille* (Marseilles, 1753).

A Four Months' Tour through France, 2 vols. (London, 1776).

Lord Gardenstone, *Travelling Memorandums made in a tour upon the Continent of Europe in the years 1786, 87, 88*, 3 vols. (London, 1791).

The Gentleman's Guide in his Tour through France (London, 1787).

The Grand Tour, containing an exact description of most of the cities . . . of Europe, vol. 4 (London, 1749).

J. B. B. Grosson, *Almanach historique de Marseille*, 21 vols. (Marseilles, 1770–90).

M***, *Voyage à Marseille et à Toulon* (Paris, 1789).

M. Margarot, *Histoire ou relation d'un voyage*, 2 vols. (London, 1786).

J. J. Mazet, *Le Guide marseillais* (Marseilles, 1789 ff).

J. Moore, *A Journal during a residence in France*, 2 vols. (Dublin, 1793).

Régibaud, *Almanach de Provence* (Marseilles, 1770).

P. Thicknesse, *Hints and Observations* (London, 1768).

P. Thicknesse, *A Year's Journey through France and part of Spain*, 2 vols. (London, 1789).

N. Wraxall, Junior, *Memoirs of the Kings of France of the Race of Valois, to which is added A Tour through the Western, Southern, and Interior Provinces of France*, 2 vols. (London, 1777).

A. Young, *Travels in France*, ed. M. Betham-Edwards (London, 1924).

(e) *Collections of Documents, Editions of Speeches etc.*

J. J. A. Abeille, *Notes et pièces officielles relatives aux événements de Marseille et de Toulon en 1793* (Paris, 1815).

Archives Parlementaires de 1787 à 1860, Première Série (1787 à 1799) (Paris, 1879–1914).

F. A. Aulard, *Recueil des actes du Comité de salut public*, 30 vols. (Paris, 1889–1951).

F. A. Aulard, *La Société des Jacobins*, 6 vols. (Paris, 1889–97).

A. P. J. M. Barnave, *Introduction à la Révolution française*, ed. F. Rude (Paris, 1960).

P. Caron, *La Commission des subsistances de l'An II*, 2 vols. (Paris, 1924–25).
A. Cochin and C. Charpentier, *Les Actes du gouvernement révolutionnaire*, 3 vols. (Paris, 1920–35).
J. Fournier, *Cahiers de doléances de la sénéchaussée de Marseille pour les États-Généraux de 1789* (Marseilles, 1908).
G. Michon, *La Correspondance de Robespierre*, 2 vols. (Paris, 1926 and 1941).
P. Moulin, *Département des Bouches-du-Rhône, Documents relatifs à la vente des biens nationaux*, 4 vols. (Marseilles, 1908–11).
L. G. Pelissier, *Un Recueil de l'Arlésien Mège (1788–1816). Documents pour l'histoire du fédéralisme marseillais* (Paris, 1913).
E. Poupé, *Lettres de Barras et de Fréron, en mission dans le Midi* (Draguignan, 1910).

II. SECONDARY SOURCES

A. BOOKS

M. Agulhon, *Pénitents et francs-maçons de l'ancienne Provence* (Paris, 1968).
H. d'Alméras, *Barras et son temps* (Paris, 1930).
Atlas historique: Provence, Comtat Venaissin, Orange, Nice, Monaco, ed. E. Baratier, G. Duby, E. Hildesheimer (Paris, 1969).
R. Baehrel, *Une Croissance: la Basse-Provence rurale*, 2 vols. (Paris, 1961).
H. Barré, *Marseille en 1787 et en 1891* (Marseilles, 1895).
P. Bécamps, *J.-B.-M. Lacombe, Président de la Commission militaire de Bordeaux* (Paris, 1953).
R. Belin, *Un Représentant du peuple en mission dans ses rapports avec la Convention et le Comité de salut public: Étienne Maignet* (Ambert, 1921).
L. Bergasse, *Notice historique sur la Chambre de Commerce de Marseille (1599–1912)* (Marseilles, 1913).
C. Berriat-Saint-Prix, *La Justice révolutionnaire à Paris et dans les départements, d'après les documents originaux*, 2 vols. (Paris, 1864–8).
P. Bertaut, *Marseille d'hier, d'aujourd'hui, de demain* (Marseilles, 1867).
P. Boiteau, *État de France en 1789* (Paris, 1889).
P. Boiteau, *La France en 1789* (Paris, 1861).
S. Bonnel, *Les 332 victimes de la Commission populaire d'Orange*, 2 vols. (Orange, 1888).
Bordeaux au XVIIIe siècle, ed. G. Pariset (Bordeaux, 1968).
Les Bouches-du-Rhône, Encyclopédie départementale publiée . . . sous la direction de Paul Masson, 16 vols. (Marseilles, 1914–37).
A. Boudin, *Histoire de Marseille* (Marseilles, 1852).
C. Bousquet, *La Major, cathédrale de Marseille* (Marseilles, 1857).
C. Bousquet, *Notice historique sur l'église Saint-Théodore (Les Recollets)* (Marseilles, 1856).
A. Bouyala d'Arnaud, *Évocation du Vieux Marseille* (Paris, 1964).
F. Braudel and E. Labrousse, *Histoire économique et sociale de la France, vol. 2, 1660–1789* (Paris, 1970).
J. B. Cantel, *Monographie de Notre-Dame du Mont-Carmel à Marseille* (Marseilles, 1874).

C. Carrière, M. Courdurié, F. Rebuffat, *Marseille ville morte; la peste de 1720* (Marseilles, 1968).

R. de Chauvigny, *Le Cardinal de Belloy et l'Église de Marseille de 1789 à 1802* (Avignon, 1930).

R. C. Cobb, *Les Armées révolutionnaires: instrument de la Terreur dans les départements, avril 1793 – floréal an II*, 2 vols. (Paris, 1961–3).

R. C. Cobb, *The Police and the People* (Oxford, 1970).

R. C. Cobb, *Terreur et subsistances, 1793–1795* (Paris, 1964).

E. Daudet, *Histoire des conspirations royalistes du Midi sous la Révolution* (Paris, 1881).

L. Dermigny, *Cargaisons indiennes: Solier et Cie*, 2 vols. (Paris, 1960).

F. Dollieule, ed. *Marseille à la fin de l'Ancien régime* (Marseilles, 1896).

J. Égret, *La Pré-Révolution française* (Paris, 1962).

A. J. E. Fabre, *Histoire de Marseille*, 2 vols (Paris, 1829).

A. J. E. Fabre, *Histoire de Provence*, 4 vols. (Marseilles, 1883).

A. J. E. Fabre, *Notice historique sur les anciennes rues de Marseille* (Marseilles, 1862).

A. J. E. Fabre, *Les Rues de Marseille*, 5 vols. (Marseilles, 1867–9).

E. Garcin, *Dictionnaire historique et topographique de la Provence*, 2 vols. (Draguignan, 1835).

E. Garcin, *Histoire et topographie de la ville de Marseille* (Draguignan, 1834).

R. Gérard, *Le 'Journal de Marseille' de Ferréol Beaugeard, 1781–1797* (Paris, 1964).

J. Godechot, *La Contre-révolution, doctrine et action* (Paris, 1961).

J. Godechot, *Les Institutions de la France sous la Révolution et l'Empire* (Paris, 1968).

J. L. Godfrey, *Revolutionary Justice, A Study of the Organisation, Personnel and Procedure of the Paris Tribunal, 1793–1795* (Chapel Hill, 1951).

D. Greer, *The Incidence of the Emigration during the French Revolution* (Princeton, 1951).

D. Greer, *The Incidence of the Terror during the French Revolution* (Cambridge, Mass., 1935).

D. Guérin, *La Lutte des classes sous la Première République, 1793–1797* (2nd ed. Paris, 1968).

G. Guibal, *Mirabeau et la Provence*, 2 vols. (Paris, 1887–91).

G. Guibal, *Le Mouvement fédéraliste en Provence en 1793* (Paris, 1908).

Histoire des prêtres du Sacré–Coeur de Marseille (1732–1831) (Marseilles, 1876).

Histoire de la Provence, ed. E. Baratier (Toulouse, 1969).

O. Hufton, *Bayeux in the late Eighteenth Century* (Oxford, 1967).

L. Jacob, *Les Suspects pendant la Révolution, 1789–1794* (Paris, 1952).

H. Jacqmin, *Les Tribunaux révolutionnaires en Provence* (Nîmes, 1907).

A. Kuscinski, *Dictionnaire des conventionnels* (Paris, 1916–19).

P. Lafran and G. Plantier, *Saint-Chamas des origines à 1851* (Les Amis du Vieux Saint-Chamas, 1955).

G. Lefebvre, *Études orléanaises*, 2 vols. (Paris, 1962–3).

G. Lefebvre, *Études sur la Révolution française* (Paris, 1963).

G. Lenôtre, *Les Fils de Philippe-Égalité pendant la Terreur* (Paris, 1907).

J. Louche, *Notice sur l'église paroissiale et cathédrale provisoire de Saint-Martin à Marseille* (Marseilles, 1871).

C. Lourde, *Histoire de la Révolution à Marseille et en Provence depuis 1789 jusqu'au Consulat*, 3 vols. (Marseilles, 1838–9).

H. Lüthy, *La Banque protestante en France*, vol. 2 (Paris, 1961).

A. M., *Sanctuaire de Notre-Dame de la Garde* (Marseilles, 1873).

P. Masson, *Marseille depuis 1789* (Paris, 1919).

P. Masson, *La Provence au XVIIIᵉ siècle*, 3 vols. (Paris, 1936).

J. Meyer, *L'Armement nantais dans la deuxième moitié du XVIIIᵉ siècle* (Paris, 1969).

A. L. Millin, *Voyages dans les départements du Midi*, 5 vols. (Paris, 1807–11).

H. Mireur, *La Prostitution à Marseille* (Marseilles, 1882).

J. R. Palanque, ed., *Le Diocèse de Marseille* (Paris, 1969).

E. Pascal, *Un Village provençal sous la Révolution* (Avignon, 1930).

B. Plongeron, *Conscience religieuse en Révolution* (Paris, 1969).

E. Pollio, *Les Papiers de Rovère* (Paris, 1931).

J. Pollio and A. Marcel, *Le Bataillon du 10 août* (Paris, 1881).

F. Portal, *Le Bataillon marseillais du 21 janvier* (Marseilles, 1900).

D. Radiguet, *Foules et journées révolutionnaires à Marseille, août 1789–25 août 1793* (unpublished *Diplôme d'études supérieures*, Faculty of Letters, Aix, 1968).

G. Rambert, ed., *Histoire du commerce de Marseille publiée par la Chambre de commerce de Marseille sous la direction de G. Rambert* (Paris, 1949 ff.) – especially vols. 4, 5, 6 and 7.

G. Rambert, *Marseille, la formation d'une grande cité moderne* (Marseilles, 1934).

P. A. Robert, *La Justice des sections marseillaises. Le Tribunal populaire, 1792–1793* (Paris, 1913).

R. Romano, *Commerce et prix du blé à Marseille au XVIIIᵉ siècle* (Paris, 1956).

le baron de Roure, *Histoire véridique de la noblesse de Provence* (Bergerac, 1912).

Le Marquis de Sade (Centre Aixois d'Études et de Recherches sur le dix-huitième siècle) (Paris, 1968).

G. Saint-Yves and J. Fournier, *Le Département des Bouches-du-Rhône de 1800 à 1810* (Marseilles, 1899).

Odon de Samatan, *Basile Samatan, épisode de la Révolution à Marseille* (Marseilles, 1894).

A. Saurel, *Dictionnaire des Bouches-du-Rhône*, 2 vols. (Marseilles, 1877).

A. Saurel, *Marseille et sa banlieue* (Marseilles, 1870).

J. Sentou, *Fortunes et groupes sociaux à Toulouse sous la Révolution* (Toulouse, 1969).

A. F. Simon, *Le Mont-de-Piété de Marseille* (Marseilles, 1939).

A. Soboul, *La 1ʳᵉ République (1792–1804)* (Paris, 1968).

M. J. Sydenham, *The Girondins* (London, 1961).

M. C. O. Teissier, *Les Anciennes Familles marseillaises* (Marseilles, 1888).

C. Tilly, *The Vendée* (Cambridge, Mass., 1964).

L. Trénard, *Lyon, de l'Encyclopédie au préromantisme*, 2 vols. (Paris, 1958).

F. Verany, *Monographie de la Chartreuse de Marseille* (Marseilles, 1860).

S. Vialla, *Marseille révolutionnaire* (Paris, 1910).

S. Vialla, *Les Volontaires des Bouches-du-Rhône* (Paris, 1913).

J. Vivent, *Barras, le 'roi' de la République, 1755–1829* (Paris, 1938).

Volcy-Boze, *Les Conventionnels en mission dans le Midi* (Marseilles, 1872).

H. Wallon, *Les Représentants du peuple en mission et la justice révolutionnaire dans les départements en l'an II, 1793–1794*, vol. 3, *Le Sud-Est* . . . (Paris, 1889).

H. Wallon, *La Révolution du 31 mai et le fédéralisme en 1793*, 2 vols. (Paris, 1886).

G. Walter, *Robespierre*, 3 vols. (Paris, 1936–40).

M. Zarb, *Histoire d'une autonomie communale: Les Privilèges de la ville de Marseille du Xe siècle à la Révolution* (Paris, 1961).

B. ARTICLES AND EXTRACTS[1]

M. Agulhon, 'La notion de village en Basse-Provence vers la fin de l'Ancien régime', *Actes du 90e Congrès national des Sociétés savantes, Nice, 1965* (Paris, 1966), *tome* I, pp. 277–301.

M. Agulhon, 'Sur l'instruction élémentaire en Provence au temps du Consulat', *Annales du Midi*, No. 57, 1964, pp. 19–26.

R. Baehrel, 'Épidémie et Terreur: Histoire et Sociologie', *A.H.R.F.*, 1951, pp. 113–46.

J. Billioud, 'Quelques industries textiles à Marseille sous l'Ancien Régime', *Marseille*, No. 48, 1962, pp. 21–7.

C. Brinton, 'Les origines sociales des terroristes', *A.H.R.F.*, 1928, pp. 522–9.

A. Brun, 'Un Collège d'Oratoriens au XVIIIe siècle, Marseille', *Revue d'histoire de l'Église de France*, 1949, pp. 207–19.

C. Carrière, 'Le commerce de draps à Marseille au XVIIIe siècle', *Con férences de l'Institut historique de Provence*, a.40, No. 1, 1962, p. 121.

C. Carrière, 'Les débuts du commerce marseillais dans la mer Noire à la fin du XVIIIe siècle', *Conférences de l'Institut historique de Provence*, a.41, No. 4, 1963, pp. 147–48.

C. Carrière, 'Les entrées de navires dans le port de Marseille pendant la Révolution', *Provence historique*, *tome* 7, 1957, pp. 200–25.

C. Carrière, 'Un hôtel de grands négociants, 42 rue Sainte, 1785–1820', *Marseille*, No. 46, 1962, pp. 3–20; No. 47, 1962, pp. 25–32.

C. Carrière, 'Les Marseillais étaient-ils des corsaires?', *Conférences de l'Institut historique de Provence*, a.44, No. 4, 1966, pp. 204–6.

C. Carrière, 'Le problème des grains et farines à Marseille pendant la période du maximum, 4 mai 1793–4 nivôse an III', *Extrait des Mémoires et documents*, No. XIII, 1958, pp. 161–84.

C. Carrière, 'Protestantisme et commerce à Marseille au XVIIIe siècle', *Conférences de l'Institut historique de Provence*, a.43, No. 3, 1965, pp. 180–1.

C. Carrière [report of a lecture], *Provence historique*, *tome* 18, Jan.–Mar. 1968, p. 193.

C. Carrière, 'Y a-t-il eu un XVIIIe siècle à Martigues?', *Provence historique*, *tome* 14, Jan.–Mar. 1964, pp. 53–68.

[1] Abbreviations: *Annales, E.S.C., Annales, Économies, Sociétés, Civilisations*; *A.H.R.F., Annales historiques de la Révolution française*.

A. Chabaud, 'Un collaborateur de Barbaroux, l'ingénieur Couédic', *A.H.R.F.*, 1935, pp. 249–53.

A. Chabaud, *Essai sur les classes bourgeoises dirigeantes à Marseille en 1789.* Extrait de la Commission d'histoire économique, *Assemblée générale de 1939*, tome I, pp. 47–144 (Paris, 1942).

A. Chabaud, 'La Marseillaise: chant patriotique "girondin" ', *A.H.R.F.*, 1936, pp. 460–7.

F. Chailley, 'La Marseillaise: Étude critique sur ses origines', *A.H.R.F.*, 1960, pp. 260–93.

J. Chaumié, 'La Révolution à Marseille vue par un Espagnol', *Provence historique*, tome 1, 1950–51, pp. 202–27, and tome 2, 1952, pp. 36–62.

R. F. Clapier, 'Aspects économiques et sociaux de la savonnerie marseillaise au XVIIIᵉ siècle', *Provincia*, No. 223, 1955, pp. 147–8.

R. C. Cobb, 'The Revolutionary Mentality in France, 1793–1794', *History*, 1957, pp. 181–96.

R. Collier, 'Essai sur le "socialisme" communal en Haute-Provence', *Actes du 90ᵉ Congrès national des Sociétés savantes, Nice, 1965* (Paris, 1966) tome 1, pp. 303–33.

E. Coulet, 'Le massacre des administrateurs du Var', *Actes du 89ᵉ Congrès des Sociétés savantes, Lyon, 1964* (Paris, 1964) pp. 419–47.

E. Coulet, 'Situation économique de Toulon pendant la rébellion, (juillet–décembre 1793)', *Provence historique*, tome 12, Jan.–Mar. 1962, pp. 72–92.

A. Crémieux, 'Le particularisme municipal à Marseille en 1789', *Révolution française*, LII, 1907, pp. 191–215.

J. Égret, 'La Pré-Révolution en Provence, 1787–89', *A.H.R.F.*, 1954, pp. 97–126.

E. L. Eisenstein, 'Who intervened in 1788?', *American Historical Review*, 71, No. 1, Oct. 1965, pp. 77–103.

P. Espert, 'Un faux complot à Marseille . . . les 21, 22, 23 juillet 1792', *Provincia*, XIX, 1939, pp. 59–92.

J. P. Ferran, 'Quelques notes sur l'esprit de la haute bourgeoisie protestante à Marseille à la fin de l'ancien régime', *Provence historique*, tome 8, Apr.–June 1958, pp. 131–49.

H. de Fontmichel and M. Vovelle, 'Deux notables provençaux sous la Révolution française', *Provence historique*, tome 14, 1964, pp. 182–203.

R. Forster, 'The Survival of the Nobility during the French Revolution', *Past and Present*, No. 37, July 1967, pp. 71–86.

P. Gaffarel, 'La mission de Maignet dans les Bouches-du-Rhône et en Vaucluse', *Annales de la Faculté des Lettres d'Aix*, vol. 6–7, 1912–13, pp. 1–100.

P. Gaffarel, 'La prise des Bastilles marseillaises', *Révolution française*, LXXII, 1919, pp. 314–25.

P. Gaffarel, 'La Terreur à Marseille', *Annales de Provence*, X, 1913, pp. 157–88, 229–62.

P. Gaffarel, 'Marseille sans nom', *Révolution française*, LX, 1911, pp. 193–215.

M. G. Gagneux, 'Un village provençal urbanisé: Marignane à la veille de la Révolution', *Actes du 83ᵉ Congrès national des Sociétés savantes, Aix-Marseille, 1958* (Paris, 1959) pp. 471–82.

H. Gay, 'Le district de Martigues-Salon: luttes politiques et luttes de "clocher" sous la Révolution', *Provence historique, tome* 14, Jan.–Mar. 1964, pp. 107–16.

H. Gay, 'Un notable de Martigues et la Révolution française; Louis Puech (1740–1794)', *Provence historique, tome* 17, 1967, pp. 256–95.

A. Goodwin, 'The Federalist Movement in Caen during the French Revolution', *Bulletin of the John Rylands Library*, 42, 1959–60, pp. 313–44.

A. Goodwin, 'The Social Origins and Privileged Status of the French Eighteenth Century Nobility', *Bulletin of the John Rylands Library*, 47, 1964–5, pp. 382–403.

E. Isnard, 'Promenade historique à travers le vieux Marseille', *Marseille*, Aug. 1943, pp. 2–18.

Y. Jouve, 'Les fermes unies de Marseille, leur déclin', *Conférences de l'Institut historique de Provence*, a.33, No. 3, 1956, pp. 32–3.

M. T. Lagasquié, 'Le personnel terroriste toulousain', *A.H.R.F.*, Apr.–June 1971, pp. 248–64.

P. Lazac, 'Marseille d'autrefois: la Grand'rue', *Marseille*, Dec. 1936, pp. 23–6.

E. G. Léonard, 'La bourgeoisie protestante et sa position politique et religieuse du XVIIIᵉ siècle à la Restauration', *Extrait de la Commission d'histoire économique, Assemblée générale de 1939, tome* 1 (Paris, 1942) pp. 171–93.

J. J. Letrait, 'Le régime du travail des ouvriers agricoles en Provence dans la première moitié du XVIIIᵉ siècle', *Actes du 83ᵉ Congrès national de Sociétés savantes, Aix-Marseille, 1958* (Paris, 1959) pp. 457–70.

D. Ligou, 'A propos de la Révolution municipale', *Revue d'histoire économique et sociale*, 1960, pp. 146–77.

D. Ligou, 'Le protestantisme français dans la seconde moitié du XVIIIᵉ siècle', *Information historique*, No. 1, 1963, pp. 8–14.

J. Louche, 'Marseille et ses habitants à la veille de la Révolution', *Revue de Marseille*, No. 37, 1891, pp. 234–62; No. 38, 1892, pp. 94–113, 192–216, 221–37, 314–31.

R. Louie, 'The Incidence of the Terror: A Critique of a Statistical Interpretation', *French Historical Studies*, Vol. III, No. 3, 1964, pp. 379–89.

A. Manfred, 'La nature du pouvoir jacobin', *La Pensée*, Apr. 1970, pp. 62–83.

G. Martinet, 'Les débuts de la réaction thermidorienne à Marseille: l'émeute du 5 vendémiaire an III', *Actes du 90ᵉ Congrès national des Sociétés savantes, Nice, 1965* (Paris, 1966) *tome* 2, pp. 149–66.

G. Martinet, 'Quelques aspects de l'émigration dans le district de Marseille pendant l'an III', *Information historique*, No. 2, 1961, pp. 64–71.

G. Martinet, 'La vie politique à Marseille en 1795 et 1796', *Provence historique, tome* 16, Apr.–June 1966, pp. 126–76.

H. Mitchell, 'The Vendée and Counterrevolution: A Review Essay', *French Historical Studies*, Vol. V, No. 4, 1968, pp. 405–19.

G. Pariset, 'Histoire du régionalisme français', *Études d'histoire révolutionnaire et contemporaine*, 1929, pp. 287–313.

C. Pellat, 'Aperçu sur le charbon en Provence au XVIIIᵉ siècle', *Provincia*, No. 241, 1959, pp. 253–4.

L. G. Pellissier, 'La délégation marseillaise à la Convention nationale', *Annales du Midi*, 1900, pp. 71–91.

G. Rambert, 'Les conditions du commerce de Marseille avec l'intérieur de 1660 à 1789', *Provincia*, a.20, No. 2, 1958, pp. 219–21.

F. Rebuffat, 'Le grand négoce marseillais au XVIIIᵉ siècle: la maison Roux', *Marseille*, No. 62, 1966, pp. 52–9.

J. B. Samat, 'La détention des princes d'Orléans au fort de Notre-Dame de la Garde', *Mémoires de l'Académie de Marseille*, 1926, pp. 106–16.

A. Segond, 'Les foules révolutionnaires à Avignon (1789–91)', *Provence historique*, tome 19, Oct.–Dec. 1969, pp. 307–28.

F. Spannel, 'Les éléments de la fortune des grands notables marseillais au début du XIXᵉ siècle', *Provence historique*, tome 7, 1957, pp. 95–130.

L. Stouff, 'Les revendications économiques et sociales de la population marseillaise dans les cahiers de 1789', *Revue d'histoire économique et sociale*, 1954, pp. 264–80.

Z. Szajkowski, 'The Jewish Community of Marseilles at the end of the Eighteenth Century', *Revue d'études juives*, 1962, pp. 367–82.

C. Taillefer, 'La guerre de course à Marseille de 1793 à 1802', *Provincia*, No. 258, 1963, pp. 113–15.

F. L. Tavernier, 'Une exposition sur la vie à Marseille au temps de Louis XVI', *Marseille*, No. 35, 1958, pp. 9–22.

F. L. Tavernier, 'Marseille sous la Convention', *Marseille*, No. 51, 1963, pp. 37–46.

F. L. Tavernier, 'Promenade à travers Marseille au temps de Louis XVI', *Revue illustrée du Musée du Vieux Marseille*, II, 1959, pp. 9–14.

G. V. Taylor, 'Noncapitalist wealth and the Origins of the French Revolution', *American Historical Review*, 72, No. 2, Jan. 1967, pp. 469–96.

G. V. Taylor, 'Some business partnerships at Lyon, 1785–1793', *Journal of Economic History*, No. 23, 1963, pp. 46–70.

G. V. Taylor, 'Types of capitalism in Eighteenth Century France', *English Historical Review*, LXXIX, July 1964, pp. 478–97.

C. Tilly, 'The Analysis of a Counter-Revolution', *History and Theory*, III, 1963, pp. 30–58.

P. Vaillandet, 'Lettres inédites de Barbaroux', *A.H.R.F.*, 1933, pp. 338–353.

E. Vellay, 'La grande peur à Saint-Rémy de Provence', *A.H.R.F.*, 1936, pp. 357–61.

J. Viguier, 'L'encadastrement des biens et droits féodaux en Provence, 1789–90', *La Révolution française*, tome 19, 1890, pp. 208–35.

J. Viguier, 'Épisodes inédits de la terreur à Marseille', *La Révolution française*, tome 28, 1895, pp. 40–65.

J. Viguier, 'La fin de l'ancien régime en Provence', *La Révolution française*, tome 20, 1891, pp. 208–322.

J. Viguier, 'Marseille et ses représentants à la Constituante', *La Révolution française*, tome 40, 1901, pp. 193–209.

H. Villard, 'La famille d'Orléans à Marseille en 1793', *Bulletin officiel du Musée du Vieux Marseille*, Jan.–Feb. 1936, pp. 1–8.

G. and M. Vovelle, 'La mort et l'au-delà en Provence d'après les autels des âmes du purgatoire(XV–XXᵉ siècle)', *Annales, E.S.C.*, Nov.–Dec. 1969, pp. 1602–34.

M. Vovelle, 'Essai d'analyse idéologique des Sections marseillaises', *Conférences de l'Institut historique de Provence*, Mar.–Apr. 1963, pp. 138–40.

M. Vovelle, 'Essai de cartographie de la déchristianisation sous la Révolution française', *Annales du Midi*, 76, 1964, pp. 529–42.

M. Vovelle, 'État présent des études de structure agraire en Provence à la fin de l'Ancien régime', *Provence historique, tome* 18, Oct.–Dec. 1968, pp. 450–85.

M. Vovelle, 'Prêtres abdicataires et déchristianisation en Provence', *Actes du 89ᵉ Congrès national des Sociétés savantes, Lyon, 1964* (Paris, 1964) pp. 63–98.

M. Vovelle, 'Le prolétariat flottant à Marseille sous la Révolution française', *Annales de démographie historique*, 1968, pp. 111–38.

M. Vovelle, 'Sade et Lacoste, suivi de Mirabeau et Mirabeau . . . réflexions sur le déclassement nobiliaire dans la Provence du XVIIIᵉ siècle', *Provence historique, tome* 17, Apr.–June 1967, pp. 160–71.

M. Vovelle and D. Roche, 'Bourgeois, Rentiers, Propriétaires: Éléments pour la définition d'une catégorie sociale à la fin du XVIIIᵉ siècle', *Actes du 84ᵉ Congrès national des Sociétés savantes, Dijon, 1959* (Paris, 1960) pp. 419–52.

R. A. Weigart, 'Quelques industries textiles à Marseille sous l'Ancien régime', *Marseille*, No. 48, 1962, pp. 21–36.

R. Ytier, 'Cucuron révolutionnaire (1788–1795)', *Provence historique, tome* 16, Apr.–June 1967, pp. 192–7.

General Index

Index of Persons

judged by the Revolutionary Tribunal[1]

[1] Men and women whose cases are cited in the text. These include *prévenus* who were sent back to the prisons without final judgement (*renvoyés*). The names of the members of some important sectionary bodies (e.g. The Popular Tribunal) are included, even if their cases are not cited individually. In virtually all instances, names have been checked against signatures but, even then, it has not always been possible to establish a definitive version.